Nothing Like a Dame

Nothing Like a Dame

The Scandals of Shirley Porter

ANDREW HOSKEN

Granta Books
London

Granta Publications, 2/3 Hanover Yard, Noel Road, London N1 8BE

First published in Great Britain by Granta Books 2006

A CIP catalogue record for this book is
available from the British Library.

1 3 5 7 9 10 8 6 4 2

ISBN–13: 978–1–86207–809–3
ISBN–10: 1–86207–809–2

Typeset by M Rules
Printed and bound in Great Britain by
William Clowes Limited, Beccles, Suffolk

Contents

Contents

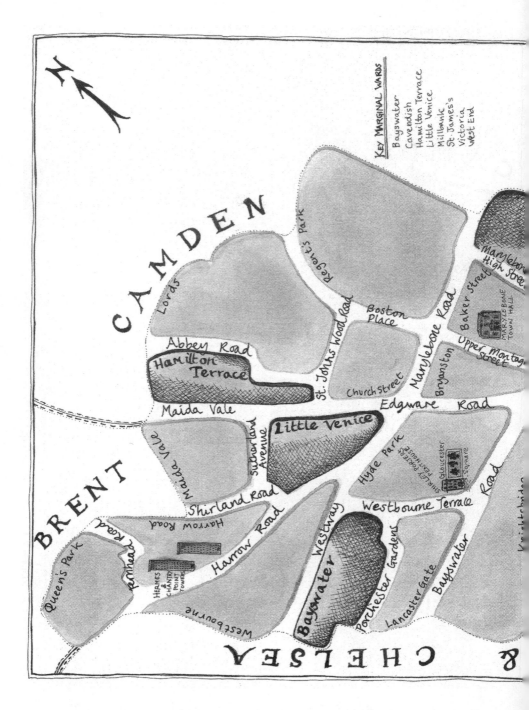

N

CAMDEN

BRENT

CHELSEA &

Regent's Park

Lords

Marylebone High Street

Boston Place

Baker Street

MARYLEBONE TOWN HALL

Abbey Road

Hamilton Terrace

St. Johns Wood Road

Church Street

Marylebone Road

Bryanston

Upper Montagu Street

Maida Vale

Edgware Road

Little Venice

Sutherland Avenue

Gloucester Square

SHELDON PRICE'S PENTHOUSE

Maida Vale

Hyde Park

Shirland Road

Westbourne Terrace

Harrow Road

Harrow Road

Westway

Porchester Gardens

Lancaster Gate

Bayswater

Knightsbridge

Penfold Road

Queen's Park

HERMES & CHANTRY POINT TOWERS

Bayswater

Westbourne

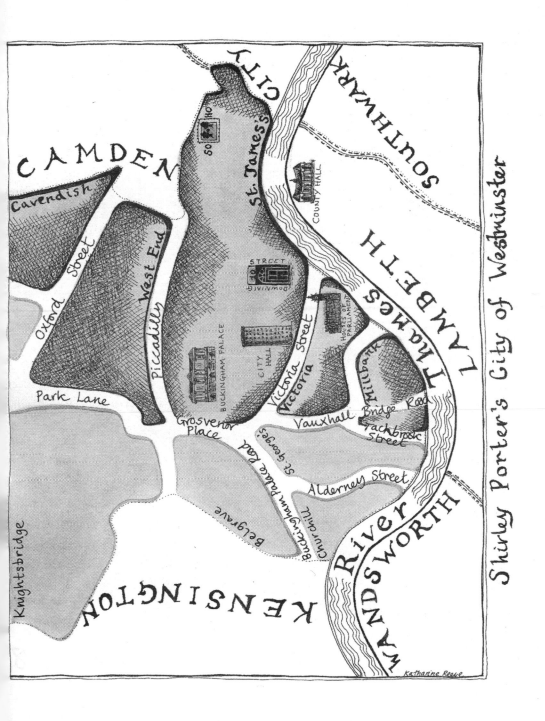

Shirley Porter's City of Westminster

Acknowledgements

This book would have been impossible without the generosity and help freely given by many people. Some spoke to me despite having to rake up painful memories. During my research, I relied on documents, letters, diaries and transcripts which constituted approximately 700 lever arch files but it was personal memory and anecdote of those involved in the Shirley Porter saga, to a greater or lesser degree, which proved particularly important. I differentiate between verbatim transcripts and my own interviews by switching tenses; if someone *says* something – I have spoken to them. If someone *said* something – I have relied on transcripts or other sources. It is hard to know where to start. I conducted more than two hundred interviews with more than 100 people. Some people gave me help and information on the basis of confidentiality or on the grounds that it was not attributed to them. They know who they are and I would like to thank them.

I received help from staff at the City of Westminster reference Library and the British Library newspaper library in Hendon, where I spent many weeks. The assistance of the Walterton and Elgin Community Homes housing association was invaluable, so particular thanks to Andy Watson, WECH Chief Executive and Debs Bourner, the organisation's community services manager. Thanks also to Tony Travers and Professor George Jones from the London School of Economics and to John Barratt, who gave me invaluable advice and help about his own inquiries into Westminster City Council as well as the foundations of the medieval trust laws governing local government which he has excavated as part of a PhD thesis on the subject, thereby answering a fundamental point: why is gerrymandering wrong? I would also like to thank the members of the Warren Old Girls' Association and staff at Worthing town archive. Thanks also to Stephen Mitchell, Head of BBC Radio News, for allowing me to write the book at a testing time, to my editor Kevin Marsh for giving me the time to write it, and to Malcolm Balen for his advice. I would also like to acknowledge the advice, enthusiasm and support of every-one at Granta, particularly to editors, Bella Shand and Sara Holloway, the managing editor Sajidah Ahmad, and sales director Frances Hollingdale, who thought that a book about Shirley Porter was long overdue. Most of all I would like to thank Katrin and our son Freddie for their patience and support while writing the book.

It took a long time and effort to recover, retrieve and reconstitute all the necessary documents I needed for the book and establish them in a central area Thanks to everyone who helped contribute to this vital resource which I called, for easy reference, 'Central Records'.

FOREWORD

The Ghost at the Feast

O n 11 February 2002 a party to celebrate the downfall of
Shirley Porter was given at the House of Commons, attended
by Labour politicians and journalists. After a meal and flowing
wine, speeches were made and the in-jokes were greeted by laughter and good-natured heckling. Porter had two months before been
found guilty of wilful misconduct and gerrymandering after
inquiries and court cases lasting for more than fifteen years.

Shirley Porter ruled as Conservative Leader of Westminster City
Council for eight catastrophic years, with responsibility for the
London borough that houses our ruling state institutions and
whose offices are only a ten-minute stroll from the Houses of
Parliament. During the 1980s Porter was Britain's second most
famous female politician after Margaret Thatcher, as much a part
of the weave and weft of the decade as Arthur Scargill and Duran
Duran. She thrived at a time when the leaders of trade unions and
councils were household names and she was lauded as the
Thatcherite antidote to the left-wing municipal 'enemies within':
'Red Ken' Livingstone, 'Red Ted' Knight and 'Red Derek' Hatton.
Porter revelled in her reputation as the mini Mrs Thatcher as she
fought the left, privatised council services, sold cemeteries and
sacked idle officials in her drive to establish Westminster City

Council, the most prestigious local authority in the land, as a Tory flagship borough. Her father was Sir Jack Cohen – the East End barrow boy who laid the foundations of Tesco, Britain's biggest supermarket chain – and her seeming invincibility as Leader of the Council was underpinned by the power derived from significant inherited wealth and a network of connections.

In nearly losing control of Westminster to Labour in the local elections of 1986, Porter was shocked to be reminded that, as an elected politician, she could be ousted by the voters, and she embarked on a disastrous course of action which resulted in what has often been described as the greatest act of corruption in the history of British local government. John Smith, the former Labour leader, said it was the 'stuff of banana republics', and Edward Heath claimed that it was the 'heaviest blow to hit the Tory Party in living memory'. Politicians often conclude that electorates make the wrong decisions but rarely, if ever, have they sought to manipulate the electoral demographic to their political advantage. Porter did exactly that. She set about replacing potential Labour voters in the borough with Conservative supporters by unlawfully abusing every resource at her disposal. She deported Westminster's homeless and earmarked thousands of council properties for sale to the 'right sort of people' she thought would vote for her. Council resources, including planning powers and environmental improvements, were misused with the same objective: 'Move in Votes'. Porter also risked the health of hundreds of homeless people by housing them in two tower blocks she knew were riddled with asbestos, as part of her extraordinary 'war' on her political enemies. For half a decade she conned the public into believing that her strategy was legal and she executed it right under the nose of Parliament and Downing Street. Porter convinced herself that she was serving the interests of the country and the Conservative Party while acting against the interests of both. And for years afterwards, she still entertained the hope of a peerage, which she was ultimately denied.

Shirley Porter's scandals were eventually exposed by the media and the authorities but her fall, although spectacular, took place in slow motion. Although her actions were recognised as corrupt by the House of Lords, she did not face criminal prosecution. Instead, under British law she was ordered to repay nearly £50 million to the taxpayers for abusing their resources. For nearly a decade she used her huge wealth to postpone ultimate judgment by making repeated court challenges until finally, on 13 December 2001, five Law Lords found Porter guilty of 'political corruption', condemning her 'history of pretence, obfuscation and prevarication'. It was, they ruled, 'a deliberate, blatant and dishonest misuse of public power'. 'Who can doubt,' they added, 'that the selective use of municipal powers to obtain party political advantage is political corruption? Political corruption, if unchecked, engenders cynicism about elections, about politicians and their motives, and damages the reputation of democratic government.'

Despite the convivial mood of the celebration at the House of Commons in 2002, a certain dissatisfaction lingered in the minds of the guests, because Porter had been judged but not punished. She lived in Israel, outside the jurisdiction of the British courts, and had hidden her wealth from the investigators in secret off-shore bank accounts and trusts. She could afford to brush aside the Lords' harsh judgment, believing that ultimately some people are too rich, too famous and too powerful to be brought to account. It would be another two years before my investigation for Radio 4's *Today* programme would unearth information about Shirley Porter's funds, resulting in a massive settlement for the council.

It is two decades since Shirley Porter embarked on an act of destruction in Westminster which consumed communities, reputations, lives and hopes and eventually herself. So why tell her story now? Mainly because it is an astonishing saga which demonstrates the depths politicians can plumb when faced with the prospect of losing power. The answer also lies in the appendices of the autobiographies and biographies of senior Tory politicians from that era. You will find no mention of Shirley Porter, even in the footnotes, despite her significant involvement in many local government policies of the Thatcherite years. Having made Porter a Dame of the British Empire and even Lord Mayor of Westminster, the party now ignores the part it played in promoting and supporting her and has never apologised. Lastly, the answer can be found in Porter's attitude to the scandal. She went to extreme lengths to lie about her actions and has shown no remorse. The full story has never been told and that was what was intended by herself and by embarrassed Conservatives. Such stories are sometimes the most interesting to tell, and frequently the most necessary.

© Philip Wolmuth

Shirley Porter on the first day of the public hearings into corruption allegations, October 1994. I'm the one in the glasses on the right, straining to hear her defence.

CHAPTER 1

Beginnings (1930–45)

Gunton Road leads off Upper Clapton Road just north of the Clapton ponds and dips into the Lee Valley towards Leyton. From there, just beyond the Millfields recreation ground, the River Lee transports its listless cargo of slime and litter south past the rotting barges and down through Hackney Marshes before joining the Thames at Bow Creek. According to records for the old Hackney parish vestry, builders called Woodruff started building houses in Gunton Road in 1894, which were acquired by Hackney Council for the poor. Number 7 is a typical late-Victorian London house with two reception rooms, a large kitchen and three bedrooms. Later, the basements became self-contained flats for au pairs or the tenants of the young professionals living above, but in the 1920s they served as storage spaces and workshops.

Jack Cohen, a market trader, bought the house from Hackney Council on 30 May 1927 and wrote out a cheque to the Mayor of Shoreditch for £1,517. It was a huge struggle to get the money for the deposit. He had £319 11s in the bank but he needed most of this to buy stock for his stall. The council agreed to lend him £1,000 and the rest he scraped together, partly from his own savings but mainly by depleting the Post Office account of his young wife, Sarah or 'Cissie'. The couple just managed to make the 5 per cent interest payments. When they sold the house eight years later, they still owed £1,000 on it.

Jack and Cissie settled down in Gunton Road with their seven-month-old baby, Irene. Three years later, on 29 November 1930, their second child, Shirley, was born at home. The news reached Jack as he was preparing the Bargain Centre, his first tiny shop, at Tooting in South London. The Bargain Centre, little more than a market stall, was the foundation stone for the mighty Tesco super-market chain which by 2005 would account for a quarter of all food sales in Britain. Cohen's entrepreneurial spirit also might explain why he chose to buy his house from the local council, one of only a very small number of people to do so. More than 50 years later, Margaret Thatcher would give council tenants the right to buy their homes, but in the 1920s the sale of council housing to private buyers was virtually unknown. Ownership bestowed respect and independence on the purchaser, even if, like Cohen, you managed to pay only the interest. It freed residents from the patro-nising interference of the municipal landlord.

Hackney Council's Housing Committee agreed to sell property in June 1926 'owing to the numerous enquiries we have received from [the] tenants'. The Ministry of Health agreed, 'subject to well-defined conditions'. But Jack Cohen never said publicly that he had been a council tenant or how, otherwise, he had been able to buy the property from Hackney. His daughter Shirley Cohen, later Porter, who was always happy to tell journalists about her father's rags-to-riches story, never mentioned the purchase, not even later when the story might have proved valuable in justifying her corrupt gerrymandering scheme to sell thousands of council houses. Perhaps she balked at using her father to promote what became known as the greatest act of corruption in British local government history, or perhaps she felt a stigma was attached to her council tenancy.

Jack Cohen was a defining influence on the life of Shirley Porter, and the growth of Tesco was a powerful determining factor in shaping its course. She gained both her wealth and her attitudes from the ruthless and driven men who built the business; her astounding, and ultimately disastrous, political career was largely a reaction against being seen as simply the daughter of the great Jack Cohen. Later, as the most powerful council leader in the country, she milked her connection with Tesco for all it was worth and claimed that it gave her the commercial acumen needed to bring about change. It also gave her the wealth and the power to overawe her colleagues and instil fear in her enemies.

Jack Cohen was born in Whitechapel, only a decade after Jack the Ripper had walked its streets, on 29 October 1898. He was registered as Jacob Kohen. His father, Avroam Kohen, had escaped persecution in a Polish ghetto and arrived in the East End some time in the mid-1880s. He set himself up as a tailor and married Sime. In 1882 alone, a quarter of a million Jews fled persecution in Eastern Europe and Tsarist Russia. If they ended up in the East End of London, they may have switched one brutish existence for another, but at least in London they were permitted to live and work. As for the Huguenots and Chinese before them, and the Bangladeshis afterwards, the East End was an initial staging post before the settlers could move somewhere better, either through luck or endeavour. Jack Cohen, as he became known after anglicising his name, succeeded in escaping the grinding poverty of the East End through a combination of good fortune and hard graft.

In the authorised biography of Jack Cohen, Maurice Corina described the founder of Tesco as a 'not particularly bright boy'. He left school at the age of fourteen and worked for his father as an apprentice tailor. In 1914 the family moved northwards to Hackney and into 26 Darnley Road, with five bedrooms and a workshop. After the outbreak of the First World War, Cohen spent two years with his father producing soldiers' uniforms and resenting every minute. Avroam was a tough autocrat and often clashed with his headstrong son, who did not want to be a tailor. At seventeen, Cohen escaped by enlisting in the Royal Flying Corps and was aboard the troop carrier *Osmanieh* when, in December 1917, it struck a mine outside Alexandria harbour and sank. He scrabbled aboard a lifeboat and survived.

After demobilisation in the late spring of 1919, Cohen used part of his £30 pay-off from the RFC to buy a small stock of foodstuffs, including Lyle's Golden Syrup and some Nestlé's condensed milk from the local NAAFI. He loaded them on to his wheelbarrow and set up a stall on Well Street in South Hackney. The profit for his first day's trading was £1, worth around £24 today. Over the next decade, Cohen worked the street markets of London and planted the seeds of an empire through a combination of hard work and costermonger charm. He bought surplus stock in quantity and sold it cheaply in smaller lots for a marginal profit. There was Pearce Duff jelly and Snowflake canned milk. 'Extra thick, creamy snowflake,' called out Cohen from his stall. 'Extra thick, extra value.' As a minor trader, he had no products of his own, so he often invested his money in obscure brand names or picked up surplus products from discontinued lines. He rebranded these products as his own and paid a printer in Cambridge Road to turn out labels for Golden Dazzle fruit and Dac Danish cream.

In 1924, six years before Shirley's birth, there were two significant events. Jack married Sarah 'Cissie' Fox, the only daughter of Benjamin Fox, a Russian Jew who had come to England at the height of the Russian Revolution in 1917. In his youth, Benjamin had stood guard outside the Tsar's palace. In England, he became a master tailor making suits from a small shop in the West End for the Aquascutum store. Jack and Cissie may have struck people as an odd couple. Cissie was an attractive and charming girl and Jack was a short squat man with a battered boxer's face and a steady stream of exuberant chatter. Benjamin was a more successful tailor than Avroam Kohen and it was Cissie who supplied the deposit for Gunton Road. But despite the apparent class divide, they proved to be a successful and loving couple, and Cissie helped provide the stability Cohen needed to succeed.

The second important event took place in the late summer of 1924, when Cohen met T. E. Stockwell, a partner in a tea-importing business called Torring and Stockwell. Cohen agreed to buy Stockwell's tea at nine pence a pound and sell it in half-pound packets at six pence each. The deal was a huge success and Cohen sold 450 lbs of tea in one day from his market stall. He said later, 'We had then and there to think of a name for the market brand [of tea] I would sell. Well, we scratched our heads and finally came up with the name TESCO, incorporating his initials and the first two letters of my surname.'

Jack Cohen made the transition from 'gorblimey' street trader to respectable shopkeeper partly through ambition and partly through necessity. In 1927 the London County Council gained parliamentary approval for a new law, known as the Costermonger Charter, to deal with the proliferation of street traders. Henceforth, all traders needed a licence from the council to work. Many costermongers were refused licences and driven out of business. Cohen saw the way the wind was blowing and gradually turned high street grocer. After his first permanent stall in Tooting, he acquired two more in Chatham and Dartford. In 1931, just months after Shirley's birth, he opened shops at Green Lane in Beacontree and Burnt Oak in Edmonton and, on 28 January 1932, Tesco was formally registered as a private limited company at Companies House. The directors were listed as Jack and Cissie Cohen and the issued capital was £1,424 divided into £1 shares. The Tesco shops were modest affairs: no front doors, only shutters which rolled up to expose a jumble of tins and boxes. Above, in weatherbeaten letters of peeling red paint: TESCO STORES LTD, THE MODERN GROCERS.

Throughout the 1930s Tesco capitalised on a population boom in the Home Counties as London spilled out and alongside newly electrified railway lines. Cohen would drive around south-east England and come back with yet more stores to be rented out at peppercorn rents. In August 1935 Tesco House, Cohen's first headquarters, was opened in Angel Road, Edmonton. At the outbreak of war four years later, Tesco had more than 100 small stores in London and the surrounding counties.

Cissie and Jack could afford a nanny and a maid to look after their daughters by the mid-1930s, and when Shirley was five the family moved out of Gunton Road for the more genteel environs of Finchley, on the outskirts of Hampstead Garden Suburb. At 27 Chessington Avenue Cohen built 'Southdene' for £3,950, complete with a billiard room. The garden at Gunton Road had been a 30ft strip of land crowded by an outside toilet and an apple tree, with a view over a scrapyard. In comparison, Chessington Avenue's garden was, according to Maurice Corina, 'landscaped'. Cohen had followed a path well trodden by successful London Jews: from the cramped squalor of Whitechapel to the more comfortable areas of Hackney and north to the leafier and desirable neighbourhoods of Golders Green or, even better, Hampstead Garden Suburb.

Shirley was close to her father and clearly loved being with him. As an adult, she spoke fondly about how she used to help out bagging raisins alongside him at an early Tesco or how she would proudly follow him down Petticoat Lane as he joked with former costermonger pals. Until the outbreak of war the Cohens were a tight-knit family unit, but when Shirley was nine Jack Cohen sent her and Irene out of harm's way, from their local state schools to a private girls' school in Sussex, the Warren. For Shirley in particular, younger and more vulnerable, the decision was shattering. The Warren provided her with an education and a home for the six years of war but she did not flourish there and clearly loathed the alien environment of privileged and well-bred girls. She admitted later that she felt utterly abandoned. She said, 'My resentment was enormous. I was a child who loved home and I didn't want to go at all. Their response was "there's a war on and everyone has to make sacrifices." It seemed to be the stock reply to any moan I had in those days.'

The school was a large Victorian manor house made of flint and stone, set in grounds on the South Downs at the edge of Worthing. In 1969, twenty-five years after Shirley Porter's departure, the Warren fell on hard times and closed. A year later an insurance company bought the building and demolished it, to the delight of Shirley Porter, who declared 'good riddance'. But in 1939 the school was flourishing, largely thanks to the war. Like the Cohens, wealthy parents were concerned that London would be bombed and thought the Warren would provide a haven for their daughters. Many of the girls at the school had fathers in the army or working somewhere in the British Empire.

The headmistress of the Warren was Miss Gertrude Ashworth, known by staff and girls alike as 'GA' – pronounced 'Jay'. For more than five crucial years, GA was the most important influence in the young Shirley Cohen's life. She was a large, imposing and well-heeled spinster, her greying red hair drawn back in a plait with a curled fringe at the front. She usually wore black or navy blue skirts but her taste in clothes was deceptively expensive. Her bills from Madame Pissot and Madame Pavy for silk blouses scandalised the school's secretary. Many girls loved GA and relished her eccentricities, but it is clear that Shirley came to loathe her.

As well as having custody of 150 fee-paying girls, GA was responsible for the Warren menagerie: a series of wire-haired fox terriers, two Friesian cows to supplement the school's milk supply and rabbits, which initially won prizes in county shows throughout Sussex, and later, as rationing bit deep, ended up on the plates of ravenous girls. GA loved the theatre and often escaped to the West End for matinees, before dining at the Trocadero.

GA's behaviour in the classroom was said to be 'extremely unpredictable'. Girls with vacant expressions were target practice for a blackboard duster, an inkpot or anything else that came to hand; on one occasion GA let off fireworks behind suspected slackers. Sometimes she would draw caricatures of the class on the blackboard. 'This is what you look like: a lot of suet puddings. Stand up! Sit down! Now run around the garden and return here ready and alert to learn something.' At the time this was just the kind of delightfully potty behaviour required by the well-meaning eccentrics placed in charge of private schools for girls. For Shirley Cohen, it was a huge culture shock.

Of the two Cohen girls, Irene was the more popular. She was considered attractive and friendly, whereas Shirley was thought by some girls to be rather surly and a tomboy. Pru Moorcroft remembers that Porter was not 'particularly fun', adding: ' I don't think anyone was a big friend of Shirley's.' Stella Williams, another Warren girl, says, 'I got the impression that popularity was not her chief asset; could you say that she tended to rub people up the wrong way? She was completely different from her sister Irene, who always came across as a very pleasant girl.' The younger girl hated being wrenched from her loving family and deposited in the alien surroundings of the Warren.

The girls wore white blouses with red polka dots under navy pleated tunics known as 'gibbahs'. In the evening there were hooded cloaks. The emphasis was on turning out sensible and sporty young women who would make sensible and sporty wives. 'A few went to university afterwards,' says Stella Coppen, one former pupil, 'but not many. It was all about common sense and a lot of girls from the Warren had that.' There was a pronounced 'jolly hockey sticks' atmosphere and sport featured just as prominently as academic studies. 'Now, girls,' GA said, 'you want to work hard and play hard and don't get them muddled up.'

In her adult life Shirley would become a fitness fanatic and even a county golf player of moderate ability. When made leader of Westminster City Council in 1983, she was asked to describe herself at school. She said, 'Thoroughly undisciplined. Likes English and History. Loves sport. Loathes being a boarder.' This statement marks the first point of contention between the portrayal of herself as a girl and her classmates' memories of her: few of her contemporaries at the Warren thought Shirley at all sporty. In part, this might have been due to her unhappiness at the school, where she found it hard to mix with the other girls, but she was also a sickly child. At the age of four, Porter had nearly died of food poisoning after the removal of her tonsils. A cousin died in the same way but Shirley pulled through. Every day until she was fourteen she had her throat coated with iodine, and it would give her trouble all her life. 'She was not sporty,' says Sheila Thomson, a Warren contemporary, 'she was not even in the lacrosse team.' Porter remained as undistinguished on the sports field as she was in the classroom.

War put a sudden brake on the expansion of Tesco but it was certainly not a disaster. Food rationing cramped Jack Cohen's methods of buying surplus goods on the cheap, but war boosted profits further. Two months after it broke out, all customers had to register with a grocer of their choice to obtain rationed products such as tea and butter. Tesco had a large stock of unrationed goods which made it attractive to people, and as it had established itself firmly by 1939 it had a set of dedicated customers. Profits increased by almost thirty per cent in the three years up to the end of 1941.

Cohen was not content for Tesco to just tick over, and now decided to pour his energy into fruit farming. He bought Little London, a farm in Goldhanger village on the Essex coast just outside Maldon, for £4,000. He converted the farmhouse into a replica of the Cohen home in Chessington Avenue, down to the first-floor veranda, and later added a tennis court and a bowling green. He bought three more farms in adjoining villages and ended up with 400 acres. The Cohen family spent many happy weekends and holidays at Little London and the girls learned to ride. Cissie learned to drive a pony and trap, which she and Shirley would often use on shopping trips to Maldon. Cohen would later sell his business, Goldhanger Fruit Farms, along with its jam-making plant, to Schweppes for a substantial profit.

At the outbreak of war Jack and Cissie Cohen also bought a small bungalow at Elinore Crescent in Worthing so they could spend the weekends with Irene and Shirley. In the Cohen fashion of combining names, it was named 'Shirene' after both girls. Wartime Worthing was no fun, particularly after the beach was mined. According to Porter, 'I remember when the wire was put on Worthing beach. I sat there with my friends thinking we're waiting for the Germans, and it didn't occur to any of us that if the Germans came, we would probably be slaughtered.'

Meanwhile, at the Warren the girls practised air-raid drills and the prefects learned to use the stirrup pump in case of incendiaries. But the fall of France in June 1940 had made the south coast a front line in the event of a German invasion, and so Gertrude Ashworth evacuated the boarders to a hotel owned by Colonel Oates at St Just near Land's End. Shirley kept a photograph of herself at this time, a small girl clutching her gas mask, with an identity label tied around her neck, saying goodbye to her parents and her dog. 'My sense of abandonment deepened,' she said. She stayed in Cornwall for a year.

Decades afterwards many girls still treasured memories of the year in Cornwall, rushing out on gusty days to see how far they could lean back on the wind without falling over. Shirley did not enjoy it. She found the Cornish 'insular' and many of the war rations, particularly the scrambled egg made from dried eggs,

revolting. 'My abiding memory of that time is one of being per-
petually cold and hungry,' she related. 'I was obsessed by food.' But
on Sundays, sometimes, there was rabbit for lunch and occasionally the excitement of baking potatoes around a campfire.

It seems that many girls were envious of Porter's access to food,
thanks to Tesco. As Moorcroft says, 'We would be hurtling around
the lacrosse pitch and she'd be sitting on the bench eating peaches,
which we had never seen, with juice running down her face.'
Another girl says, 'We used to salivate looking at her but she never
gave anything to anyone.' Although on one occasion Moorcroft
does remember Shirley bringing a chicken to a midnight feast
among the gas burners in the school laboratory.

The boarders returned from Cornwall in the autumn of 1941
when the threat of invasion receded. The staff and girls followed
the progress of the war. 'At school,' Porter wrote, 'we were orien-
tated to everything that was going on. We plotted movements and
followed battles. It was part of school lessons.' While other girls
knitted scarves for sailors, Shirley became something of an expert
plane spotter and could tell the difference between a Heinkel and a
Lancaster as they flew over Worthing.

The war had also brought an increase in the number of pupils
with the arrival of a large contingent of Jewish girls from Germany,
escaping Nazi persecution. Pam Kinch, who attended the school at
the same time as Shirley, said, 'She tended to hang around in a little
clique of other Jewish girls and I just remember she was a little bit
bossy but there were one or two like that at school.' The clubbing
together of the Jewish girls suggests that the Warren was not
immune to a cultural anti-Semitism which was widespread in
England and elsewhere in Europe. The school welcomed Jewish
girls but they were certainly identified as such by the others, and
tended to stick together. One old girl remembers being reprimanded by a teacher for making anti-Semitic remarks. During the
war years news of the atrocities in Europe filtered out of Germany
and it was an unsettling time for the Jewish pupils. Shirley Cohen's
experience at school made her acutely aware of anti-Semitism,
whether real or imagined, throughout her life.

Forty-five years after leaving the Warren, she accused the school and particularly Gertrude Ashworth of anti-Semitism, claiming that she was overlooked as a potential head girl because the head-mistress did not want the name Cohen on the school board of honour. In July 1989 the *Observer* reported, 'Jack Cohen arrived to fight the battle on his daughter's behalf and it ended with her leaving without a single examination passed.'

Stella Williams, elected head girl in 1945, never knew that Shirley Porter was in the running. She says, 'I don't know what she's talking about because frankly I never heard rumours of her being head girl when I was at school.' Stella Coppen, another contemporary, says, 'I think she left under a bit of a cloud; I don't think she was happy, and I never heard anything about her wanting to be head girl. She was far too young anyway!'

Shirley Porter's story is almost certainly untrue but it is worth mentioning simply because she repeated it many times. Something strange had undoubtedly occurred, as Jack Cohen abruptly removed Shirley from the school, but it is unlikely that she was ever recommended as head girl, based on her performance and obvious dislike for the school. Ten Warren contemporaries, interviewed for this book, had never heard the story before it appeared in the press. To the growing irritation of her former classmates, the claims were repeated by successive newspaper feature writers.

Porter once described 'passing examinations' as the 'most over-rated virtue' but when she became a successful politician her senior officials detected a deep insecurity about her lack of education. The head girl saga would certainly help to explain to her colleagues why her education was cut short but she may well have used the unstated anti-Semitism at the Warren as a cover for her lack of academic success. In any event, her old classmates thought they recognised a self-serving slur when they saw it. In 1989 they dropped Shirley Porter from their old girls' mailing list.

CHAPTER 2

Family Fortunes (1945–74)

Shirley Cohen spent two years after leaving school at establishments which catered for the non-academic daughters of the wealthy. First there was a stint at La Ramée finishing school in Switzerland, for lessons in elocution and etiquette and the opportunity to brush up on French and skiing. 'I disliked it intensely but endured seven months,' she said. She returned home and enrolled on a course at St Godric's Secretarial and Languages School in NW3.

By the age of eighteen, Shirley had grown into an attractive young woman; photographs from this period show a petite woman with dark curly hair. In 1948 she returned from a family trip to South Africa and, at a friend's wedding, met Leslie Porter, a short, stout man with startling blue eyes, ten years her senior. Shirley thought Leslie looked like the actor Paul Newman. Years later, when he was well into his sixties, she fondly claimed, 'Women still swoon.' Leslie asked her out to the Chelsea Arts Ball and proposed three months later. They were married in under a year at the St Petersburg synagogue in Bayswater on 29 June 1949. The wedding reception took over the Dorchester Hotel and the couple honeymooned in the Grand at the Lido in Venice. 'At the time,' Shirley said, 'I wished I had known more about sex. It would save the embarrassment one went through.' Perhaps more surprising was the admission that at the age of eighteen she could 'barely boil an egg'.

Leslie Porter was much more self-sufficient. Born in 1920, he left Holloway County School in North London aged fourteen to become a car salesman. During the war, he served in the King's Royal Rifle Corps in North Africa, Greece and Italy, initially as technician and finally as quartermaster sergeant. 'My boy,' he once told a dinner companion, 'there was a moment when I thought Hitler was following me around the Mediterranean.' After the war Porter joined his father, John, in the family's textile firm, J. Porter and Co. He built up the business by trading in tea towels, pillow cases and other items for which there was a large demand and within a decade had transformed the company out of recognition. He enjoyed working for his own family business, where he had achieved a high level of autonomy, and for more than a decade he rebuffed entreaties from Jack Cohen to work for Tesco.

Leslie Porter did allow Cohen to buy the couple their first house, Porter Ho, on the outskirts of Hampstead Garden Suburb in Lyttelton Road, close to the Cohen family home. The area had a large Jewish community, was well-heeled, well-to-do and True Blue. Jack Cohen ordered his solicitor, Bernard Lazarus, to complete the purchase within one day. 'Please do what I ask. I want it done, today,' commanded Cohen, who was growing increasingly demanding. For the next two decades, Shirley Porter's life revolved around her family in north-west London. She had two children in her first four years of marriage – Linda when she was twenty, followed by John two years later. She settled into life as a wealthy housewife, playing golf, working for charity and raising her family. But she did not, as she often suggested, completely eschew political ambition and activity during this period.

Shirley Porter applied to become a parliamentary candidate for the Conservative Party in her late twenties but was rejected. In 1957 Alan Dawtry was appointed the Chief Executive of the City of Westminster Council and shortly afterwards became good friends with two senior London-based Tories, Arnold and Lillian Silverstone. Lillian was then the chairman of a regional branch of the Conservative Party which included Kent, Surrey and Sussex;

Arnold was a successful property developer who would become party treasurer under Edward Heath, and later a life peer. Dawtry dined with the couple regularly at their home in Lowndes Square, Knightsbridge. One evening, before the general election in 1959, Lillian Silverstone said she had been vetting potential female parliamentary candidates. 'Perhaps I shouldn't be telling you this,' she told Dawtry, 'but today I turned down as a candidate Jack Cohen's daughter Shirley, because I didn't think she was bright enough.' Dawtry remembered the exchange when Porter turned up as a councillor at Westminster in 1974. According to some of her former political associates in Westminster, Porter always felt she had to struggle for acceptance from the Tories and had a love–hate relationship with the party. It may well have stemmed from this rejection. Alan Dawtry heard that Porter was so angry about it at the time that she left the Conservatives and joined the Liberal Party.

Porter did indeed join the Liberals in Finchley within a year of this rejection, but she was not an active party member. Gerald Hirsch, secretary of the Finchley Liberals, remembers collecting annual subscription payments from Porter at her home in Lyttelton Road. Hirsch says, 'Once you've paid your subs, you're a member of the Liberal Party.' Porter never mentioned her former membership of the Liberal Party either before or after she became a committed hard-right Thatcherite firebrand. She remained silent too about her participation in a campaign between 1958 and 1960 led by the local Liberals which proved particularly embarrassing to the Conservative Party and their new parliamentary candidate in Finchley, Margaret Thatcher.

In 1958 Frank Davis, a local Liberal councillor and a former mayor of the borough, accused Conservatives of tolerating the blackballing of Jews at the Finchley Golf Club. Gerald Hirsch says the issue of suspected anti-Semitism helped the Liberals take control of the local council from the Conservatives in 1959. Margaret Thatcher contested the parliamentary seat of Finchley for the first time at the general election in October 1959, and she was clearly anxious about the impact of the Liberals' campaign.

Alan Cohen, the then Liberal Leader of Finchley Council, says, 'We arranged for two or three members of the Jewish faith, competent golfers with a good handicap, to apply. We managed to find someone to nominate them, and of course what happened was that they were turned down.' One of the campaigners was Shirley Porter, who, along with her friend Freda Gold, extended the campaign across North London by applying to ten golf clubs including Hampstead and North Middlesex. They were turned down each time, fobbed off with lame excuses such as that there were 'no vacancies' or that, unaccountably, the ladies' section had become suddenly filled.

Alan Cohen says, 'The council then had the evidence,' and told the golf clubs in its area that their licences would not be renewed if they continued discrimination. In March 1960 the *Jewish Chronicle* started a three-part inquiry into the scandal. 'In general,' the *Chronicle* said, 'it would seem that many clubs throughout the country, especially in areas where there are sizeable Jewish communities, indulge in subtle discrimination against Jewish applicants. In some cases clubs have a quota system for Jews.' The *Chronicle* went on, 'An extensive campaign conducted during the past two years by Mrs Shirley Porter (of Hampstead) and Freda Gold (of Golders Green) has yielded some interesting results.'

Tesco was emerging from the doldrums of the immediate postwar period. Self-service, where customers picked goods off the shelves themselves, had been established in the United States for decades, but the late 1950s saw the start of the supermarket revolution in Britain. By 1958 144 of 150 Tesco stores were self-service and there were plans for ten fully fledged supermarkets, big self-service stores, for the early 1960s, by which time Leslie Porter would be a senior director of the company.

Jack Cohen, despite having two daughters, would eventually be succeeded as Tesco Chairman by their husbands, first Irene's, Hyman Kreitman, and eventually Shirley's, Leslie Porter. Cohen did not believe in mixing women with business. There was one exception: Daisy Hyams, his secretary in 1932, went on to become the company's senior buyer. When a relatively junior board member, Ian MacLaurin, who would later end up as Chairman of Tesco, discovered he was being paid fifty per cent more than Hyams, whose rise through the company was by then a Tesco legend, Cohen said dismissively, 'Oh, she's married. She doesn't need the money.' 'It was not simply meanness,' observed MacLaurin in his autobiography *Tiger by the Tail*, 'more his belief that women should know their place in the order of things, and that their place was subordinate to men.' Jack Cohen was born thirty years before women were given equal voting rights and it seems that he expected little more of his daughters other than that they fulfil their roles as wives and mothers. In any event, neither Irene nor Shirley was asked to play any part in the fortunes of Tesco except to support their husbands in their rise to the top of the organisation. Irene appears not to have been concerned. But for her driven younger sister, Tesco was her inheritance and the fact that she was allowed no part in its running clearly grated over the years.

Shirley Porter was extremely close to her parents but she resembled her restless and ambitious father far more than her gracious and gentle mother. Cissie Cohen spent her time with her family or on charity work and seemed content to leave the running of Tesco to the men. A senior member of London Jewish society knew the Cohen family well during this period. 'Their mother was the most delightful, wonderful woman, a real lady. But I think both girls were influenced by their father, particularly Shirley. Jack Cohen was a really tough man,' she says. 'He built up a really fantastic business and he didn't have a son. My mother used to say, really not of Shirley's sister, but of Shirley herself, "If I saw the Cohen girls walking down the road, I'd always move to the other side because I was always so terrified of them!" I don't know if Shirley was always politically ambitious but she always wanted to be not just Jack Cohen's daughter. She wanted to justify herself.'

In 1959 Leslie Porter relented to a decade of pressure from Jack Cohen and joined the Tesco board as a part-time consultant, advising the company on expanding its non-grocery lines. He continued to run his family's textile business for another year, after which he joined the Tesco board full-time and took on the job of building up the company's new non-food division, known as 'Home 'n' Wear'. Leslie Porter arrived at a time when the relationship between Jack Cohen and Hyman Kreitman, his other son-in-law and deputy, had soured. Cohen himself summed up the problem, 'I want something yesterday; he is planning ten years ahead.'

According to David Powell's history of Tesco, *Counter Revolution*, Cohen saw Kreitman as one of the new men 'sapping at his power and usurping his authority'. Kreitman found it hard to cope with 'the Governor's' despotism and bullying. Leslie Porter was not such a pushover. He had not simply married the boss's daughter, he had built up his own successful business by the time he joined Tesco, and was ebullient and self-confident. He was often seen with a fat cigar, which he was said to chew rather than smoke. Occasionally during an inspection of a Tesco store he would cast the remains on the floor, leaving someone else to sweep them up. Leslie Porter liked his whisky, which he drank straight, in three-finger measures. In fact, he was a lot like Cohen. The pair often clashed, sometimes violently, and ultimately victory went to Leslie.

Tesco's rapid growth created wealth but with it came greater responsibility, pressure and rows among the ruling family members which pushed family relationships to breaking point. Despite these tensions, the family would gather before sundown every Friday evening at Cohen's home in Chessington Avenue to celebrate the start of the Jewish Sabbath in the traditional way. There would be the five traditional blessings. Cissie, Shirley and Irene would each receive a blessing from their husbands. All would bless the wine. The Motzi, the blessing of the sweet, braided Challah bread, completed the prayers with the words: 'Blessed are you, Eternal One, Ruling Presence of the Universe, who brings forth bread from the earth.' The family would break the bread and consume it with the customary sprinkle of salt, and the Sabbath was greeted with 'Shabbat Shalom!' Then, over a hearty candle-lit meal, the conversation would be dominated by Tesco: which products were in or out; which managers were in or out. The wine would flow and the air would become thick with cigar smoke. Later, Shirley Porter would tell profile writers on national newspapers how she listened with rapt attention to the Tesco table talk as the three men plotted the expansion of the supermarket chain. Some writers thought Shirley Porter derived her drive and her love of the raw simplicities of commerce from these family get-togethers. During her political

career it was clear that, predominant among the characteristics that
rubbed off on her at these gatherings, were the hard talk of the
dealer and the pitiless consecration of the bottom line. There was
also, of course, Shirley Porter's often emphasised genetic inheritance. Ian MacLaurin saw both Jack Cohen and Shirley Porter at
close hand for years. 'In many ways they were very similar, Jack
and his daughter Shirley,' he once said. 'Ambitious and ruthless,
they made dangerous enemies, though none more dangerous than
to themselves!'

As Leslie made his way up the company hierarchy, becoming
assistant managing director in 1963 and later deputy chairman,
Shirley raised the children and concentrated on golf and charity
work. She did voluntary work for WIZO, the Women's
International Zionist Organisation, which provides care for disad-
vantaged Jews in Israel and the Diaspora. She was captain of three
golf clubs and in the early 1960s played five times for the
Hertfordshire Women second team. But she may have seen this as
a subservient role and bridled at her exclusion from the affairs of
Tesco. Her family found her difficult and affectionately called her
'Chippy'.

Tesco expanded rapidly throughout the 1960s, mainly through
the acquisition of rivals such as Irwins and Victor Value and with
the introduction of Green Shield stamps, a loyalty voucher which
customers saved until they had enough to trade in for some household goods they wanted. In 1965 alone, fifty-one stores were
opened, usually by Cohen and the chimpanzee which starred in TV
adverts for Brooke Bond tea. Tesco quadrupled in size in little more
than a decade. By 1967 the business which had started from a
wheelbarrow was a supermarket chain with 834 shops and a
turnover of £200 million. Jack Cohen coined a saying later quoted
by Shirley Porter, 'You can't do business sitting on your arse.' He
had brass tie clips made up with the initials YCDBSOYA. He even
presented one to Harold Wilson.

By the late 1960s it was clear that Tesco had outgrown its cre-
ator. Cohen's policy, to 'pile it high and sell it cheap', no longer had
the same resonance. Cohen, nearing seventy, was out of fashion
and out of time. Since 1947, when Tesco became a public company,

© Getty Images

Jack Cohen, 'You can't do business sitting on your arse.'

investment was found elsewhere and Cohen's influence waned. Although the family's stake in the company became ever more valuable, it also became proportionally smaller. By 1967 the family owned just 18.4 per cent of the shares and held trustee interests in another four per cent. Jack Cohen became increasingly irascible and bitter as it dawned on him that he was being edged out of the business by his two sons-in-law. Even Daisy Hyams, a loyalist from the early days, described Cohen as 'restless', 'impetuous' and 'single-minded to the point of distraction'. She was being diplomatic.

On 6 October 1968 Shirley Porter and Irene Kreitman organised Cohen's seventieth birthday party at the Dorchester Hotel. Seven weeks later he received a knighthood from the Prime Minister, Harold Wilson, in the New Year's Honours List. The razor company Wilkinson's Swords presented Cohen with two swords which were hung in the boardroom. Within a year, on 16 December 1969, he was deposed as chairman and replaced by his son-in-law, Hyman Kreitman. Leslie Porter became deputy chairman. Cohen was made Life President and, according to the minutes, '. . . requested the board confirm his duties'. There was a brief discussion and a decision: 'The board confirmed that he was responsible for public relations and there being no further business, the meeting was closed.'

Cohen haunted Tesco House, the company's new headquarters at Cheshunt, and meddled incessantly in the family firm. Ian MacLaurin likened Tesco board meetings to gatherings of the Chicago Mafia, '. . . with Jack in the role of Godfather, all the while scheming to curb Hyman's power'. By September 1973 Kreitman had wearied of Cohen and retired. Leslie Porter took over as chairman, but he also squabbled constantly with the old man. On one occasion, the pair grabbed the Wilkinson's swords off the wall in the boardroom and had a duel, with Cohen shouting, 'One more crack like that, and I'll kill him.' When some Harlow wine merchants awarded Leslie a carriage clock instead of Cohen, the Life President started a brawl with his son-in-law in a Rolls-Royce on the A3. By 1976, Leslie Porter's control of the business was secure enough for him to emphasise Cohen's irrelevance publicly. He informed one journalist with bluff ruthlessness, 'I think Sir John took a long time to get the message. He has the message now. We value him going out and visiting branches but as far as the day-to-day running of the business is concerned, he merely comments. We meet every Monday morning and I would say that we get through most of the agenda by the time Sir John arrives.'

By 1970 Cohen and his family held personal trust interests of forty million shares, enough to yield a total gross annual income of £500,000. By average stock market prices, the family holdings at that time were valued at more than £22 million. Although it is not clear how much of Tesco the thirty-nine-year-old Shirley Porter personally owned, there is no doubt that she was a seriously wealthy woman.

Both Shirley Porter's children left home and she found herself with time on her hands. John was going to university and Linda had married young and settled in Israel. Porter suffered an acute mid-life crisis. She admitted later, 'I was amazed to find at the age of thirty-nine I had become a mother-in-law. I found it rather shattering.' She filled the vacuum with charitable work, organised charity sales at Tesco stores and became a prison visitor. In 1962 Jack and Cissie Cohen had moved out of their home in Chessington Avenue and into a luxury apartment in Cumberland Terrace, overlooking Regent's Park, in the City of Westminster. Life in the Garden Suburb had palled, and on 2 September 1970 Shirley moved closer to her parents. She and her husband bought a luxury penthouse duplex apartment at 19 Chelwood House in Gloucester Square, overlooking Hyde Park. The Kreitmans took the apartment below. The family was once again living in close proximity. More significantly, Porter's flat lay within the City of Westminster, which meant she could stand for election to the local council, if she wished.

Porter was still thirsting for some kind of role. In 1972 she was asked to become a magistrate, a natural progression for a prison visitor. For twelve years she sat on the Bench on Talgarth Road in West London, where she handed out fines and occasional short prison sentences to petty thieves and drink-drivers. She claimed later that her interest in politics was whetted during an argument with a left-wing magistrate. She realised she did not know enough about politics so she 'started reading up on the subject'. She also claimed that she got involved in local politics because she was disgusted by the litter and dirt in central London. Her break into politics seems to have been more dependent on her wealth than her political beliefs however. Her local Conservative Association, based in Paddington, was strapped for funds and had developed a nose for hard cash. One day Porter was asked for a contribution for a fundraising tombola. Gradually she became involved in her local party and, ever restless like her father, decided to enter local politics.

In the spring of 1974 she applied for selection as a Tory candidate in the imminent local council elections. Reg Watts, another hopeful, remembers coming across her just before the selection meeting at the Association offices in Bishopsbridge Road, not far from Porter's home. Watts, who served as a councillor in Southend-on-Sea for nine years, chatted to Porter before they both went in to be interviewed. 'She was a little nervous,' he said, 'and we just exchanged pleasantries. There was that feeling that you may be competing with each other, but she was very pleasant.'

Porter's interview was only twenty minutes long. The questions were fairly predictable and not particularly challenging: 'Why do you want to be a councillor? Why do you want to represent this ward?' No one ever became a local councillor for the money; the attendance allowances were feeble. She told the panel that she wanted the council to 'develop strong links with local arts amenity groups' and argued that it did not do enough to keep people informed about its activities. She wanted action taken against the nuisance of coaches parked off Park Lane and drivers to be prevented from using the quiet streets around Hyde Park as rat-runs.

Work as a magistrate and involvement with charity organisations were fairly standard precursors for anyone wanting to be a Tory councillor. By the time of her interview, Porter had also worked as a fundraiser for the first of the two general elections in 1974 called by the Labour government. She had time and energy, and she was rich. One former councillor said, 'The Paddington Conservative Association was in financial trouble and I think they were hoping she would bail them out, but to her credit, as far as I know, she never did.' Porter's application was successful, but after her selection someone at the Association noticed that she was not actually a member of the Conservative Party. One party worker says, 'It was gently suggested to her that, as she had been selected to represent the party on the City Council, she might like to consider joining.' Porter quickly did so and became one of five Tory candidates for the Hyde Park ward, which, with twenty-two other mini-constituencies, made up Westminster. The local elections for the City of Westminster and the thirty-one other borough councils in London were held on 4 May 1974. Porter could be seen on the campaign train handing out leaflets or driving around in her chocolate-coloured Mini with the licence plate JP1, after her son John. Hyde Park was a safe Tory ward and she secured an easy victory by polling 2,602 votes, a majority of more than 1,000 over the Labour candidates.

Shortly afterwards, Porter attended the ceremony at the Marylebone Council House to witness the robing of the new Lord

Mayor. It was her first important municipal event as a Conservative councillor. Jack Cohen, now sick and rapidly ageing, was also present. He sat next to Simone Prendergast, a member of the dynasty which founded Marks and Spencer and a prominent Tory who was made a Dame in 1986. 'Isn't it wonderful that my girl is a councillor?' Cohen said to Prendergast. So began one of the most extraordinary, and most calamitous, political careers in the history of British local government.

CHAPTER 3

Little Britain (1974–8)

The City of Westminster comprises the greatest concentration of power and wealth in Britain. Its eight and a half square miles, stretching from Victoria and Pimlico in the south to Paddington and Queen's Park in the north, encompass the country's most important symbols and institutions. The streets of Kensington and Chelsea in the west may boast the chic of Notting Hill and the status of a royal borough, and the ancient City of London immediately to the east may lay claim to St Paul's Cathedral and the Bank of England, but in Westminster, the Abbey, Parliament and Buckingham Palace represent the three great estates of Church, government and monarchy.

For centuries, Parliament itself oversaw the running of Westminster. The historian George Trevelyan wrote, 'Neither London nor the court nor parliament had ever wished to deal with a Lord Mayor of Westminster. So Westminster was never permitted to enjoy self-government or to acquire a corporate sense.' Perhaps, as things turned out under Shirley Porter, they were proved right all along. The Establishment was always deeply concerned about what would happen if Westminster were allowed its own authority. A council with sway over an area occupied by the government and the monarchy could get ideas above its station and grow into a rival power; such an authority, privy to great secrets held by the important instruments of the state within its boundaries, could fall into the wrong hands. By 1901, such fears had relented, and following a general reorganisation of local government in London, Parliament formed the first Westminster City Council from a motley collection of one district board and several old parish vestry councils such as St George Hanover Square and St James's.

For sixty years the councillors met in Carvell House, their tiny city hall just off Trafalgar Square. Once a month at two o'clock they would gather in their formal gowns to register their approval or, less frequently, their disapproval of the decisions and actions taken by the city's officials, over such services as street cleaning and rubbish collection. Tea would be taken at four-thirty and then, usually, they would retire to their clubs in St James's to dine.

By the early 1960s the phenomenal expansion of London into the Home Counties meant a second reorganisation of its local government. The London County Council, which had provided essential services across central London, such as fire, ambulance and housing, was abolished and replaced by the Greater London Council, which took on a less defined, strategic role across a much greater area encompassing all of Middlesex and parts of Kent, Essex and Surrey. The second tier of borough councils like Westminster was merged to form new authorities.

Cross-river mergers were vetoed, so common sense dictated the amalgamation of Westminster with its two northern neighbours, Marylebone and Paddington. The Thames would form the southern border of the new city as it had the old. A walk across the new city from Parliament in the south to Paddington in the north would take you up Whitehall, past Downing Street, to Trafalgar Square and Soho, then across Regent Street in the West End through Mayfair to Marble Arch and Bayswater Road, which formed the border between the old City and its two new partners. From there, you could go westwards to Bayswater before heading up across the Harrow Road into Maida Vale, where, just north of the Paddington Recreation Ground, the City dissolved into the urban landscape of the London Borough of Brent.

The sedate neighbourhoods of Marylebone around Lord's

cricket ground and Regent's Park were in tune with the mansion blocks and mews of Mayfair and Victoria; the same was true of south Paddington around Hyde Park and Bayswater. North Paddington was a different matter from its wealthier neighbouring postcodes. Since the war, Paddington had been controlled by the Tories, except for one term in the 1940s, but there was always a forceful Labour opposition which drew its support from the slums and council estates off the Harrow Road. The main preoccupations of Paddington's councillors, particularly the Labour members, had been the shocking housing conditions in the north and the activities of notorious private landlords like Peter Rachman, who had bought the leases for run-down houses from the Church Commissioners. They then used vicious dogs and violence to force out established tenants so the properties could be let for higher rents, mainly to new immigrants from the Caribbean desperate for somewhere to live. The merger with Paddington injected active and vibrant socialism into the bloodstream of the new city of Westminster and was something of a shotgun wedding for many in the old City. Dame Simone Prendergast says, 'It only became political when it became a much bigger authority because it brought in Marylebone and Paddington, and Paddington was a hotbed of really left-wing people; it produced Ken Livingstone and before him Illtyd Harrington.'

On paper it was a merger, but in reality it was a gentle annexation by the old City of its northern neighbours. Until 1983, three of the council Tory Party leaders of the new City were drawn from the ranks of the old one. The first chief executive of the new city, who managed the council officers, was Alan Dawtry, the town clerk for the old one.

Sir Hugh Cubitt, the Conservative leader when Shirley Porter joined the council, says, 'When we had the merger there was no doubt that Westminster was regarded as London borough Number One, and Marylebone and Paddington were quite delighted to be joined up to Westminster, and I think, and this is a very immodest thing to say, we probably had a higher calibre of councillor on Westminster than they had on Paddington and much the same on Marylebone.'

The new council was not only three times the size of the old, it was given extra powers. The town halls which had served the three component boroughs were too small for this grand new entity and, in any case, Paddington town hall at Paddington Green stood in the way of the new Westway extension of the A40. Marylebone's town hall on the Marylebone Road was kept for council meetings, and Dawtry entered into negotiations to rent a new building in the heart of the old city as the headquarters of the new council. He approached Sir Harold Samuel, chairman of the property developer Land Securities, to lease a stark, grey, twenty-floor tower block nearing completion in Victoria Street and told him that work had to be completed by 1 April 1965. Jack Taylor of Taylor Woodrow was in charge of the building project and managed the task with just a day to spare. The 1,500 officials of the new authority moved into City Hall.

The top two floors were reserved for the Tory councillors and their Labour opponents. These part-time politicians were elected to represent the twenty-three wards which made up the City. The other floors were occupied by council officers. They were the civil servants of the City Council. For them, the council was not just an outside interest, or even a ticket to get a parliamentary seat, as it was for the councillors. City Hall paid their rent or mortgage; it was their profession. They served the councillors in control, but were themselves required by law to be politically neutral. In Westminster the majority had always been Conservative, but decisions had to be taken by committees made up of councillors of all parties, and often ratified by meetings of the full council. Officers implemented decisions made by the controlling political party, but they also had to assist the Opposition with advice and information. By law, their first duty was to the public. Like the councillors, the officers acted as trustees who managed the council's assets, whether those assets were housing estates, dustcarts or rat catchers, for the common good of the people of Westminster.

In City Hall there were entire floors for different departments: for the planners who approved and rejected applications for demolitions or new buildings, or closed down dirty restaurants and dubious hotels; for the City Treasurer's office which collected a vast wealth in rates from the stores in the West End and some 200,000 residents; for the housing officers who cleared slums, built new homes and collected the rent from good tenants or evicted bad ones when they failed to pay; for the social workers who managed children's homes, cared for the elderly and kept an eye on problem families; for the City Solicitor who made sure that the council, its officials and politicians kept on the right side of the law. The big strategic functions such as transport were not housed here; they were the responsibility of the Greater London Council and the schools that of the GLC's quasi-independent Inner London Education Authority, the ILEA.

In their first full meeting in 1965 the councillors of the new City stood for a minute in silence to mark the recent death of Winston Churchill, before settling the crucial question of their ceremonial dress. They decided to wear the blue robes worn by members of the three old Westminster boroughs. The Aldermen, an ancient title enjoyed by senior councillors – the elder statesmen of the City – would wear the scarlet robes of St Marylebone and Paddington. The Lord Mayor would wear the blue Chancellor's robe with gold embroidery and the black tricorn hat. All the costumes were tatty and needed replacing. A quote by Ede and Ravenscoft Ltd, who specialised in making such things, had been accepted: £913 and 4 pence.

The new City was ruled by Tory patricians with little time for the hurly-burly of politics. Their status as aldermen meant they did not have to stand for election. Aldermen usually had a long history as elected candidates on the local council but in their senior years the status was bestowed upon them by the party. In a dated system, they were chosen not by the voters but by the elected councillors and then invited to assume the supreme position. The leadership of the City would be surrendered by an Alderman to his anointed successor after a decent period of five years or so. As the Tories always held the majority of seats, their leader ran the council and would be required occasionally to spar with his counterpart on the Labour benches. There was little dissent as the power passed from Group Captain Sir Gordon Pirie to Arthur Barrett to Hugh Cubitt and then to David Cobbold.

Hugh Cubitt not only ran the City – with the help of Chief

Executive Alan Dawtry – but his great-great-great-grandfather, the builder Thomas Cubitt, had developed a significant portion of it: Belgravia, Mayfair and Pimlico. According to Cubitt, the City was 'eighty per cent good management and twenty per cent politics, at the most'. He and his colleagues thought of themselves more as non-executive chairmen of the board than as leaders of the council. This suited the paid officials under Alan Dawtry. Cubitt would pop into City Hall occasionally to see how Dawtry and his team were getting on and acknowledges, 'It was very effectively run by Alan Dawtry, in the way of things in those days. The officers under Alan ran the council and really devised the policies and the councillors sort of listened, and decided, and then the officers carried them out.'

The relationship between the Tories and their Labour opponents was at first extremely cordial. Cubitt and the leader of the Labour councillors, Illtyd Harrington, were close friends and would get together before meetings of the full council. Harrington, an elected councillor, would dine each month with the Conservative leader to sort out any differences. 'We would go through the agenda,' says Cubitt, 'and agree the things we agreed about and even agree about the things we disagreed about! If we didn't agree on something, we would have a bit of a bargey in the council chamber and then we sorted it out.'

Robert Morcom-Harneis, the Tory chief whip at the time, believed the City was run by an 'inner circle' of predominantly rich men like Cubitt, who saw their roles on the council as a duty and revelled in the grand events, whether it was attending Westminster Abbey for the annual council service or displaying their medals at St James's Church in Paddington on Remembrance Sunday. Morcom-Harneis remembers the difficulty he had in trying to arrange a meeting of Tory activists, including some local councillors, to select a new parliamentary candidate for South Westminster. 'They were all anxious to get it over with,' he says. 'They were all going to the Opera and I couldn't hold it on certain days because something was happening at Eton or there was racing at Epsom, and there wouldn't be anyone around. It was slightly unreal as far as I was concerned.'

The City Fathers expected to see new councillors when required, but not to hear them. Porter said later that she found her first years on the council 'the most frustrating period of my life'. She said, 'Naturally I was very keen, desperate to do things, to get on with the job, to put right the wrongs I'd seen. But I felt every good idea I suggested vanished into a black hole.'

Porter was placed as a junior backbencher on two committees, Housing Management and Highways and Works. At first she found the machinations of the committees baffling and the council in general a puzzle. After meetings she would often give a fellow Hyde Park councillor, Trixie, later Baroness Gardner, a lift home. Gardner says, 'Shirley always used to say to me, "I don't understand how this council works, do explain things to me."'

Porter pushed for promotion fairly early in her first term as a councillor. She began phoning the home of Morcom-Harneis. His wife, Martine, made it clear that the calls were 'not appreciated' and they stopped. Porter realised that badgering people was not the way to get on at Westminster and tried to be patient. The tactic paid off six months after she was elected when Cubitt made her a deputy whip, a job which meant running errands for Morcom-Harneis and making sure some of the older and lazier councillors turned up for votes at important council and committee meetings. She admitted later that her promotion was probably to keep her quiet, and she was right. Cubitt cheerfully admits, 'I put her dainty foot on the first ladder of advancement.' Morcom-Harneis remembers Cubitt saying that if Porter was going to push for advancement, it would be better to have her inside the tent peeing out, than the unseemly alternative.

By the mid-seventies the political climate was turning distinctly chilly and events would soon destroy the avuncular self-satisfaction which emanated from the wood-panelled meeting rooms of City Hall. Labour governments under Harold Wilson and Jim Callaghan, surviving on slim or non-existent parliamentary majorities, lurched from one financial crisis to another. The planet seemed to hang on every word of the Saudi Oil Minister, Sheikh Ahmad Zaki Yamani. A swift rise in oil prices coupled with inflationary wage demands by the unions would bring the country to bankruptcy. In November 1976 the Chancellor, Denis Healey, was forced to negotiate a loan from the International Monetary Fund.

Unemployment in Britain rose from 625,000 in February 1974 to 1.5 million by August 1976, by which time inflation had hit fifteen per cent. Thanks to the stores along Oxford Street and elsewhere in the City, Westminster was so rich that just a hike of one penny on the rates – the property-value-based local tax collected by councils at the time – would generate £3 million. Most of the money raised by Westminster was dispensed by the government to the GLC and ILEA, or to poorer boroughs.

In 1975 the Labour Environment Secretary, Tony Crosland, reminded councils that they accounted for a quarter of all government spending and that they would have to tighten their belts. 'The party is over,' he told them. Town halls would have to cut spending.

Jonah Walker Smith, Westminster's Housing Chairman, told the council, 'There hasn't been such an economic crisis that this government has got us into since the 1920s.' He and other City Fathers started to look for cuts. The crisis finally hit home in Westminster, despite its wealth, and began to affect the once impregnable fortress. Labour councillors protested about the cuts to services such as council housing repairs because they impacted on the poor. They also argued that Westminster was wealthy enough to avoid causing hardship. Inevitably, cracks started to appear in the political consensus enjoyed by Labour and the Tories at Westminster. The cosy lunches of Cubitt and Illtyd Harrington were becoming a distant memory.

In this more arid political climate early impressions of Porter were mixed. From her first appearances in the council chamber at Marylebone Council House, her Tory colleagues observed that Porter was always immaculately and tastefully turned out and regularly weighed down by expensive jewellery. She stood a shade over five feet tall in her high heels and, thanks to golf and regular exercise, was slim. She was rarely without a tan acquired while playing golf and on regular trips to Israel and California, or a recent cut and blow-dry. As a politician in the chamber, however, Porter was not so impressive. There was always a high standard of debate during council meetings at Westminster, but Porter did not

strike Alan Dawtry or her fellow councillors as a good speaker. She
was not a quick thinker and she relied on notes prepared earlier. It
would be a constant criticism throughout her political career. The
more sophisticated operators on both sides of the council chamber
concurred with Dawtry that she lacked spontaneity and mental
agility, and possibly humour. Her initial ignorance of politics and
how the council worked clearly robbed her of the self-confidence
needed for public speaking. Her chronic throat complaint did not
help either and she could sometimes sound shrill and rather nasal.
To some of the snootier patricians, wreathed in their old money,
Porter's slightly manicured accent bore the unmistakable taint of
elocution lessons.

Incapable of cutting a dash in the council chamber and apparently unwilling to dive into the political controversies of the hour,
Porter decided to make her way up through the ranks by focusing
her attention on the Highways and Works Committee, which handled chores like rubbish collection, street cleaning, road works and,
importantly as things transpired, the maintenance of the council's
cemeteries. In late 1976 Porter discovered something which would
become a lifelong friend and foe: litter. Although she later claimed
that she joined the council because of the filth in central London,
there is no record of her ever mentioning rubbish until the autumn
of 1976, when she and Leslie went on a trip to the Soviet Union
and made an astonishing discovery in Leningrad and Moscow:
both cities were spotlessly clean. It was then that it occurred to her
that Westminster was not. On her return to London, Porter made
clear to the local paper, the *Paddington Mercury*, her contempt for
the Soviets. 'But one thing they must be given credit for is the cleanliness you find everywhere,' she said, before adding a note of
concern. 'I should hate to think that we need such a repressive
regime to get our cities cleaned to their standards.' She told people
to shun 'places with litter', advice which, if taken to a natural conclusion at that time, might have necessitated the self-imposed house
arrest of every resident of the City. Up until then, Porter's only
recorded public utterance was a demand that something be done
about the illegal salesmen proliferating on Oxford Street, selling
shoddy toys and lingerie out of their suitcases.

Porter was no political ideologue at that time, but her campaign against litter clearly gave a focus to her drive for advancement at City Hall. 'Westminster was a shithole,' says one former Tory councillor, 'and at least Shirley wanted to do something about it.' Porter had hit a raw nerve; the City, particularly the West End, was filthy. Although the council was responsible for street cleaning, blame was pinned on messy tourists and the remorseless spread of fast-food outlets. She was careful not to attack the senior Tories for their failure to tackle the problem, although she later said she was privately dismayed at the growing sense of inertia and malaise at City Hall.

Porter joined the 'Clean Up London' campaign which had been started by other like-minded people fed up with the tidal wave of rubbish drowning London. She tried to cajole hoteliers near her flat in Bayswater to get together to fight the squalor which was beginning to affect their business. It was at this time that a senior position became free at the top of the Highways and Works Committee. Alderman Herbert Sandford had resigned the committee chairmanship to devote more time to his role as a councillor on the GLC. Tom Whipham, Sandford's vice-chairman, took his place, leaving the number two spot open. Porter was one of only three Tory councillors eligible, and her enthusiasm to clean up Westminster, as well as the time she had to devote to the task, made her the obvious choice. On 28 June 1977 she became vice-chairman of Highways and Works.

Porter's promotion could not have come at a better time for her. The top positions were reshuffled every four years following council elections, and the next polling day was set for May 1978. Many Tory councillors wanted advancement and Porter was no different; she wanted to replace Whipham as Chairman of the committee in the reshuffle. Whipham liked Porter and thought she was an energetic deputy at committee meetings and she continued to hit the headlines as an anti-litter campaigner. She had clearly inherited her father's gift of publicity and love of the photo call. In November 1977 the *Paddington Mercury* carried a photograph of Porter at the top of a stepladder feeding rubbish into 'Mr Clean-up', a ten-foot-high plastic litter bin with a happy face, a hat and a bow tie.

The *Mercury* said that Porter was 'fast winning a reputation as Paddington's Mrs Mops'. The paper described how Mrs Porter, Mr Clean-up and forty schoolchildren 'had caused quite a stir in the Lord Mayor's show', where they marched, brooms flung over their shoulders like rifles, singing 'Pick up your litter and put it in the bin.'

In the months before the 1978 elections Shirley Porter was becoming more confident at City Hall. Illtyd Harrington, who by then had resigned the Labour group leadership to concentrate on his career as a senior councillor at the GLC, witnessed a strange scene at the tea bar in the Marylebone Council House. He overheard Porter interrogating the tea lady about where the council bought its biscuits. The answer was Sainsbury. 'Well from tomorrow,' said Porter, 'you're ordering them from Tesco.' 'I never took her seriously,' says Harrington. 'I suppose I should have done.'

CHAPTER 4

'What Rubbish!' (1978–81)

The year 1978 was a significant one for Westminster and for Shirley Porter. The deep unpopularity of the Callaghan government had led to benefits for the Tories in the local elections across the country on 4 May 1978. Their victories would herald the arrival of Margaret Thatcher at Downing Street exactly a year later. In Westminster, the Tories were safely returned to power, but there was a great sea change in the political make-up of the Council. Of the sixty Council members elected in 1974, no fewer than twenty-five – almost half the total number – had hung up their robes, and a new generation of councillors took their places. Also in 1978 the law which abolished the position of Alderman came into effect. In practical terms, it meant that senior Tories in Westminster had to stand for election as councillors. The departure of the Aldermen seemed to herald the arrival of real party politics at City Hall and town halls throughout the country.

The Westminster Tories also experienced a deep shock in the heartland they had always taken for granted. For the first time in their history, the Conservatives lost the ward of Mayfair to two independents, Brigadier Gordon Viner and Lois Peltz, who had become dismayed at the council's inability and idleness in dealing with the sex barons whose activities daily encroached on the

families who lived there. The Mayfair ward included Soho, where
there was real anger among residents at the council's inaction. The
grander neighbourhood of Mayfair itself also suffered from the
overspill of the pimps, their prostitutes and the porn. The loss of
Mayfair to a new political force alarmed the Tories, who had come
to see control of Westminster as their right; surely if Mayfair was
vulnerable then nowhere was safe.

This fear played into the hands of a new breed of councillor who
had arrived on both sides of the chamber following the 1978 election. For Labour, there was still room for taxi drivers like Joe
Glickman and welders like Joe Keogh, but 1978 saw the emergence
of much more political candidates who were community relations
officers, business economists and even 'political education officers'.
They were younger and often more ideological than their political
forebears at Westminster. Their attitude towards their politics and
their Tory opponents was tougher, more professional and less
wedded to the dying concept of compromise between the political
parties. In January 1977, sixteen months before the council elections, Labour councillors had taken the rare decision to boycott the
Lord Mayor's reception in protest over £2 million worth of budget
cuts. Ironically, these had been imposed on the council by a Labour
government. Following the arrival of the new intake, such demon-
strations and protests became the norm.

On the Tory side, the new Conservative councillors clearly
reflected the right wing trajectory undertaken by the party since
Margaret Thatcher defeated Edward Heath for the leadership in
February 1975. Thatcher's municipal outriders in Westminster
were new Conservative councillors such as Francis Maude and
Michael Forsyth, who would later lead successful parliamentary
careers. Significantly for Shirley Porter and the council's future
direction, there were also new Tory councillors such as Peter
Hartley and Barry Legg, men who proved to have less talent and
judgement.

According to Rachael Whittaker, elected a Tory councillor in
1978, the new intake were not satisfied with remaining silent while
they 'learned the ropes'. They blamed the loss of Mayfair and the
potential threat from Labour on the indolence and exhaustion of

the paternalistic old guard, and they swiftly formed a backbenchers group which agitated for change. Perhaps the most dramatic example of this new breed of municipal Tory could be seen just across the Thames from Westminster in Wandsworth. In 1978 a group of radical young Tories seized control of this run-down South London borough from Labour and started to implement policies later associated with Thatcherism, including privatisation of council services such as rubbish collection and the sale of council houses, a year before Thatcher herself entered Downing Street.

In this new political atmosphere at Westminster, Alan Dawtry's former deputy, David Witty, was now chief executive. Dawtry had received a knighthood and retired as chief executive after eighteen years in charge. Hugh Cubitt, the Conservative leader, had been succeeded by David Cobbold, a wealthy solicitor. A serious war wound had left him with a limp and he was often seen resting his shattered leg on a chair in the council chamber during debates. A kind and clever man, Cobbold was respected by Labour and Tory members alike for his gentle stewardship of the council's affairs. He softly accepted the 'enthusiasm' shown by the strident new Tories that was now causing a rapid deterioration in consensus at City Hall, a breakdown which had started in town halls up and down the country. John Whatmore, a Tory councillor of the old guard, had detected change in the wind shortly before 1978. 'Local government has become highly polarised,' he said. 'I am not sure that is what people want.' He was right to be concerned but helpless to stop it.

Shirley Porter was promoted to Chairman of the Highways and Works Committee by Cobbold; Tom Whipham moved sideways to chair the Planning Committee. In the habitual post-election reshuffle, it was sometimes convenient to promote the vice-chairman to the top position, and the leader felt that Porter had proved her effectiveness through her anti-litter campaigns and her willingness to take on extra responsibility. One long-serving Tory councillor who knew Cobbold and Porter says, 'I blame him really for creating the monster.'

At this stage in her career, Porter had even higher political ambitions than the council. Shortly after her promotion, the political parties picked candidates for the 1979 European Parliament elections. Porter made it on to the shortlist for the central London seat. She did not shine at her interview. One senior Tory who sat on the panel says, 'We were stunned at Shirley Porter's profound ignorance of European matters.' She was not selected, nor did she make any further attempts to leave the council for higher office elsewhere. From then on, she resolved to make her name in the world of local government.

Highways and Works had always been considered a fairly safe non-political committee compared to those of finance or housing, but it would prove to be Porter's springboard to greater things. Over the next four years she would use the unglamorous area of street cleaning to demonstrate her flair for action and publicity. Within nine months of taking over the committee, Porter was attracting the attention of the national media. In the autumn of 1978 the Labour government tried to restrict pay increases for all workers, both in the private and public sectors, to five per cent while inflation hovered around seven per cent. From December 1978 many public sector workers went on strike in protest. Manual council workers demanded a wage rise of forty per cent and other manual workers, including oil tanker drivers, submitted claims of up to thirty per cent. When the demands were rejected, they also went on strike. 'Each night the television screens carried films of bearded men in duffel coats huddled around braziers,' wrote the Chancellor of the Exchequer, Denis Healey. 'Nervous viewers thought the revolution had already begun.'

On Monday, 22 January 1979 a period of strikes known as the 'Winter of Discontent' began in earnest. Its legacy would help keep the Labour Party out of government for eighteen years. Rubbish was uncollected across the country and the dead were left unburied in Liverpool. In Westminster, 700 ancillary workers belonging to the National Union of Public Employees (NUPE) walked out of St Mary's Hospital and marched to Hyde Park for a protest rally. Then 2,500 Westminster Council employees, including dustmen, street sweepers and lavatory attendants, came out on strike. As the rubbish piled up across the city, Shirley Porter made her first impact on the national consciousness.

Nowhere was the chaos caused by the rubbish strike more visible than in the West End of London, nor more accessible to the media. The streets quickly filled with litter and, before long, there were sightings of rats. Porter opened thirty-three emergency rubbish dumps across Westminster. The huge one in Leicester Square provided a tremendous backdrop for interviews with the new Chairman of Highways and Works. Porter threatened to privatise rubbish collection if the strikers did not return to work. Standing in front of piles of black bin bags overflowing with rotting refuse and infested with vermin, she told the newsmen, 'I am fed up with pussy-footing around. If I gauge public opinion right, the public want to see positive action taken. The private contractors will have to run the risk of being confronted by the pickets and, if necessary, run the gauntlet.' Porter was gaining a reputation as a doer, rather than a talker, and this was securing her admirers among the new intake of right-wing Tories. Her use of private contractors and the implicit threat to privatise refuse collection, which she later carried out, were well received by right-wingers like Francis Maude, who said, 'Surely we have to think about putting operations like refuse collection out to private contractors on a permanent basis.'

In early March, as the Winter of Discontent limped to an end and manual workers drifted back to work, Sir Jack Cohen died aged eighty. A decade earlier he had survived cancer, and in the period before his death he had been declining gradually. 'The chutzpah remained but little else,' MacLaurin recounted later. On the day before Cohen's heart stopped from his ailments and old age, MacLaurin received a call from the Governor's chauffeur: 'Sir John's planning to visit Pitsea today.' MacLaurin arrived at the new Tesco superstore at Pitsea in Essex before Cohen's Rolls-Royce. He pushed Cohen in his wheelchair around the store, where he was greeted by shoppers who recognised him. For lunch, Cohen had his favourite snack, a smoked salmon sandwich and a glass of whisky. He asked MacLaurin to push him on to the balcony overlooking the shopfloor. MacLaurin noticed him quietly weeping and asked, 'Are you all right, Governor?' Cohen replied, 'I never imagined that this was how it would be.' MacLaurin took him back to his Rolls-Royce, and waved him off as it pulled away.

Jack Cohen influenced and dominated Shirley Porter's life more than any other person. Both Jack and Cissie were occasional visitors to functions at City Hall and took a great pride in their daughter's growing prominence. He had gone just as she was coming into her own. Of all the family members, Jack and Shirley had been the most alike. She inherited her father's ruthlessness and flair for publicity; she also inherited his obsession with power, his meddling capriciousness and his bullying methods. But she lacked her father's easy charm and street wisdom, the two qualities which might have saved her from herself.

Cohen's death, although long anticipated, plunged the family into deep grief. His funeral took place at the private Jewish cemetery in Willesden. Shortly afterwards Porter threw herself back into her council career, and just a couple of weeks after Cohen's death chaired a committee meeting, where she considered her officers' reports on the dirty strike and decided to renew the contract for the organist at East Finchley crematorium. She always missed her father and referred to him repeatedly in conversations with her friends and newspaper profile writers. In many ways he was her guiding light.

On 4 May 1979, three months after the great Westminster rubbish strike and two months after Cohen's death, Margaret Thatcher won her first general election. Shirley Porter would be compared to the Prime Minister but, at this point, Porter was no Thatcherite ideologue. Her admiration for Thatcher came later because the example of the Prime Minister helped boost her own profile and justify her hard-line council policies.

A politician in Westminster much more in tune with the times than Shirley Porter was Patricia Kirwan, a feisty intelligent Tory with a sharply defined ideology who was already a leading light in Porter's local Conservative association of North Westminster. She would come to play a vital role not only in Porter's story but eventually in the destruction of her political career and reputation. In the late seventies Kirwan had worked as a publishing consultant for the Centre of Policy Studies, the radical right-wing think-tank run by Alfred Sherman and Keith Joseph which developed many of the tough monetarist policies later known as Thatcherism. Kirwan even helped write some of Thatcher's speeches.

She was born Patricia Hacking in Lancashire in 1942, and attended thirteen schools in England, Switzerland and Kenya before working as a journalist. She moved to Paddington in 1963 and became a press officer, and five years later married the City broker Peter Kirwan, a former army officer. She became active in politics after running a residents' association in Westbourne Grove. She first met Porter in 1974 when they both fought seats on Westminster; Kirwan lost, but in 1977 she was elected as the Conservative member for Paddington on the GLC.

Kirwan was a colourful character, fond of gossip over a cigarette and a glass of wine. She was blonde, emotional and tough. She disguised a ruthless streak and keen intelligence behind the frocks, bows and blouses traditionally worn by Tory women, but there was always a glint of steel in her blue eyes to warn the wise that she was not a woman to be crossed. Kirwan enjoyed the rough and tumble of politics and could often be seen striding along the corridors of County Hall with her two Cairn terriers, Pompidou and Disraeli, in tow. Occasionally she would point at Ken Livingstone, then a young left-wing councillor at the GLC, and tell the dogs, 'Kill Ken!'

The local newspapers often reported Kirwan's views on politics, housing and the new Tory thinking. In 1976 she told the Paddington Young Conservatives that Thatcher was 'the right leader at the right time'. She added, 'Conservatism must mean we conserve what's good in society, not that we stand for narrow or backward policies.' Peter Hartley was a close associate of both Kirwan and Porter later at City Hall. He said of Kirwan, 'Intellectually, she was streets ahead of Shirley.' A senior figure at Central Office described Kirwan as a 'very, very good politician'. If bookmakers had taken bets on who would become the first woman to lead Westminster City Council, the smart money would have been on Kirwan rather than Porter.

Increasingly, the council filled a huge void in Porter's life. Her father was dead, both children were living away from home and her husband was busy transforming Tesco into the country's biggest supermarket chain; she immersed herself in the problems and complexities of Highways and Works. She wrestled with the introduction of new parking meters and fretted over road schemes to alleviate the gridlock in central London. She complained about the traffic jams caused by the Queen's summer garden parties at Buckingham Palace and suggested they should be held at Windsor Castle instead, advice which was haughtily rejected.

Following Thatcher's victory, cuts in public services bit deeper as the new government tried to balance the books. Porter's response to her reduced budget was to close more than thirty public toilets across the City from St John's Wood NW8 to Rochester Row SW1. Her decision angered Labour councillors and caused concern among her Tory colleagues, particularly the more elderly members, who wanted to spare themselves the indignity of pleading with pubs and hotels in Westminster for permission to use the lavatory. Porter's answer to the problem was innovative and was initially greeted with contempt by members of both parties at City Hall. Strange new cubicles sprouted in the City: the Automatic Public Convenience, or APC. Porter had visited Paris with her Conservative colleague Peter Hartley to inspect the unusual-looking APC, popular with the French. 'I can think of better things to do in Paris!' scoffed one senior Tory, on hearing of the Porter fact-finding mission.

Porter loved gadgets and thought the APCs were wonderful. They were not cheap, but in the long term they would save money on the meagre wages paid to lavatory assistants and they would not go on strike for better conditions. At first, the cubicles were alien, even startling arrivals to the Westminster streetscape. They were far less accommodating than the subterranean, beautifully tiled, sometimes ornate Victorian lavatories which were gradually shut down and padlocked. On payment of a coin, the doors of the APC would slide open to reveal a toilet and a micro climate of perfume and piped music, including 'Chariots of Fire' by Vangelis and, perhaps more fittingly, 'Dark Side of the Moon' by Pink Floyd. Porter had a growing love for the photo call and so declared the first one open. At the photographers' request, she entered the APC. She later admitted that, as the doors slid behind her and the music started, she could not quite bring herself to put it to the test. She waited for what seemed an appropriate time before stepping out with a triumphant smile for the waiting flashbulbs. Illtyd Harrington, the former Westminster Labour councillor, said of the APC that 'for ten pence people could be showered in their own urine'. Stores in Oxford Street thought they were ugly, and prostitutes used the one in Queensway to entertain clients.

By 1978 Porter's first anti-litter campaign 'Mr Clean-up' had clearly been retired on grounds of general ineffectiveness and she launched the 'Cleaner London Campaign', which by March 1980 was superseded by the 'Cleaner City Initiative'. The campaigns were ill-defined and amounted to the deployment of extra street sweepers in a particularly grubby part of the West End for a two- or three-week period, with, naturally, photo opportunities for the newspapers. Rubbish was now collected more frequently in Westminster and Porter persuaded some local firms to sponsor litter bins, ranging from £25 for a small, lamppost bin to £100 for the luxury free-standing variety. The bins allegedly raised £30,000, a tiny contribution compared to Westminster's annual street cleaning bill of £8.5 million. However, it did help increase public awareness about rubbish and also raised Porter's public profile. In May 1980 Porter persuaded the Duke of Edinburgh to inspect the bins and the work of the sweepers in Soho. Whenever he saw her afterwards, the Duke would accost Porter with 'How are the litter bins?' The proliferation of the bins was shortlived. Following IRA outrages in London during 1981, many were withdrawn on the advice of the security services to prevent them being used by bombers.

Some of the newspapers sensed that Porter's cleaning-up campaigns were more gimmickry than substance. Labour councillors were furious to discover that she and her Tory colleagues were refusing to charge the city's businesses, the main culprits for the mess, for taking away their rubbish, and that this failure was costing local ratepayers £2 million a year. The decision not to charge businesses was taken before Porter took over the committee but she continued the policy. The new intake of Labour councillors complained to the District Auditor, Sir Douglas Morpeth, the senior independent accountant responsible for making sure

council funds were spent properly and legally. They objected on
the grounds that the council was acting unlawfully by effectively
subsidising businesses at the cost of local taxpayers. In 1981
Morpeth agreed that the council was breaking the law and said it
should start charging. Astonishingly, Porter rejected the Auditor's
findings on the grounds that such charges would be 'too complex'
to collect, despite the fact that other boroughs seemed to manage
it, and Westminster carried on picking up commercial rubbish free
of charge. Morpeth continued to demand charges but he threatened no penalties against the errant councillors. He was rebuffed
again in October 1983 and it was only when his successor, John
Magill, put his foot down in 1986 and insisted that business pay
its way that Porter finally relented. By that time the council had
missed out on an estimated £10 million since Morpeth's first edict.

In 1980 the council hired only 800 staff to do the dirty work of
litter collection, ten per cent fewer than in 1965, although the
amount of rubbish, mostly generated by business, had increased by
eight per cent a year. In September 1980 *The Times* carried a picture
of a litter-strewn Piccadilly Circus, and its correspondent John
Young said, 'The Clean-up Westminster Campaign, which began this
summer, is claimed to have been a great success; but there is little
sign of that at night. Waste bins are full to overflowing and boxes of
rubbish have been dumped on the pavements. Few things are more
depressing to anyone who loves London than the decline of the once
thriving and glamorous West End into its present squalor.'

A week later Porter threatened to resign if Cobbold reduced her
budget by £1 million as planned, as part of a £3.4 million package
of cuts to Westminster's services. She told the *Paddington Mercury*,
'I will resign in the event that they cut our basic services and that
means keeping our frontline services and a clean and litter-free city.'
The row split the Tory group and demonstrated Cobbold's weak-
ness in the face of the confident new right-wing councillors who
thought the council was lazy and wasteful and equated cuts with
efficiency. They threatened to cause 'mayhem' if the cuts were not
implemented. Francis Maude accused officials of trying to 'preserve
their jobs and empires', adding, 'We all know that the administration at City Hall carries a great deal of fat.'

Photographs © Associated Newspapers/Solo Syndication

Porter on the litter trail in traditional Sioux Indian dress.

Ironically, the row placed Porter in opposition to this emerging new Thatcherite force on the council, whose support she would cultivate two and a half years later in her bid for the leadership. But in autumn 1980, more than a year after Thatcher's entry into Downing Street, Porter was no right-wing idealogue: she was simply bound up in the parochial problems of tackling rubbish in Westminster and was so desperate to succeed that she risked alienating the Thatcherites. Cobbold respected her commitment but had long concluded that she was a difficult person to work with. Porter backed down and did not resign as threatened. She allowed Cobbold to make the cuts needed to placate his right-wing councillors and slowly came round to their way of thinking. Later, after they had helped her become Leader, Porter would take an axe to services and the voluntary sector with the zeal of the newly converted.

During this period Porter developed a fierce contempt for the leadership under Cobbold in general, and for the senior officials at City Hall. In a broadcast years later for Channel 4, she said, 'Minds and corridors were both blocked by dust . . . For years residents had complained of red tape and bureaucracy. But generations at the Town Hall had fine-tuned the art of passing a complainant – or a complaint – from office to office with no one willing to accept responsibility. It seemed that the bureaucrats were only good at passing the buck, at making excuses and doing nothing.' Francis Maude had heard rumours that the senior official and councillors were members of the same Masonic lodge. 'It was very patrician, very stuffy,' says Maude. 'We young Turks thought that the leading councillors were basically all in hock to the officers and the officers ran it. It was a very unpolitical place.' But Maude thought Porter was different, 'She was a stylish, flamboyant lady with quite a lot going for her; I thought she was fun.' Rachael Whittaker says, 'During my first four years on the council when Shirley was Chairman of Highways and Works, she was very able, although difficult. She was determined to get some of her ideas through and they were innovative and creative. She was really feisty about some of the things she wanted and that was an admirable part of her work on the council.'

But a certain ambivalence towards local government ethics started to accompany Porter's determination to get things done. In the spring of 1981 Porter's committee awarded a contract to a sports company called Racquets to build three new tennis courts on top of a football pitch in Westbourne Park in North Westminster. She had supported the proposals despite opposition from local people, including the headmaster of a nearby school, who insisted that the children in this working-class area preferred football to tennis. Porter had backed similar plans involving the same company six months earlier in the Paddington recreation ground which had been successfully opposed by the locals, but the scheme for Westbourne Green went ahead.

Shortly after building the courts, Racquets became insolvent, owing the council money in rates and rents. Porter never mentioned that the managing director of Racquets, Zulfiqar Rahim, had been her tennis coach. When the truth did come out much later, Labour councillors were outraged and spluttered that she should have declared this obvious conflict of interests. Porter dismissed their concerns about the fiasco as being of no importance; there was no need for her to declare such an interest as her relationship with Mr Rahim was 'purely limited to his being a tennis coach and my being one of his pupils'. For the Labour councillors that was precisely the point.

But her main focus remained litter. In May 1981 Porter campaigned yet again against rubbish, this time with the launch of 'Operation Spring Clean', another short term cleaning blitz in the West End. The *Paddington Mercury* was wearily dismissive of this latest operation. 'There is no doubt,' it said, 'that Westminster is a filthy city compared to say, Amsterdam and Paris ... This [Operation Spring Clean] is patently not enough and only covers central London. What about the bulk of Westminster?'

As usual, the effectiveness of Porter's litter campaign came down to money and how much City Hall was prepared to spend on cleaning up. Gimmicks and photo opportunities were not the answer to the problem. The local paper could whine as much as it liked about the cleanliness of other European capitals, but Paris spent up to ten times as much on cleaning her central streets, and there was nothing that either Mr Clean-up or the Duke of Edinburgh could do, despite their good intentions, to alter the stark arithmetic. However, thanks to rubbish, Porter was becoming a well-known public figure, and on her way to leading the council herself.

CHAPTER 5

Ken's Coup (1981–2)

On 7 May 1981 Londoners went to the polls and elected a new Labour administration for the Greater London Council under a moderate and uninspiring leader, Andrew McIntosh. McIntosh had less than twenty-four hours to enjoy his victory over the Tories before he and his colleagues were toppled from their senior positions in an internal coup led by Ken Livingstone and other left-wing GLC councillors. For nearly two years Livingstone and his fellow socialist hard-liners had openly plotted to get themselves elected on to the GLC, overthrow McIntosh and the rest of the moderate Labour leadership and implement a radical left manifesto. By the end of 8 May Livingstone and his co-conspirators had sprung their well-oiled trap and were in control of County Hall and its £1 billion-a-year budget. In a similar operation the following day, the plotters took control of the GLC's mighty semi-autonomous Inner London Education Authority, the ILEA.

The events at County Hall shocked the political establishment, particularly the Labour Party. McIntosh had been given a personal letter of endorsement by the party's leader, Michael Foot, who was anxious to prevent a Livingstone takeover. The reaction was widespread; the event even inspired the novelist Frederick Forsyth's bestselling conspiracy thriller *The Fourth Protocol*. Livingstone's takeover had serious implications, not only for the future of London local government, but also for Westminster City Council and Shirley Porter. It triggered a chain of events which hardened her political views and propelled her into the leadership of the ruling Tory group at City Hall. Shirley Porter might never have taken City Hall if Ken Livingstone had not taken County Hall.

There is no better example of the rise of the urban left than Ken Livingstone. Livingstone had left school with four O levels and worked as a laboratory technician at the Chester Beatty cancer research unit in Fulham Road. He joined the Labour Party in Norwood, a part of Lambeth in South London, at the age of twenty-three, just months after disastrous local election results for the party in 1968. 'It was one of the few examples of a rat joining a sinking ship,' he says. He prospered under the wing of the veteran hard-left 'Red' Ted Knight and over the next decade served as a councillor for the borough councils of Lambeth and Camden, as well as the GLC.

One hot August day in 1979, three months after Mrs Thatcher entered Downing Street, two young radicals, Keith Veness and Chris Knight, were in Kings Cross with time to kill. They decided to visit Livingstone in his councillor's office at Camden Town Hall. Veness and Livingstone had become firm friends after meeting at the Labour Young Socialist football tournament in 1975 at Brockwell Park in South London. 'At first I thought he must be terribly suspect,' says Veness. 'We were teenagers and we thought anyone over twenty must be a reactionary, and to make matters worse, he was a councillor and we thought no self-respecting revolutionary would be a councillor. A lot of people on the left were completely humourless and thought the worst crime of all was to be "unserious", but Ken thought there was no harm in having a joke in politics, particularly at his own expense.' The conversation at Camden Town Hall turned to the GLC and the next County Hall elections less than two years away in May 1981. Veness said to Livingstone that the GLC had a lot of money and power, and it was incredible that so few people took it seriously. He added wistfully, 'Can you imagine a really socialist GLC? That would be unbelievable!' Livingstone had already been thinking along the same lines.

During the next eighteen months a plot took shape. Labour activists chose candidates and drew up radical policies in the event of victory, including plans to cut the price of Tube travel. Livingstone knew it could succeed only if left-wingers got selected for and then won critical marginal seats in London; the plotters had to oust the Tories and put enough of their own people in place to form the new socialist administration. Livingstone wanted a seat in inner London, where he felt he would be better able to influence the make-up of the ILEA. He decided to fight for a Paddington seat against Patricia Kirwan. He gave up his safe seat in Hackney North and rented a bedsit at 195 Randolph Avenue in Maida Vale. He was selected as the Labour candidate for the GLC election in 1981.

The Paddington election was a curious affair. Patricia Kirwan remains convinced that officials at Conservative headquarters in Central Office did everything they could to make sure Livingstone was elected. The Thatcher government's attempts to bring down inflation were so unpopular by the time of the election, mainly due to the mass unemployment they helped to create, that few expected the Tories to retain control of the GLC. In the event, the Tories abandoned Kirwan. There is little question that she was denied any central support: neither canvassers nor campaigners were sent to Paddington to help her. Her husband, Peter, was forced to dragoon his work colleagues into knocking on doors and handing out election leaflets. The Kirwans were so outraged that they wrote a letter of complaint to the party chairman, who belatedly dispatched some workers, but the damage had been done. It was too little, too late. Kirwan believes it was a deliberate tactic by Central Office to ensure Livingstone's election so that he could effect his takeover and implement 'loony left' policies, which would harm the long-term prospects of the Labour Party. And so it was that, on 7 May, Livingstone defeated Kirwan by a majority of 2,397 and the Tories were swept from power at the GLC.

The following day the plotters moved swiftly to County Hall for the crucial leadership battle between Livingstone and McIntosh. 'It was like the gunfight at the OK Corral,' says Veness, 'We had our "minders" there to talk to any potential waiverers and so did McIntosh's people. People were being offered peerages and all the rest of it to vote for him.' At 5 p.m. the GLC Labour councillors moved to Room 166 to choose a new leader: Livingstone beat his adversary by thirty votes to twenty. Within forty minutes, Livingstone's radical supporters had been voted into the most important committee chairmanships at County Hall. ' London's ours!' proclaimed the left-wing leaflet *Labour Briefing*, which led with an article by Livingstone: 'No one will be left in any doubt that the GLC is now a campaigning organ and a bastion of power for the Labour movement within a national context . . . Part of our task will be to sustain a holding operation until such time as the Tory government can be brought down and replaced by a left-wing Labour government . . .' It was a declaration of war on Thatcher's government and the Conservative Party.

The GLC had not enjoyed the stability of its predecessor, the London County Council, because its powers were never consistent and, therefore, its purpose was never obvious. The LCC had had clear and defined responsibilities. During the war, it had organised the evacuation of children from London, its fire engines had tackled the Blitz and its ambulances had taken the wounded to hospital. Everyone knew what the LCC stood for. The GLC was a different matter. During its short and troubled existence, it had failed to make itself a relevant force in the lives of Londoners, or gain their affection. Brought into being alongside a second tier of thirty-two new London boroughs, like the new City of Westminster, it all too often duplicated the powers of the boroughs, such as planning, housing and road maintenance. This fact was used by Shirley Porter on her assumption of power at Westminster to argue that the GLC could be safely abolished with little noticeable impact on people's lives.

County Hall was a self-contained, hermetically sealed world with twenty-eight restaurants and seven miles of corridors, just across the river from the City of Westminster and the Houses of Parliament. Shortly after their takeover Livingstone and Keith Veness toured their new domain. On the fifth floor they came across a strange room with a huge chain and padlock securing the door. Their guide, a senior officer, claimed he did not know the purpose of the room and nervously suggested that they move on.

Veness was suspicious and threatened to cut the chain with the bolt croppers he always carried as the manager of a housing estate in Hackney. A key was hastily produced and the door was opened revealing a huge Masonic temple, simply another facility on offer in that vast complex alongside the cinema and after-hours chess club. The temple was swiftly turned over to the newly formed Women's Unit. It was the first of Livingstone's many challenges to the Establishment.

From the start, Livingstone's takeover of County Hall outraged right-wing Tory politicians and elements of the media. He represented a particular threat to Westminster City Council. County Hall glowered at Westminster over Westminster Bridge and Livingstone's personal power base in Paddington seemed to spy on City Hall from the north. To make matters worse, Livingstone would have ready access to seventy-two per cent of Westminster's wealth. The City was so rich that it collected £320 million a year in rates from residents and businesses but by law it had to give twenty-one per cent of it to the GLC and fifty-one per cent to the ILEA, now under the control of Livingstone's friends. Livingstone also knew that it did not matter if the government withdrew funding from a profligate GLC to curb its spending programmes; he could simply raise the money he needed from rich boroughs such as Westminster.

Livingstone proved to be a dream bogeyman for the press. He was not only politically dangerous, but eccentric. Neighbours would tell inquisitive journalists of his nocturnal trips to collect slugs and woodlice to feed his pet salamanders. Occasionally, reported one newspaper diarist, Livingstone was spotted stopping off to buy a bag of chips 'on the way to his room and his seven cold-blooded friends'.

As far as the government was concerned, Livingstone displayed more dangerous eccentricities such as drawing attention to its economic failures. On 29 May 1981, within a month of his takeover, he had greeted the 'People's March for Jobs' at the outskirts of London; 6,000 unemployed people had marched from Liverpool in protest at rising unemployment. Livingstone invited the demonstrators to stay at County Hall and provided them with refreshments. He refused an invitation to the wedding of Prince

Charles and Lady Diana Spencer, and on the day itself released black balloons over County Hall in support of IRA suspects who were starving themselves to death in the 'H' blocks of the Maze prison in Belfast.

At the time both Labour and the Tories were in trouble. Nationally, Labour had just been through the trauma of its civil war between the right and the left. Michael Foot, who few thought would make a credible Prime Minister, had replaced Jim Callaghan as Labour leader. Denis Healey had fended off a hard-left challenge and secured the deputy leadership by the narrowest of margins from Tony Benn, another left-wing hate figure for the Tory-backing

© Getty Images

Ken Livingstone (left) at County Hall under his banner showing London's unemployed, December 1981.

press. Meanwhile, recession was eating into the Tories' support. In January 1982 unemployment would pass three million for the first time since 1933. Livingstone's banners across County Hall proclaiming the latest London unemployment figures were known to make Margaret Thatcher seethe.

Westminster was the first borough to bear the onslaught of the Livingstone revolution. He planned to cut fares on the London Underground by around twenty-five per cent and to raise the £117.3 million shortfall through an extra local tax called the Supplementary Rate. Twenty per cent of the money would come from ratepayers and businesses in Westminster. The council was forced to issue the demands to its local residents. Jonah Walker Smith, deputy leader to David Cobbold, requested that 'the ratepayers of this City, who bear approximately twenty per cent of the total . . . be asked to make their cheques to WCC (Greater London Council/ILEA) Supplementary Rate,' so they 'may more readily recognise the profligacy of the new administration at County Hall'.

Livingstone's presence galvanised the hard-right wing of the Tory Party and the think tanks which gave it ideological sustenance. Among them was Aims for Industry, a think tank which represented 'business interests' under threat in Westminster from the high rates demanded by Ken Livingstone. It was run by Michael Ivens, who befriended Shirley Porter in 1981 and would have a significant influence on her political career. A charming, witty man and a talented poet, Ivens was one of the first people to articulate the right-wing vision which would be fashioned into Thatcherism. He was a signed-up member of the 'Libertarian Right Wing', along with other men such as Sir Alfred Sherman, who had an enormous influence on Margaret Thatcher and would also advise Shirley Porter. They believed in free enterprise and privatisation, not trade unions and high taxation. Ivens and other right-wingers concluded that Livingstone was a danger, and that he had to be stopped.

The dynamism and clarity of Ivens's message appealed to Shirley Porter, who was becoming increasingly frustrated with what she saw as inertia and muddle at City Hall. Until then, she had been a member of the City Council for seven years and had essentially kept out of trouble, and her anti-rubbish crusades had been supported by press and public alike. In October 1981 she made a dramatic entrance into politics under the influence of Ivens. She declared war on Ken Livingstone.

Porter launched a campaign called 'War against Reckless Spending', or WARS, run from City Hall. The stated policy of WARS was deliberately hazy; most people were against reckless spending and Shirley Porter could not lawfully declare that her target was Ken Livingstone because she planned to dragoon the resources of the City Council to a party political cause aimed at GLC abolition. The WARS campaign bore the hallmarks of Ivens, and was undoubtedly conducted with his encouragement and advice.

WARS marked the start of a five-year conflict that transformed local government politics in London, as well as the fortunes of Westminster City Council. It demonstrated for the first time Porter's attitude to fundamental local government law. She was prepared to use neutral officials for her political ends, and she discovered that, handled the right way, they would go along with it. She demanded that the City Council contribute £10,000 to the campaign, but that was too much for Cobbold and Jonah Walker Smith, his deputy, to stomach. Cobbold, who admitted privately that he was embarrassed by the matter, agreed on the derisory sum of £250, the maximum a local authority could spend on such a brazenly political campaign without fear of a surcharge from the District Auditor. The Labour leader, Joe Hegarty, described even this pitiful sum as 'a supreme example of the very kind of reckless spending which this campaign is supposed to be about'.

By November real damage had been inflicted on Livingstone by Tories from the outer London Borough of Bromley who successfully challenged in the House of Lords his 'Fares Fair' plan for cheaper Tube travel. The Bromley Tories argued that because the Tube did not reach their borough, their residents would not benefit from reductions in fares, making it unfair and possibly unlawful for the GLC to force Bromley to help finance the plan. It was an argument with which the Law Lords happily concurred. In December 1981 'Fares Fair' and the Supplementary Rate to pay for it were declared unlawful. Livingstone's revolution was in trouble and Shirley Porter cashed in the undeserved credit.

During the winter WARS adverts started to appear in the local newspapers: 'The Blitz didn't bring London to its knees ... the GLC could.' It was soon clear that the token £250 council funding could not cover such an extensive advertising campaign. Under pressure from Labour to explain who was financing the campaign, David Cobbold answered cryptically, 'Mrs Porter's heart is involved in all this.' The suggestion was that Porter was using her own money. Politicians are not expected to use their own money to supplement their politics. Porter's willingness to fund her political activities was an unhealthy development. It gave her a dangerous self-sufficiency which made her feel that the normal rules and protocols governing municipal life did not apply to her.

Porter held a WARS meeting at Porchester Hall in Bayswater on 11 March 1982 to argue for the abolition of the GLC but left-wing activists disrupted proceedings and the meeting rapidly dissolved into what the local papers described as a 'mess' without Porter having the chance to make her point. On 23 March she held one of her greatest publicity stunts to advertise the campaign: she led a camel to Downing Street to demonstrate her message. The camel is proverbially capable of having its back 'broken by the last straw', the last straw in this case administered by the profligate Greater London Council. She did not ride the camel herself but nevertheless the event received a lot of publicity and entered into the Porter legend.

Porter was so desperate to advance her campaign that she bypassed council meetings, picking up the phone and directly ordering senior City Hall officials to help with the campaign. She instructed Anthony Spelman, the City Architect, to fix WARS banners on council-owned buildings, including City Hall, the Queen Mother's sports centre in Pimlico and the Council House in Marylebone. Not only was it unlawful for council officers to participate in blatantly political campaigns, Porter had no personal authority to issue them direct instructions.

Banners also appeared across libraries, between trees on the Victoria Embankment facing County Hall and Leicester Square. The churchyard at St John's in St John's Wood now sported a WARS banner which declared: 'I love London but it's over rated.

WARS. Westminster against Reckless Spending.' For many people
the message, disguised in non-political language and therefore only
implicitly targeting Livingtone's extra taxes, was obtuse and baffling. Dawson Jackson, a resident who lived opposite St John's
churchyard, was furious. He wrote to the *Paddington Mercury*: 'I
am opposed to waste and inefficiency on part of the Council both
of which these posters illustrate: they cost money; and they are a
classic case of bad drafting – comprehensible if you know what
they mean but hardly so if you do not. "WARS" – what "wars"?
Or who "wars"? Westminster against reckless spending – what
does that row of words mean?'

Porter also insisted that WARS posters were plastered on every
dustcart and van in the council's fleet. A union official was angered
that council staff and resources were being misused for party political purposes. He protested to Ian Cooper, the Director of
Cleansing, about this 'absurd situation'. The official wrote later:
'Mr Cooper pointed out to me that it was out of his hands as it was
a decision taken by Councillor Porter who was, I believe, behind
this particular campaign.' Nalgo, the union representing white
collar workers at City Hall, called on members to boycott 'all work
connected with WARS, as it forms no part of normal council function'. The statement added: 'It is not part of your job! Refer all
inquiries regarding WARS to Councillor Mrs Shirley Porter at City
Hall.' In a portent of things to come, Dylanie Walker, the union's
publicity officer, spent the next two years urging Sir Douglas
Morpeth, the District Auditor, to surcharge Porter for misusing
council resources for political purposes and ban her from public
office. The Auditor decided that the sums of money involved with
WARS were so small that it would not be in the public interest to
take action.

In May 1982, after the council elections, Porter challenged
David Cobbold for the leadership of Westminster Council. WARS
had advanced her in the eyes of the right-wingers as someone who
could counter Livingstone and the new threat from the left. Porter
had whipped up feeling and tapped into a base of supporters. By
March 1982, two months before her first attempt at the leadership,
it appeared that she was introducing a new dimension to life at

City Hall: hysteria. Alistair and Camilla Sampson, both SDP activists, attended a meeting of Westminster Council and described it in a letter to the *Paddington Mercury*: 'The "WARS" campaign was in full swing. Indeed, almost every Conservative councillor wore either a badge or an emblazoned sweatshirt. To such an extent did it appear required wearing that we were relieved to see the Lord Mayor still immaculate in his tailcoat.' However, the Lord Mayor's 'control of the vociferous banner-waving demonstrators from [Conservative] Central Office in the gallery was far from immaculate and their disgraceful cheering, jeering and shouting all but drowned out the sonorous readings of Mr Cobbold and the tasteless interjections of the socialists.'

The sums of money involved in the WARS campaign were tiny and there was more than a hint of the ridiculous about the whole affair but a precedent had been set. Senior members and officers decided it was better to humour Porter than uphold a critical principle which demanded that council officers remain politically neutral. Her contempt for this absolute requirement of officers and their acquiescence to her improper demands was a recurring pattern of the 1980s. Once out and allowed to roam free around Westminster City Hall, this particular genie would not be squeezed back into its bottle.

CHAPTER 6

Sex and the City (1982–3)

The local elections of 6 May 1982 marked the end of political consensus at Westminster. The huge Tory victory paved the way for a takeover of the council by right-wingers under Shirley Porter twelve months later. Of the sixty councillors elected in 1982, only a third had been members when Porter joined in 1974. There was a further intake of Thatcherites, including Theresa Gorman, Andrew Greystoke and Patricia Kirwan, who became a councillor in Westminster for the first time a year after losing her GLC seat to Ken Livingstone. There was also an influx of new left-wing Labour members who would become her ruthless and determined enemies for the next two decades: Neale Coleman, Paul Dimoldenberg and Andrew Dismore all joined the council. The Tories had lurched to the right, Labour to the left.

Local elections took place at the height of the Falklands War and, although victory was far from certain, patriotic feeling led to a surge in support for the current Conservative government which benefited town-hall Tories at the local polls. The results also wrecked Ken Livingstone's plans. After taking power at County Hall, Livingstone had planned similar takeovers of key London boroughs. Westminster had been on the list. The plan 'Target Westminster' had been proposed under a general strategy called

'Target 82'. Keith Veness says, 'If it wasn't for the Falklands, we would probably have won Westminster. We thought it was marginal, because there were a lot of Labour strongholds in the north of the borough and some in the south.' 'Target 82' meetings were held at County Hall, and occasionally attended by Livingstone in person, but Labour candidates knew their plans were dashed when Union Jacks sprouted all over Westminster, even among the homes of Labour's natural supporters on the council estates. 'We knew we didn't stand a chance,' says one Labour candidate.

David Cobbold was ill, with heart problems and his old war wound. He had already been Leader of the Council for more than four years and was expected to retire with dignity before long. He had in fact decided to resign his leadership twelve months after the elections but had not advertised the fact. His chosen successor was Jonah Walker Smith, a witty barrister with a busy family life and the experience of chairing three of the council's most important committees, highly regarded at Westminster by councillors from both parties for his warm personality and political astutenes.

But shortly after the local elections in 1982, to the surprise of most, Shirley Porter tried to depose Cobbold; she stood against him at the annual leadership election, which was usually considered a formality. The right-wingers may not have objected to the challenge but the old guard was appalled. Although Porter was within her rights to challenge Cobbold, standing against an incumbent Leader at Westminster was considered disloyal. One former Tory Lord Mayor says, 'I knew that David Cobbold was not well at that time, suffering as a direct or indirect result of the wound he received in Burma, and it was a poor show that she stood against a man who I greatly respected and who was plainly not a hundred per cent.' Loyalty won the day and Porter was roundly defeated, but she had put down a marker for the top job.

Cobbold was personally hurt by Porter's challenge but was too much of a gentleman to show it or bear grudges. He respected her energy but was privately contemptuous of her inability to depart from her pre-prepared notes in the council chamber. A former Tory councillor says, 'A City Father such as David Cobbold would not have made head nor tail of someone like Shirley Porter.' Cobbold decided to give her a new role: he put her in charge of the General Purposes Committee, with responsibility for those council functions, such as running laundries and licensing street markets, which did not fit in with the portfolios of the other chairmen. Theresa Gorman, a new member in 1982, called it the 'odds and sods' committee, but Cobbold had a specific task in mind for Porter. She was to switch her attentions from rubbish to the Soho sex industry.

Since the early days of the old City Council at the dawn of the Edwardian age, Westminster councillors had wrestled with the borough's endemic vice. In 1902 the Chairman of the City's Watch Committee, the Duke of Norfolk, sent a petition signed by 8,500 electors to the Home Secretary and asked for help to 'ameliorate the moral condition of the streets, which is at present a reproach and disgrace to our City and to civilisation, by the removal of the constant danger of temptation to young and inexperienced persons, caused by the open solicitation therein carried on and tolerated, whereby such streets are rendered objectionable to respectable citizens'. After congratulating the councillors for the 'clearness and brevity' of their petition, the Home Secretary spurned the opportunity to act. Displaying compassion, and possibly drawing from personal experience, Charles Ritchie said prostitutes inspired feelings of 'great pity', adding, 'It must also be remembered that in places like Piccadilly, it is not only that a considerable number of women collect there at certain times of the night, but that there are a considerable number of men who go there and are not in the least annoyed by what takes place.' The Establishment ignored the problem for the next eight decades until Shirley Porter became Chairman of the General Purposes Committee.

As London's predominant red-light district from the late eighteenth century onwards, Soho, at the heart of Westminster, had always been a headache for the authorities. A seedy succession of what the Duke of Norfolk described as 'notorious persons' had ruled the vice industry with a firm grip until, inevitably, they were arrested or escaped into exile, leaving their empires of prostitutes and porn to characters who were equally as, and often more, dubious.

By the end of the Second World War, this small area of narrow winding streets lined with buildings from every era of the last 200 years had fallen under the sway of the 'Maltese Mafia'. The five Messina brothers – Carmelo, Alfredo, Salvatore, Attilio and Eugenio – set up brothels in Soho after being chased out of Egypt before the outbreak of hostilities. They made a fortune during the war, when demand from servicemen was at its peak, but their empire fell apart after their rackets were exposed by the *People* newspaper. Their place was taken by 'Big Frank' Mifsud, another Maltese pimp, and Bernie Silver, once described by the *People* as 'one of the most evil men in Britain'. During the sixties and seventies Silver corrupted members of the Metropolitan Police Vice Squad, paying officers working for the Obscene Publications Unit up to £14,000 to allow them to open new sex shops, and £500 a week to turn a blind eye to their operation. Silver's men were even permitted to buy back pornography seized by detectives in 'raids' mainly designed to keep up appearances. In 1974 an inquiry was held into the corruption: seventy-four officers were investigated, twenty-eight 'retired', eight were fired and thirteen went to jail. In the vacuum caused by the turmoil, a new generation of pornographers moved in.

In the late 1970s the sex industry was still having a miserable effect on the residents of Soho; it was the main reason why they vented their anger on the City Council in 1978 by electing two Independents, Lois Peltz and Brigadier Viner. 'The situation was absolutely disgraceful,' says Peltz. 'Labour councillors were reluctant to act because Soho wasn't one of their seats and they didn't want to be seen to be meddling in people's freedom; and the Tories were reluctant to act because they didn't want to be seen as prudes.' The red-light barons made such vast profits that they were able to pay any rent demanded. Unscrupulous landlords in Soho harassed long-standing tenants out of tenements so they could be let out to prostitutes or porn merchants for greater profits. Land in Soho had become so expensive that the council could not even afford to buy the slums it wanted to demolish to create new housing for local people.

The number of sex shops had doubled in little more than a decade: from thirty-one in 1969 to sixy-five by 1982, plus another

100 establishments including sex cinemas and bars with strippers. Any enforcement action was governed by Parliament's inadequate planning laws. Lois Peltz had campaigned on the problems for years with organisations such as the Soho Society, and managed to see Willie Whitelaw, the Home Secretary. 'We urged him to give extra power to councils to allow them to take action,' says Peltz. Terry Neville, then City Solicitor, says, 'It was a disgrace. There was no moral high ground. The sex industry was having a detrimental effect on living conditions and business and the drive was on to restore Soho.'

The answer lay in legislation which would enable the council to close down the sex shops and put most of their operators out of business. Angela Killick, who along with Porter had joined the council in 1974, suggested to the newly appointed General Purposes Chairman that, although the police had to deal with prostitutes and pimps, the sex shops could be tackled by a change in the law giving the council the power to license them. The council could then refuse any operator a licence. Shirley Porter decided to see the situation in Soho for herself and was taken on a tour of the area on a hot day in July 1982. Terry Neville and his new deputy, Matthew Ives, accompanied her. Neville introduced Ives, who received a terse acknowledgement. It was Ives's first view of Porter and he was not impressed by her manner.

At the West End Central police station each was assigned their own senior detective for the vice tour. Porter entered sex shops and perused the smutty videos and sex toys on offer, all the time questioning her policeman and ignoring the male clientele. She inspected the strippers' bars and bleaker establishments with cubicles stinking of bleach and strewn with used tissues. According to Neville, Porter was completely unfazed, and appeared relaxed while chatting to prostitutes about the problems they were having. Neville says, 'These tarts thought their trade was being affected as well, because there was a gay porn shop beneath their brothel that was deterring customers. That was one of her attributes, Shirley could talk to anybody.'

After the visit, Porter urged the Home Secretary to change the law, enabling Westminster to license the sex trade. Whitelaw had listened sympathetically to Peltz and her fellow campaigners but was particularly impressed by Porter's forceful arguments. He agreed to act and asked her help in drawing up new legislation which would give all councils the necessary powers to tackle pornographers. Shirley Porter cooperated closely with Neville and Ives. They were aware that they were up against an unscrupulous industry which would exploit any possible loophole, and knew the proposed new law had to be detailed and watertight. Neville and Ives set to work drafting a parliamentary bill known ponderously as the Government Miscellaneous Provisions Act 1983. Once the law was passed, if Westminster wanted to close down a pornographer, it could withhold a licence on virtually any grounds it thought fit. For the first time, councils would have the power to crack down on the dirty mac brigade.

Porter had ruled that there should be no more than twenty sex shops in Soho and two in Paddington. The new legislation stipulated that any successful applicant had to have a clean police record and six months' residency in Britain. A register of employees had to be kept and name badges worn. Many sex shops had slatted blinds to hide the premises inside; Ives legislated even for the position of the blinds. By February 1983 only twenty-nine sex shops had bothered to apply for a licence and a year later only thirteen remained. By the spring, Porter had achieved something which eluded the City Fathers all the way back to the Duke of Norfolk: control of the sex industry in the West End. The initiative was a stunning success. One porn baron took one look at the new legislation drafted by Neville and Ives and remarked despondently, 'The man who wrote this was a fucking genius.'

Matthew Ives had trained as a Jesuit before deciding to become a lawyer. He and Neville made a good team, despite their different personalities. Neville, jovial and smiling, was tough and knew how to handle Porter; Ives, gentle and cerebral with a quiet sense of humour, felt oppressed by aggression, which Porter had in abundance. As deputy and then City Solicitor, Ives saw Porter regularly at close quarters. To many people, Porter appeared tough, but Ives detected a deep insecurity. He believed that she was conscious of her limited education and undeveloped intellect which she disguised with bluster and force. In her role Porter had to sign off documents and comment on decisions, and she would do so in a terse, often incoherent way, leaving others to make sense of her meaning. When she read a report by Ives or Neville, she would sometimes scribble in the margins 'not my style'. As Ives never saw a report written by Porter, he would struggle to redraft the sentence, or in his confusion leave it as it was. One note, referring to the layout of furniture in meeting rooms, read: 'Not how it should be done. This isn't good enough.' The missive ended, literally, 'signed Shirley Porter'.

By April 1983 Westminster City Council was like a vintage car: still running with its old parts but breaking down more and more. When Terry Neville became City Solicitor in 1981, he was amazed at how chief officers like himself were treated. His predecessor, Edward Woolf, had been a captain in the Royal Artillery and had served the City, according to the praise on his retirement citation, 'as a most excellent officer'. When Neville took his place, he was ushered into a palatial office with a huge leather-covered desk, en suite loo and a couple of worn fireside chairs. Neville's new secretary asked if he would like to take an afternoon nap, as had been Mr Woolf's habit. The City Architect and the Director of Cleansing had their own 'grace and favour' flats in the best parts of town; one senior officer started his week by asking for a supply of the latest books from the City Librarian and spent the rest of the week, when not inconvenienced by meetings, reading them. Neville says, 'I'm not saying they didn't work, but it was all very genteel and leisurely before Shirley Porter.' One clerk remembers, 'It was fossilised, in the past, totally antiquated and chronically overstaffed.'

On 25 April David Cobbold resigned as leader. The fight to succeed him was between Shirley Porter and Jonah Walker Smith: the Tesco heiress versus an Oxford-educated barrister, the son of a Tory peer. Walker Smith was a self-confessed 'non-Thatcherite' who promised 'the minimum of dogmatism, the maximum of pragmatism'. He was Cobbold's deputy and was considered by far the most able and articulate of the two candidates, so he was irritated and bemused at the suggestion that candidates should circulate a manifesto. Clearly, he underestimated the threat posed by Porter.

He believed it was 'Buggins' turn', and adds, 'I forget if it was specifically forbidden or not, but it certainly wasn't the done thing to canvass for votes; after all, one's fellow councillors knew one's qualities, or the lack of them, so to be quite honest, I wasn't really campaigning. Shirley Porter was and that obviously did her a lot of good. She was able to promise committee chairmanships to people.'

Porter's campaign was run by Peter Hartley and Patricia Kirwan. Kirwan had been on the council for only a year but believed it was time for change. 'It did need bumping into the twentieth century,' she says. 'It needed changing and it did need sorting; I thought she was the right person to do it. I was wrong.' Porter promised Hartley and Kirwan that she would lead the council for three years only; then she would resign, serve for a year in the ceremonial role as Lord Mayor, and finally 'bail out', leaving open the possibility that either might succeed her. The critical intervention in the campaign was made by Angela Killick, an experienced and respected councillor who was considered the touchstone of common sense by the majority of the Tory councillors. Both Porter and Walker Smith asked her to run for election as their deputy. Killick chose Porter, mainly because she was anxious about Ken Livingstone and the danger he represented. Walker Smith was 'too nice', says Killick. 'I didn't think he was sharp enough to deal with the "sharks" in the sea circling Westminster, because he was a straightforward gent, a barrister and a judge and all the rest of it', she adds. That's where dear Jo had missed it, because the world was changing out there, and he didn't have the political 'savvy'. Porter asked Killick to write her manifesto, promising change and renewal at City Hall, and Killick agreed because she privately thought Porter 'couldn't string two sentences together'.

On 28 April, the day before the election, David Witty, the urbane Balliol man who had succeeded Sir Alan Dawtry as chief executive, told his chief officers, 'If it's Jo, it'll be business as usual; if it's Shirley Porter, then God knows what will happen.' On the following day, 29 April, the *Paddington Mercury* described the election as a fight between the 'old guard' and the 'new'. The paper added, 'Shirley Porter is very keen to give a new political direction to the council and put Westminster back on the map.' The election was overseen by Rachael Whittaker, who was by then David Cobbold's chief whip. She thinks Walker Smith 'missed the boat'. He had underestimated the importance of the growing band of right-wingers agitating for change. Francis Maude, who was one of them, voted for Porter. He says, 'I liked Jo, I thought he was able, and a good and thoughtful man. I just thought the council needed shaking up. It needed to get more political, to get more edge.'

The forty-three Tory councillors gathered at City Hall that evening to vote in the secret ballot. The result was a tie at twenty-one each; one councillor had abstained. There would have to be a second ballot. The abstainer was one of the old guard, a well-connected and charming man who had witnessed Walker Smith a few days earlier being 'prickly' to a fellow councillor, which he considered 'rather poor form'. On the second ballot the councillor voted for Shirley Porter. The result was Porter twenty-two, Walker Smith twenty-one. The jubilant Porter supporters celebrated at the Albert Pub near City Hall.

Kind words greeted the retirement of David Cobbold, with Walker Smith leading the obsequies for the old regime. 'We have been faced with decisions we would have preferred not to have faced,' he said, indicating his clear regret at the cuts in council spending and the anxiety accompanying what he saw as the stark creed of Thatcherism. Joe Hegarty, the leader of the Labour group, praised Cobbold's integrity and honesty. He said, 'Those qualities are not universal and they will merit emulation from his successor when she takes over.' For Shirley Porter and her supporters, Hegarty's concern was simply affirmation of all that was wrong at Westminster. The more Hegarty praised the virtues of Cobbold, the more Porter became convinced there would be no parley with the apostates of Livingstone in the council chamber and that there would be an end to the political consensus.

Over the following years the former custodians of the City would grow ever more aghast at Shirley Porter's policies and ever more powerless to act against her. Through age or dismay, their numbers withered. The rump survived through studied courtesy towards the new regime and by voting, time and again, in support of decisions which left them feeling anxious and bewildered. Increasingly they took comfort in the ceremonial life of City Hall, attending the Abbey in their gowns for the annual service of Thanksgiving, polishing their medals on Remembrance Sunday or, at the annual Lord Mayor's reception, donning their funny hats, the ermine-trimmed residue of the old City.

CHAPTER 7

Mrs Porter's Putsch (1983–6)

The comparisons with Margaret Thatcher began in the press from the moment Shirley Porter took over City Hall. Both were women with centres of power in Westminster, both were the daughters of grocers who married successful businessmen a decade senior to themselves, both were viewed as Tory conviction politicians and baiters of the left, both were bossy and strident, both paid regular visits to the hairdresser and carried large handbags. However, while Shirley Porter hero-worshipped Margaret Thatcher, the feeling was not mutual.

Porter would sometimes boast that she was the 'other grocer's daughter' with the caveat that her father had been rather more successful than Alderman Alfred Roberts and his small shop in Grantham. In fact, Porter and Thatcher could not have been more different. Thatcher was an Oxford-educated chemist and a qualified barrister who insisted on mastering detail; Porter had done poorly at school and was notorious throughout City Hall for her butterfly mind. Thatcher followed a coherent political ideology; for Porter, her ardent Thatcherism was mainly a way to ingratiate herself with the Tory Party and also a device to shake up City Hall and, through cuts in spending and privatised services, get rid of lazy or tired officers. Thatcher was known for her courtesy to junior members of staff at Downing Street; the same could not be said of Porter.

Roger Bramble was one of the old guard at City Hall, a well-connected former Tory councillor at Westminster and an acute observer of the political scene. He often saw the two women together at functions. He noticed how Porter seemed to go 'into neutral gear' and become 'like putty' in the presence of real

Photographs © Associated Newspapers/Solo Syndication

Maggie in the driving seat. Two grocers' daughters clean up Downing Street in Porter's latest cleaning gadget, 1989.

political power. Thatcher, on the other hand, appeared indifferent to Porter and gave the impression that she considered her something of a nuisance and was once reported to have described Porter as 'scary'. Patricia Kirwan says, 'Shirley obviously wanted to do things, to run something. Tesco had passed her by and Westminster was the next best thing possible. She wanted to make a big impression on Mrs Thatcher, so she learned all the "in" management accounting terms, but she couldn't read a balance sheet, or any complicated paper, or understand the ramifications of her actions.'

The most significant thing Porter had in common with the Prime Minister was contempt for the bureaucracy of government. In 1991, after Thatcher's fall, Porter wrote of her heroine: ' To put it bluntly, she was an inspiration . . . they called us bossy. Autocratic, difficult. They howled if we bypassed second-rate people or challenged old-fashioned methods.' A favourite television programme of both women was *Yes Minister*, in which a hapless Cabinet minister, Jim Hacker, was constantly thwarted by devious civil servants when he attempted change. Of their equivalents at City Hall Porter said, 'The more self-important the bureaucrats, the more it riled them that women were in charge – in Parliament, in the Palace of Westminster and in Westminster Town Hall.' Both women had their enemies and critics, but, although Thatcher was often accused of an arrogant self-sufficiency, her eleven-year rule was rarely tarnished by allegations that she personally misused power. In comparison, Porter came to believe that the ends always justified the means, that the possession of power came with the right to abuse it, and that it would protect her from censure.

In June 1983, a month after Porter was voted in as Leader of Westminster Council, Leslie received a knighthood in the Queen's Birthday Honours. Since becoming Chairman of Tesco, Leslie had rescued it from decay and turned it into Britain's most successful supermarket chain; few could deny that he had earned his accolade for services to the grocery trade. His knighthood entitled Shirley Porter to use the honorary title of 'Lady Porter', which she did without hesitation.

At City Hall Porter was known by a more important title: 'Leader'. Officially, she was simply the leader of the Conservative

© Philip Wolmuth

Leader Shirley Porter: 'Vote Conservative!'

group, which controlled the council due to its majority. Constitutionally, she was neither the leader of the Labour councillors nor the leader of the officer corps whose political impartiality was a legal requirement. However, many senior officers slipped casually into referring to Porter as 'Leader', and gradually she started to believe that this status allowed her to issue orders, without needing approval from council committees. During one spat, city solicitor Matthew Ives told Porter, 'You have no personal power in this organisation; you can't so much as order a cup of tea.' Porter considered Ives stiff and stuck-in-the-mud, and ignored him. Enough officers believed that power rested with her and her advisers, and they did what they were told.

Porter made many poor judgements in the first days of her leadership, not least in her choice of lieutenants. David Weeks was elected as Porter's deputy by Tory councillors, despite her preference for Angela Killick. After leaving university, he was a manager for a furniture company and later for an urban regeneration firm. He was first elected in 1974 with Porter and started off as a whip before rising through the ranks to become Chairman of the Housing Committee. Weeks was thirty-six at the time of his advancement to the deputy leadership and possessed a flat in Dolphin Square, wore a large pair of glasses, had a wife called Heather and an appalling temper. At first, he was considered by some a colourless presence at City Hall but appearances were deceptive. His contempt for officers was deep and inexplicable, as were his rages, which seemed to grow in frequency and ferocity over the years. Once he addressed a junior female member of staff as a 'cunt' and threw a book at her. To him, officers were a 'motley crew' and he once observed how 'bloody difficult it is to get them to do anything'. The council was 'a bloody beast' and 'a lump of unresponsive organisation'. 'One is not necessarily driven [to do] rational things to get this machine to do anything,' he once said, seemingly oblivious to the fact that the alternative was irrationality. Patricia Kirwan thought he was a 'pathetic little bully'. Peter Bradley, a future Labour adversary, described him as 'Weeks by name and weak by nature'. Weeks considered himself Porter's loyal 'details man'.

Porter's chief whip was Barry Legg, then aged thirty-three. Legg had ambitions to become an MP, which he realised nine years later, albeit for just one parliamentary term. Alongside his duties as a councillor, Legg worked as an accountant for the food giant Hillsdown Holdings. Using his accountancy skills he gained mastery over the complexity of the council's finances. Hywell Williams,

David Weeks, Porter's loyal deputy.

a former Conservative Party political adviser, once described him as a 'lugubrious accountant sedulous in the avoidance of charm'. Opinions among officers and councillors were divided on Legg. Some considered him the actual brains – and even the real power – behind Porter's regime. Some thought Barry Legg unpleasant; others found him unsettling. Porter, Weeks and Legg quickly formed what was later described by the District Auditor as the 'ruling triumvirate', with Weeks as Caesar to Porter's Augusta, and Barry Legg providing enforcement as chief praetorian. Individually, they

Barry Legg, Porter's chief praetorian and financial wizard.

may have turned out to be fairly innocuous local politicians, but as with the separate components of nitroglycerine, the combination of the three would prove explosive.

Patricia Kirwan and Peter Hartley were rewarded for running Porter's successful election campaign with committee chairman-ships: Kirwan took charge of Housing and Hartley Environment.

Both appointments would prove disastrous for Porter: Kirwan's because she refused to cooperate with corruption; Hartley's because he went along with it. According to Kirwan, Hartley was a likeable man who did not think too hard about what he was doing. 'He just did, did, did,' says Kirwan. 'I always used to say to him, "Now come on Peter, think!"'

Committee chairmanships and officer appointments made in those first weeks established the cast of characters who would witness, ignore and in some cases collude, in the unfolding scandals of Porter's leadership years. She chose Rodney Brooke, a forty-four-year-old council solicitor, to replace David Witty as chief executive. Brooke was then Chief Executive of West Yorkshire, a metropolitan council facing abolition. He was a reserved and thoughtful man who smoked a pipe and, among his friends, enjoyed a good gossip and fine claret. From the start, Porter and Brooke struggled to get on. She became exasperated by his clever asides and strained to hear his low mellifluous voice. Brooke had formed a poor impression of Shirley Porter at their first meeting. She struck him as 'a forceful woman who didn't know very much about local government'. His contempt for her deepened within days. In his first week Brooke saw Porter shouting at Matthew Ives, who had dispensed some sensible advice she did not like. Witty, who was about to retire, told Brooke, 'It's just as well you've seen that so you can see what she's like.'

Perhaps the most extraordinary of all the characters around Porter was Roger Rosewell. A short man with glasses and thinning hair, he was persuasive yet discreet, and could be charming. Michael Ivens had introduced Rosewell to Porter shortly after she became Leader. At that time Rosewell was a right-wing hero, known by the *Daily Mail* as the 'Turncoat Trot' and by the *Socialist Review* as the 'worm that turned'. In the early seventies Rosewell had been one of the most senior Trotskyites in the country, the industrial organiser of the International Socialists. However, he became disillusioned with the far left while at Oxford as a mature student in the late seventies. By the end of the decade, he had swung to the right and was paid by companies such as British Leyland to root out former comrades in the unions who were calling for strikes. In an interview for the *Daily Mail* he said, 'I know this bunch we have found are just the tip of the iceberg,' adding, 'The Reds are there, burrowing in, biding their time, I know.' The late Paul Foot, the investigative journalist, remembered Rosewell from the days when they were both members of the International Socialists. He said, 'It's an amazing story really, how Roger ended up as chief bottle washer to Shirley Porter. He would have loved the thought of being the *Éminence Grise*.'

Rosewell always seemed to be at Porter's side, but officially had no role: he was neither a councillor at Westminster, nor an officer. Council clerks were told that Rosewell's name must not appear in any official council documents and to excise it should it do so. The excuse once given for his constant presence was that he was writing a book about Porter. The book never emerged. Rosewell became known by councillors and officers alike as the 'Man With No Name', and when Porter employed further unofficial aides, he became the 'Man With No Name Number One'. Because he shunned the main lifts at City Hall and instead ascended to Porter's office on the eighteenth floor in the goods lift, along with the repaired photocopiers and boxes of carbon paper, he soon earned a second nickname, 'The Thing in the Lift', shortened for convenience to 'Thing'.

Rosewell says he would attend meetings between Porter and her officials to help 'decipher' what they were telling her, but he was no mere adviser. He had the strongest influence over Porter's political beliefs and was still at her side long after she had been abandoned by everyone else. Under local government law of the time, which frowned on the involvement of outside political advisers in council business, he should not have been at those meetings at all. Rosewell's critical role for Porter was demonstrated to Patricia Kirwan in the early eighties. Alone on the eighteenth floor one day, Kirwan was nosing through Porter's papers and came across a document she says was written by Rosewell. It outlined a three-year strategy detailing how Shirley Porter might get a seat in the House of Lords. The paper advised her to revolutionise City Hall and attract publicity. Then she would be assured a peerage. Porter's desperation to obtain a peerage was an open secret and even a source of merriment among senior members and officials. It was a driving force in her career and, always impatient, she felt it had to be accomplished within a ridiculously short time. The daughter of a self-made man, Porter felt insecure about her status. Her father and husband had received knighthoods, and for Porter, a title, particularly a peerage, would represent the ultimate symbol of success and acceptance from the British Establishment.

Rosewell was Porter's most important adviser and employed personally by her, but there were others who would dispense advice for a fee or for free. Michael Ivens and Sir Alfred Sherman were regular visitors to City Hall, as was the management consultant Michael Silverman, useful to Tesco and later to Porter for sorting out tricky personnel situations involving the hiring, but more often than not the firing, of employees. The advice may have been sound but it was dispensed by men not accountable to the people of Westminster. Before long, many of Porter's Tory colleagues began to feel that power was slipping away from City Hall and its committees. Rachael Whittaker was so concerned she raised the issue with her fellow Tory councillors. 'I never met Roger Rosewell,' she says. 'I never knew about him officially, I was no longer in the inner circle. When I heard about it, I was very upset and I raised it at a party meeting, that we should not take advice from people who weren't bound by local authority officer rules and the code of conduct [for councillors], and that was where I met a brick wall.'

Senior officers felt the same way when Porter introduced a cadre of 'policy assistants' to the chairmen of the major committees. They were mainly bright young political activists with little or no knowledge of local government. Before long, they were meddling in the affairs of the various council departments and the seasoned officials who ran them. Many chief officers thought the policy assistants were there to spy on them. Bill Ritchie, the Director of Social Services, argued against their appointment, but was ignored. He says, 'They were bringing in people who were given more power than senior officers. It was up to you personally to curb policy assistants or they felt that they were running you. I told them, "This is my department, not yours and anything that's done in my department is done by me.'" Within a year, Porter had established a less accountable power structure at City Hall with outside advisers, policy assistants, officers and councillors all jostling for her wavering attention. Increasingly, Labour and Tory councillors became worried at the way power was concentrated around Porter and often exercised through secret meetings. Within months of her leadership victory, the *Paddington Mercury* voiced concern: 'When decisions are made in secret at "inner" cabinet meetings and passed on to committees for rubber-stamping ... one is tempted to wonder: is this "open government" or "government by diktat"?'

Only weeks after she was elected Leader, Porter became embroiled in the first of the many scandals which would tarnish her regime. As Chairman of General Purposes, she had allowed the BBC consumer TV programme *Watchdog* to film two of the council's trading standards officers at work. Alan Sharpe and Roger Dennis made the mistake of inspecting a Tesco store in Portobello Road, where they discovered some risible discrepancies in the weight of some vacuum-packed meat. Porter was convinced they had deliberately set out to embarrass her and demanded an apology from them. Both men left the council's employment shortly afterwards: Dennis got a better job elsewhere but Sharpe opted for redundancy after being rejected for two posts at Westminster. Porter had sat on one of the interview panels. The BBC followed up the story and suggested that they had been forced out after falling foul of the Leader. Porter dismissed the allegation as 'ugly and completely untruthful' and threatened libel proceedings against the BBC unless she received an apology. The Corporation refused to back down but she did not sue. 'Shirley was hopping mad,' says Terry Neville. 'It was funny, of course it was, but she couldn't see it.'

Shirley Porter used fear to effect change at City Hall. Within days of her becoming Leader all 5,000 council officers, from the humblest part-time secretary to the chief executive, received a letter from Porter at their home by first class post, threatening them with the sack unless they sharpened up their ideas: 'We have got to make savings and we are going to do so. For those who are inefficient and don't pull their weight there may well be demotion or redundancy.'

Some of the council's most senior officers dismissed the note as nonsense, and mocked the odd syntax and poor standard of punctuation. Further down the pecking order, the more canny junior employees and their unions were outraged. There was hollow laughter in particular at the observation by an heiress that 'redundancy is an unpleasant fact of life', and that 'we cannot be immune from it'. In retaliation, Nalgo, the main union for office workers at City Hall, sold their members dark blue ties with a wasp motif and the initials WASP, 'Westminster against Shirley Porter'.

Porter's letter was no idle threat though; she and her followers had nothing but contempt for the City Hall they had inherited. They were determined to take on the unions and privatise the services they thought inefficient. Rumours soon swirled around City Hall that Porter planned to make cuts of around £6 million and sack 500 staff.

Porter started to push through plans to privatise the Council's Architects and Valuers Departments in the teeth of fierce opposition from the unions and Labour councillors. She used her large Tory majority on the council to force through job cuts. On 24 October 1983 there were scenes unprecedented in Westminster when 500 people marched from Little Portland Street to the Council House in Marylebone in protest over job losses and cuts. They carried with them forty coffins symbolising each of the architects facing the sack at City Hall. Joe Hegarty reported, 'It was apparent that the new Tory regime in City Hall had achieved in a few months what the Labour Party has been pursuing for years – bringing together the Labour Party, Labour group, trade unions, voluntary bodies in a common cause.' Dylanie Walker, the union official who had tried to persuade the District Auditor to take action against Porter for her WARS campaign, had left Westminster Council but still felt moved by the protests to write a prescient letter to the local press: 'The Council cannot function when its staff have no faith or trust in it . . . Unless steps are taken to restore some sense into what is occurring at City Hall then I fear the Council is on a collision course with disaster. What worries me is the fact that it may already be too late.'

Porter then antagonised Labour councillors and a number of

Tories with her decision to close down the Portland library in Little Portland Street, near Oxford Circus, which the council claimed was underused. Labour councillors and librarians staged a nine-day occupation, which ended only after Porter threatened court action. When a young Tory councillor, Stephen Govier, abstained in a crucial vote following a debate on its closure, Porter hauled him outside the council chamber and sacked him as vice-chairman of the Grants Committee. 'Never mind that you're an elected councillor; never mind you have a conscience,' Govier said afterwards. ' Shirley Porter wants "yes men".'

By early 1984 Porter's conduct was causing such alarm among her Tory colleagues that a plot formed to depose her. There was concern about her ruthless management style as well as the cuts and redundancies. In April the *Daily Telegraph* observed: 'Porter, the dynamic leader of Westminster Council and a great favourite at 10 Downing Street, is proving less popular with her top council bureaucrats . . . In less than a month, no fewer than four chief officers of the council have tendered their resignations . . .'

Jonah Walker Smith's wife, Aileen, fielded calls from Tory councillors urging him to stand against Porter for the leadership. In May 1984, against his better judgement, Walker Smith stood against Porter a second time and was defeated. He had misjudged the mood among the majority of Tory councillors, who still thought Porter's shock therapy was the only way to shake Westminster Council from its apathy. After her second leadership victory, the men and women of the Westminster Conservative group started singing a chant usually reserved for the football terraces: 'Here we go, here we go, here we go!'

City Hall began to revolve around Porter's whims and the frenetic pace of her life. Officers and members would be phoned late at night after a long day in the office and ordered to report for one of Porter's notorious breakfast meetings the following morning in her flat in Gloucester Square, a lavish apartment over two floors connected by a marble staircase. Breakfast meetings were held in the dining room around a marble 'Lazy Susan' revolving table, which would be spun round by Porter to dispense cold Tesco croissants, coffee or documents. Adjoining it was Porter's own private reception room, filled with dolls, teddy bears and gonks. Witnesses attest to huge mirrors and a profusion of vulgar ornaments. By common consent, the fittings, furniture and kitsch paintings represented a victory of wealth over taste, and it was a sign of her unpopularity that people laughed about her bad taste behind her back. Porter became so acutely aware of the cowardly mockery of 19 Chelwood House that she was reluctant to allow newspaper interviewers to use the lavatory in case they wrote about gold-plated taps.

Occasionally Porter would arrive at City Hall for an early-morning meeting, usually dressed in a brightly coloured tracksuit, and flushed after a 'power walk' across Hyde Park from her apartment, sometimes accompanied by a wheezing retinue of eager-to-please officers. Later in the day, sometimes after a spot of tennis at the Queen's Club or a steam at the Porchester Hall Turkish baths, she would turn up for meetings at the council. Senior officers were called on to attend discussions and one particular victim was Ian Lacey, the Planning Director. 'Send for Lacey!' became one of Porter's favourite instructions and later a joke among his colleagues. Lacey soon learned that Porter often forgot the reason for her summons and would stay put. Other officers obeyed the call, only to be given a list of impossible tasks to be completed by an absurd deadline. But there was a good chance Porter would forget all about it if they just kept out of her way for long enough.

In her haste to bring about change coupled with her devotion to outside advice, Porter destroyed the very thing which Parliament and the courts had developed down the ages to protect politicians from themselves and the public from disaster: the necessary political independence of public servants. In the four-year period which preceded Shirley Porter's election as Leader, just four senior officers retired from the council, after a long service, with a decent retirement package and the best wishes of the City. In the four years following Porter's succession, forty-eight officers of the first and second rank left, often pushed out by Porter, usually after a short service.

Edward Steen was the first journalist in the national press to identify a problem in City Hall. In his column in the *Daily Telegraph* he observed Porter's disregard for the rules by which the council was run. She was 'impatient with standing orders', said

Steen, adding, 'staff turnover is costing a small fortune, morale appalling: the eggs are not yet a happy omelette.' According to Patricia Kirwan, the situation only deteriorated as time went by. 'A lot of older officers chose to take early retirement. In some cases a good thing; they were too stuck in their ways,' she says. 'The problems started when their replacements "failed" in Shirley's view and were also chucked. Also the redundancies were appallingly handled and morale plummeted.' Angela Killick was also dismayed by Porter's treatment of officers: 'She would make impossible demands of them, by which I mean demands that would be impossible to meet, but she wouldn't see that. She would make improper demands of them, she would waste their time, she would change her mind, she would be inconsistent, she would be all over the shop, and she would drive them mad.'

Pamela Whitford-Jackson, who left the Civil Service in 1984, was appointed assistant chief executive to Rodney Brooke and became a favourite of Shirley Porter. She quickly realised that Porter had no head for detail so she reduced complex reports to simple graphs and diagrams, which she described to colleagues as 'finger painting for Shirley'. She witnessed close up Shirley Porter's effect on other officers. She saw one senior officer break down in tears after being criticised by Porter. Whitford-Jackson protected herself from the stress around her by appreciating the ridiculous side of life at Porter's City Hall. In late 1985 the Leader was flying off on holiday to the US and Whitford-Jackson asked Porter's assistant, Lawrie Smith, to notify City Hall the moment she was safely in the departure lounge at Heathrow so they could all relax. When the call came through, Whitford-Jackson breathed a sigh of relief and kicked off her shoes. One of Porter's last suggestions had been to supply successful officers with new leather filofaxes; the underachievers were to be given plastic ones. It could wait until she returned, Whitford-Jackson decided, by which time there was a chance Porter would have forgotten about it. Suddenly the phone rang. 'Pamela!' It was the familiar voice of command. 'Now I don't want you slacking while I'm away.' 'No, Leader.' 'I want you to develop an Adopt-a-Granny scheme.' 'Yes, Leader.' 'And I also want to award the top ten time managers with leather personal organisers.' 'Yes, Leader.' 'Oh, I've got to go now;

the pilot wants to take off.' The affairs of state having been concluded, the pilot asked Porter for the return of his radio before
taxi-ing the Concorde out on to the runway for take-off.

Whitford-Jackson became increasingly involved in the consequences of Porter's growing paranoia about the press. Porter was
obsessed by her media coverage, something which City Treasurer
David Hopkins believed should be the ' icing on the cake'. 'But,' he
said in mild despair over the ever-increasing press office budget,
'the icing is thicker than the cake itself.' Porter should have had few
complaints. In September 1985 *The Times* profiled her, suggesting
she was a municipal version of Margaret Thatcher. Porter is
described striding through Bayswater, kicking a dropped paper
tissue under a car 'with a brief snort of displeasure'. The writer
Shirley Lowe observed when she entered City Hall with Shirley
Porter that 'the staff seems to flinch slightly as she passes and the
temporary secretary looks wan.' Most council leaders were lucky
to receive a mention in a national newspaper, let alone a whole profile. But Porter was never happy with her press office. By her own
calculation, Whitford-Jackson spent twenty-five per cent of her
time interviewing candidates to replace press officers who had been
sacked or forced out by Porter. Whitford-Jackson says, 'The record
was one day. A woman who had won a Pulitzer Prize lasted a
month; a former *Sunday Times* reporter, for three months.'

On 21 October 1985 Porter opened the council's new 'One Stop
Shop' in Victoria Street next door to City Hall. Inspired by Tesco,
it would be a sort of supermarket for residents who needed something from the council, whether it was planning permission for a
loft conversion or an answer to a query about their rent. Hitherto,
people had to tackle a faceless and seemingly disinterested bureaucracy if they wanted anything done, and might end up being
shunted from one council department to another, often with little
to show for it. The One Stop Shop provided a desperately needed
interface for the public and local council. Porter insisted that senior
officers spend a few hours each week there dealing with people
one-to-one. Tact did not accompany the edict, but few observers
could deny the importance of removing the mandarins from their
wood-panelled offices at City Hall and exposing them to the people

who were affected by their decisions, and who paid their salaries. The initiative was copied by councils up and down the country.

The year 1985 marked the 400th anniversary of the first primitive form of local government in Westminster and Porter devoted much energy in planning how to commemorate the occasion. Soon, council stationery bore the insignia of the Westminster Quatercentenary and each department at City Hall was instructed to appoint its own '400th' liaison officer to co-ordinate events, which included fun runs, concerts and a gala performance of *Orpheus in the Underworld*.

Despite some successes, 1985 was a bittersweet year for Shirley Porter. Running the council was her way of proving that she could run Tesco, which she believed was her rightful inheritance after the death of her father. In July 1985 she tried to become a Tesco board member on Sir Leslie's retirement as chairman. At a board meeting, she orchestrated a series of interventions by her friends to secure her place on the board. Amie Raphael spoke for her: 'There are no ladies at the top table; to my way of thinking something is very wrong with that.' Porter stood before the meeting and, to the ill-concealed embarrassment of her husband, pleaded for a place on the board, citing her experience as a council leader. 'I have chaired meetings, negotiated with unions, fixed budgets,' she said. 'I believe I can bring a different perspective . . . for the benefit of customers.' Mike Boxall, the company secretary, knew the rules. 'They can't elect anyone today. They have to give the meeting twenty-eight days' notice of such a proposal,' he told Sir Leslie's successor Ian MacLaurin, who disliked Shirley Porter for meddling in Tesco while Sir Leslie was in charge. MacLaurin remembered how Sir Leslie, usually the most easy-going of men, would arrive at Tesco House on a Monday morning after being nagged all weekend by his wife, and grumble his way through to lunchtime. In the process, MacLaurin said later, '[she] made his life and ours a hell.'

After the board meeting, Porter accosted MacLaurin at his office and demanded a seat on the board. 'The more she raged, the more venomous she became,' MacLaurin wrote later. 'I was "anti-Cohen", "anti-Semitic", anti-just about everything, all punctuated by her qualifications for a place on the board. Wasn't she Jack's daughter? Wasn't she Leslie's wife? Wasn't she the chairman of this, the patron of that, and wasn't that enough for me?' MacLaurin looked at her, 'marooned in silence', before calmly informing her, 'Look Shirley, you'll just have to accept that as long as I am Chairman of Tesco, you'll never get a place on the board, which is the end of the matter as far as I am concerned.'

MacLaurin said later that his only regret in blocking Porter was that if her attention had been focused on the family business she might not have gone on to destroy Westminster City Council, although of course from his perspective it was preferable to her wrecking Tesco. He wrote with hindsight but towards the end of 1985 Porter was already sowing the seeds of destruction. After nearly three years of sackings and resignations, every chief officer owed their position to Porter either by appointment or sufferance. City Hall now rewarded the dubious qualities of sycophancy and obedience, which were of limited value in executing good policies, worthless in opposing bad ones and dangerous when commanded by a capricious and arrogant Leader.

Margaret Thatcher was among those to harbour serious doubts about Shirley Porter. On 6 October 1985 the country was shocked by the brutal murder of PC Keith Blakelock during a riot at the Broadwater Farm Estate in Tottenham. The Haringey Council senior housing officer for the estate was Neale Coleman, a Labour opponent of Porter's. Foolishly, Porter exploited the tragedy for a purely parochial political advantage on national television in front of the Prime Minister at the Conservative Party Conference. She defamed Coleman by implying that he was responsible for the disturbance. 'What was he doing on the night of the riot?' she shrilled, adding, 'I shudder to think.'

As Porter descended the rostrum to polite applause, she was brought up short by an anxious Margaret Thatcher, who told her, 'You need to be careful; I hope you've got your facts right.' Immediately, Porter rang Matthew Ives, who had replaced his boss, Terry Neville, as City Solicitor, for reassurance. Ives was unable to give it and told Porter that the council could do nothing if Coleman decided to sue for libel. But Coleman did not sue, and was satisfied with a public apology. 'I have regretted it ever since,' he admits. It is uncertain that Porter could have survived such a public humiliation if Coleman had successfully sued.

By early 1986 a number of key figures at City Hall concluded that Porter had to go and that the cleanest way to effect her departure was to arrange for her be given what she wanted: a peerage. Rodney Brooke and Roger Bramble, the Lord Mayor, had come to the same conclusion. Brooke knew Thatcher's then parliamentary private secretary, Michael Alison, Conservative MP for Selby in North Yorkshire, and made an appointment to see him. Alison sat in baffled silence as Bramble and Brooke praised the merits of Porter and tried to persuade him that she would be a great asset to the House of Lords. Alison heard them out before leaning forward and emphatically giving Thatcher's view on Porter: 'She can't stand the woman!'

CHAPTER 8

The Great Cemeteries Sting (1984–7)

The decision by Shirley Porter to sell three council cemeteries for five pence each to ruthless asset strippers who then abandoned them to vandals, drug addicts and devil worshippers has entered political folklore. Even the passage of time has done little to dull the sense of amazement and contempt felt by the public about all parties involved in the transaction. It was possibly the most witless, the most heartless and the most ludicrous disposal of an asset in the history of local government. Before it blew itself out, the scandal would engulf Margaret Thatcher, two Chancellors of the Exchequer, Queen Beatrix of Holland, thousands of grieving relatives and the Billy Fury Fan Club.

The decision demonstrates the widening gulf between the myth of City Hall under Shirley Porter and the reality. On the surface, Porter was the bustling 'Westminster Whirlwind', blowing away the cobwebs of City Hall and transforming it into an efficient, commercially driven Tory flagship. But within the council itself, there was a rapid collapse into dysfunction caused by fear, and the dread which accompanies the realisation that unreasonable people are in charge. Fewer and fewer officers were prepared to stand up to Porter, and those who proffered sensible advice were ignored, or worse.

Porter's family background and aggressive approach persuaded many people outside City Hall of her business acumen. They listened as she referred to residents as 'customers' and argued the need for the council to be run along 'business lines', and concluded that the magic of Tesco had rubbed off on her. But Porter had no real business experience aside from running the occasional charity stall and the knowledge of Tesco she gained in conversations with Leslie. 'She hadn't run a piss-up in a brewery,' says one of her former senior colleagues. 'She couldn't analyse activities, set targets, start implementing them nor draw conclusions. There was no time for reflection. Everything had to be done immediately.'

In her growing recklessness, Shirley Porter laid the seeds for the great cemeteries fiasco with a dogmatism which seems perverse in hindsight. Time and again, she ignored the advice which would have prevented it. The disastrous sale of the cemeteries was largely due to her political naivety, and also due to the kind of ruthless business attitude that she had witnessed in her father, and that she affected to imitate.

Porter grew up close to one of the three graveyards she would later sell for five pence, a large wooded Victorian cemetery at East Finchley, a few minutes' stroll from the second family home in Chessington Avenue. Hers and Leslie's first house in Lyttelton Road was also nearby. All three cemeteries were situated in what had been virgin Middlesex countryside where land was cheaper and more available. For decades, they were lovingly tended by the three constituent boroughs which merged to form the new City in 1965. Hanwell was the responsibility of the old City since its opening in 1935; East Finchley and Mill Hill both started operating in 1854 for Marylebone and Paddington. The graveyards were also used by the two boroughs where they were situated: Hanwell lay within Ealing; Mill Hill and East Finchley were both contained within the London Borough of Barnet.

Westminster City Council assigned the running of the cemeteries to the Highways and Works Committee when it assumed responsibility for their upkeep in 1965. As the committee's chairman for four years, Porter had been concerned with expenditure on the cemeteries and each month she stared uncomprehendingly at the

mounting costs itemised in the accounts. It cost £4,400 a year just
to dig the graves; 'equipment and materials' came to £12,240. It
seemed a lot of money to spend on shovels, pruning shears and
lawnmowers. The annual total for the three graveyards came to
more than £400,000.

The cemeteries were immaculately maintained by a total work-
force of twenty-six, including gatekeepers, gravediggers and
gardeners. They cleaned the chapels and the monuments or tended
the cedar trees and crocuses with loving diligence. Their working
conditions were hardly punishing, as a professional valuer once
described to a subsequent inquiry into the circumstances of their disposal: 'It was a real council bonanza and these guys disappeared in
the morning, down into the overgrown rhododendrons and so forth,
never to be seen again. They go off and work on cars, paper rounds,
come back to sign for overtime, and disappear again.' Others would
reveal how workers, 'sober or not', would turn up lethargically at
funerals, switch on the tape of sombre music and return to the pub.

Porter's predecessors took a fairly relaxed approach to this type
of working practice endemic at that time in local government and
elsewhere in the public sector. They were astute enough to realise
the dangers inherent in meddling with graveyards, the repositories
of so many emotions and memories. Westminster was rich and, by
common consent, the cemeteries looked pristine. By the time of
Porter's takeover in 1983, Conservatives were taking on the bas-
tions of union power and the ugly by-products of profligacy and
over-staffing. Privatisation, closure and disposal appeared the most
suitable remedies, although none of these solutions could realisti-
cally be applied to municipal cemeteries. Porter was not alive to the
sensitivities and blundered on where even other hard-line municipal Thatcherites feared to tread.

The cost of the cemeteries may have rankled Porter when she
chaired Highways and Works, but a year into her leadership it had
become an obsession. Even the high level of maintenance counted
against them. In Porter's opinion, the dead, and those who
mourned them, were not entitled to the highest standards of civic
care. She later told an inquiry by the District Auditor, 'I remember
all this talk about how beautiful it was and wonderful and [I] said,

"Look this is ridiculous. We've got to be an acceptable standard but we don't have to be the most beautiful cemetery in England."' Porter also resented the fact that relatives in Ealing and Barnet used the three cemeteries. 'We were told there were minimal Westminster ratepayers in this cemetery,' she said later. She admitted 'screaming' at the officers, 'Who's actually in the graveyard?' She was furious that they did not know and that she could not get a 'straight answer'.

Porter's competitiveness with Wandsworth, the Tory flagship council across the Thames, was well known throughout City Hall. Neale Coleman, the Labour councillor who investigated the cemeteries affair, says, 'They were competing with Wandsworth, and it was a case of "Which service can we privatise next?" They wanted to do one which Wandsworth hadn't done.' Despite their Thatcherite zeal, Wandsworth Tories were too smart to get into the cemetery-selling business.

Two men bore the brunt of Porter's fixation: Peter Hartley, the Chairman of the Environment Committee, and George Touchard, the council's Director of Property Services. In particular Touchard, the senior officer in charge of the council's property portfolio, came under pressure to sell from both Porter and Hartley, who bullied and harried him down the path to catastrophe. Touchard later said in defence to the District Auditor as both men surveyed the political wreckage left by the sale of the cemeteries: 'Whenever . . . [you] put caveats forward against policy, even before it was executed, when it was still in a gestation period, if you put any opposition up, you were either "not one of them", or you were opposed to them politically . . .'

Rodney Brooke warned Porter and Hartley that the enterprise would end in tears. He tried to scare off Porter by telling her that one of the cemeteries, at East Finchley, lay within Margaret Thatcher's constituency. In the later inquiries, Brooke remembered his advice to Porter: 'Cemeteries are basically loss-making activities. When local authorities have sold them in the past any development land is sold off by the purchasers who keep the profit and the cemetery is passed on to a shell company which either goes into receivership or maintains the cemetery inadequately, since the

income from opening graves is rarely sufficient to keep it in order.'
'Who cares about that?' Porter replied, before dismissing his advice
on the grounds that, because the cemeteries lay outside
Westminster, they could be 'safely' off-loaded.

In September 1984 Touchard was ordered to see if anyone
wanted to buy the three municipal cemeteries. From the start, it
was an impossible task. 'Judged by strictly economic standards,'
the *Daily Telegraph* observed later, 'graveyards are bad investments.' Not surprisingly, there was little interest. The Institute of
Burial and Cremation Administration advised Touchard there was
no hope of finding a buyer, and a major crematorium company
called the Great Southern Group added: 'The most caring and careful private organisation would find the total financial burden
beyond its capability to bear, and there would never be a lightening
of the load. In the end it would be economic ruin.' Touchard hoped
Porter might forget the whole thing or change her mind, but she
did neither. Patricia Kirwan remembers Porter periodically barking
at Hartley, 'Have you sold those cemeteries yet?' Hartley winced
and blustered, and simply passed the buck to Touchard. Touchard
pleaded with Hartley not to sell the freehold of the graveyards,
giving a purchaser freedom to dispose of them in any way it saw
fit. But Porter and Hartley wanted rid of them, lock, stock and
barrel. By the following April Peter Hartley had tired of Touchard's
excuses and instructed him to 'actively market' the three cemeteries for sale.

Touchard's only sensible option lay with the councils in whose
domains the cemeteries were located. He wrote to one of them,
pleading, 'I'm under great pressure from my Chairman to expedite
the disposal of cemeteries generally, and unless I have some indication from you within the next ten days of a positive interest . . .
I am instructed to take active steps to secure disposal elsewhere.'
Ealing and Barnet Councils wisely turned down the acquisition of
a pointless extra financial burden. By the end of June 1985
Touchard had hit a brick wall, so he could scarcely believe his eyes
when, on 23 July 1985, a letter arrived from Messrs Lewis and
Tucker, Surveyors, Valuers and Estate Agents, based in North
London, 'to submit an initial offer on behalf of our clients, the

Western Synagogue'. Clive Lewis, a senior partner of the firm, urged the council to 'bear in mind in considering this offer that this Synagogue has considerable experience in dealing with the type of land in question . . .' He said later that he had heard about the sale from the secretary of the synagogue.

Clive Lewis knew people at the Western Synagogue and may have attended services there, but he was not representing it, only himself, as became obvious the further the deal advanced. He was a shrewd surveyor and businessman, who saw something the council in its folly had missed. He realised that the loss-making cemeteries included a valuable lodge at Hanwell cemetery, four houses and a crematorium at East Finchley, later valued at £250,000, as well as twelve acres of potential development land at Mill Hill. All Lewis had to do was carve off the valuable assets for himself, pass on the responsibility for the cemeteries to others, and he had a profitable deal which would be perfectly legal.

It might at least have occurred to the City Council that the Western Synagogue, or indeed any synagogue, would have no interest in buying three Christian cemeteries. 'But,' a later inquiry said in disbelief, 'the question was not even asked'. The synagogue in fact had no knowledge that Clive Lewis had used its name to capture the attention of the desperate Touchard, and it was later horrified to be associated with what its president, Sidney Jake, described as the 'desecration of the dead'. By September 1985 Lewis had stopped claiming that he represented the Western Synagogue and told the council he was now representing Royel Investments Ltd, also known as Growish Ltd. The council made a cursory investigation into Royel Investments and discovered that the company had been dissolved almost nine years earlier. Two of the directors were Phillip and Lillian Lewis, the parents of Clive Lewis. Astonishingly, the council did not ask what had happened to the Western Synagogue, why Clive Lewis's parents were interested in buying three cemeteries, nor why it was selling three cemeteries to a company which had been dissolved. Instead, Hartley and Touchard pressed headlong through every warning signal.

There was just one other possible offer on the table and it was the only deal which might have worked. A company called

Chancery Lane Estates proposed to set up a charity to run the cemeteries. In return, it asked for council-owned land, then occupied by a propagation nursery at East Finchley which provided flowers, not only for the cemeteries but for all the City Council's floral displays and hanging baskets. Chancery Lane Estates wanted to sell the nursery unit for residential development and use part of the profits to finance the maintenance of the cemeteries, but the City Council had agreed to sell the nursery to another company and rejected the offer from Chancery Lane. In September 1985 Chancery Lane stated that, without such a deal, it was 'inevitable that the cemeteries would fall into decline and misuse'. 'If this happened,' the company warned the City Council, 'I am sure that Westminster could be criticised as such a consequence could be easily foreseen.'

Shirley Porter's plan was voted through by the council's Tory-dominated Environment Committee, who arrogantly decided that the cemeteries could be disposed of because 'the City Council had no legal obligation to provide and run a cemetery.' This arbitrary ruling was made in spite of the fact that the City Council had received money from relatives to bury their loved ones in the graveyards, and to maintain them. There was a clear duty to consult relatives about the sale but no consideration was given to them. Shirley Porter set another hasty deadline, demanding that the cemeteries be sold by Christmas 1985. For good measure, she pressurised the officers to make the sale by cancelling the budget set aside for the cemeteries' maintenance. Porter was convinced that they were worthless, as she later stated to the District Auditor, 'As far as we were concerned . . . there was no value, absolutely minimal. We were getting rid of a liability to Westminster ratepayers.'

At the end of the year Clive Lewis's offer was the only one available. To choreograph every stage of the deal as it evolved over the months, or record for posterity its every clause and sub-clause, as contained within the vast quantity of material gathered by subsequent inquiries, would be neither illuminating nor entertaining. Suffice to say that both parties thought they were getting a bargain, and only one of them was right. By now, Touchard had assigned the finer details of the transaction to a junior valuer whose inexperience, according later to the District Auditor, 'was exploited by Clive Lewis at every turn'. Essentially, the auditor would add, 'the council ". . . eased the path for Clive Lewis to set up" his asset-stripping venture at the expense of and to the detriment of rate payers'.

At the end of January 1986 Clive Lewis demanded that his contract with the City Council be amended. This would enable the sale of the cemeteries to one company, and the land and houses to several other companies either associated with him or members of his family, thus separating out what Lewis perceived as the commercially valuable from the commercially worthless. The desperate officials at City Hall, worried at the prospect of Lewis walking away from the deal, agreed to this request without demur or suspicion.

A last-minute hitch could have wrecked the whole transaction. One worker at East Finchley cemetery, already distraught at his redundancy notice, refused to move from his home in East End Road. The council had no option but to withdraw the property from the sale. In compensation, almost supplication, Westminster sent a cheque of £70,000 to Clive Lewis.

Just before the contracts were exchanged in April, the council received another warning. The Commonwealth War Graves Commission did not have the full details of the proposed sale but was worried about the 1,000 war graves in the cemeteries, including those of 254 Dutch servicemen at Mill Hill. The Commission warned Westminster: 'Should there be any marked deterioration in the state of our graves due to neglect, we shall certainly be looking to your council to make good, either by carrying out any necessary work directly or in compensating us for any additional payment we may need to make to any other person or body to bring the graves to an acceptable standard.' The warning was ignored and the deal kept on rolling.

The final contract between Westminster City Council and Clive Lewis, or companies associated with him and his family, agreed these terms: three graveyards sold for five pence each to Royel Investments Ltd (Growish Ltd); the lodge at Hanwell sold for forty-five pence to Royel Investments Ltd (Growish Ltd); the development land at Hanwell sold for five pence to Bestwood Property Ltd; twelve acres of grazing land at Mill Hill sold for five pence to Bestwood Property Ltd; the worker's lodge at Mill Hill sold for five pence to Marsha Interiors Ltd; the crematorium at East Finchley (subject to lease) sold for five pence to Clive Lewis; the foreman's flat and car park at Mill Hill sold for five pence to Platmede Ltd. The total sale price was eighty-five pence.

Essentially, Lewis got the assets for nothing and, taking into account the City Council's cheque of £70,000 for the failure to gain vacant possession of the East Finchley house, made a straight profit of £69,999.10 before the ink on the contracts was dry. Eventually, Lewis sold the crematorium freehold for £250,000 and the lodge at Hanwell for £170,000. He rented out the two remaining lodge houses at East Finchley and Mill Hill. Others would also make profits through the sale of the cemeteries in a clever and complex deal.

The City Council was satisfied with the sale because, although it had essentially given away the cemeteries and had to pay Lewis £70,000, it had rid itself of a service which cost £422,000 a year. Porter and the rest believed that they had protected themselves from future complaints about the graveyards' upkeep, which they thought would now be maintained by Lewis under a legally binding covenant. Porter was mistaken however: the covenant applied only to the immediate purchaser of the cemeteries and not to subsequent owners.

On 28 April 1986 the contracts were exchanged and Clive Lewis had assigned the properties and the twelve acres of land to companies which either he or members of his family controlled. Both parties agreed to postpone the actual completion of the deal for nine months to give Westminster time to clear tenants from the remaining cemetery properties. Lewis now began the process of disposing of the few assets he did not want to keep: the cemeteries and the twelve acres of land at Mill Hill. If what happened until this point was astonishing, it was nothing compared to what happened next. To dispose of the cemeteries, Lewis dealt with two sharp businessmen: John Whybrow, a property consultant, and his solicitor

Rodney Hylton-Potts. Lewis still refuses to talk about his links to the two men, although there was nothing illegal about the deal they would strike.

Whybrow, according to Hylton-Potts, was a qualified barrister and 'a very, very remarkable dealer. Beak nose. Violent mood swings. He could be very amusing and then suddenly turn. An extraordinary character. But very, very shrewd.' Despite his talents, Whybrow was not flourishing at the time, and as Hylton-Potts puts it, 'Whybrow hadn't got a pot to piss in.' He looked successful and was living in a six-bedroom house in St John's Wood where he threw big parties, but in fact rented the house for £400 a year thanks to a cheap tenancy under rent legislation.

Just as Lewis was agreeing the exchange of contracts with the City Council, Whybrow visited Hylton-Potts's offices at Cheval Place in South Kensington. Hylton-Potts recalls, 'He came to see me one day and said, "We've got a very good deal." He said he had bought three cemeteries from a man called Clive Lewis.' Neither Hylton-Potts nor Whybrow could at first believe that Westminster was selling off the freeholds, allowing a purchaser to dispose of the graveyards in any way he saw fit. It was the height of irresponsibility by Westminster, but it had the makings of a very profitable deal.

Whybrow agreed to buy the cemeteries once he had found someone to whom they could be sold. He knew they had no financial value, but things might be different if they were part of a business package which included a huge incentive to any prospective buyer. Lewis was keeping the valuable assets such as the properties and the crematorium freehold for himself, but was prepared to sell the twelve acres of undeveloped grazing land, known as Milespit Hill, adjoining Mill Hill cemetery.

Also technically worthless, Milespit Hill was designated Green Belt land and Barnet council was unlikely to allow houses to be built there, but if the council changed its mind, the land would be worth an estimated £5.5 million. Whybrow's aim was to convince a buyer that there was a possibility that Barnet would allow homes to be built on Milespit Hill. The purchaser would have to take the cemeteries as well, but it was under no legal obligation to maintain them because the covenant would not be binding. Whybrow thought buyers would be convinced by the deal if he could tell them he was acting as a 'receiver' to a company which owned the cemeteries, and that his job was to sell them off. 'People think, "receivership; fire-sale: cheap",,' says Hylton-Potts bluffly. Hylton-Potts purchased a company, based in Panama, called Chelwood Holdings, to pose as the company in receivership. He recalls, 'I picked Chelwood Holdings for Whybrow quite by chance. It was a nice name. Unbeknownst to any of us, Lady Porter lived in Chelwood House and had a company called Chelwood Nominees. I'd never met Lady Porter, Whybrow never met Lady Porter. But the press later got hold of it and thought it must be Lady Porter! It's as simple as that. Had I chosen "Bloggs Holdings" there would have been much less shit. Pure chance!'

Whybrow now just needed a buyer. He told an inquiry in 1988, 'We hit what we thought were the eight major companies, and excuse the expression, in the "death business". The response came back: "No interest at all, we think it's absolutely worthless." As for the maintenance agreement,' remembered Whybrow, 'I don't think anybody bothered with it.' In the course of his business ventures Whybrow met a mysterious Swedish businessman who lived behind high security fences in a mansion at Bourne End in Hertfordshire. And, because he was a Swede, Whybrow and Hylton-Potts knew him simply as 'The Turnip'. In December 1986, seven months after Lewis exchanged contracts with Westminster, Whybrow had concluded a different property deal in Islington with the Turnip, and the pair went for a drink in the Loose Box wine bar in Cheval Place. 'Have you got anything else, Whybrow?' asked the Turnip. 'No,' replied Whybrow. 'It's a bit quiet really. I've got three bloody cemeteries.' The Turnip asked if he could have a look at them. Whybrow demurred, 'I'm awfully sorry but you're a bit late.' The Turnip pressed on, 'Well I have overseas clients who are desperate to get money into this country, please give me a chance.' Whybrow did not ask the Turnip why his clients were desperate to get money into the UK and why more orthodox avenues were denied to them; it was probably wise not to. He simply reiterated, 'Look you're wasting your time.' Brilliantly, Whybrow further tempted the Turnip by offering to sell him Milespit Hill. For the

Turnip, the graveyards and the twelve acres of grazing land made a good package: his clients could get their money into the country; there was no legal obligation to maintain the cemeteries, and Milespit Hill would be worth a fortune if Barnet Council ever granted planning permission to build houses.

The Turnip planned to purchase the cemeteries from Whybrow for £1.25 million, through Wisland, one his companies based in Switzerland. Whybrow also sold Milespit Hill to Wisland, sold by Westminster to Clive Lewis for five pence, reportedly for £1.75 million. Whybrow stood to gain £500,000 from the sale of the cemeteries and an extra £100,000 from the grazing land; according to Hylton-Potts, the rest of the profit passed down the line to Lewis. Hylton-Potts was struck by how desperate the Turnip was for the deal. 'He couldn't wait to exchange and complete early,' says Hylton-Potts. 'The Swede was so frightened of losing the deal. He thought it was a good deal for him. And he had no idea that Chelwood didn't own it. He didn't know they'd just owned it for a day; and that was the skill in the deal.' Shortly before completing the deal with the Turnip, Whybrow took fleeting possession of the cemeteries. At ten o'clock one Sunday evening, a taxi drew up outside his house in St John's Wood. The cab driver handed Whybrow an envelope. 'Here mate, these are for you.' Inside were the keys to the three cemeteries.

In April 1986 the council had exchanged contracts with Lewis, but the deal had not been completed. Completion took place nine months later, at the end of January 1987, between businesses such as Whybrow and Wisland of whom the council had no knowledge. Lewis had handed the cemeteries to Royel Investments (Growish Ltd), his parents' dissolved company, which in turn had passed them on to Cemetery Assets Management Ltd, another shell company, whose company secretary was Rodney Hylton-Potts, and whose directors were 'associates' of Whybrow. Cemetery Assets had agreed to sell them on to Chelwood Holdings, whose receiver was Whybrow, which had in turn agreed to sell them on to the Turnip's Wisland company. Contracts were exchanged and completed on the same day among the various parties, and ownership of the cemeteries passed like a greased rugby ball down the line of four offshore companies. Whybrow constructed the deal 'back to back' to pay off Lewis once the Turnip had signed for £1.25 million. Operating as Chelwood, Whybrow used the money he received from Wisland to buy the cemeteries off Cemetery Assets for £750,000 and pocketed the £500,000 difference. Hylton-Potts believes the bulk of the profit went to the inscrutable Lewis but Lewis refuses to comment on the details of the deal. On the same day, the council lost any control it might have had over the welfare of the graveyards, and Porter was completely at the mercy of the mysterious businessmen who now owned them. Wisland promptly abandoned the cemeteries to the elements and the fly-tippers and submitted plans to build houses on Milespit Hill.

To celebrate his triumph, John Whybrow treated himself to a holiday at the Monte Rosa Hotel in Zermatt, Switzerland. He paid the pianist at the bar to play Tchaikovsky's *Funeral March* over and over again, and tipped him each time. It was only later that he realised he had made a mistake over the exchange rates and had paid the pianist £10 each time instead of £1. He just laughed, flush with money. Later, he bought himself a villa in Spain.

In 1996 John Whybrow and his solicitor, Rodney Hylton-Potts, were jailed at Southwark Crown Court for swindling two Scottish banks. They had used an offshore company to purchase three Scottish hotels, conned the banks into lending more money than they were worth and pocketed the difference. The company was called 'Magus Inns', a play on the words 'major sins', according to the Prosecution. Both men spent two years in jail, after which Hylton-Potts earned national notoriety by winning a television programme called *Vote for Me*, in which he called for a total ban on all immigration and the castration of convicted paedophiles. In the 2005 general election, he stood as a candidate for his Get Britain Back Party in Folkestone against the Conservative leader, Michael Howard, and polled 153 votes. Hylton-Potts last heard that Whybrow had fallen on hard times and was living in a bedsit in Surrey.

In February 1945 the first Town Clerk of the old City of Westminster, Sir John Hunt, had died at the age of eighty-five. The City Fathers and their officials held a memorial service at

Photographs by Eileen Sheppard

The desecration of Mill Hill cemetery, 1988.

St Martin-in-the-Fields near the old City Hall off Trafalgar Square, and Sir John was buried at Hanwell cemetery with appropriate pomp. His grave and those of 200,000 other souls would soon disappear beneath long grass, brambles and discarded syringes. Porter's folly affected thousands of London residents, but her later response demonstrated her desire to get her own way without regard to the consequences or the feelings of others. 'I was amazed to see all the millions [the cemeteries] were supposedly worth,' she said years after the deal. The grass grew unhindered through the spring and summer of 1987, but it did not whisper in the breeze; it ticked like a time bomb, primed to go off at the most inconvenient time in the political career of Shirley Porter.

CHAPTER 9

Shirley Versus Ken (1983–6)

A few days after Mrs Thatcher's second general election victory on 9 June 1983, a delegation of Labour councillors from the GLC arrived at the ferociously ugly 1960s office block in Marsham Street which then housed the Department of the Environment. They had been invited for tea by the Secretary of State, Patrick Jenkin. 'There were biscuits from the Army and Navy store,' recalls Illtyd Harrington, the exuberant GLC Chairman, 'and tea in bone china.' After politely asking which councillors took milk and sugar, Jenkin revealed Mrs Thatcher's plans for the GLC: 'She's going to get rid of you.' The abolition of the GLC had made its way into the Tories' election manifesto, but many people considered it a hollow threat. Thatcher had in fact moved abolition to the top of the agenda and decreed it must happen by April 1986. What little remained of any political consensus was over: the GLC and the government would fight each other tooth and nail, and the battle would in many instances take place at the local borough level. Tony Travers, an expert in local government at the London School of Economics, says, 'You had Ted Knight in Lambeth, Derek Hatton in Liverpool and Ken Livingstone at one end, and Shirley Porter at the other. It was a mad period for local government. It's very difficult to find another example of it internationally; this intense ideological rivalry between right and left using local government as a battlefield has no parallel anywhere.'

Livingstone fought the proposed abolition of the GLC with a remarkable publicity campaign, transforming the GLC from an increasingly irrelevant force in the lives of Londoners into an expression of their contempt for what was perceived as an act of political malice. Livingstone's 'Say No to No Say' proved highly effective in turning the tide against the government. Posters appeared all over London, showing the Houses of Parliament and declaring: 'What kind of place is it that takes away your vote and leaves you with no say?' The government bungled its response to Livingstone's counter-attack so completely that John Grigsby, writing in the *Daily Telegraph*, said that Livingstone had begun to appear 'a champion of sanity and moderation'. According to a poll by MORI in October 1983, fifty-four per cent of Londoners were against GLC abolition. By the summer of 1984 the number climbed to seventy-four per cent. The days when Livingstone had caused outrage by breaking bread with the Sinn Féin leader, Gerry Adams, or by funding organisations such as Babies against the Bomb receded in the public consciousness in the face of Thatcher's determination to close down County Hall.

Margaret Thatcher was concerned that voters would register their fury over abolition at the next GLC elections, due to take place in May 1985, by voting Labour in greater numbers and she could not afford a Livingstone victory. She was determined to cancel the elections and pass an Act of Parliament to hand the functions of the GLC to representatives of the thirty-two London boroughs in April 1985 for the last year of its life. As the majority of boroughs were Tory-controlled, her plans would mean a transfer of power from Labour to the Conservatives without an election. Some Tory grandees were outraged; Edward Heath told the Commons in April 1984 that it amounted to 'a negation of democracy', adding, 'it immediately lays the Conservative Party open to the charge of the greatest gerrymandering of the last 150 years.'

Thatcher would not countenance the obvious alternative, which was to extend the life of Livingstone's administration for the last year of the GLC's existence. However, on 28 June 1984, the House

of Lords inflicted a savage defeat on the government, passing a
wrecking amendment allowing the 1985 elections to proceed – the
last thing Thatcher wanted. The government was forced to change
its strategy. The GLC elections would still be scrapped, but there
would be no handover of County Hall to Tories such as Shirley
Porter. Instead, Ken Livingstone would continue to run London for
another year. The *Daily Express* said Patrick Jenkin's tactics had

© Philip Wolmuth

Porter launches the ill-fated EfILG campaign.

'dismally failed', adding 'It is a sad and sorry story of complacency compounded by incompetence.'

Porter entered the fray three days before the Lords' vote. On 25 June, at the Waldorf Hotel in the Aldwych, she launched a new campaign against the GLC, 'Efficiency in Local Government' or EfILG. Porter and Roger Rosewell were the only directors of EfILG Ltd, a company set up to raise money from businesses to aid the cause, and there was also an advisory committee, whose members included Michael Ivens, the suspected brains behind WARS. EfILG was simply a new improved version of WARS, with the same objective of GLC abolition and, by the same stroke, the defeat of inefficiency. Porter hammered home her message by distributing T shirts and balloons sporting a motif of GLC sinking beneath the waves.

EfILG was a disaster well in advance of its launch. Two months before the Waldorf press conference, Ken Livingstone leaked to the local press a begging letter from Porter to businessmen which declared that the campaign had the full and active support of the Prime Minister and the government, and that sponsors would have the chance to meet Thatcher at Downing Street. All this was news to Margaret Thatcher, whose spokesman emphatically informed the *Paddington Mercury*, 'There is no involvement on our part at all.'

EfILG headquarters were at 25 Radnor Mews, a small house owned by Porter behind her apartment in Gloucester Square. Livingstone was the first to spot that she did not have planning permission to use it as an office. 'I'm glad to see that Lady Porter's second home at Radnor Mews – the one equipped with a word processor – is not infringing any planning permission,' Livingstone wrote in the *Mercury* three months before the EfILG launch. When Paul Dimoldenberg, the Labour councillor, started asking questions, 25 Radnor Mews was given planning permission for use as an office by Westminster City Council in a record fifteen days. *The Times* wondered 'why Lady Porter felt it necessary to set up her company when there is so much efficiency in local government already'. Shorn of Thatcher's support and embroiled in controversy about her campaign headquarters, Porter could only watch as her balloons drifted gently over the Aldwych, out of sight and out of mind, taking the Efficiency in Local Government campaign with them.

On 2 August 1984 Ken Livingstone upped the stakes. Because the GLC elections had been cancelled, he and three other councillors at County Hall would resign their seats and stand for re-election, giving people a chance to register their protest at the polls. Porter was desperate to stand against Livingstone in Paddington. Illtyd Harrington says, 'Shirley Porter saw herself as the White Knight to bring the Red Knight crashing down. Ken Livingstone would be the Demon King and she would be the very small Brunhilde. She saw it as a way of advancing herself in the Tory Party.'

Livingstone relished the possible contest. 'I think she would be a wonderful candidate,' he told the local press. But senior Tories at Central Office were convinced Porter would be annihilated if she stood. To the anger of local Tories, the party did not field a candidate for the by-election, which Livingstone won by a huge majority of the small number of voters who turned out on a rainy day in Paddington.

Thatcher now took refuge in brute force. During 1984 the government obtained parliamentary approval to strip County Hall of responsibility over buses and the London Underground, and handed it to a quango, London Regional Transport. The GLC was banned from selling off land and ordered to obtain government agreement for any building or engineering work costing more than £250,000.

Porter took every opportunity she could to thwart Livingstone through the courts. On her accession to the leadership, Westminster took repeated legal action against the GLC to prevent it from adopting new policies or from defending itself against abolition. First Porter challenged Livingstone's spending budget for 1983, which included subsidies for travel on public transport. The courts ruled in Livingstone's favour on this occasion, but Porter did score some victories over her rival. One former senior official at Westminster says, 'Shirley became a bag carrier for the Tory Party in fighting actions against the GLC and cramping Ken Livingstone's style.' As City Solicitor, Terry Neville had to fight most of the cases against the GLC. He says, 'The big politics were encouraged by Downing Street through Michael Ivens who influenced Shirley.'

Porter tried to silence the GLC by challenging its right to campaign against abolition using ratepayers' money. She challenged the 'Say No to No Say' campaign on the grounds that it was party politicking on the rates. In October 1984 Brian Skinner, District Auditor for the GLC, declared that most of the £10.2 million spent by the GLC on its anti-abolition campaign was unlawful. In early January of the following year Terry Neville threatened the GLC with court action unless it cancelled its campaign. Later that month, the High Court ruled that councils could seek only to inform but not to persuade and granted Westminster an injunction preventing the GLC from using campaign slogans such as 'Keep the GLC working for London'. On the day of Westminster's triumph, Rodney Brooke noticed that a corridor in City Hall was cluttered with boxes of anti-GLC propaganda leaflets ordered by Porter and paid for by Westminster ratepayers. Brooke was horrified; it was exactly the type of illegal publicity the courts had banned the GLC from using. Brooke told his officers, 'Shred all that straight away.' He warned Porter, 'You can't actually take on Livingstone and do the same stuff yourself.'

Porter celebrated the day that the bill abolishing the GLC received royal assent with one of her more notorious photo-calls, appearing on Westminster Bridge with a man dressed as a jailbird. A former press officer says, 'We got one of the young lads in the office and dressed him up as a prisoner to symbolise Westminster shackled to the GLC. He posed on Westminster Bridge chained to a ball marked "GLC". Porter ceremoniously cut it off. It was just tacky and populist hype.'

The fight became increasingly nasty. Porter further provoked Livingstone and the Labour councillors at Westminster by threatening to lay waste the bedrock of their support among the voluntary organisations in their Paddington heartlands by cutting the grants to Law Centres and tenants' associations. Following GLC abolition in March 1986, Westminster would assume the responsibility for their funding. 'It's obvious,' Porter pronounced to the local press, 'that many of these so-called voluntary groups are political and only object and shout when they think that a party political point can be scored.' Many groups did support the GLC, but Porter's actions only reinforced their allegiance.

Her fears increased when Livingstone gave £32,084 to the Westminster Voter Registration Project, a new voluntary organisation set up to encourage more people from ethnic communities to register for voting. 'Westminster is one of a number of London boroughs who need the cobwebs dusted off their electoral registers,' Livingstone said at the time. He knew that many members from the ethnic communities voted Labour, as he told the *Paddington Mercury*: 'Who knows what effect this could have on the representational colour of Westminster and the services it provides?'

Labour Paddington formed a base of the resistance against Shirley Porter. A 'Save Westminster Services' news-sheet, carrying attacks on Porter and her senior colleagues such as Patricia Kirwan, was clandestinely printed in Emmanuel church and distributed throughout Westminster. It was run by Jill Selbourne, a local Labour Party member and community worker, but was funded secretly by the GLC. Norman Grigg, minister at Fernhead Road Methodist church, says, 'That was a big thorn in the flesh for the Tory councillors and they could never work out where it was coming from or who was funding it and how it got all this news about the services being decimated.'

Porter finalised cuts during a rowdy meeting in November 1985 at the Marylebone Council House, convened to decide Westminster's budget following the abolition of the GLC in the coming April. Police dragged ten protesters from the meeting and a mother, Susan Kirby, was so distraught at plans to cut the grant to a crèche at the Covent Garden Community Centre, that she entered the council chamber and dropped her baby into Porter's arms with the words, 'Well there's no one to look after him now, so you'll have to.' Porter soothed the crying baby and, turning to Matthew Ives, newly promoted to City Solicitor, said, 'Whatever other people may think, I'm very good with children and animals.' Among the seventeen organisations to lose their future funding that day were the crèche, two Law Centres, the Voluntary Action Westminster group and Grigg's Methodist church.

During the politically volatile autumn of 1985 Porter opened up another front against Livingstone and Labour Paddington which would mutate three years later into her greatest scandal.

Patricia Kirwan, the Housing Chairman, had been wrestling with the deplorable housing conditions off the Harrow Road, and two estates in particular. On the Walterton estate, more than 1,000 homes needed new roofs, and over a fifth had wet or dry rot. On the nearby Elgin estate, Hermes Point and Chantry Point tower blocks had fallen into disrepair. Even more seriously, they were filled with asbestos which the council claimed it could not afford to remove.

In September 1985 Patricia Kirwan announced controversial plans for the privatisation and redevelopment of both estates. Around 850 Victorian slums on Walterton would be handed over to a developer called Bellway who would rehouse the existing council tenants, demolish the houses and build 1,800 new flats. Six hundred of the new homes would be sold off; the rest would go to a newly created charitable trust for rent.

Private money would also be used to remove the asbestos from the two tower blocks and refurbish them. Hermes Point would be sold to the Trust House Forte hotel company; Chantry Point would be split in two. The bottom half would become a youth hostel and the top half would be used to house homeless families. For Kirwan, the scheme was the best way of improving the estates and, in particular, funding the expensive costs of removing the asbestos from the towers. Kirwan says, 'The government imposed very tough limits on what we could spend on repairs and building new homes. This scheme was an imaginative way of improving the area and people's lives.'

The plans caused uproar among the council tenants on the estates and escalated the already ferocious war between Porter's Westminster and Labour and Livingstone. For Labour the plans represented a major assault on their heartlands. Two days after the announcement, Labour councillors wrote to the tenants: '. . . we have just been told of council plans to sell your flat to a private company . . . we are staggered by these proposals.' Kirwan responded immediately, describing Labour's letter as 'a pack of lies aimed at scaring you'. She told residents that the council wished to 'create a new community', which only provoked them into demanding what was wrong with the old one.

Neale Coleman, the Labour group's housing spokesman, says, 'The plan was disastrous from the point of view of the residents, and would have ended in complete financial disaster because it relied on rising house prices, which crashed a few years later.' On 24 September, with Coleman's help, a group of tenants set up a campaign against the proposals. The Walterton and Elgin Action Group or WEAG was run by a twenty-eight-year-old history graduate, Jonathan Rosenberg, who moved into the area in 1978 and later became a council tenant at 203c Shirland Road. He joined the Labour Party and even provided his home and his services to Ken Livingstone during the by-election campaign in the summer of 1984. Livingstone gave the group a GLC grant of £8,000 to run the campaign.

On 10 October 1985 a meeting of the Westminster Housing Committee hastily convened by Kirwan to agree the scheme ended in disarray after Livingstone turned up with 150 WEAG tenants and several TV cameras. He tried to make a speech but Kirwan ordered him to leave, and called the police. Livingstone invited the tenants to County Hall for a meeting. His parting shot to Kirwan was, 'You will one day answer for this; it will follow you to your political grave.' On 5 November, at the WEAG fireworks party, a strange guy with a blond wig, a cigarette in one hand and a plastic bottle marked 'gin' in the other was cast into the flames. It was an unconvincing effigy of Kirwan. Within weeks, the scheme collapsed in the face of the opposition and Bellway pulled out. But Kirwan refused to be beaten and began to think of ways to resurrect her plans with different developers.

Towards the end of its life the GLC disintegrated. Keith Veness, Livingstone's close friend and political associate, remembers the final days. 'The task was to get as much money as possible out of County Hall,' he says. County Hall was stripped of typewriters, telephones and photocopiers. Lorries, cars, bikes and vans were used to take away the spoils of defeat. 'That stuff kept the left going for years,' says Veness. 'One night we took out 2,000 boxes of paper. As the clock ticked down, it looked like a flock of vultures had been through the place.'

Four days before the GLC passed into oblivion, it once again tried to provide voluntary organisations in Paddington and elsewhere with funds to survive. Cheques for around £25 million were signed and given to motorcycle dispatch riders outside County Hall. Matthew Ives found out and on Maundy Thursday, 27 March 1986, obtained a temporary injunction to prevent it. The following day, the High Court ruled in Westminster's favour.

Twenty-one years earlier, the abolition of the London County Council had been marked by a solemn ceremony on the Thames at Festival Pier. Herbert Morrison, the great Labour leader of the LCC, had died three weeks earlier. After a memorial service at Westminster Abbey, where Harold Wilson read the lesson, the task of scattering his ashes into the river at Westminster Bridge was assigned to the LCC tugboat *Firebrace*. Then the Aldermen and councillors returned to County Hall for the last rites of the LCC itself.

The demise of the GLC was less dignified. After the GLC farewell party at the South Bank Centre, fourteen plumbers had to unblock the lavatories and seventeen brand-new industrial cleaners had to go back for immediate repairs. Meanwhile, security guards hired by the government cleared County Hall. Porter, who was not invited to the wake, remarked sarcastically, 'Great party, pity about the bill and the mess.' The day after abolition, Livingstone joined his friends from the Westminster Labour Party on their campaign in the marginal wards to wreak their revenge on Porter in the borough council elections scheduled for May 1986. At the moment of her triumph over the GLC, Porter had no clue that her own position at City Hall was in jeopardy.

The Labour campaign to wrest control of Westminster from Shirley Porter at the polls had been running for nearly eighteen months by the time of the GLC's abolition. The plan was hatched at a meeting on 4 August 1984 in North Paddington in a large Victorian house owned by the Labour Party activists Steve Hilditch and Jen McClelland. Three senior Westminster Labour councillors were present: Joe Hegarty, the Labour leader, Neale

Coleman, Labour's housing spokesman, and Paul Dimoldenberg, a committed Labour stalwart. They gathered to consider how to take control of Westminster for the first time in Labour's history. Hegarty had spotted something important: Tory Westminster was in decline.

The Conservatives had always considered Westminster a birthright. Since the days of the old City, they had simply taken it for granted that they would remain in charge. Even during Labour governments, the Tories always took comfort in the fact that they still held some sway over the country's most important institutions and they always considered the buildings and power bases as part of their heritage. Yet Westminster is a deceptive city. In 1984 it was easy to stand in the grandeur of Parliament Square and forget that, only a few streets away, teenage children on the decrepit Grosvenor council estate were sleeping three to a room and having to bathe in the kitchen. The Tories took reassurance from the mansion blocks and town houses of Park Lane and St James's and, imagining they would always remain in power, overlooked the 23,000 council homes which provided Labour with its support.

Housing determined political allegiance. George Tremlett, a former Tory Housing Chairman for the GLC, wrote in 1979: 'It became the great misfortune of British democracy to have one of its major political parties, the Conservative Party, identified with home ownership and its rival, the Labour Party, with the interests of the council tenant. This was not repeated in the same form anywhere else in the world.' When Margaret Thatcher gave people the right to buy their council house a year later, she was striking at Labour's core constituency as well as extending the gift of home ownership. For Tremlett and others, housing divided Londoners politically and encouraged divisions between communities. This rift was particularly acute in Westminster during the highly charged period of Porter's leadership.

The Tory population of Westminster was gradually shrinking. The main problem was the City's prominence: landlords could demand virtually any rent they wanted for apartments. There was a huge demand for short-term lettings in and around the centres of economic and political power usually situated in the Tory strongholds. Increasingly, multinational companies, political parties and embassies were prepared to pay high rents to house staff who often needed accommodation for short periods and would rarely bother signing on to the electoral register. Traditional Tory homes were now occupied by residents whose votes were registered outside the borough and often outside Britain. In the 1980s the non-permanent professionals came and went so quickly that at any one time a third of the huge mansion blocks in safe Tory areas around Oxford Circus or Victoria were empty. The demand for short-term accommodation, coupled with high salaries, also drastically reduced the availability of housing which might otherwise have been affordable by people wishing to make a permanent home in Westminster. Another factor in the changing face of Westminster was that in the decade following the census of 1971, the number of professional males in Westminster fell by more than twenty-six per cent. They were just the sort of people who were more likely to vote Conservative. Only twenty-eight per cent of Westminster residents owned their own home, compared to the thirty-two per cent who were council tenants and the rest who rented from private landlords. Hegarty says, 'Basically, the demographics had been changing over a long period. I was reasonably interested in statistics so I was noticing that electorally we were doing considerably differently; whenever there was a swing to Labour, it was a bigger than average one.' In 1982 the Tories regained Westminster comfortably, winning forty-three seats to Labour's fifteen, but ominously their share of the vote had fallen to below fifty per cent for the first time.

Labour's electoral strategy to beat Porter and take Westminster in 1986 took shape over the autumn of 1984. Councillors and activists formed the '86 Campaign Group'. Their plans were ambitious. In a good electoral year for Labour, it was possible to secure twenty-seven out of the total sixty seats on the council if they could win marginal seats in Millbank and in parts of south Paddington such as Bayswater. If they managed to clinch another two seats, they would have twenty-nine seats to the Tories' thirty. The balance of power would then effectively be held by the Independent Councillor Lois Peltz, who was more sympathetic to Labour and loathed Shirley Porter. Porter would no longer have overall control of the council. Another three seats would be even better, leading to an overall Labour majority of two.

The Labour councillors set their sights on three vulnerable Conservative wards: St James's and Victoria in the south, which had two seats each, and the Cavendish area around Oxford Circus, which held three seats. If any one of these wards fell to Labour, the Tories would lose control. Ken Livingstone said, 'We thought by putting much effort into the election . . . in those wards, we might have just one chance of snatching a couple of them and taking control of the council. We said among ourselves, "We shall only get four years. We shall catch the Tories only once because they will canvass afterwards and rebuild those neglected wards."'

In each of the target wards an experienced Labour councillor managed the campaign. Neale Coleman was put in charge of Victoria; Hegarty was given St James's and Paul Dimoldenberg would run the Cavendish campaign, which would prove critical. In a report for the group, Dimoldenberg wrote: 'All the areas we need to win have idle Tory councillors . . . Local people should be reminded of this often through news letters, advice sessions and membership drives . . . Labour Group to highlight particular issues in those wards we need to win in council and committee meetings . . .'

With the GLC's resources behind him, Ken Livingstone was crucial to the campaign. According to the minutes of one meeting, it was agreed to 'fix up meeting with Ken re how GLC can help us in these wards . . .' On 9 December 1984 it was reported that the meeting had taken place: 'Ken is keen to help, and will help get priority for particular projects in the key wards, if they apply for funding. Voluntary projects in these areas should be informed of this . . .' A month later cards and leaflets were already being sent to voters, and key figures in the national Labour Party were being approached for funds to pay extra campaign workers. By the end of January Labour candidates were out campaigning in the three target wards, signing potential Labour supporters on to the electoral register for the May 1986 vote.

In February 1985 an 86 Campaign Group report noted that Labour candidates had been chosen to fight the key wards, giving them plenty of time to get to know their electorates. Each weekend, Labour would set up a stall in their wards, hand out leaflets and offer help to local residents. Joe Hegarty remembers, 'There was a group of people who designed the week-to-week tactics. There was no constitution and no officers, but I always say it was the most effective body I've ever been a part of and good fun. We were all younger then, with fewer responsibilities.'

Hegarty's team would hit the streets of St James's every week-end, targeting potential Labour voters in the pockets of council housing or housing association accommodation. They also can-vassed hostels for the homeless. The biggest in St James's was Bruce House, made famous by George Orwell's book *Down and Out in Paris and London*, which housed 400 residents at the time. Wards are small constituencies and a few dozen votes can make the dif-ference between victory and defeat. If all 400 residents at Bruce House had signed on to the register and voted Labour, that would have been enough to seize St James's and control of Westminster. 'We had to make a special effort at Bruce House,' says Hegarty, who knew that many of the occupants might get drunk and forget to vote. 'We'd tell them, "Vote early and get down to the pub!"'

Neale Coleman's team in Victoria, home to Porter's City Hall and Parliament, focused on the big Peabody housing association estates scattered discreetly throughout the ward. 'We flogged our guts out, almost every weekend,' says Coleman. 'It was worth a try. Even in the periods when Thatcher was quite dominant, there were times when the Labour Party did very well, particularly in local elections.'

The Cavendish ward was looking particularly promising. It stretched from Marylebone High Street in the west to Cleveland Street on the Camden border in the east, and included many beau-tiful mews filled with Tory voters, as well as the expensive doctors' surgeries along Harley Street. But there were also pockets of social housing, including 240 council flats in Holcroft Court. Paul Dimoldenberg had set up his stall at the corner of Great Titchfield Street and Langham Street, close to BBC Broadcasting House, and soon started making a big impact among the local residents and traders with his warm character and easy-going manner. Porter's

closure of the Portland library had been a talking point, and there
was growing contempt for her campaign against the GLC. 'We
were very popular with shoppers on a Saturday morning,' remembers Dimoldenberg. 'Local restaurants used to bring us out coffee.
We took up issues on behalf of local residents, getting their trust
and working to improve very small things like uneven pavements
and getting cobblestones re-laid in mews.' In March and April
1986 the Labour campaign was particularly intense; leaflets were
sent out each week to voters in the target wards.

Shirley Porter remained ignorant of the seismic changes going on
around her. Before the elections there is no evidence that she was
interested in demographic change or housing tenure or what was
happening in Cavendish, St James's or Victoria. She was too com-
placent and bound up with her own obsessions: fighting
Livingstone, obtaining a peerage or a seat on the Tesco board, selling the cemeteries, the Quatercentenary and running Westminster.
But the foundations on which the edifice stood were cracking and
buckling beneath her.

In contrast to Labour's, the Westminster Tories' election campaign was flaccid. Peter Bradley, a new Labour candidate
campaigning to take Millbank from the incumbent Tory councillor
Teresa Gorman, says, 'Teresa Gorman's campaign leaflet said that
people on the Grosvenor estate were fortunate to be living near the
Tate Gallery, which for hard-pressed working people with a bath in
their kitchen wasn't really something they considered would add
much to their lives.' Neale Coleman says, 'The Tories seemed to be
very moribund and disorganised. They just weren't used to fighting
in those wards.'

The elections were held on 8 May 1986, the count on the following day at Porchester Hall, the sports centre in Bayswater. 'It
was a marvellous atmosphere; we were winning ward after ward,'
says Dimoldenberg. Labour held the marginal Maida Vale ward,
gained Millbank and won Bayswater for the first time. They won
Little Venice on a recount and even took a seat in Churchill. Lois
Peltz regained her place in the West End. Labour needed just three
more seats to achieve the unthinkable: control of the Tories' most
important borough. They failed to win St James's and Victoria, but

their third target seat was looking promising. All attention now focused on the table where the votes for the three seats in Cavendish were being counted. Many senior officers were at City Hall watching the results on television. 'It was so exciting,' says Pamela Whitford-Jackson. 'It's not that we were Labour supporters, it was just the extraordinary prospect of Westminster going Labour!'

As the morning wore on and the results were announced, panic gripped Porter and the Tories. Elizabeth Flach, a Tory councillor, remembers Porter striding up and down 'in a terrible state', muttering to herself, 'We've got to do something about this, this isn't on.' Flach said, 'What do you mean it's not on? It's just politics, democracy; this is how it is. People have a vote.' Porter's mood grew more hysterical and dangerous. She poked a threatening finger in Rodney Brooke's chest and twice threatened to fire him on the spot. 'If we have lost this election, it's your fault.' Porter then turned on her Housing Chairman and added, 'It's your housing policies which are turning Westminster socialist.' 'I thought that was a bit rotten,' says Kirwan.

At the Cavendish table, it seemed too close to call. There were two recounts and finally the result was announced. The Tories had hung on to the ward and therefore Westminster by just 106 votes. 'There is general agreement,' wrote John Magill, the District Auditor, some time afterwards, 'that the result of the election was closer than many people had anticipated.'

CHAPTER 10

Wet Rot (1986)

Paul Beresford received a summons from Shirley Porter a few days after the election: his attendance was required at City Hall. Beresford was raised on a farm in the harsh climate of North Island in New Zealand. In 1971, shortly after qualifying as a dentist, he arrived in England with £5 in his pocket and soon found work at a surgery in the East End. Within fifteen years he had his own successful practice and had become the Conservative Leader of Wandsworth Council. He was an imposing giant of a man: quietly spoken, stocky and ruddy-faced with huge hands more than capable of snatching a lamb from the perils of a wintry gale and carrying it to the security of a hillside barn. He was no less formidable as a politician.

Beresford led a right-wing team of Tories who had campaigned vigorously against the ruling local Labour Party and had been elected to power in 1978. In eight years they had transformed a tatty and poorly run part of South London: they smashed corrupt union practices, sold council houses, slashed local taxes and privatised failing local services. Beresford would sometimes tease Thatcher, 'Maggie, no matter how long you've been in power, we've been in power a year longer.' The Wandsworth Tories unleashed a tidal wave of gentrification across the borough and, according to the old joke, turned Clapham into 'Claahm' and Battersca into "Bart-ur-seah'.

Porter was extremely envious of Wandsworth, which had achieved Tory flagship status in an unglamorous part of town with little fanfare. The Wandsworth Tories viewed their counterparts across the river as faintly ludicrous. They would read in the *Evening Standard* of Porter's latest publicity stunt, usually involving some new cleaning gadget, and laugh. 'Her championing of these guys on motorbikes rushing around with vacuum cleaners and squirter things picking up dog poos was just so funny,' says one Wandsworth Tory. 'Nowhere else in the world has anyone rushed around with a vacuum cleaner like that! '

Porter had summoned Beresford because she wanted to know how he and his colleagues had effected such a transformation so quickly: how had his council changed Labour-voting Battersea into Tory-voting "Bart-ur-seah'? Both council leaders hoped the meeting would be brief. Beresford admired Porter's chutzpah and was amused by her antics but he knew he would find her impossible to work with and wondered whether Leslie Porter, who was supportive of her council activities, had got her into politics to keep her out of Tesco. Beresford gave Porter some documents – freely available in Wandsworth's archives – setting out the housing and planning policies he had used to reverse decline in his borough.

They contained details of the extensive sale of council houses which many people, including Porter, suspected was the real reason behind the growth in the number of Tory voters in Wandsworth, although subsequent enquiries unearthed no evidence of an unlawful purpose. Beresford left City Hall and thought no more about the meeting until much later when a great deal would be made of it by the media and Labour MPs once they discovered the details. He just remembers thinking that Porter was 'in too much of a hurry'. Later, Patricia Kirwan, who was also present, said the Beresford meeting was 'definitely, 100 per cent, the beginning' of the unlawful schemes that Porter was about to let loose on Westminster.

Behind the rictus-like grimace for the photographers at the election count in Porchester Hall, Porter's eyes betray fear. Had 54 people voted Labour instead of Conservative in a few streets around Oxford Circus, Westminster City Council would have been lost. The scale of the disaster was obvious at the first council meeting after the poll, when the new Labour councillors physically encroached on Tory space in the chamber. Their presence emphasised how close Porter had come to political oblivion. Peter Hartley, one of her closest political associates, remarked later, 'To lose the most important local government [sic] in the UK would have been an unmitigated disaster.'

Shirley Porter's three-year plan to shock the council into change and retire with a peerage had come off the rails; she would have to stay and make Westminster safe for the Tories to achieve her personal goals. Over the next four years, panic intensified among Westminster's Tories. If anything could be more incredible than the council's descent into corruption, it was the breathtaking speed with which it happened.

Herbert Morrison, first elected as Labour Leader of the London County Council in 1934, once boasted, so the myth goes, that he would 'build the Conservatives out of London'. He embarked on a massive programme of slum clearance as part of a drive against poverty and disease. One Morrison election slogan talked of 'building a socialist London', but according to Professor George Jones, the co-author of a biography of Morrison, there is no evidence that he had ever said he would use council housing as a way of increasing the number of Labour voters in London. However, the Tories believed he had said it and it became an article of faith among their ranks.

For years the Labour Party accused the Wandsworth Tories of 'doing a Morrison' in reverse, claiming that they had set aside 15,000 council homes for sale out of a total stock of 37,000 to build the Tories back into the borough. Whether by design or chance, it had happened. The Labour MP Alf Dubbs lost his marginal seat in Battersea after Wandsworth had moved tenants off the Livingstone estate – where asbestos had been discovered – and sold it to private developers. There had been 400 Labour voters on the estate; the newly redeveloped property had hardly any. 'Afterwards I found just two Labour voters,' says Dubbs. 'I'm not whingeing. It's a tough old world but they succeeded in shifting me.'

The rumours about both Morrison and the Wandsworth Tories were that they were engaged in gerrymandering: they were using public resources, in this case their respective councils' housing stocks, to secure a party political advantage, but there was never any documentary proof to support the suspicions. The term 'gerrymandering' was originally coined in 1812 by Gilbert Stuart, a cartoonist on the *Boston Sentinel,* to accuse Elbridge Gerry, the Republican Governor of Massachusetts, of redrawing county voting districts in his party's favour. Stuart thought one of the new districts, Essex, was shaped like a salamander, so he drew it as one, put Gerry's face on it and called his creation a 'Gerrymander'. The term took on a wider meaning to describe all suspicious political behaviour, particularly in marginal seats. If a Labour council demolished houses and replaced them with tower blocks in a marginal ward, the Tories would accuse it of gerrymandering; Labour councillors would do the same if a Tory council sold off homes or rejected plans for social housing in one of their target seats. The charges were rarely proven mainly because, even if such actions were deliberate, the guilty parties were never foolish enough to record their real motives on paper.

Gerrymandering is not just harmless political point-scoring. Since the evolution of its most primitive forms in the Middle Ages, and later through the great reforms and landmark court judgments of the 1820s and 1830s, local government essentially developed as a trust. By law, councillors hold the common assets of the local authority in trust for the good of all local taxpayers. When councillors take decisions affecting resources such as housing, libraries and even the local swimming pool, they have to bear in mind the common good. It is acceptable, for example, for councillors to cut local taxes shortly before an election because, although the measure is aimed at retaining power, the whole community benefits. But the abuse of public resources to service the narrow advantage of a particular political party is not only unlawful, it strikes at the central tenet of local government itself, that it acts for all voters regardless of their affiliation. Gerrymandering is designed to benefit a particular sector of the community and therefore must act against the common good.

Political neutrality in the use of public assets is woven into the fabric of local government. Few opportunities are missed in driving the point home to councillors when they are first elected. Councillors cannot even use their authority's headed notepaper and free postal service to elicit support for their political parties; they can be used only in the performance of their official council work, such as addressing the concerns of their constituents. After the May elections in 1986, all councillors at Westminster were issued with a copy of the members' manual, which told them: 'Council stationery and photocopying despatch and postal facilities, wherever provided, are available to provide support to Members of the Council. However, in making use of the facilities, Members must take account of their distinction between their official duties as councillors and their wider political role.' Shirley Porter, after twelve years' experience as a councillor, would hardly need to be reminded of such wisdom. Yet after the elections, she was so determined to retain power, that she ignored her responsibilities to the public.

At her first post-election meeting with senior officials on 15 May she blamed them for nearly losing the Conservatives control of the City Council. It was a measure of Porter's state of mind that she levelled the accusation in the first place at council employees who were required by law to be politically impartial, and testimony to how far she had destroyed their political independence that they accepted the ridiculous charge without demur. 'SP thinks result is CE's [Rodney Brooke, the chief executive] fault plus Chief Officers' . . . noted the then Planning Director James Thomas. He recorded ominously that Porter wanted 'a change of direction'.

Porter, with her love of quick fixes and influenced by what she thought the Wandsworth Tories had done, was convinced that Tory rule over Westminster would be protected only by gerrymandering in general, and the sale of council housing in the marginal wards in particular. On 3 June she met with her senior Tory chairmen, and officers were yet again blamed for the results. Brooke was on holiday, so his assistant chief executive, Pamela Whitford-Jackson, was present in his place. 'It was extremely hostile and unpleasant,' she says. 'At that meeting it was first discussed that what we needed to do was to get all the buggers out of the marginal wards and sell them [council houses] to yuppies. It was absolutely clear what they were talking about and, as soon as Rodney was back, I reported it to him. They wanted to shift the political balance.' None of the senior Tories at the meeting opposed the plan.

Porter's main obstacle to her unlawful plan was the decision-making structure of the City Council itself. By law, decisions and policies had to be arrived at in public by the various committees and often ratified by a meeting of the full council. Obviously, any new policy underpinned by a secret gerrymandering motive could not be implemented in the same way. Porter resolved to usurp the legal process by a simple expedient. In future, secret meetings held by Porter and her committee chairmen, the so-called 'Chairmen's Group', would decide the new initiatives; then officers would be ordered to introduce them to the committees so they could be processed, debated and disguised as legitimate policies. A record of the meeting on 3 June says that, in future, 'major policies would come down from the Group . . . rather than coming up from service committees . . .'

Senior officials such as the City Treasurer, David Hopkins, took refuge in supposing that the new system, operated with the ignorance of Labour councillors and the outside world, 'regularised what tended to happen'. In reality, Porter's new directive was a *coup d'état*. The real policy-making power of the Council had been transferred to an elite group of Tory politicians who would only meet in secret. Peter Hartley remembered Porter's mood at the time. 'It was, "Right, lads and lasses, you've buggered this thing up; we nearly lost the Council. I gave you your rope and you nearly hung us. I am now going to take charge of it all. I'll call it something else and we'll dress it up so that the public will not realise what is going on . . ."'

Also at the meeting of the Chairmen's Group on 3 June was Graham England, the Director of Housing, whose compliance was essential for the success of Porter's gerrymandering plans. England would become one of the most important chroniclers of the unfolding scandal. Present at many critical secret meetings, he always kept personal notes, which would later prove crucial when officials deliberately destroyed the minutes of these encounters to thwart subsequent inquiries. England had started his career as a committee clerk for the London County Council, where his job was to keep a record of meetings. 'It's a habit you get into,' he said later. He had worked his way up the career ladder until he was appointed Director of Housing for Westminster in September 1985, just seven months before his role took on a new significance. England was ambitious; he had hopes of eventually becoming a chief executive. He wore large tinted glasses, which lent a slight inscrutability to his appearance. His knowledge of housing was unquestioned and expressed in a confident, South London tone and with a broad smile. Socially, perhaps, he lacked a certain security. On his appointment to the top housing job in Westminster he invited Patricia Kirwan to a dinner at the Institute of Housing and her husband, Peter, diplomatically took him through the rigours of tying a black bow tie.

Over the following year a conspiracy took shape at a series of secret meetings in hotels, conference centres and City Hall, where plans to gerrymander the most important eight square miles of Britain evolved under the noses of the country's greatest democratic institutions. On 22 June 1986 Porter held a meeting at her country retreat, Corner Cottage, in the tiny hamlet of Worton just off the A40, a few miles north-west of Oxford. England recorded Porter's objectives, which were now clearly focused on the sale of council housing in the marginal wards: 'social engineering inc [luding] housing'. Policies would be dictated 'via Leader's group ... Chairmen's group'. Just two days later a special meeting of senior officers reiterated the objective. Porter demanded to know which properties were owned by the council in 'key wards', in other words, the marginal seats in Westminster.

The word 'gerrymandering' was recorded for the first time by England at a meeting six days later on 30 June, during a working lunch held by Porter for her senior councillors and officers. England took notes of Porter's increasingly manic observations: 'Who is a Tory voter?' She had decided to sell council houses to attract likely Tory voters into Westminster, but she needed some phoney reason to legitimise the policy in public. She wanted, as England recorded, an 'Economic justification for G [erry] Mander on housing'.

Events were now developing at speed. A Law Lord, Lord Bingham, later said, 'From July 1986, if not before, concentrating on marginal wards was majority party [Conservative] policy. The intention of the majority party was to develop council policies which would target marginal wards, including such housing policies as could affect the make-up of the electorate in those wards.' During the late summer and early autumn Porter dispatched senior officers from both the council's housing and planning departments on fact-finding missions to Wandsworth. Labour councillors were kept in the dark about such delegations, as they were over the development of policies aimed specifically at lowering their vote.

On 3 September a document of supreme importance – a product of feverish secret activity – emerged from the council's planning department. It was a 'strategy paper' looking ahead to the next local elections in 1990, and was called 'The Wandsworth Experience'. It not only articulated Porter's own conclusions but clinically spelled out both the 'problem' and the 'solution': 'The sale of council houses is much more difficult to achieve in Westminster than Wandsworth because the city holds less stock, demand in the borough is high and options to rehouse are limited.' The report remained within legal parameters until the next dynamite paragraph: 'Unlike other London boroughs therefore the sale of council houses offers little opportunity to socially engineer the population of Westminster. This remains a longer term objective, but there is an immediate need to socially engineer the population in marginal wards.'

The paper was sent to Bill Phillips, who had joined Westminster as head of the Policy Unit in July 1986, shortly after the elections, on secondment from his duties as a civil servant at the Department of the Environment. Porter had lost confidence in Rodney Brooke long before the election results. Too often in the past, the chief executive had tried to block her. After the elections, her faith in Brooke and several other senior officers simply collapsed. They could not be trusted to participate in the gerrymandering. For these special tasks, she needed a new breed of 'highly motivated' officer, and with that view in mind she held talks with Sir Terry Heiser, the most senior civil servant at the Department of the Environment.

She did not spell out precisely why she needed someone special and Heiser may not have asked; he was accustomed to lending his civil servants to councils for short periods. He suggested Bill Phillips.

Pamela Whitford-Jackson had been a civil servant with Bill Phillips at the Department of the Environment and told Brooke he was 'mad' to allow the secondment. She thought Phillips would try to take Brooke's place: 'He's very dangerous to you, Rodney.' Beneath Phillips's suave veneer, Whitford-Jackson detected pent-up frustration and a highly ambitious drive. In 1985 Phillips had been promoted to assistant secretary grade in the Civil Service and according to his bosses had probably hit the glass ceiling. One former higher-ranking civil servant at the Department of the Environment says, 'He was a nice, clean-cut young man, not very wise, not very good judgement, but active. He was just the sort of person you would want as a bag carrier. It was fairly clear that he wasn't really making progress. Bill, even with his level of naivety, must have begun to suspect that he didn't have a glittering, long-term career at the Civil Service.'

Porter was deeply impressed by Phillips, possibly because she detected a malleable character who would do as he was told. He in turn saw a path to speedy advancement. 'He insinuated himself into Shirley's affections and got between Rodney Brooke and Shirley,' says one former senior officer. When the planning department sent 'The Wandsworth Experience' to Bill Phillips, he took his opportunity to impress Porter. His Policy Unit produced a paper called 'Homelessness/Gentrification', which suggested that moving homeless families outside Westminster would 'assist in . . . gentrification . . .' It went on: 'What is gentrification? In short, it is ensuring that the right people live in the right areas. The areas are relatively easy to define: target wards identified on the basis of electoral trends and results. Defining "people" is much more difficult and is not strictly council business.' Phillips would orchestrate the gerrymandering for Shirley Porter and he was generously rewarded with the new post of managing director shortly after joining the council.

Porter unveiled her evolving gerrymandering strategy to Conservative Party councillors and activists over the course of the following year at a series of secret Saturday seminars in a lecture theatre at the London Business School by Regent's Park. She held the first meeting on 6 September 1986 and handed the participants a note she had prepared setting out plans to win the local elections scheduled for May 1990. 'In fact, when you have read the documents and after we've had our discussion,' she wrote, 'it would be helpful if you'd swallow them in good spy fashion otherwise they might self destruct!!' Porter's plans, which she described as 'very sensitive', included the sale of council houses in marginal wards to bring in more Tory voters. 'What is gentrification?' she asked, simply regurgitating Bill Phillips's report. 'In short, it is ensuring that the right people live in the right areas . . .'

Porter also spelled out plans for the homeless who were more likely to vote Labour, suggesting that the council 'use property outside Westminster' and 'target homeless accommodation on specific and appropriate wards'. Homeless families were emerging as the greatest barrier to Porter's plans. Wandsworth had a much greater number of council houses and could afford to sell many thousands while retaining enough to meet its legal duties to house the homeless. Westminster, on the other hand, did not. The City Council had only 23,000 council houses, compared to Wandsworth's 37,000, and these were in much greater demand due to Westminster's central position and the proximity of railway termini such as Paddington and Victoria, a magnet for homeless people from all over the country. There were 10,000 people on the waiting list for a council house in Westminster. Porter's dilemma was how to sell thousands of council flats to potential Tory voters and still provide homes for people in need. She could not do both so she planned to mitigate the huge extra costs of housing the homeless by seeking less expensive accommodation outside the City.

At another meeting that September, Porter made clear to her chief officers what she had in store for the homeless. 'Homelessness,' wrote Graham England during the discussion, 'Be mean and nasty.' The plan was to export homeless families out of Westminster and sell off council housing which would otherwise be made available to them. This would mean extra work for the City's social workers who would have to deal with the misery and dislocation caused, hence England's jotted reference: 'implication – social services'. A former senior officer at Westminster says, 'She was actually rather naive. I'm afraid she treated people a bit like litter problems and that's where it all went horribly wrong.'

Porter's other dilemma was how to disguise the gerrymandering plans and avert the attention of Labour councillors and those authorities such as the District Auditor, who carefully audited the council's books every year to ensure funds were spent legally. Her need grew for an 'economic justification for G-Mander on housing'. Without some kind of cover, she knew she could be vulnerable to public disgrace and punishment by the District Auditor, who had the power to force councillors and officers to repay money they had deliberately misused in the abuse of public resources.

Porter hoped she would find protection from PA Cambridge, a new consultancy company. On 15 September she summoned the consultants to a meeting at City Hall and commissioned them to write a report on 'housing and planning policy' in the City. She did not want them to come to their own conclusions. A record of the meeting was taken by Dr Mark Kleinman, one of the consultants, a young Cambridge academic. His notes display how far the language of gerrymandering used by Porter and her entourage had degraded into a mixture of sinister euphemism and brutish gangster talk. Kleinman listened with mounting astonishment to the discussion led by Porter. There was a need 'to push Labour voters out of marginal wards' and to 'privatise/gentrify council blocks in marginal wards', she said. There would have to be 'area strategies for housing policies' – in other words, council house sales in marginal wards. On the population decline in central Westminster, which had brought about the electoral disaster, Porter raised the question, 'Is loss a bad thing?' Clearly she thought that population decline was acceptable if it involved Labour rather than Tory voters. 'Who are you losing? Concentrations of ethnic minority. Social imbalance. Social problems from concentration.' Porter insisted that any future new policies would be 'electorally driven'. Kleinman also noted Porter's acute fear about 'moles within the City Council', an indication of her growing paranoia that the details of her conspiracy would leak. She concluded the meeting by telling the consultants: 'We want the right answers.'

Porter was badly mistaken in thinking Kleinman would give her a report recommending the sale of council houses in marginal wards; he had his reputation to protect and he was determined to produce an independent professional study. He concluded that the greatest problem affecting the City's housing and planning policies was the high turnover of population, mainly caused by high rents and property values. He studied census data and carried out an exhaustive survey of porters in blocks of flats, asking questions about the permanence or transience of residents. Kleinman drew up a list of five wards where there was a particular problem: Baker Street, Lancaster Gate, St George's, Bayswater and the West End.

Porter was not pleased by the report; only two of the eight wards she wanted to gerrymander were on the list: Bayswater and the West End. She asked one of his senior colleagues to pressurise Kleinman into including more marginal wards. He said later, 'I was approached and asked if I could include certain named wards in the target category, either in addition to, or as substitutes for, the five I had chosen. It was clear that this approach had come from the "18th floor".' But Kleinman refused to budge, and to make matters worse, concluded that the solution to population decline lay in the provision of more social housing. He planned to deliver his report to the council early in 1987. Porter ignored the report and continued with her plan to sell council houses in the marginal wards. Her decision to fly in the face of Kleinman's report was later used as powerful evidence of her wilful determination to continue unlawful policies despite advice to the contrary. Kleinman's report was a catastrophic own goal for Porter.

She doggedly pressed ahead. In one of her 'Leader messages', she instructed the chief officers: 'Now we know policies – do them.' On 25 November she called a meeting at the YMCA in the City of London, which the 'Top 70' council officers at Westminster were ordered to attend. They were told that the council was going to sell council property in marginal wards to help guarantee the Tories victory at the 1990 elections. Other council activities, including environmental improvements, were also going to be targeted at the same wards. In most other local authorities such an announcement would have produced outrage, opposition and possibly calls for the

resignation of the Leader of the Council, yet there appears to have
been no challenge from the Top 70. Porter announced that the new
policies would be given a name: 'Building Stable Communities', or
BSC. Peter Hartley accurately described BSC as 'one of Shirley's
smokescreens'. Some officers present at the meeting claimed later
that they had wearily dismissed BSC as yet another Porter initiative, or as 'political clap trap'. But Bill Ritchie, the Director of
Social Services, knew Porter was in deadly earnest. He thought,
'We're in a different ball game here.'

Ritchie says, 'I think we realised what we were dealing with. All
the directors, all the deputies, all the assistant directors, the very
top management structure, the Top 70 were there. The meeting was
addressed by Shirley Porter personally and David Weeks, her
deputy. It was where everybody was brought together and told
what these new policies were going to be. Shirley Porter's role was
to spell out that these policies were being introduced and our
involvement was meant to make sure these policies were going to
be successful. What was also to be done at that time was to ask
service departments like mine to prioritise spending in the marginals.' Robert Lewis, who had recently joined Westminster as deputy
City Solicitor to Matthew Ives, was also there. 'Everyone knew
what was going on,' he said. 'Everyone knew it was not proper.
The whole atmosphere permeated the place.'

On the way to the YMCA meeting in a taxi, Porter had
brusquely informed Rodney Brooke that Bill Phillips was to be
given a new role as managing director of Westminster. She knew
Brooke would never have carried out the tasks she would now
assign to Phillips. The move sidelined the chief executive and
greatly diminished his importance at City Hall. Brooke was
shocked but was so out of favour with Porter that he was powerless to prevent the appointment. Matthew Ives, who had formed a
low opinion of Phillips, was angry with Brooke for not standing up
to Porter over the promotion. 'He should not have let it happen,'
he told a colleague.

Pamela Whitford-Jackson was furious when she found out and
told Brooke she would never report to Phillips. She says, 'The aim
was to keep the officer centre – people like me and Rodney –

destabilised through changing duties and changing organisational structures.' Brooke remained titular head, but effectively he was out; Phillips held the power. Labour councillors, ignorant of the drama being played out behind the scenes, mocked the chief executive as a 'king without a kingdom'. Brooke was allowed the occasional glimpse of an increasingly nasty game being played out while he occupied himself with activities unconnected to BSC.

Porter knew she had embarked on a dangerous course but sought comfort in the thought that she was keeping Westminster safe for the Conservative Party. On 19 December 1986 Shirley Porter met Margaret Thatcher to try to persuade her to change housing laws which would reduce the council's legal duties to house the homeless. Porter feared that her brutal plans for the homeless, central to the gerrymandering, would be unlawful, and hoped Thatcher would rewrite the statute book to get her off the hook. She prepared a note for the Prime Minister: 'We in Westminster are trying to gentrify the City. We must protect our electoral position which is being seriously eroded by the number of homeless that we have been forced to house. We wish to pursue policies for increased home ownership, but how can we achieve this when we are forced to house over 1,500 families a year, seventy per cent of whom are already in receipt of State Benefit? I am afraid that unless something can be done, it will be very difficult for us to keep Westminster Conservative . . .' Thatcher's response remains unknown.

Robert Lewis later observed, 'One either stopped the rot, in the authority, or one did one's best to live with it.' By Christmas 1986 most officers and Tory councillors were prepared to live with it. Nothing short of Porter's removal as Leader could prevent the rot spreading into every corner of City Hall.

CHAPTER 11

Dry Rot (January–July 1987)

In her determination to implement her gerrymandering schemes, Porter suppressed all copies of Kleinman's report and turned to Alex Segal, a wealthy solicitor who had been appointed vice-chairman of the Housing Committee shortly after the 1986 elections, to produce an alternative which would keep the plot on course. On 27 January 1987 he presented Porter with a report called 'Home Ownership Proposals', providing her with the arguments she needed. It stressed the need to act against the Labour threat at the local elections in 1990, citing figures which showed there were more council tenants than home owners in Westminster. 'If it is accepted that owner occupiers are more inclined to vote Conservative then we approach the City Council elections in 1990 with an enormous handicap.' It added: 'The short term objective must be to target the marginal wards and, as a matter of utmost urgency, redress the imbalance by encouraging a pattern of tenure which is more likely to translate into Conservative votes.'

Segal supported Porter's plans to sell council homes in the marginal wards. People already had the right to buy their own council house at a substantial discount under legislation introduced by Margaret Thatcher in 1980, but this could not help Shirley Porter in the marginal wards. Crucially, to guarantee a swift sale of council houses in time for the 1990 election, Segal urged Porter to expand an obscure council scheme called 'Designated Sales', which produced only ten sales of council housing a year in Westminster. When a council flat fell vacant on the death or departure of a tenant, it could be sold on the open market to a Westminster resident instead of being re-let to someone from the housing waiting list.

Segal warned there was no time to experiment: 'The urgency of these proposals cannot be overstressed. We are already twenty per cent through the life of this Council. Many of the policies will take time to implement and longer for their effect to be felt. If we delay we shall be too late. Political opposition to change and disruptive action must be anticipated and should be countered by a clear demonstration that we will not be deflected and a realisation on our part that non-action is not a viable option if we are to retain control of the Council in 1990.'

The report was a blueprint for the widespread and unlawful abuse of the council's resources to service a party political advantage. It articulated Porter's thinking and intentions. On the day after Segal's presentation, Bill Phillips sent the report to Graham England and ordered him to 'see where and when specific actions might be targeted', or, in other words, how council homes could be sold in the marginal wards. During February 1987 England's officers identified the council estates in the eight marginal wards from which homes could be sold. By acceding to this improper instruction, England was committing himself and his department to a dangerous and foolhardy enterprise.

On the weekend of 14–15 February Porter held a clandestine conference at the University Arms Hotel in Cambridge with her senior officers and councillors, where they discussed how to get the gerrymandering plans passed by the council's committees without Labour councillors discovering the real motives behind them. Phillips was ordered to provide as much information as he could in relation to eight marginal wards: Bayswater, Cavendish, Hamilton Terrace, Little Venice, Millbank, St James's, Victoria and the West End, including demographic changes. Porter wanted profiles for each area, and initiatives to promote her objectives involving planning permissions, council house sales and environmental improvements. On his return to City Hall, Phillips demanded the information from his senior colleagues in the housing, environment and planning departments.

On Saturday 14 March Porter held another secret meeting in an empty City Hall to consider the information gathered by Bill Phillips. She confirmed that the managing director would oversee the gerrymandering strategy, 'Building Stable Communities', by leading and directing 'the officer input to BSC'. The main component would be designated sales, but other council services, including planning permissions and environmental improvements, would also be targeted in the marginal wards. Porter and her deputy, David Weeks, decided that 2,200 new potential Tory voters had to be brought into the City before the electoral register closed in October 1989 prior to the May 1990 elections. Weeks handed Phillips a note listing the eight marginal wards and the number of required new voters in each one: Bayswater, 350; Cavendish, 250;

Protesters ambush Bill Phillips as he sells BSC to a conference, December 1987.

Hamilton Terrace, 250; Little Venice, 250; Millbank, 450; St James's, 250; Victoria 150; the West End, 250; total: 2,200.

These extra voters could make all the difference in marginal seats where a hundred votes could swing the result. At an average of two people per dwelling, it would mean that Porter would have to sell around 1,100 council houses. Council homes under designated sales were also sold at an average discount of £30,000 each as there would be few buyers if the properties went for their full market value. Councillors were personally liable if they wilfully abused public money or public assets and could be forced by the District Auditor to pay back the squandered funds from their own pockets. Porter's unlawful motives put her at risk of a potential surcharge, just on the sale of 1,100 houses at a £30,000 discount each, of around £33 million. The secrecy surrounding the evolution of the plot strongly indicates that she knew she was playing with fire.

The developing conspiracy placed intolerable pressure on the relationship between Porter and her Housing Chairman, Patricia Kirwan, who had helped Shirley Porter into power in 1983. Since then, their relationship had deteriorated due to a series of spats and slights, small in themselves, which had accumulated to create a mutual loathing. Kirwan was an ebullient and emotional woman; Porter came across as taciturn and socially ill at ease. Kirwan felt competitive towards Porter. Shortly after the 1986 elections, when Porter was feeling acutely vulnerable, Kirwan told the *Paddington Mercury*, 'We all treat Shirley with a healthy degree of respect,' adding enigmatically, 'but naturally I am ambitious.' Kirwan admits, 'I would love to have been leader.' But she understood that Porter derived much of her support from Tory councillors who were impressed by the Tesco millions and the publicity they attracted from the media. Kirwan sought to downplay Porter's wealth, and when Porter once asked her why she appeared so underwhelmed by it, replied callously that new wealth was often lost with the same speed it took to acquire it. 'We have a saying in Lancashire,' Kirwan told her. '"Clogs to clogs in three generations".' She also had a low opinion of Porter's intellect and failed to disguise her irritation at the Leader's inability to grasp detail. 'Shirley was always insecure, so she didn't know what to say,' says

Kirwan. 'I was always sure of myself because of my wide experience in politics, my education and because of my personality. I don't give a stuff what people think about me.'

Their feuding began in the early days of Porter's leadership when the senior Tories at Westminster would meet regularly at each other's houses. In 1984 it was Kirwan's turn to host dinner at her home in Ledbury Road, Notting Hill. Porter walked into the kitchen and snapped her fingers at Kirwan's husband, Peter, demanding, 'Water! Water!' Peter Kirwan stormed upstairs to his study. When Barry Legg followed, he turned on Legg, 'Get that woman out of this house now!' Legg managed to patch up a fragile peace, but it did not last. The final break came at the election count in 1986, when Porter blamed the result on Kirwan's housing policies. 'I know she talked a lot,' Porter said later, 'but it was all "jaw, jaw" and no war, in the sense that she was just not talking

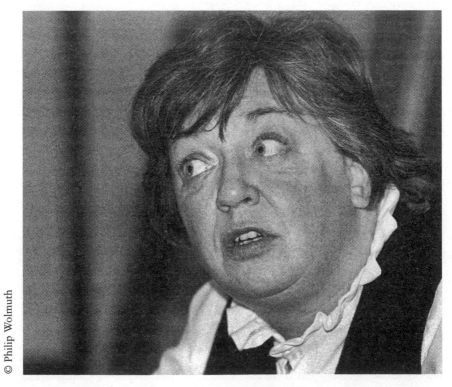

© Philip Wolmuth

Patricia Kirwan, Porter's great rival and nemesis.

enough action and her housing policy was not good enough.' Peter Hartley, who was close to both women, said, 'Shirley had been trying to get Patricia out for years. They hated each other's guts.'

By 1987 the housing department was of paramount importance to Porter. To subjugate the housing officers to her will, she wanted to force out the department's commanding presence, Patricia Kirwan. The Housing Chairman was too dangerous to fire outright so Porter's plans to remove her started, as had been the case with so many others, with calculated and unspoken ostracism. From the outset, Kirwan knew what Porter was thinking but underestimated her intentions. 'I thought, this is panic,' says Kirwan. But Porter was in deadly earnest. Kirwan tried to cool the situation by suggesting the privatisation of council housing estates, similar to her badly stalled scheme in Paddington. Porter was not interested, and, gradually, secret meetings to discuss 'housing issues' started to be held without the Housing Chairman. Kirwan was convinced the plans to target marginal wards amounted to gerrymandering sales and placed councillors and officers at serious risk of surcharge by the District Auditor. She decided to defeat Porter's proposals due to be debated by Westminster Tories at a Saturday seminar in the London Business School on 21 March 1987.

It seems remarkable that a large number of respectable Tory activists – and a few unscrupulous ones – would sit in a lecture theatre, complete with flip charts and plates of chocolate bourbons, and insouciantly discuss the pros and cons of such obvious corruption as if they were choosing a new carpet for the Lord Mayor's parlour. Perhaps they were prepared to contemplate anything to beat Labour in 1990; perhaps they did not care; perhaps they concluded that such a fearless and open discussion of Porter's plans legitimised everything; or perhaps, as a senior barrister put it later, it was like standing so close to an elephant that you could not actually see what it was.

Kirwan tried to shake the Westminster Tories from their apparent insensibility. At the meeting she warned against the misuse of officers for such blatantly political purposes, and insisted that there was nothing which could justify a massive extension of designated sales in marginal wards. She also used the word Porter used only in

private. 'I do recall Patricia Kirwan using the word "gerrymandering",' says one former senior Tory councillor. 'She said, "You can't
do this because it is gerrymandering; you have to take proper purposes into account." Shirley was chairing the meeting and she just
ignored it.' But the Tories failed to see sense. The former councillor adds, 'There was a total lack of training for councillors about
what was and was not proper and there was this new intake of
Tory councillors at the meeting who did not understand what was
going on.'

Angela Killick also objected to the policy, expressing concern at
the impact such a vast sell-off would have on the homeless and
people on the housing waiting list. She was 'howled down' by
Porter, Barry Legg and David Weeks. Another Conservative councillor, Anthony Prendergast, an elegant and urbane Tory patrician
with swept back grey hair, a ruddy face and a jovial manner, married to Dame Simone, the former chairman of the London
Conservative Party and a friend of Margaret Thatcher, also
attacked the proposals. He was appalled that council housing
would be denied to the children of existing tenants. He, too, was
shouted down.

A few days later Kirwan plotted a coup attempt against Shirley
Porter. Over dinner at a nearby Italian restaurant, she and three
fellow committee chairmen discussed Porter's deteriorating conduct
towards them and senior officers. 'We decided we couldn't cope
any more and that it's got to stop and somebody had to stand', she
says. Kirwan agreed to stand against Porter for the leadership;
Simon Mabey, Social Services Chairman, and Peter Hartley,
Porter's apparently loyal Environment Chairman, decided to stand
against her deputy, David Weeks. 'Weeks was actually even more
irritating than Shirley,' says Kirwan. According to the Westminster
Conservatives' rules, the Council leader had to submit to re-election every year. Usually, it was just a formality. Porter would be
standing for re-election on 13 May. The group would strike then.

Meanwhile, Porter planned to replace Kirwan with Peter
Hartley, little realising that he was plotting against her. Hartley had
masterminded the sale of the cemeteries – at the time considered a
triumph – and proved to Porter his credentials as a doer. 'That

Hartley should be rewarded for his cemeteries' sale,' says Neale Coleman, 'just shows how mad they all were.' 'I did not want to become Chairman of the Housing Committee,' Peter Hartley said later. 'I was forced to.' Porter pressurised Hartley into taking the post, telling him, 'You're the man for the job, I want you to do it . . . you're going to be fabulous.' In early April Barry Legg introduced the Director of Housing, Graham England, to Hartley, 'Here is Peter. He is going to sort this out. He is going to get on with home ownership and your chairman is going to be phased out.'

Hartley's presence at the Housing Committee on 1 April 1987 first alerted Labour councillors that something was afoot in the Tory camp as he was not a member of that committee. Before the meeting, Ken Hackney, one of England's assistant housing directors, approached Neale Coleman, Labour's housing spokesman, and warned him that the Tories were planning something 'extreme'. During the meeting Alex Segal planted a seemingly harmless question: 'How many designated sales were there a year?' He was told 'ten'. Then, as quick as a flash, as arranged by Porter, the Tories on the committee used their majority to force through a resolution instructing Graham England to 'report back to the Committee on means by which designated sales can be increased without delay to annual level of at least 250'. Labour councillors were horrified at such a huge housing sales programme and their suspicions were aroused. The next Housing Committee would be on 8 July. Then, finally, Porter would reveal her hand.

As Housing Director, Graham England was placed in an intolerable position. He knew there was no justification for the proposed sales but he was caught between backing Kirwan, whom he liked, and Porter, whom he feared. Bill Ritchie, then Director of Social Services, says, 'I felt sorry for Graham England, knowing that he was between a rock and a hard place in a way that nobody else was, because of their absolute determination to do what they did, even against the advice of the solicitors, that was ignored. He was in his early forties, he had a family. He was placed in a very invidious position. I don't know how he didn't have a breakdown.'

During April Kirwan became increasingly confident of victory over Porter, who had now heard about the challenge. At least a dozen Tory councillors had promised their vote. Kirwan told the worried England, 'Don't worry about this. This is not going to happen because I'm going to oust Shirley. The support for me is growing and we will put a stop to it.' England pinned his hopes on a Kirwan victory but still had to deal with Porter's systematic bullying. She sent him a list of questions which contemptuously addressed him in the third person. 'How does he propose to achieve the voter figures in the eight relevant wards by 1990? Can the Housing Department not be more like an estate agent and create its own sales list of properties?' In a rare display of resistance, England faxed back: 'There is little support that officers can give to the eight target wards as opposed to the policies in other wards without the PA Cambridge Report.'

That month Pamela Whitford-Jackson left the council. She saw her colleagues become unbearably stressed and felt her health would go if she stayed. 'The rot had set in by then,' she says. Rodney Brooke was upset when she resigned. 'Don't go. I'll protect you,' he said to her. She replied, 'You'll be the next to go. Bill Phillips is going to get you out and then he planned to get me out.'

The strains of the gerrymandering plot coupled with the Kirwan challenge created a toxic atmosphere. Porter and her senior associates now routinely bullied senior officers. On 30 April the chief officers met in City Hall and discussed their deep concerns that they had been 'subject to political intimidation by the majority party and prevented from giving impartial, professional advice'.

At the start of May the gerrymandering plans had all the appearance of a runaway train. Porter's conspiracy had been taking shape for a year: the Building Stable Communities strategy was being finalised and the jewel in the crown, designated sales, had been sneaked on to the public agenda. The policies were ready to be placed before the council's committees, disguised as legitimate and radical initiatives aimed at arresting the City's population decline. However, there was still an opportunity for the plan to be derailed. On 5 May Shirley Porter, under acute pressure, was forced to seek external legal advice.

The day started badly for Porter when she received a negative report on designated sales from Paul Hayler, one of Graham

England's deputies, who had arrived only six months previously. Paul Hayler was yet another official to warn Porter about her scheme in his report innocuously entitled 'Discussion Paper – Designated Sales'. He had obtained a copy of Mark Kleinman's paper and concluded in his own report: 'The PA Report suggests a need to supplement the rented supply. There is nothing in the PA Report which would justify a designated sales programme on the scale presently proposed.' Porter had already ignored a similar warning from Graham England and had been told by Matthew Ives that arguments in support of the sales must be 'soundly based', and 'anything which smacks of political machinations will be viewed with great suspicion by the courts.'

When Porter received Hayler's report on 5 May, she suspected Kirwan's influence. At 9.45 a.m., Hayler was summoned to the 18th floor for his first ever meeting with the Leader. 'Had this been an instruction from others?' she asked. He denied it. 'The report is not what I wanted,' said Porter. Hayler asked if her proposed sales programme included tenants who were already legally allowed to buy their own council houses. 'It does not!' Hayler suggested that advice from a senior Queen's Counsel should be sought. 'Get it!' snapped Porter. 'You know what is required. Get on and do it! I do not need obstacles and options and things. Come back with solutions by the end of the day.' A conference with Jeremy Sullivan QC, an eminent expert on housing law, was hastily arranged for 3 p.m. The unhappy trio of Graham England, Paul Hayler and Robert Lewis jumped into a taxi and raced to Sullivan's chambers in Gray's Inn Square. Porter wanted a summary of Sullivan's advice on her desk by 5 p.m. for a meeting with her chairmen.

The fate of the whole sorry enterprise now hinged on a hastily snatched meeting lasting under an hour between three scared municipal officials and a busy QC, ignorant of the complexities of Porter's plot. It was the best opportunity the officers would ever have to destroy the conspiracy; all they had to do was lay the cards on the table and Sullivan would tell them that Porter's scheme to sell off council housing in marginal wards was unlawful. But they bungled it.

Lewis did initially try. He opened the conference by telling
Sullivan, 'It is my understanding or belief that the Conservative
Party, the leading members of the Conservative Party, wish to
secure electoral advantage by adopting a policy to designate [sales
of council housing] in marginal wards.' Sullivan told the three men
that it would be unlawful to concentrate sales in the marginal
wards or to select properties for sale by reference to party political or electoral considerations. Any sales must be for valid reasons
and apply to all the wards across the City. The officers might just
as well have asked Sullivan if it was OK for them to rob a post
office. No one needed a senior barrister to tell them that what was
being proposed was unlawful. Porter certainly knew it. Even if she
had initially forgotten, she had received repeated warnings.
Indeed, the Sullivan conference had been precipitated by just such
a warning from Hayler. As Robert Lewis said later, 'I cannot
believe that the kind of people who represented the leadership of
the Conservative Party needed telling of that point. It is an obvious
point.'

But fear stepped into the uneasy silence which followed
Sullivan's unequivocal advice. One of the officers now suggested to
the QC that justification for an expansion in designated sales could
be found in the PA Cambridge report, despite the fact that both
England and Hayler had specifically told Porter the complete opposite. It is likely they were influenced by Porter's volatile mood.
Robert Lewis spelt out the awful dilemma later, 'It would not have
been possible for an officer to say "No, you cannot do this. You
must forget the whole idea." It was the officer's job to say, "You
cannot do it that way; I will now explore the matter to see if there
is a legitimate way to achieve what you are trying to do."'

On learning of a legitimate 'justification' for the sales programme, Jeremy Sullivan's advice changed. The QC said, in that
case, there could indeed be a lawful basis for the sales. There had
to be real 'justifications' for the policy, such as preventing polari-
sation of owner-occupiers in Westminster into rich and poor, or
enabling skilled workers to live in Westminster. As 'justifications'
existed in the Cambridge report, the policy could be 'completely
judge-proof', as long as the advantages and disadvantages of the

scheme were properly set out in public, and there were no references to 'irrelevant considerations'. The three officers now deceived themselves that they had a legal opinion Porter could use despite the fact that there was no justification and the secret overriding purpose of the policy remained the same: gerrymandering.

The clear hypocrisy of the tactic employed by Lewis, England and Hayler was demonstrated within minutes of the conference ending. In the frenzied rush back to City Hall, Graham England scribbled a quick calculation on the back of his copy of Paul Hayler's report. Sullivan had said that the sales had to be spread across all twenty-three wards, not just in the eight marginals. England worked out roughly how many sales there had to be across Westminster to produce more than 200 in the marginals. He wrote: '395 [across the City]. 202 – Marginal wards.' It was a complete reversal of Sullivan's advice. England was suggesting a smokescreen of a City-wide sales policy to disguise the gerrymandering in the marginals.

Back at City Hall, England revised his calculations slightly and delivered a summary of the advice to Porter at 5 p.m.: 'Counsel advises that designated sales should be identified in both marginal and non-marginal wards in order to protect the Council. The Group will, therefore, need to decide whether the 250 target [a year] applies across the City or whether in fact 250 sales in marginal wards are required in which case following Counsel's advice, somewhere in the region of 300–350 properties will need to be sold across the City.' England had shown Porter the escape hatch. She could do what she wanted, as long as she created a smokescreen by selling housing elsewhere in the City, in safe Labour and Tory seats, where it would make no difference to her political objective in any case. There was one pathetic caveat: 'This will clearly exacerbate the problems of dealing with housing demand.' Porter was delighted. 'We've cracked it!' she told England.

At 6 p.m., England reported directly on Sullivan's advice to a secret meeting of Porter and her chairmen. She resolved to disguise the scheme, at England's suggestion, by selling properties in the non-marginals, as well as the marginals. They would have to sell significantly more housing than they had originally planned to

produce the sales they wanted in the eight seats, and as a consequence deny housing to even more people in need of homes. So be
it. 'Such an important date,' the District Auditor said when reflect-
ing on 5 May. Porter would use the events of that day to defend
herself against charges of gerrymandering; for the Auditor and the
courts 5 May 1987 was above all others the day that proved her
flagrant contempt for the law.

The House of Lords later ruled that Porter knew that 'a policy
adopted for the purpose of electoral advantage in the key wards
would be unlawful. Nothing in Graham England's note of what
Sullivan had said or what Sullivan had actually said indicated that
the adoption of the city-wide policy in order to achieve the electoral
purpose in the eight key wards would be any less unlawful than the
adoption of a policy in respect of the eight key wards alone'.

Patricia Kirwan was the last obstacle to stand in the way.
According to Hartley, Porter feared she would be defeated: 'I think
Shirley was so frightened about what might happen, the ramifications of Patricia.' But in the days before the leadership election,
Porter consulted the card index file she kept on her colleagues. Her
greatest advantages over Kirwan were her personal wealth and the
power of patronage she enjoyed as Leader. She used both to quell
the revolt. Two of the councillors who had pledged support to
Kirwan were in financial straits, a third wanted to be Lord Mayor,
a fourth wanted a senior committee post on the council and a fifth
was anxious to prevent the troubled business affairs of her husband
from being exposed. Gradually rumours surfaced of back-room
deals. One senior former Tory councillor says, 'I heard all these
rumours. There is nothing illegal about offering people incentives.
Again, it's all about integrity issues. That would be classic Shirley:
horses for courses.'

The two councillors with money problems discovered they had
less to worry about; the councillor who wanted to be Lord Mayor
did realise the dream, as did the councillor who wanted a senior
committee job. The fifth councillor was pathetically grateful for
Porter's discretion about her husband's business affairs. Crucially,
Porter's leadership campaign was bolstered by the Sullivan advice,
which she wrongly claimed made her policies 'judge-proof'. As a

result, other Tory councillors now thought Kirwan's campaign, which criticised Porter's policies, struck 'the wrong note'.

The vote took place at 6.30 p.m. on 13 May. Kirwan's supporters came on time but some of Porter's were late. Killick urged Legg to count the votes, but he refused until more councillors arrived. Still, only twenty-four out of the total of thirty-two Tories voted. The result was Porter, sixteen; Kirwan, eight. The five councillors, persuaded by Porter to switch their votes, made the difference. If they had stayed firm, the result would have been Kirwan, thirteen; Porter, eleven. 'It was a wipe-out; people were bought off,' says Kirwan. 'I lost it in the last few days.' She offered Porter her congratulations. One witness said, 'I saw Patricia Kirwan offer an olive branch; it must have taken her some effort to say it. I believe she meant it, but Shirley was vicious and went for revenge. She did everything she could to be nasty and marginalise her.' Porter sacked Kirwan as Housing Chairman and banished her to the backbenches.

Having seen off internal opposition, Porter got on with the serious business of gerrymandering. One immediate effect of Kirwan's defeat was that it stripped Graham England of hope that the policy would be abandoned. Until the Kirwan challenge, he had tried to run with the fox and hunt with the hounds; afterwards, he felt he had no option but to throw in his lot with Porter. Ultimately, he was quarry for the District Auditor.

At the end of May twenty-nine-year-old Nick Reiter arrived at Westminster as the new head of the Policy Unit following Bill Phillips's promotion to managing director. Reiter had worked closely with Bill Phillips at the Department of the Environment in drawing up the so-called Enabling Bill to abolish the GLC, by common consent a botch. Phillips considered Reiter a 'very bright guy' with strong writing skills. Certainly, Reiter would pen some of the most astonishing documents ever to emerge from a British public authority. He saw Porter and her associates on a daily basis during the most intense period of the corruption. Academically he was bright, but he was naive and rather hesitant, and she reduced him to bumbling incoherence during his early presentations, by snapping, 'Come on! Spit it out!' As head of the Policy Unit, Reiter was given the job of preparing many of the secret papers on the

Building Stable Communities policy and soon became a deft hand
at using the BSC euphemisms. Within ten days of arriving, Reiter
was already making tacit references to Porter's plans to deport
Labour-voting homeless families out of Westminster: 'BSC requires
very careful placement of homeless families . . . Our long-term aim
must be to move out as many homeless families out of Westminster,
and indeed out of London.'

Reiter prepared three important documents setting out the ingre-
dients of the gerrymandering that Porter presented to her chairmen
at a hotel in Oxford on the weekend of 13–14 June 1987. Two
days before the gathering she formerly announced Peter Hartley
would replace Patricia Kirwan as Housing Chairman. It was the
same day that Margaret Thatcher won her third general election
with a majority over all other parties of 102. By her third term,
Thatcher had enabled a million council tenants to exercise the right
to buy their own homes. 'There was a real mood of triumphalism
among the Tories at Westminster at the time,' says Neale Coleman.
'They exuded this feeling that they were unstoppable; that they
could do anything they liked.'

In her introductory note for this 'Strategy Weekend', Porter
wrote: 'We face a tremendous challenge. The electoral register for
the 1990 elections will be compiled in just over two years' time.
Some very ambitious policies must be implemented by then: providing a great deal of affordable housing in key areas; protecting
the electoral base in other areas.' The first of Reiter's papers was
called 'Targeting Key Areas' and listed the eight key marginal
wards with the number of new potential Tory voters required.
Another called 'The Quality of Life' reported on the council's plans
to target the eight seats through the misuse of environmental
improvements. Action would be taken against dog mess in Little
Venice, uneven pavements in Victoria, rubbish in St James's, and
builders' skips in Millbank, with a stream of other measures to
woo the floating voter. The council's planning powers were to be
used to bring in more potential Tory voters through 'co-operation
with the real estate industry'. Another document, 'Protecting the
Electoral Base', contained detailed plans to safeguard Tory
Westminster by exporting Labour-voting homeless families. As a

council officer, Reiter knows that he should not have written any of these papers. 'I was naive, and I possibly allowed myself to be flattered that I was actually doing a job where quite a lot of trust was placed in me by people who I perceived as being pretty powerful.' He quickly realised that the council was 'deeply, deeply dysfunctional'.

Porter's efforts were now focused on authorising the designated sales programme at the Housing Committee on 8 July. She told Hartley before the meeting, 'All the donkey work for designated sales has been done and all you have to do, because you have the personality, is to take it through committee.' Porter and Hartley aimed to sell 250 council homes a year for at least three years in the marginal wards to secure re-election, and a total of 500 across the City to disguise her plan. England was shocked because he had hoped fewer properties would be designated but Porter thought a greater number of sales would further conceal the policy's true purpose. Hartley's new vice-chairman, Michael Dutt, snarled at England, 'Well, don't look surprised because . . . we could go for 750 [a year] if we wanted to.'

The scale of the whole plan was breathtaking. Approximately 9,800 of the 23,000 council homes in Westminster were to be designated for sale once they fell vacant, instead of being let to the 3,400 people declared homeless and another 10,000 on the waiting list. Because the homes belonging to the public were being sold at an average discount of £30,000 each for an unlawful purpose, it meant a potential loss to ratepayers of £294 million, plus interest but minus subsequent rises in property values, over two decades. By 26 June 1987 England and Hayler had identified 71 per cent of all the properties in the eight marginal wards for sale, a total of 4,401 homes, producing an estimated 269 sales a year. They then made a list of 3,807 in the remaining fifteen non-marginal wards, 22 per cent of the total, producing the smokescreen of an extra 220 sales per year.

The report presented by the housing officers to the full council meeting on 8 July was a shabby exercise in deception. They sold the policy as a way of extending home ownership to reverse population decline. England and his officers further disguised the gerrymandering by listing the council estates to be designated not by wards but by reference to one of the four council housing district offices responsible for their management. Elsewhere, the report played down the appalling effects that such a loss of public housing would have on the homeless and long-term sick. Naturally, there was no mention of the real purpose behind designated sales. 'It was the love that dare not speak its name,' Robert Lewis said later. England and his cohorts demonstrated their pusillanimity by failing to either endorse or criticise the report to the councillors.

Neale Coleman, the Labour spokesman on housing, had expected some kind of bombshell following the curious events at the previous Housing Committee on 1 April and was not easily fooled. He had extensive knowledge of housing in Westminster and he knew where all the marginal wards were. He quickly scanned the list of the designated estates and estimated that more than half were in the marginals. 'It was obvious to me then that this was gerrymandering,' says Coleman, 'They tried their best to hide the fact, but it was absolutely obvious; we just did not have the evidence to prove our suspicions.'

Shirley Porter had once likened Westminster City Council to an oil tanker which took a long time to turn around. In changing course, the Tory flagship had lost its bearings. The frantic crew had forced decency to walk the plank and would cast adrift the most vulnerable people in society. Thanks to the Tories' slim majority, the scheme was approved by the committee. It had taken just fourteen months since the local council elections to set the scene for the greatest act of corruption in the history of British local government.

CHAPTER 12

The Import–Export Trade (From July 1987)

The deportation of the homeless began on 6 July 1987, two days before it was authorised by the Housing Committee. David and Margaret King had already been moved around the borough three times in the previous week, from one grim bed-and-breakfast to another. Their fourth residence was a fairly dingy hotel in Bayswater. They had just unpacked when there was a knock at the door. It was a housing official from Westminster Council. The Kings were ordered to leave the borough the following morning and move to accommodation in South London. David King had just got a new job and faced the sack if he did not live locally. 'You can't do this to me,' he said. The brutal eviction was indeed unlawful, coming two days before the policy was 'sanctioned' by the Housing Committee, but the order had been made early in their enthusiasm. After 8 July, Westminster could claim committee approval to export its homeless, but as with designated sales, the purpose was gerrymandering and the deportation policy remained unlawful.

In the confines of their secret chamber, Porter and her chairmen often indulged their contempt for the thousands of homeless people dependent on Westminster for their housing. Porter once asked Graham England, 'Could some of Westminster's problem people –

such as homeless families – be transferred to special needs units in rural/coastal areas, where life is less stressful?' In fact, she would exacerbate the stress of thousands of people by selling homes which would otherwise be let to them, and by exporting them to temporary accommodation in alien neighbourhoods. England recorded some of the methods by which Porter meant to be rid of the homeless: 'Boot them out', 'try to ship them out', 'export them'. The minutes of Porter's Chairmen's Group on 23 September 1986 gave instructions to 'determine if more [homeless people] can be exported'. And officers were ordered to 'seek Counsel's opinion on legality of deporting'. To save breath and time, some documents referred to homeless people simply as 'HPs'. Most of them were in hotels and other forms of temporary accommodation, waiting to be allocated a council flat or house when one became available. But under designated sales, council properties were to be sold off to people with tenuous links to Westminster, including those who had merely been offered a job in the City.

Porter's disdain for the homeless was exacerbated by the fact that they were entitled to vote and were likely to support Labour. In one of her most absurd documents, 'Keeping Westminster Conservative', she displayed not only a lack of compassion, but also her ignorance of the London Irish and Asian communities in her borough: 'neighbouring Labour boroughs are deliberately trying to stack the electoral rolls by dumping their homeless families, many [un]educated people from Eire and Bangladesh, into hotel and residential accommodations in the key wards. These families bring enormous social problems with them and create problems for the police and schools. They generally know nothing of living in central London and have little respect for the environment or the well-being of long established Westminster residents.' Her order to Bill Phillips was succinct: 'Clear hotels in Westminster of all homeless families.'

Labour councillors debated passionately against the deportations, arguing that the actions broke up families and deprived them of a home in a borough where they had relatives and friends. They were deeply suspicious of the Tories' motives, but once the policy had been given the go-ahead by the July Housing Committee,

Porter and her chairmen were able to instruct the housing department to: 'move most families to temporary accommodation out of Westminster, starting with key wards, by end of 1988'.

David and Margaret King were 'booted out' of Westminster because they represented a threat to the 'electoral base'. They were moved to the Leigham Court Hotel at Streatham in South London, which had been block-booked by Graham England to house the first of Westminster's deported families. Porter was kept closely informed of progress as families were deported from the marginal wards. A memo sent to Porter on 9 July, the day after the fateful Housing Committee, said: 'families have been moved from existing hotels to accommodation in Streatham. So far twenty families have been moved out.'

Steve Platt, a reporter with *New Society* magazine, got wind of the move and hurried down to the Leigham Court when the first deportees started to arrive. He spoke to the Kings, as well as Thomas and Bertha Holt, who had been forced to live in a Bayswater hotel after a fire destroyed their flat in Vancouver Square. 'We were told to get out this morning and come here,' Thomas Holt told Platt. Another confused family were dragging their suitcases up the hill. The husband wondered, 'It's something to do with a new Act of Parliament, isn't it?' Sean McTigue had been made homeless by a fire. He was a frame-maker who had lived in Westminster for twenty years. He could not have known what was going on behind the scenes but he guessed. 'It is a form of deportation,' he said. 'You can expect these sorts of things to happen in a totalitarian country but not here. The council is creating refugees in a democracy.'

Deporting the homeless was the one part of Building Stable Communities which could be implemented straight away; it immediately cleared the marginal wards of potential Labour voters and contributed significantly to Porter's hopes of winning in 1990. To sell the houses and flats would take time. Extra staff would have to be recruited and an estate agency established to promote the sales and it would take several years through planning permissions to build new properties and fill them with new residents. The beauty of deportation lay in its speed and effectiveness. Three days after the first deportations, the front page of the *Paddington Mercury* announced : 'Exodus of the Borough's homeless', along with the lie it had been fed by the council: 'Westminster is moving over 300 homeless families out of bed and breakfast guest houses in the City because of soaring hotel prices and the influx of tourists.' Internal housing department documents now talked about 'combating homelessness'. It was yet another cynical Westminster euphemism. From the start, it was a war on the homeless themselves.

By 16 July the group of officers overseeing the deportations, the 'Homelessness Review Group,' met at City Hall, and heard that 'Westminster were beginning to move homeless families out of the City . . . The principal area of concern remained obtaining suitable properties outside Westminster.' The group also considered legal action to force hotels in Westminster to stop taking in homeless families from councils elsewhere in London. The officers were determined that hotels emptied of Westminster homeless were not 'filled by homeless families from other boroughs'.

The deportations would place severe stress on the department of social services at City Hall and its director, Bill Ritchie. Ritchie was a traditional local government man who thrived in the avuncular environment which preceded Porter. In the good old days, he and David Witty, Rodney Brooke's predecessor, were considered the strongest players in the annual golf match between officers and councillors, and they played together against Shirley Porter, then just a committee chairman. After the 1986 elections Ritchie had observed the alarming change which came over Porter, to the point where he could scarcely recognise in her the keen golfer with whom he could cheerfully discuss a misjudged putt at the fifteenth hole.

The homeless families became the responsibility of the borough councils in whose communities Porter dumped them. Often, these boroughs either did not know Westminster was moving families into their area or they were powerless to stop it. Housing officers were careful to use either hotels which already had planning permission to accommodate homeless people, or private landlords, who did not need it. The introduction of designated sales would mean homeless families spending years in bed-and-breakfast and other low-grade temporary accommodation. As the deportations continued, Ritchie worried about vulnerable children on the At Risk Register; they would remain his temporary responsibility until their files could be handed over to the recipient council. Ritchie demanded, and received, additional social workers from City Hall just to deal with those children placed miles from Westminster. As Graham England had predicted at the outset of the plot, there was indeed an 'implication – social services'. In a memo to England, Ritchie wrote: 'the use of hotels or other similar inadequate accommodation for families with small children, or for the socially vulnerable, rapidly leads to excess stress and deterioration in family relationships.' And he warned England that 'The stress caused by long periods in unsatisfactory temporary accommodation is increasing the incidence of child abuse and neglect.' However, as the months went by, Porter demanded more and more deportations. In October 1987 she ordered: 'Homelessness – must move more out.' This had to be done 'urgently'. She demanded a report each week on progress.

Councils across London soon found out what was going on. Bill Ritchie says, 'I got a lot of criticism from my fellow Directors of Social Services in London when this policy became known throughout London. We used to meet four times a year and when these families were being shipped out, I got stick from my fellow directors: "What the hell do you think you're doing putting your problems out in our patch?"' Ritchie says, 'They were shipping out children who needed day nursery care, and educational psychological help, and effectively Westminster Council made the decision "We don't care about that."' Ritchie's own social workers were up in arms, but there was nothing he could do to stop Porter and the housing department.

Westminster City Council told the world that it was cheaper to house the homeless outside Westminster, but this was another lie. At one meeting chief officers discussed the rising costs of housing the homeless. The minutes record that 'Buying blocks in Westminster would save money but is less attractive in policy terms than housing outside Westminster.'

The rising costs of housing the homeless outside Westminster led to more and more ridiculous plans for cheaper alternatives.

Months before the deportations started, the council entered secret talks with private companies 'about the use/development of mobile home sites within a twenty-five-mile radius of London'. Miles Young, one of Porter's senior Tory colleagues, said later, 'We spent some time looking at a whole series of options . . . including New York-style options of temporary shelters, aircraft hangar shelters on derelict ground, including leasing buildings in Essex and all sort of other measures.' Porter later revealed to the District Auditor that one option was to house people in trailers in car parks far from Westminster.

In early September 1987 the news broke that Westminster planned to build a settlement of plasterboard prefabricated homes on a derelict site in the outer East London borough of Barking and Dagenham. George Brooker, the Labour leader of the borough, was furious. Barking had taken pride in being the first council to get rid of all its wartime prefabs – within five years of VE Day. 'To bring them back in that way was completely wrong,' said Brooker. Architects at City Hall had drawn up the plans in great secrecy. Westminster wanted to erect forty-three prefabs, a type of temporary house called a 'Terrapin Home unit – 804', next door to Barking power station at Ash Lagoon. There would be two new roads, a sewage pumping station and a play area for children. The total cost was £1.4 million. The prefabs would be surrounded by a jumble of timber yards and warehouses. If the new residents wanted to stroll along the Thames, the nearest accessible point on the river near Barking Creek was at a place marked on the map, 'Mud'.

Confidential Westminster documents talked about the need to 'create reservoirs for the homeless' in places like Barking, but housing officers warned that the councils in these areas would 'undoubtedly wish to thwart our efforts . . . when they learn what we are up to'. England warned Porter to expect protests, although he said 'there are no areas beyond Westminster in which we should not be looking.' But the ferocity of protests in Barking caught her by surprise. Two thousand local residents signed a petition opposing the plans and their local councillors argued that the local schools were full and other important services were already overloaded. Porter wrote to Brooker: 'I hope that you will recognise that our proposals are a humane way of helping the homeless have decent accommodation. They will not overburden the services of your borough and, indeed, will contribute to its rate income. I do hope that your planning committee will feel able to support this small attempt to ease the problem of the homeless.' Brooker's Planning Committee rejected the plans, and the prefabs were never erected, but Westminster did not give up in the interim to move hundreds of homeless people into Barking.

Whenever possible Westminster would try to dump homeless families without letting the recipients know. But many councils required planning permission from hotels eager for the vast sums on offer to take in the growing number of homeless people from their neighbouring London boroughs. Councils were alerted when a hotelier submitted the necessary planning application. When Westminster planned to place homeless families in a Conservative-controlled South London borough, one City housing officer wrote: 'Officers were advised to proceed up to exchange of contracts without any contact with the host authority.'

Porter also acted against hotels in the marginal wards which were being used to house homeless families from other London boroughs. Westminster took planning enforcement action against thirty-one hotels in Sussex Gardens in the marginal Bayswater ward to prevent them from becoming hostels. The council threatened the licences of the hotels unless they agreed. At a secret BSC gathering, senior officers decided that 'cheap hotels' should be 'put in safe hands'; in other words, the council should use whatever power it had to ensure that the hotels were owned by people who would not hire out their rooms to homeless people, even if that meant refusing planning permission to obstinate owners and awarding it to compliant hoteliers. Porter had once asked Graham England, 'What about WCC [Westminster City Council] purchasing hotels in non-Tory wards or preferably outside of Westminster to provide short term accommodation for single parent families?' But even the Housing Director baulked at the suggestion that the City should exchange its duty as a landlord for that of a doss house keeper.

'Carrots and sticks' was the phrase used by officers when describing rewards and punishments meted out to hotel owners. A housing department schedule reported: 'Move WCC homeless out of hotels which are subject to planning enforcement.' The issue was of such high importance that Porter approved the use of private detectives to spy on hoteliers to see if they continued to take in homeless families despite the edict. The investigators reported any infringements back to City Hall, which would then take action against the guilty hotelier. The pressure worked, as one internal council report made clear: 'A number of hoteliers have indicated that they would be prepared, in return for planning permission as a hotel, to enter a S (ection) 52 agreement specifically excluding use as a hostel.' Shortly afterwards, a housing officer was able to report: 'All Westminster families now removed from hotels which were subject to planning action.'

The hostels scattered throughout the key wards were another focus of Porter's obsession. Hostels were used by students, by nurses and worst of all by homeless people; all were more likely to vote Labour. At yet another secret weekend meeting on 5–6 September 1987, she laid down a policy stipulating that as many hostels as possible should be brought into 'BSC residential use'. Hostels would be identified 'for purchase and conversion to residential units'. 'Get hostels into right hands,' Porter ordered, as she had with hotels. At the meeting, she specified the targets: 'Seventy-two hostels have been identified in the eight key wards . . . targets should be to assess each hostel for potential action.' She again authorised the use of private detectives to gather information on hostels, as well as the secondment of a solicitor and four additional planning officers to force as many hostels as possible to close. From now on, there would be constant demands for action against hostels from Porter.

Bruce House, in the marginal ward of St James's, was the large and famous hostel for the homeless visited by Joe Hegarty's canvassers during Labour's campaign for the local elections of 1986. Although few of the down-and-out residents would have voted, Porter considered them an electoral threat. In September Porter and her chairmen ordered officers 'to look at the implications of emptying Bruce House as quickly as possible and disposing of the property . . . for conversion into yuppie flats'. But Bill Ritchie felt there was a real need for Bruce House and opposed the move as long as he could, despite coming under serious pressure. 'They wanted to get rid of it, pull it down under the pretext of rebuilding it,' says Ritchie. 'It didn't proceed then because at that time they were just fishing, and because we needed those resources. I argued against it fairly forcefully. But they did it in the end, after I left in 1988, as part of BSC.'

Another hostel, Ambrosden, was in the marginal Victoria ward near the Roman Catholic cathedral opposite City Hall. The young people who lived there heard rumours that it would be closed and protested. Even Cardinal Basil Hume implored Porter, 'The first message I would like to give to her and to the council is, please don't sell this hostel which is needed for young people. I believe fundamentally that there is, in human beings, a side of them which is generous and decent, and I would have no doubts that I would find all that among the councillors.' On this occasion, the cardinal's faith in human nature was misplaced. The council even wrote to the residents to 'assure' them that 'there are no plans to close the hostel,' although Porter and her chairmen took the decision to do so a little later in May 1988. The Ambrosden, worth £2.62 million, was sold to a developer for just £630,000. This decision lost local taxpayers £2 million and the young people their home; the District Auditor later found evidence that 'properties such as the Ambrosden, which were in residential use, but which were occupied by individuals who were regarded as less likely to vote Conservative, were emptied and disposed of for redevelopment.' Porter was as obsessed with exporting the homeless from the marginal wards as she was with importing Tory voters into them. Before the 1990 elections, developers began turning the Ambrosden into 40 new flats, to be sold as *pieds-à-terre* for the wealthy. The sale and conversion of the hostel went a long way towards Porter's target for Victoria of 150 new voters.

Westminster was not the only agency providing homes in the City for people in need. Porter fretted constantly about housing associations, because they were willing and able to build homes in Westminster for people who she was convinced would vote Labour. Despite the apparent independence of the associations, Porter had powerful levers to use against them. These included the power to give them money to house homeless families on behalf of the City Council, and the right to reject planning permissions for their housing schemes. She would not allow the associations to develop social housing in her precious key wards and she tried to discourage them from building homes anywhere in Westminster.

On 1 September 1987 Porter held a meeting with her chairmen where housing associations and those which might support her strategy were discussed. Officers assured her that they would 'make sure that the "right people" in the "right" housing associations were identified'. On 18 February the following year the housing associations were summoned to a meeting at City Hall, where Peter Hartley addressed them. Tony Bird, a manager for the Family Housing Association, recalled, 'People were generally quite shocked at the tone of the meeting. It was intimidatory in a crude and subtle sense because it was about promoting the understanding that either you do this, or you won't get borough support, which means you're not going to develop as a housing association.'

By then Bird and his fellow housing association colleagues knew about Westminster's designated sales policy and came to what at first felt like an extraordinary conclusion: the City Council was determined to move out an entire class of residents. 'It wasn't in the interests of the people who needed rented housing. I think that's the most important thing to say,' Bird said, before likening the policy to events in the former Yugoslavia . 'I would describe it as ethnic cleansing.'

Some friendly housing associations helped Westminster achieve its objectives by the back door. The council would pay the housing associations to house homeless families outside the City. The housing associations applied to build estates in their own names without the local council realising that the new homes would be used for Westminster families. At Barking, George Brooker discovered that Westminster had deported 227 families including 170 children – more than 700 people – into his borough by placing them in privately-rented accomodation. He said, 'We were not aware of them. These poor families were dumped over here, most of them couldn't speak English; they spoke about thirty-five different languages. They were in a terrible state and . . . [we had no] . . . proper service to give these people. I blame Westminster for this; they were shifty.'

Shortly after he found this out, Brooker was at a meeting of the London Boroughs Association, a body mainly representing Tory councils in London, and spotted Anthony Prendergast, a supporter of Kirwan at Westminster. Brooker said to Prendergast, 'What the hell are you doing in Westminster, exporting your people down into my borough?' Prendergast was appalled: 'What are you talking about? We don't export people.' 'Oh yes, you do,' said Brooker. Prendergast promised to investigate. He went to the housing department and asked an official, 'What the hell's going on?' The official responded matter-of-factly, 'We've pushed all these people down into Barking and Dagenham.' Prendergast said, 'Well, you haven't told Barking and Dagenham Council about it. No one's consulted them. I've just had the leader shouting down my throat.'

Other councils got the same treatment. Over the next five years housing associations would build estates for the Westminster homeless in other London boroughs, including Redbridge and Hillingdon. The council would create further scandal by writing to councils outside London offering them money to take their homeless.

As well as ridding the borough of potential Labour voters, Porter concentrated her efforts on moving in those residents she was convinced would vote Conservative as she began to implement designated sales. This was the most expensive gerrymandering scheme. In order to deter squatters, across Westminster solid steel doors were fitted to flats which had become empty until they could be sold to likely Tory voters. By August 1987, although the council had yet to establish its estate agency to make the sales, 170 flats were sealed until a purchaser could be found. By early November this number had risen to 500.

A company called Sitex was awarded the contract to fit the security doors, charging Westminster £300 for each installation and £50 a week for hire. Within six months, Porter and her associates started to fret about making their own doors to save money. These costs, combined with lost rent and the additional costs of housing the homeless in shoddy temporary accommodation, crippled the council finances within a year of the sales programme starting. Paul

Dimoldenberg, who replaced Joe Hegarty as leader of the Labour group in autumn 1987, told the local press, 'It is obviously ridiculous to have 500 flats empty and bolted up with steel doors and iron grilles when hundreds of Westminster families are living in bed-and-breakfast hotels.' The financial costs of the policy were already spinning out of control and endangering Porter's gerrymandering strategy. Ironically, the United Nations had designated 1987 as the 'International Year of the Homeless' to focus attention on a world-wide tragedy. The campaign made little impression on Shirley Porter; her policy of selling public housing made her an important contributor to homelessness in central London. And, although the District Auditor later estimated the many millions lost by Porter's policies with impressive accuracy, the personal cost to thousands of homeless people always proved incalculable.

CHAPTER 13

The Lady Vanishes (1987–8)

L abour councillors suspected from the start that Building Stable Communities was corruption by another name, although it was not until 1989 that they began to appreciate the extent of it. On 27 July 1987, three weeks after the designated sales policy was voted through, Joe Hegarty, leader of the Labour councillors, wrote: 'Despite warnings from council officers of the disastrous consequences, Westminster has decided not to let homes on nearly half of its council estates. There appears to be an underlying aim of encouraging "yuppies" at the expense of those in need in order to enhance the Conservatives' prospects in future elections.'

The statistics made sobering reading for a party which drew the bulk of its support from the council estates. Quite simply, Labour faced extinction in Westminster. In the long term, designated sales could account for 41 per cent of Westminster's council housing and Porter hoped a similar number of council tenants would be encouraged to buy their own homes under 'Right to Buy' legislation which they might sell on later to potential Tories. Porter even offered £15,000, so-called 'Assisted Purchase Grants', to existing tenants to vacate their council homes so they could be sold off. More than 130 tenants took the money. It was a recipe for the virtual eradication of a Labour voting class in Westminster.

Porter would later write of her fear of 'socialists running Buckingham Palace' or 'militants lording it over Parliament', but her Labour opponents were more prototype Blairites than red flag carriers for the 'loony left'. Many had attended public schools and were lawyers, PR consultants and accountants. Paul Dimoldenberg, who succeeded Joe Hegarty as Labour leader in 1987, worked as a senior consultant for the company Good Relations, part of the public relations empire controlled by Tim Bell, Margaret Thatcher's favourite PR executive. Peter Bradley, a newly elected Labour councillor in 1986, also worked there. Andrew Dismore, the Labour chief whip, was a personal injuries solicitor; Gavin Millar a barrister who would later become a QC; David Pitt-Watson an accountant and a future treasurer of the Labour Party. But perhaps the most formidable of Shirley Porter's Labour opponents was Neale Coleman, who had earned a First in Classics at Oxford before joining the Civil Service as one of its brightest graduates. He became a housing officer for Labour-controlled Haringey in North London and, in 1982, was elected to Westminster City Council in marginal Maida Vale, where he soon impressed both Labour and Tory councillors with his intellect and his command of housing policy. Some of the wiser Tories detected that Coleman was not a man to be crossed.

Peter Bradley says, 'The Labour group of 1986 to 1990 was very talented. That's what scared Porter and the Tories.' Within weeks of the 1986 election results, Porter ordered officers to compile secret reports on the conduct of new Labour councillors at committee meetings. One committee clerk says, 'We were told to make a note of Labour councillors at meetings, what they said and how they behaved.' Peter Bradley discovered a copy of an intelligence report about him, carelessly left on a photocopier. The Labour councillors were appalled at such an abuse of council resources and kicked up a fuss. They were assured the surveillance would cease. However, within eighteen months, Porter asked a group of professional political consultants to compile dossiers on her political enemies.

In February 1987, five months before the launch of designated sales, Patricia Kirwan tried to resurrect plans to privatise the Walterton and Elgin estates. Westminster hired Project Management

International (PMI), consultants which specialised in managing big building projects. The previous deal had collapsed mainly because of intense opposition, partly because it was too complex. Now Kirwan proposed an allegedly less complicated 'barter scheme'. It was her last act before she was sacked by Porter. The council would sell 256 of the houses on the estate cheaply to a developer who would refurbish the homes and sell them for a profit – in return for modernising 776 other homes in the area for rent to council tenants. The developer would make a clear £6 million profit; the community would lose 256 homes. It would also involve a mass eviction of the existing residents while building work was carried out.

The Walterton and Elgin Action Group again declared war on the council. 'It's back to the barricades!' WEAG's co-ordinator Jonathan Rosenberg told the *Paddington Times* when the scheme was announced. 'We will have an intense campaign against the scheme.' Soon Rosenberg was rounding up his battalions, including large numbers of elderly residents who had time on their hands. He hired coaches to take his troops into action and they became a regular feature of council meetings. Rosenberg's wife, Jackie, was a newly elected Labour councillor in 1986 and Rosenberg himself was a Labour Party member. Increasingly, Porter and the Tories saw Rosenberg and the WEAG as the 'provisional wing' of the Labour councillors.

Police were called to a meeting of the Housing Committee on 1 April 1987 which not only passed the PMI plans, but more significantly, fielded the planted question from Alex Segal: How many designated sales were there a year? When he was told 'ten' as planned, he asked for the report which laid the groundwork for the extension of the policy three months later. Proceedings were reduced to a farce by 100 WEAG residents. Patricia Kirwan adjourned the meeting and reconvened in a room three floors below. Again the WEAG disrupted proceedings, as Rosenberg wrote in his diary: 'The small room was a stuffy jumble of chairs and desks, with the council and its associates cowering in a couple of corners surrounded by angry residents engaging and challenging them.'

Porter announced a special meeting on 23 April of the council's main policy committee to discuss 'disorder at council meetings'.

She hired consultants to draw up plans for a glass screen to separate councillors from the public and threatened to turn cameras on the public gallery to quell opposition to her policies. The WEAG turned out in force, paradoxically disrupting the meeting. Peter Hartley accused the campaigners of being a 'rent-a-crowd rag-bag of extremists'. William Rae, an eighty-three-year-old tenant on the Walterton estate, stood up and challenged Hartley, 'What did you do in the war, sonny?' When there was no apology, Rae rolled up his sleeves and again challenged Hartley. There was uproar. Porter adjourned the meeting and the police arrived. According to *City Limits*: 'Lady Porter called the police who persuaded councillor Hartley to explain that his remark was directed at the Labour Group, not the public gallery. The meeting was reconvened with the Police in attendance. A vote was passed approving recommendations to ban all photographs, recordings and banners from future meetings, to eject members of the public who were not "quiet" and to "name" councillors judged by the Chair to be contributing to "disorder".'

The Housing Committee's July meeting which voted through designated sales led to a major escalation in the conflict between Labour and Tory councillors. Labour councillors, who could only guess at the plot behind the decision, did everything they could to rally opposition against the sales. Gavin Millar, the Labour councillor and barrister, wrote to Matthew Ives: 'I am concerned that the procedure adopted by the Housing Committee may have been unlawful. I am also concerned that the substance of the decision may be unlawful in a variety of respects.'

Ives had been away on 5 May when Jeremy Sullivan QC's advice on the legality of designated sales had been sought and, although he had his suspicions, says he was kept in the dark about Shirley Porter's gerrymandering strategy. Robert Lewis, Ives's deputy, had been dealing with the legality of her proposals, and told Porter there was no great risk from her policies. She was able to fend off Millar by dispatching a note to her fellow Tories: 'our legal advice is that our policy is completely judge proof . . . We all know how important the designated sales policy is to the success of our overall objectives. We are completely sure that it carries no risk of legal challenge.'

Labour councillors also used less orthodox channels to try to stop the sales. In July 1987 approximately 100 people from forty organisations from across the City, including tenants' groups, met and formed the 'Westminster Housing Forum'. Posters were produced to stick on the Sitex steel doors which were springing up like mushrooms across the City. Some said: 'This door costs you £50 a week – Tory waste'; others asked simply: 'Where are your children going to live?' The most famous appeared around the Walterton and Elgin, designed by John Phillips, a Paddington printer. It showed a man with bulldozer jaws for a face, wearing a suit and a bowler hat. Beneath the Iron Man, were the words 'We are a little worried about our landlord.'

Labour councillors were prepared to go to great lengths to defeat designated sales. In a speech at a public meeting in North Paddington on 21 July 1987, Neale Coleman advocated that

photo © Andrew Wiard/reportphotos.com

Designated for sale. The Sitex door says it all.

squatters should occupy empty flats designated for sale. 'Coleman came out publicly in favour of squatting,' records of the meeting state. He said that council caretakers should be asked to provide keys to empty flats and suggested that the assistance of some housing officers who were also union activists might be discreetly forthcoming. Opposition to the sales grew and intensified as more Sitex doors appeared. Some squatters even managed to get into the empty flats. On 2 September unions at City Hall staged a half-day strike in protest against the sales, and instructed their members not to cooperate with the implementation of the policy.

The Tories had seriously miscalculated at the July Housing Committee. They had agreed to sell 500 homes a year, but they had no administrative mechanism to facilitate the sales. They still needed official committee approval to spend £4 million on a new council estate agency called the 'Home Ownership Centre', to advertise and sell the homes, as well as help arrange mortgages. No centre, no sales, no victory in 1990. But Porter was fast running out of time. Even if she managed to get approval that autumn for the Centre, it could not be up and running until January 1988 at the earliest and the first sales would take a few more months to complete. She had a target of 2,200 extra voters to reach by the closure of the electoral register in October 1989; precious time was passing.

The attention of both sides now focused on the Housing Committee meeting of 22 September 1987 which would authorise Porter's new estate agency. Late on the night of 21 September, less than twenty-four hours before the meeting, there was a curious, and even sinister, event. Residents on the Walterton estate heard a clattering letter box and saw on the doormat a leaflet from Rosenberg revealing that he had accepted help from politically extreme organisations including Militant Tendency, the Workers Revolutionary Party, Lesbians against the Bomb and even the neo-Nazi National Front. Rosenberg urged residents to attend the meeting the following day with 'rotten eggs and tomatoes or even stones and bricks'. The leaflet added: 'Don't forget that we have promised the Tories the worst riot they have ever seen if they decide to sell off our homes.' The leaflet was a fake. Rosenberg says, 'It was a very clever smear;

photo © Andrew Wiard/reportphotos.com

Designated sales draw protests from young and old.

some of the residents were at first taken in because of the relative degree of sophistication in the forgery, because it made use of WEAG phrases and slogans. We immediately went round to people's homes to tell them, but it did scare some of the older ones away.' Westminster City Council would have had access to the addresses of council tenants on the estate, but no one saw the people who delivered the leaflets to hundreds of homes in a few hours.

The following evening there were barricades outside City Hall and a heavier than usual police presence for the meeting. The campaigners noticed that Porter had installed more security doors on the seventeenth floor of City Hall where the meeting would take place, but they did not anticipate too much trouble. Usually, the police were local and well used to sorting out the spats at Westminster City Council. But hidden out of sight was a police force of a different breed. They were the battle-hardened men and women of the Metropolitan Police Territorial Support Group who had long experience of dealing with public disorder.

Within a few minutes of the start of the meeting, Peter Hartley managed to provoke another octogenarian, who climbed on to a table and started shouting. The other residents invaded the committee area and the local police came in to restore order. During an adjournment, the police tried to pull Rosenberg away from the public gallery and a tug-of-war followed, with residents keeping hold of their man. Labour councillors went up to the gallery to calm things down and people gradually returned to their seats. There had been no violence until then, just loudly proclaimed anger at Westminster's policies, but it was clear that the bogus leaflet had heightened tensions on both sides. Hartley adjourned the meeting and ordered the public gallery to be cleared. Right on cue, the Territorial Support Group [TSG] entered in full riot gear. Rosenberg says, 'When they went in, some people stayed sitting where they were or shrank back into the corner. One by one people were dragged out of the room.'

Six Labour councillors, four council workers and Rosenberg were arrested and thrown into the police vans by the TSG. Andrew Dismore remembers, 'I was just going into City Hall and caught the fag end of it; I heard all this shouting and then suddenly there was this rush. It was a bit like a cartoon. Suddenly I was splattered on the pavement and then there's no one there.' He asked, 'What the bloody hell's going on?' and was told, 'They've nicked loads,' including Linda Julian, his partner and fellow Labour Councillor. Dismore adds, 'I went down to the police station, got out my lawyer's cards and bailed them all out.' Paul Dimoldenberg says, 'It was a set-up. The Conservatives knew what would happen. They called on the police and the police came in. We were very angry that the police were willing to be used in this way. There was no need for it.'

It was a triumph for Porter. In the absence of the Labour councillors, Hartley was able to get the necessary committee approval for the Home Ownership Centre, and, although most of the charges against them would later be dismissed, nearly a quarter of all Labour councillors were arrested and thrown into cells. The *Sun*'s headline the following day was a bonus for the Tories: 'Lefties held in punch-up at town hall . . . more than 100 ranting lefties in the public gallery were thrown out.' The Labour councillors were unknowingly trying to prevent an act of unlaw-fulness on an epic scale and yet they had ended up in court.

By the autumn of 1987 Porter was under intense pressure from all sides and her paranoia, never far from the surface, increased. She ordered her office be swept for bugs. Every fortnight for around two years, an officer from the council's technical mainte-nance department would make checks while the Leader pointed out a vase, a lampshade or the telephone. 'The operative didn't have the nerve to tell her that he had the wrong gadget for the job,' says one City Hall official. 'He swept Porter's office anyway but if there had been any listening device, there's no way he could have detected it. Who would want to bug her anyway?' Nick Reiter, who saw Porter most days, says, 'She certainly wondered who was with her and who she could trust.' Later, the paranoia spread to senior officers, who suspected that their phones were being tapped by Porter.

On the night of Thursday, 16 October a great storm hit Britain. Winds of up to ninety-four mph caused widespread damage and blew down more than a million trees across the country, including about a thousand trees across the City. Within hours, Porter launched a campaign to replace them. Then a week later, an unex-pected thing happened. Shirley Porter simply disappeared. From the weekend of 25 October 1987, she was absent from City Hall for three months, precipitating the second leadership challenge that year. The *Evening Standard* reported that Porter was ill and 'has been told to rest for the next two months . . . doctors believe she contracted a virus several years ago which caused a serious attack . . .' Rumour swept City Hall that Porter had either suffered a nervous breakdown or had collapsed from mental exhaustion. Whatever the truth about the mystery virus, Porter's leadership was seriously in doubt. The wobble could not have come at a worse time for the conspiracy or her cronies. Hundreds of council flats were sealed behind Sitex doors but not a single designated sale had been made. Plans were under way to extend the gerrymandering into other areas of the council's activity. The whole enterprise was vulnerable.

A last-ditch attempt was made to bring down the Porter regime and put an end to the rampant wrongdoing. With Porter out of the way and her little-respected deputy David Weeks in charge, the time was ripe for another putsch. The attack came from the diminishing band of sensible Tory councillors at City Hall. Anthony Prendergast CBE had come to the view that 'the way that Shirley Porter was running the council at the time was bordering on the criminal.' Later Prendergast would tell the District Auditor that 'It did not seem to me to be discharging the moral responsibilities of a local authority for the council to try and change the political balance in particular wards through council policies.' The chief executive Rodney Brooke says, 'Tony was an old style Tory, a very great gentleman, enormously wealthy, and he just didn't soil his hands with dirty politicking. He didn't go around offering people jobs saying, "If I become leader, you will be chair of this that and the other," the sort of patronage which normally gets people connected; I think Tony would be too gentlemanly to do that. He just disliked Shirley intensely and simply stood.'

Prendergast wrote to his fellow Tories urging them to see sense. His letter was for public consumption, so for the good of the party he made only cryptic references to the BSC policy. Instead, he focused his attack on Porter's treatment of officers: 'The morale of the staff is at an all-time low and this has been brought about by a series of events which have sapped confidence. Once upon a time officers would fight their way to get a job in Westminster; no-one worth his salt wants to apply for job vacancies that we advertise.'

Prendergast attached a list of the forty-eight senior council officials who had left in the first four years of Porter's rule. The roll of honour included a chief executive, four assistant chief executives, three heads of press and public relations, a city engineer, a deputy city engineer, three assistant city engineers, a city planning officer and three assistant city planning officers. There was also a reference to George Touchard, the Property Services Director harangued into selling the cemeteries. The description of Touchard's departure was short but illuminating: 'Retirement: ill health.' 'It resembled a casualty list from the Great War,' says a former Tory councillor. Prendergast also referred to Porter's failure to pay large bonuses to a number of senior officials. He criticised her plans to strip Rodney

Brooke of his few remaining powers and transfer them to Bill Phillips, who had failed to impress a large number of the Tories. Prendergast hoped that such obvious examples of Porter's tyrannical leadership would be enough to break her authority and persuade her colleagues to elect a new leader. On 14 November a special meeting was called to discuss Porter's behaviour. Her cabal of supporters played for time and made a tactical retreat in her absence. They agreed to pay the promised bonuses and back-tracked on her plans to further humiliate Brooke.

Details of the growing revolt found their way into the *Independent* on 18 November along with the list of officers who had left Westminster. 'Yesterday,' the paper reported, 'Lady Porter was unavailable for comment. Asked why so many staff had left, a Westminster press officer said: "I couldn't tell you. I'm new here."' Patricia Kirwan was blamed for the leak by some of her colleagues. 'I hadn't leaked it,' she says, 'but the paranoia was amazing. It was then agreed by the party group on a majority vote that we should swear an affidavit on a bible that we hadn't leaked to the press. It was also suggested by someone that we should take a lie-detector test.'

Porter was forced to attend a second emergency meeting called on the day the *Independent* broke the story to face down the rebels. According to the *Guardian*: 'a very determined Lady Porter forsook her sick bed to be there.' Her henchmen again directed their anger at Patricia Kirwan whom they falsely blamed for the press coverage, and eventually cowed the rebels into abandoning their takeover attempt. A vote on the leadership was averted. Ten days later a sick Porter re-emerged momentarily to grant an interview to the *Evening Standard*'s Dick Murray. She told him, 'There is no coup attempt now.' Murray described her as looking 'tired, unusual for her, and gaunt'. She told the reporter that she believed she had contracted the virus on holiday in Kenya and that it could have had an inflammatory effect on her heart known as myocardis. She added that she might resign in the New Year but would 'base her decision on medical advice'. Thanks to concession and bluster, the challenge to Porter's regime had evaporated by the end of the year. A former press officer at City Hall says, 'It was a half-hearted backbench coup and as soon as she came back they all cowered again. The Tories got what they deserved.'

Then, Porter disappeared again. Some of the Tories received letters from her with a Florida postmark. At one time Rodney Brooke heard she was convalescing at Champneys health farm. Wherever she was, she would not reappear at City Hall until February 1988, when she announced, 'I'm back. Having survived a serious illness, I feel that life is beginning for me again. I intend to use it to the full. Watch this space.' The *Evening Standard* said Porter's doctors had given her the all-clear, adding that she was 'determined to stay until she has secured her peerage'. Porter would spend the next ten years compounding every single error she had made in the previous twenty months.

CHAPTER 14

Losing the Plot (1988)

From 1988 Shirley Porter was essentially the master of two strange worlds. There was the disturbing Building Stable Communities underworld with its secret agenda and endemic paranoia. Then there was the public face of Westminster with its rowdy meetings and its emerging scandals. The great cemeteries débâcle had already started to unravel in 1987.

Nigella Lawson, the future celebrity cook and daughter of Thatcher's Chancellor of the Exchequer Nigel Lawson, was one of the first relatives to raise questions about the cemeteries within a month of the exchange of contracts. Her mother, Vanessa, had died of cancer in August 1985 and was buried at Mill Hill. Her last request to Nigella was to have flowers planted on her grave. In her letter of complaint to the council on 21 May 1986, Nigella said: 'While I was planting the seeds a gentleman approached me and told me I was wasting my time because the grave was going to be turfed over and mowed.' This sort of behaviour naturally upset the relatives of those buried; they had paid for the plots and wanted to tend them.

Within weeks of the sale's completion, a panicky internal memo from the council's leisure department revealed City Hall's ignorance about who actually owned the graveyards: 'Mr Whybrow is out of the country, letters . . . are not being answered. As far as the

public is concerned the cemeteries have been abandoned. Gates at
Mill Hill are . . . left open all night and clearly [there is] vandalism
of graves, fly tipping and vandalism of toilets, shelters and staff
accommodation. The press implications of this in Mrs Thatcher's
constituency are considerable.' During the spring and early summer
of 1987, the grass reached waist-high. In June Jo Mahoney visited
the grave of her father, Owen, at East Finchley with her brother
Eugene and was shocked by the neglect: 'My brother actually took
a ruler out of the boot of the car and the grass was over 4ft tall. On
that particular day, there were a lot of people wandering around
and it was very difficult for people who had graves two or three
rows back to find out where their loved ones were buried.'

The cemeteries scandal was eventually broken by the
Paddington Mercury on 24 September 1987. The headline read:
'Cemetery Disgrace' and the paper carried an interview with Harry
and Lillian Upton, who had buried their son at Mill Hill. Harry
Upton told the *Mercury*, 'It was disgusting. We come here every
month and we couldn't find our son's grave.' Alongside the article
was a photograph of some undergrowth with an arrow pointing
out an approximate location of their son's plot. The story was
beginning to gather pace.

On 29 October Paul Foot became the first reporter to reveal the
fifteen pence price tag. Foot's piece in the *Daily Mirror* ran under
the headline 'GRAVEY TRAIN'. He disclosed: 'In January this
year, Westminster Council sold three superbly kept cemeteries for
15p.' Two forces would combine to turn the 5 pence cemeteries
into a totemic scandal of the Thatcher era. On 10 November Paul
Dimoldenberg, the Labour group leader, met up with Stewart
Payne, a newly appointed investigative reporter on the *Evening
Standard*. Payne says, 'John Lees [the editor] felt it was an
appalling example of selling assets without any regard whatsoever
for the feelings of people concerned, in this case, the relatives of
those who were buried there. That's why he wanted it investigated.'

No one could quite believe the Foot story, so Dimoldenberg rang
Peter Chesters, one of the City's valuers. Payne whispered, 'Ask
him how much they sold them for.' Chesters' reply was: 'Five pence
each.' Dimoldenberg 'couldn't believe it'. He and Neale Coleman

immediately demanded the council's file on the sales. 'It was absolutely staggering,' says Coleman.

On 2 December the *Evening Standard* carried the feature: 'The Haunting Tale of the 5p Cemeteries'. The rest of the press pack was not far behind. If anything could be more extraordinary than the affair which was now breaking, it was the fact that it effectively diverted attention from a scandal on a much grander scale which still lay hidden from view.

The year 1988 was a bad one for cemeteries salesmen but a vintage one for gerrymandering. On 12 January 1988 the Home Ownership Centre at 91 Victoria Street was opened. This was the council's great machine of social engineering, an estate agency that would sell thousands of council properties to prospective Tory voters. Westminster employed an actual estate agency called Ellis and Co. to run the Centre, and building societies were offering buyers 100 per cent mortgages; a West End solicitor had agreed to cut his conveyancing fees. On the day before the opening the Centre was visited by a WEAG raiding party, which made its protest peacefully and then promptly left.

Demonstrators were outside the Centre for its grand opening, while inside the celebrations were attended by the two local Conservative MPs, John Wheeler and Peter Brooke. There were trays of wine and snacks for the hubbub of estate agents, lawyers and mortgage brokers, who mingled with Tory councillors and officers, and discussed the exciting offers in the window. For example, there was a council property in St John's Wood at Robin House in Newcourt Street, described as an: 'extremely well located two-bedroomed first floor flat in purpose built block in need of internal redecoration . . . Regent's Park is literally a stone's throw. Leasehold 122 years. Real value: £67,500 (minus the maximum 70% Westminster's tenant discount of £35,000). Asking price: £32,500. 100% mortgage is available.'

To buy the flat, all you needed was a job offer within the City. Designated sales would allow first-time buyers and others on middle incomes to settle in Westminster, or so Porter proclaimed. But the government had told Porter only six months previously that she had no power to limit the resale value of any property, destroying at a stroke her stated aim of helping people to stay in Westminster. From day one, the council's housing stock was wide open to property speculators looking for a quick profit by buying up a council flat at a huge discount and then selling a few years later at full market value. Once the property had been resold, it

photo © Andrew Wiard/reportphotos.com

Peter Hartley in his favourite checked sports jacket, opening the Home Ownership Centre. (John Wheeler MP cuts the cake)

would be beyond the pockets of first-time buyers, but Porter – if she gave it any thought at all – thought it a price worth paying for Tory control of Westminster. At the time, Peter Hartley – who had managed the opening of the Centre – told a *Guardian* reporter, 'I wish to nail the lie that the only interest of this council is to bring in a load of yuppies.' Clearly he had forgotten attending a meeting four months earlier where it was decided that Bruce House was to be emptied and 'converted into yuppie flats'.

It took spectacular nerve by Porter and Hartley to ask Peter Brooke officially to open the Centre. Brooke was not only the Chairman of the Conservative Party nationally, but one of the most decent and affable men in Parliament. The image of Brooke cutting the ribbon with a giant pair of scissors in the shape of a key oblivious to the sinister purpose behind the new estate agency provides one of the most enduring images of the Porter scandal. But Hartley would not have long to enjoy his triumph.

On 21 January 1988 approximately 800 outraged relatives of those buried in the three graveyards gathered at Porchester Hall in Bayswater. Reverend Norman Grigg chaired the meeting organised by the Labour councillors. Paul Dimoldenberg, their group leader, says, 'I'd never addressed a bigger meeting; there were hundreds. We got a list of all the people who had written to the council complaining. So we had this huge database. They came from all over southern England.'

Harold Sheppard had died on 25 April 1986 and his widow, Eileen, had paid £1,200 to bury him at Mill Hill cemetery. The council exchanged contracts three days later with Clive Lewis on 28 April without telling her or anyone else, and Harold Sheppard was buried on 2 May 1986 in what was now a private graveyard. She was absolutely distraught when she found out about the five pence price tag of the cemetery, 'It was a huge meeting and people were cross, devastated and heartbroken. Everyone felt the same, that the cemeteries had been taken off us and they were all overgrown.' The meeting decided to set up a campaign organisation to force the council to buy back the cemeteries and hold the guilty accountable. Jo Mahoney was appointed press officer and Linda

Taylor became secretary. Other senior posts in the campaign went to Eileen Sheppard and Lew Lurie. Ominously for Porter, it was called the 'Westminster Association of Relatives', or WAR. For the next five years WAR would haunt Shirley Porter's every move. She attempted to shield herself by announcing an 'internal inquiry' into the affair. Who else but Bill Phillips would carry it out?

During January the unimpeded weeds of Mill Hill cemetery began inexorably to choke the fortunes of Peter Hartley. There was little to fear from Bill Phillips's endeavours, but now there were rather more serious investigators on the scene. Both the Local Government Ombudsman and the District Auditor set up inquiries, and then the Fraud Squad took an interest. Chief Inspector James Wadd told the *Standard*: 'We will interview anyone we feel can help with our inquiry. Obviously, this may include Lady Porter and Councillor Hartley.'

On 19 February Peter Hartley sent Porter a rather hysterical letter, resigning as Housing Chairman and councillor: 'I am doing this partly to protect my family. I have been subjected to anonymous telephone calls in the middle of the night threatening my life and I have hate mail.' Porter would later display the extent of her gratitude for his self-sacrifice: 'Peter Hartley was a man who lacked certain qualities, as we saw through the cemeteries fiasco.' Years later at the High Court, people who knew Hartley found it hard to reconcile their memories of the dapper and bluff soul with the shambles of a man weeping in front of three judges. It was clear to anyone who witnessed the spectacle that, in the intervening years, Hartley had come to regret bitterly his association with Shirley Porter.

The macabre tragi-farce of the cemeteries saga captured the imagination of the press. At East Finchley the grave of PC Keith Blakelock, murdered in the Broadwater Farm riot of 1985, disappeared beneath the grass, as did the grave of a former Tory Chancellor of the Exchequer, Austen Chamberlain. The *Daily Mirror* took up the cause of the 1960s pop idol Billy Fury, buried at Mill Hill. The paper's correspondent William Marshall described a scene at the graveside: 'A lady in black passed by. "Wasn't he some sort of singer?" she asked. "Lady," I said, "he was one of the all-time greats. And they're selling him for fifteen lousy pennies . . .'"

The scandal was reported internationally and caught the attention of Queen Beatrix of the Netherlands. At Mill Hill, there were graves of Dutch servicemen killed in the Second World War. She demanded news of their condition and dispatched Colonel Jacob Smit, military attaché at the Dutch embassy, to find out what was going on and report back. The Commonwealth War Graves Commission, which had repeatedly warned Westminster about the folly of its actions leading up to the sale, had taken matters into its own hands, and was keeping a careful eye on all 1,000 war graves in the three cemeteries. Colonel Smit reported that the Commission was doing a good job, but 'the pathway leading up to the Dutch Field of Honour had been a depressing sight.'

At first Porter attempted to placate the relatives. When that did not work, she went out of her way to offend and intimidate them. In early February she arranged a meeting with senior WAR representatives, who were demanding a public inquiry. Eileen Sheppard says, 'I thought Shirley Porter was very overpowering and she clearly thought you should bow and scrape to her because of who she was. I was in tears. She said I would "get better". I had lost my husband twenty-two months earlier but I had not been allowed to grieve; all my energy was going into sorting out the cemetery and it turned into a long fight. She was vindictive and arrogant and obviously she thought I had no right to say anything.'

Porter started packing the public gallery at meetings in the Marylebone Council House with her own supporters, mostly young right-wing Tories who got a kick out of jostling the relatives. These unpleasant young men were known as the 'Poison Acolytes' by a few of the more sensible Tories, quietly appalled at their antics. When Neale Coleman read letters from relatives during a council meeting, a group of them began to simper and snigger. Jo Mahoney poked two of them in the back and said, 'If you had someone buried there you wouldn't find it funny; the place is like a jungle.'

The relatives would arrive at the Council House or City Hall for

7 p.m. meetings an hour early and protest peacefully with their placards outside. Porter insisted that they be hemmed in behind barricades and that policemen keep a close eye on them. Then the relatives would be searched by council security guards before going into the meetings. Porter always made sure that any item for debate on the cemeteries would be the last thing on the list. 'We would sit there for hours without so much as a cup of tea,' says Mahoney. 'It was particularly tough on some of the relatives who were old and frail. They became angry waiting for the item to be reached and when it wasn't reached, they would become agitated; there would be snide comments from the Tories and they would become distressed.'

During a debate, one of Porter's colleagues referred to a television report which showed a relative laying flowers at her husband's abandoned grave and accused her of 'peddling cheap emotion for the cameras'. The woman became so upset she had to be helped out of the Council House. Jo Mahoney shouted down from the gallery, 'At the next council meeting you are going to need the St John's Ambulance.' Mahoney meant St John's would be needed to minister to relatives but Porter accused her of threatening physical violence. When Mahoney demanded an apology, Porter replied, 'I am pleased to have your assurance that you were not threatening me.' Porter would also jab her pen menacingly at relatives in the gallery, and she did not hesitate to have them thrown out if they displeased her. Leslie Furr, whose wife was buried at East Finchley, was hastily bundled out by security at one meeting, but not before he told Porter, 'I've said what I wanted to say and I've been thrown out of better places than this.'

On 2 March WAR assembled their forces at the Council House for a special debate on the cemeteries. They carried placards reading: 'HONOUR OUR DEAD! DON'T BUILD ON THEM!' and 'EUROPEANS LOOK AFTER OUR WAR DEAD! WHY CAN'T WE LOOK AFTER THEIRS?' Three hundred packed into the public gallery and the proceedings were relayed by video to another 400 at St Edward's Roman Catholic School in Lisson Grove.

Porter announced that she wanted to buy back the cemeteries, which prompted WAR to write its own anthem to the tune of the

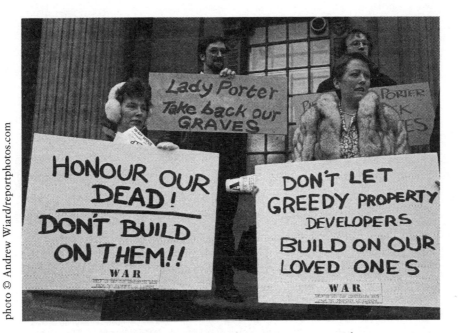

It's WAR! Cemetery relatives protest outside
Marylebone Council House.

old music hall number 'Oh Mr Porter!': 'Oh Lady Porter, what will
you do? You've promised to buy back the cemeteries, but we don't
believe it's true. Give us that inquiry, the public one we'd like, or in
1990, we'll tell you "On yer bike".' But there were major problems
with Porter's buy-back plan: how to do it and for how much? Clive
Lewis, Rodney Hylton-Potts and John Whybrow were completely
untouchable. The deal had been legal and so cleverly orchestrated
that none of the speculators could be held accountable. By now,
Lewis, the original architect of the deal, had sold the elegant lodge
at Hanwell cemetery for £170,000 and there were rumours that the
gatehouse at Mill Hill would fetch £300,000, but he had decided to
rent it out instead, along with the one at East Finchley. He would
also receive £250,000 for the crematorium at East Finchley. As the
scandal unravelled, Porter sent out an instruction: 'Nail Clive
Lewis.' She never could – and she never did.

Shirley Porter was at the mercy of the mysterious Turnip and his
company Wisland. They owned the freehold and, as predicted by

Rodney Brooke, the maintenance covenants proved utterly useless. The value of owning both the cemeteries and the twelve acres of land at Mill Hill became clear from the moment Porter said she wanted the cemeteries back. Wisland had already submitted a planning application to build houses on Milespit Hill and demanded £5.5 million from Westminster, saying the land would be worth that much with planning permission. Although Tory-controlled Barnet Council would not grant permission, Wisland hoped that Westminster could persuade Barnet to change its mind. Porter was in a terrible dilemma. She could not pay the amount demanded by Wisland because she might risk being surcharged by the District Auditor for such a huge loss to the public purse; there was the same risk if Barnet did grant planning permission for houses because that would transform an apparently worthless piece of countryside sold by Westminster for five pence into an asset worth in excess of £5 million.

Porter blustered and threatened to use a Compulsory Purchase Order, which the government could issue to force property owners to sell their land. The government made it clear that, although there were grounds for CPOs in extreme cases, for example in buying houses which stood in the way of a new motorway, political incompetence was not one of them. The CPO was refused.

Many Tory councillors became deeply concerned. Rachael Whittaker remembered how both she and Angela Killick had asked questions about the sale when it had first been suggested, but had been assured that the issue would come back to the Tory Councillors Group for further discussion. It never happened. Whittaker discovered that the minutes of that meeting, glued into a large bound book, had disappeared. She never saw them again.

The council was mocked for the scandal and the joke went that Westminster was the only place where you could buy three cemeteries and a pint of beer, and still have change from a pound. In March 1988 the *Evening Standard* sent its drama critic, Milton Shulman, to a council meeting to have some fun at Porter's expense. He reviewed it as if it were a weird and grisly West End show: 'A grave mystery or the Tale of the Disappearing Cemeteries'. He described the two tribes fighting over the graveyards in the Council House: 'The costume designer emphasised the

The dead have their revenge, according to Nicholas Garland of the *Daily Telegraph*.

class distinction of the characters by dressing the Conservatives in well-tailored business suits with Tory women in pearls and floral frocks while many Labour councillors conveyed their proletarian credentials in sweaters, jeans and open-necked shirts.' During the meeting itself, 'absurdity piled upon absurdity like so many custard pies being flung by drunken clowns'. He described an address by the relatives: 'Their spokesman, pounding the table with the resolution of a scolding headmaster, spoke of foxes having a field day because graves were dug only two and a half feet deep and of the distress of relatives who had come across bones on the overgrown paths.' As for Porter, Shulman said she was 'no sleep-walking Lady Macbeth washing the blood of guilt from her hands' but a tough leader who resolved that 'appropriate action would be taken after several inquiries had been held, negligence of council officers or advisers would be disclosed, serious misjudgements would be reported'.

Paul Foot was the first reporter to name John Whybrow as one of those involved and appealed for help in tracking him down. The council, also desperate to find out what had happened, located him and he consented to an interview in the office of his lawyer, Rodney Hylton-Potts. Whybrow appears to have enjoyed the experience, and still claimed to be a receiver for the worthless Chelwood Holdings Company; he said he had simply disposed of the assets of a company which was in receivership. He told Phillips's inquiry nothing of the quick fortune he had made selling the cemeteries or how the receivership had simply been a ruse to disguise reality. 'I am here to help, sir, as I always have been,' Whybrow said courteously. He then admonished the men from the council: 'It was not our decision, it was yours. I am a Westminster ratepayer and aggrieved at the situation. I don't believe you had any right to sell these cemeteries in the first place. You cannot sell people that have served this community in two world wars.' Phillips and his team were left none the wiser from their encounter with Whybrow. Hylton-Potts says, 'Of course, in reality, Whybrow couldn't give a stuff.'

Until the cemeteries fiasco, Porter had been lionised by the media as the hyper-efficient and no-nonsense Tesco heiress who was introducing long overdue commercial awareness to local government. The cemeteries revelations shattered Westminster's reputation as a model Tory council, and it is likely that the government would have heaped instant retribution on City Hall had it been Labour controlled. But the silence from the government was deafening. Dale Campbell Savours, Labour MP for Workington, lodged eighty-three separate objections with the District Auditor over the sale and accused Porter and her cohorts of 'wilful misconduct and gross negligence'. John Gorst, Tory MP for Hendon North, called on the government to hold a public inquiry.

Before too long, the Prime Minister was pulled into the storm. East Finchley cemetery was in her constituency, and Martin and Louise Cave, whose son was buried there, were her constituents. At first Thatcher refused to see them but relented when they threatened to go to the press. News of the meeting was, however, leaked to the *Evening Standard*. When the couple arrived at Thatcher's constituency office in Finchley, they were met by her agent Mike Love. He held up the *Evening Standard* article, which revealed that the Caves were due to see the Prime Minister later that day, and told the couple, 'This is very serious; you realise you're jeopardising the security of your MP and our Prime Minister.' Thatcher's opening gambit was: 'You do realise this is a serious situation. Why did you leak this information to the *Standard*?' Louise Cave told the Prime Minister she did not feel the need to apologise for something they had not done and she would not have her using it against them.

Thatcher backed down and sat uncomfortably as the couple made their way through their list of prepared questions. It was clear that the Prime Minister was acutely embarrassed of a fiasco perpetrated by her own municipal *doppelgänger*. Martin Cave says, 'Margaret Thatcher was very cold and precise and blocked virtually everything; she did thank us for coming and she did offer us a rather cold hand. It was quite an ordeal. We had asked a number of questions which we hoped would achieve something and in every case she gave exactly the same answer. What she said was, "I'm not in a position to deal with the matters which are the responsibility of my ministers and therefore I cannot give you any answer on this point."' Thatcher refused to hold a public inquiry and later wrote to the Caves, listing the numerous ongoing inquiries into the saga. She added, 'I understand a considerable amount of remedial work has been done in the cemeteries and generally their condition has been much improved. May I repeat once again I fully understand your concern about this whole matter?'

Bill Phillips was the first to produce a report into the affair. As expected, it lamely offered up Peter Hartley as the fall guy. Later, it emerged that there were 'gaps' in the transcripts of some critical interviews. A council spokesman said the tape recorder had 'malfunctioned'. Neale Coleman remarked, 'I think the similarity with Watergate is clear.'

Some senior Tories saw a funny side to the whole business, despite the damage done to the party. After the scandal broke, Ken Baker, the Secretary of State for the Environment, held a meeting of Tory council leaders to discuss the abolition of the Inner London Education Authority and the dispersal of its assets. Porter arrived late with two huge prototype mobile phones which resembled army walkie-talkies. As the meeting drew to a close, she got ready to leave. 'She was always much busier than us, even the Secretary of State!' says a council leader. Baker said, 'Is there anything else we should discuss before Shirley goes?' Paul Beresford, the Wandsworth leader, said, 'Yes. If ILEA have got any cemeteries, can Westminster have them?' As Baker and his officials struggled to restrain their laughter with barely muffled snorts and guffaws, Porter left the room in a huff. 'It was very funny,' says Beresford. 'It was worth it just to see her flounce out!' Max Hastings, then editor of the *Daily Telegraph*, remembered sharing a panel with Porter for BBC Radio Four's *Any Questions?* He wrote later: 'Shirley Porter arrived one day with sheaves of papers, determined to deliver her defence of Westminster's cemeteries. She insisted upon delivering her apologia on the air, even though no one in the audience asked her a question about it.'

It would be another five years before the cemeteries, minus the valuable assets, were returned to the City Council for a nominal fee and after thousands of relatives had gone through needless suffering. But for now, Wisland held firmly on to its possessions as bargaining chips in an attempt to get planning permission for Milespit Hill or a good price from City Hall. When Westminster argued with Wisland about shoddy maintenance or the CPO, it ordered cemetery workers to down tools and the graveyards were abandoned once again; drunks moved into Hanwell and drug addicts and vandals into Mill Hill. Devil worshippers placed a black cross on the grave of Wendoline Mackrell's son in East Finchley. In a later half-hearted attempt to appease the council and the relatives, Wisland operatives sprayed the cemeteries with a special growth-retardant chemical, which turned the grass brown overnight. Neither the annual crops of crocuses at Hanwell nor snowdrops among the graves of paupers and infants at East Finchley ever appeared again.

CHAPTER 15

Tree Tubs in Paddington (1988)

The cemeteries crisis ironically proved extremely useful to Shirley Porter in diverting attention away from the deep malaise which now consumed the City Council. Gerrymandering infected virtually every department and activity to the extent that later, the District Auditor's investigation team wondered whether there was any section of the authority not involved in the endemic abuse of public resources. Porter had often complained that the council's departments acted as private fiefdoms and that City Hall lacked the corporate ethos of Tesco. But the corrupt policies of BSC required all departments to work together to keep Westminster Conservative. According to an internal policy memo, BSC was nothing less than 'an expression of a complete, corporate approach to everything that the City does and the services which it provides'.

Many of the components of BSC were cynically dressed up as legitimate policies for public consumption. Designated sales extended the gift of home ownership; the deportation of the homeless to boroughs where accommodation was allegedly cheaper saved ratepayers' money. But there was also the so-called 'Quality of Life' initiative, designed to focus the council's resources on tidying up and improving the eight marginal wards. Despite all the importing and deporting, there were still thousands of fickle voters in the marginal wards. The solid Labour and Conservative areas could be treated with contempt; the only electorates which mattered now were those in the 'key areas'. The 'task' according to one secret document at the time was 'to change residents' attitudes in key wards'.

By the spring of 1988 it was almost impossible to tell where the gerrymandering ended and proper council activity began, if such a distinction could now sensibly be made. To promote the Quality of Life initiative, in April 1988 Porter launched a crusade against potholes, a problem across the City but in her view particularly acute in BSC terms for the residents occupying the marginals. She hired a bus to inspect the problem and demanded the attendance of senior officers. Representatives of the utilities responsible for the blight were summoned with a day's notice and journalists were invited along for the ride to witness their ritual pillory and humiliation.

Holding a microphone, Porter stood at the front of the bus as it bumped around the City, and on sighting a pothole ordered the man from Thames Water, the London Electricity Board or British Telecom to explain himself. The *Paddington Mercury* reported: 'They were forced to fend off what one of them described as a "diatribe".' Matthew Ives, who was on the bus, says, 'Many stout parties collapsed in the face of Porter's withering criticism. They were hauled up to the front to explain why these potholes had been dug and re-dug . . . for most of us it was just a day out because we weren't on the anvil as a result of anything. This was somebody else getting a roasting. We quite enjoyed seeing this happen and how other people reacted to this.'

The Quality of Life initiative also targeted the plagues of estate agents' boards, broken pavements, discarded breeze-blocks, piles of rubble and, according to the local papers, 'wastelands of litter'. During 1988 and 1989 Porter threw council energy into the offensive against all these blights. There were the 'Pothole Eater Squads' (PES), the 'Zoned Improvement Patrols' (ZIP), the 'Westminster Initiative Summer Patrols' (WISP), the 'Summer Blitzes' and the 'Brighter Buildings Initiatives'. It was a ferocious campaign, often

praised by sections of the press, and all of it driven by gerrymandering.

Although these problems affected the whole of Westminster, the
initiative was particularly targeted at the key wards. Nothing was
overlooked: not the builders' skips in St James's or the wheelchair
ramps in Victoria or the abandoned bags of cement in Bayswater.
No job was too small or too unimportant when it came to the marginals. They would be cleaner, smarter and safer than the rest. 'It is
amazing,' Shirley Porter once said, 'what a hanging basket will do.'
The marginal wards would get as many hanging baskets as were
required for victory in 1990. A total of seventy-four environmental
schemes, costing more than £4.5 million in the first year, were 'targeted as far as possible into the key areas', according to a report by
the council's department of leisure services.

Building Stable Communities had become an industry within
City Hall requiring its own separate and secret administrative
structure which bypassed and eventually consumed the City
Council. Porter and her senior committee chairmen, the so-called
Chairmen's Group, stood at the apex of the BSC machine. Porter's
deputy, David Weeks, was fulltime at the helm, as 'lead member on
BSC'. Beneath the chairmen came two BSC steering committees
one made up of senior officers, the other of senior Tory councillors.
Under the steering committees mushroomed a plethora of BSC
subcommittees for activities from publicity to deporting the homeless. Every council department had its own 'BSC Action Plan' and
its own BSC liaison officer to police the gerrymandering. Senior
officers were ordered to 'think BSC' and to demonstrate 'BSC initiative'. Everything had to fit in with the 'total BSC concept'. For
example, the Housing Director, Graham England, would later
describe the accelerating costs for the temporary housing of the
homeless as 'Category 1 BSC'. 'What are we going to do to ensure
that residents are BSC?' asked members of the BSC Officers
Steering Group at their first meeting on 22 January 1988, as they
pondered their task of replacing thousands of Westminster citizens
with the 'right sort of people'.

Nick Reiter was the head of the Policy Unit at the epicentre of
the plot. He says, 'It almost felt that we'd become some sort of

© Philip Wolmuth

Graham England (right), Director of Housing and reluctant gerrymanderer jokes with Assistant Director Ken Hackney.

strange cult. It had nothing to do with the management of a major city council. You get a group of people who get intense about something, and they're bouncing this off each other all the time. The more they're bouncing it off each other, the more they feel that this belongs to them and they can't share it too much outside with anybody else and the less they can trust anyone else. Was it spinning out of control? To be honest I didn't think it was ever very much in control.'

The council and the committees were meaningless talking shops where Labour councillors let off steam. The senior officers took their orders directly from the BSC infrastructure and the Chairmen's Group in particular. Nick Reiter says, 'There was no protection from management lines of command. Members like David Weeks felt perfectly able to say to an officer, "Well you're working on this, where is it? We must have it tomorrow." It was constant chasing and chivvying without any clear hierarchy.'

A paper called 'The Machinery for Implementation' prepared for the BSC Members Steering Group laid the ground rules for this informal and unlawful structure. One critical function assigned to the BSC machine was to 'monitor' and record its achievements and results, as Bill Phillips made clear in a confidential note at the time: 'It is intended that each department will provide information, a written commentary, on their key BSC programmes and their flagship projects, together with, as appropriate, statistics on a ward-based level.' Porter did not trust her BSC machinery to carry out the gerrymandering and so she demanded evidence in the form of monthly reports from each department on what had been achieved in each of the eight key wards. The marginal wards would be scrupulously checked for progress: every new resident, every deported family, every hanging basket, would be counted in or out or up. A database was established to compile the information.

As the BSC machine whirred into action, it collected more information and spewed out more papers, often in triplicate, which flowed in an unceasing stream through the in- and out-trays of City Hall. Whether you were a committee clerk, an assistant divisional engineer or a chief officer, it became impossible to avoid the memos, graphs and documents. Through arrogance and carelessness, Porter lost control of the information and eventually the conspiracy itself. The widespread dispersal of documents gradually stripped the plot of the secrecy necessary for its survival and left the conspirators vulnerable. Reiter says, 'It wasn't consistent. Papers would go out to all and sundry and then a week later she'd decide that maybe that paper shouldn't be circulated to quite so many people. But by that time, it had gone out anyway.'

Bill Ritchie, the Director of Social Services, was besieged from all sides by BSC. He was already handling the deported homeless and now he and his staff were told that extra money would be available to help disabled people and other vulnerable groups only in the marginal wards. There was a BSC central slush fund to which departments had to apply, but only schemes for what Bill Ritchie now called 'the magic eight' stood a chance. He says, 'I had four area teams across the City based in Victoria, Bayswater, Paddington and Marylebone, and attached to those teams were 12 occupational therapists. They were responsible for any disabled person asking for bath aids, wheelchair ramps etc. They were unearthing need in the community no matter where in the City.

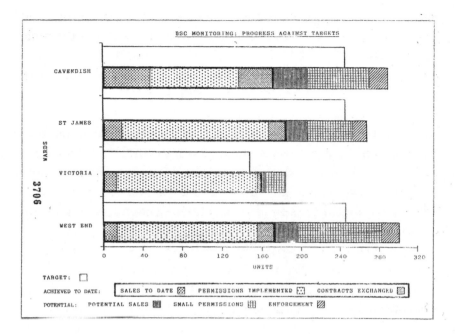

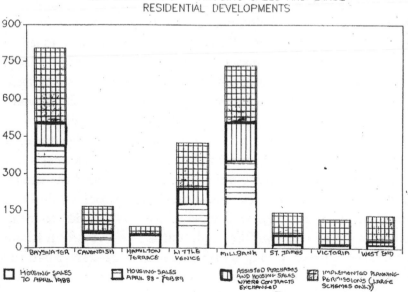

Gerrymandering at a glance. Secret BSC papers show
how officers monitored council house sales and
planning permissions in the marginal wards.

And that's when they ran into the priorities of the time: the eight marginal wards.' Ritchie's therapists continued to care for people as best they could with the resources they had but they were fed up at being told in meetings that disabled people could not get help because they lived outside the eight key wards.

The absurdity of the policy was demonstrated by a memo written by a middle-ranking manager in the council's planning and transportation department headed 'DISABLED MOBILITY SCHEMES'. It reads: 'All schemes under this heading and those relating to tree planting and Pavement trouble spots are to be specifically angled to the eight key wards.' The first two wards to get the treatment were Cavendish and Victoria: 'street seats for the elderly, crossings for the partially sighted, ramps and crossovers . . . a network for the disabled'. The planning and transportation department started building a network of wheelchair ramps and dropped kerbs for the elderly and disabled in the marginal wards of Millbank and Victoria, taking in Marsham Street, home to the Department of the Environment, Great Peter Street and Horseferry Road. A further memo revealed: 'The streets were chosen from the Key Wards, which for this purpose, have an agreed ranking . . . Cavendish, Victoria and Millbank. The remaining five will be treated in a similar manner as the programme develops.' Streets which formed ward boundaries presented a particular problem for the engineers. What if someone in a wheelchair crossed from a marginal to a non-marginal ward? Should there be a ramp to receive them? The conundrum was never satisfactorily sorted out. Sometimes it happened; sometimes not.

Bill Ritchie confronted Shirley Porter about her behaviour: 'I said that instead of allocating resources in this way, why don't you allocate resources across the City so all wards have their chance to get extra services through the funding that's being made available? I said, what you're doing is building a two-tier system where if you're in Place A, you've got a chance of getting something, but if you're in Place B, you haven't got much chance.' Ritchie said, 'You're creating what we call in Liverpool a house with a "Queen Ann front and a Maggie-Anne back".' 'I find that very offensive,' replied Porter.

The ZIP teams spearheaded the clean-up in the eight marginals. They had their own uniforms and vans at a cost of £550,000 a year. Robert Davis, a Tory councillor, wrote a paper recommending deployment of the ZIP teams and said their efforts must be concentrated in 'target wards in line with BSC Strategy and Majority Party [Conservative Party] direction'. Porter had high expectations of the ZIPs. One objective set for them in wards such as Hamilton Terrace was 'to reduce dog fouling by March 1989'.

Porter dictated the problems which had to be addressed in the document she wrote in the spring of 1988, 'Keeping Westminster Conservative'. She listed the eight wards and the action which needed to be taken in each to curry favour with the voters: Little Venice: 'increase surveillance on builders to prevent unsocial behaviour. Continue crackdown on [removal of] estate agents boards . . .'; Millbank: 'environmental improvements to older council estates . . . improve traffic . . . investigate provision of open space and youth facilities . . .'; Victoria: 'traffic management schemes to protect area from intrusion by tourist coaches . . . Parliament Square improvements . . .' According to the District Auditor later, expenditure on the improvement schemes in the eight wards was just under £2 million, double that in the remaining fifteen.

Many documents relating to environmental improvements in the marginal wards were destroyed in 1994 but those which survived the shredders show that the monitoring of the activity in the key wards was pervasive. On 25 March 1988 a monitoring report detailed the excellent progress on the 'Disabled Mobility Network' in three marginals. Workmen had built thirty new dropped kerbs and installed forty-four street ramps in Cavendish, Victoria and Millbank. A monthly report on actions in marginal Maida Vale revealed that the ZIPs had tackled twenty-five skips and six estate agents' boards and dealt with two 'dog fouling incidents'. WISPS were deployed in Bayswater. According to the monitoring schedule, they had removed forty-eight bags of ballast or cement, twenty scaffolding fence boards and one wheelbarrow.

Residents in the marginal wards saw daily improvements. Noisy neighbours were more likely to be dealt with in the marginals than elsewhere. Council inspectors were ordered to respond faster to complaints from residents in 'key areas'. Monitoring reports revealed how inspectors responded to 160 complaints about nuisances from people living in St James's. Buildings and statues in the marginal wards were smartened up. The real purpose behind the 'Brighter Buildings Initiative', another BSC scheme, was 'to secure the restoration and cleaning of a number of buildings in target areas . . .' Westminster Abbey and Parliament Square, both in marginal Victoria, received the same treatment. Someone walking through the West End noticed that the John Lennon statue in Carnaby Street was looking a bit grubby. That too got the BSC treatment. Cost: £16,500.

Remarkably, Porter decided to publicise the activities of the WISPs, ZIPs and Pothole Eaters in a council publication called the *Rate-Payer Reporter*. There were 'Ward Inserts' and, of course, the first ones publicised BSC initiatives in marginal wards. Although the public remained largely ignorant about the political marginality of the wards which constituted their city, the Labour councillors were growing suspicious. When, during a council meeting in April 1988, Paul Dimoldenberg asked Porter about the Ward Inserts, she lied. 'The special inserts in the last edition of the *Ratepayer Reporter* were aimed at wards where particular Quality of Life schemes are being undertaken,' she said. 'No decision has been taken yet about which wards will be dealt with in this way in the future.'

Bill Ritchie was a disillusioned man. He says, 'Certainly the stress of the latter years under Shirley Porter increased dramatically and I was getting bad migraines, so much so that on one occasion I had to go out of the meeting and just vomited. It changed from when Shirley Porter was this dynamic person coming into the leadership to a situation which was totally wrong, because these policies were wrong, and they were known to be wrong.' In spring 1988 Bill Ritchie took early retirement.

Even officers who had naively collaborated began to feel uneasy about what was happening. After a year as head of the Policy Unit, Nick Reiter was coming to an unsettling conclusion. 'I think it was an example of an organisation that had gone bad,' he says, 'because all the established rules and cultural artefacts of local government had collapsed and what you ended up with was an attempt to turn a council into a party machine. On the whole there were not bad people there, even the councillors were not embodiments of evil, and certainly the chief officers were as good a bunch of guys as I have ever worked with. Something had gone wrong with people's understanding of where their true responsibilities and loyalties lay, and I am as guilty of that as anybody else.' Who was responsible? 'A fish stinks from the head,' answers Reiter.

Not everybody in the marginal wards was delighted with the attention being lavished on their neighbourhoods. Norman St John Stevas, Baron St John of Fawsley, a former Conservative cabinet minister and chairman of the Fine Art Commission, took grave exception to the sudden appearance of trees in large wooden tubs in some marginal wards. The tubs were part of Porter's 'Greening the City', another Quality of Life initiative, but they had quickly become used as litter bins and even as something for late night revellers to throw up in.

A report by the Commission in November 1988 said: 'The Commission was appalled by the sudden appearance of large wooden tubs containing trees of different species in the central ceremonial streets of Westminster including Lower Regent Street, Pall Mall, St James's Street and Piccadilly.' Porter dispatched her deputy, David Weeks, and Sid Sporle, then Acting Director of Planning and Transportation, to appease Fawsley. They arrived at the Commission, were ushered into the chairman's presence and sat down at his Georgian card table. Fawsley ordered the two men to withdraw their wretched tree tubs forthwith and preferably sooner.

Sporle and Weeks inspected the tubs. 'Weeks thought the tubs were bloody awful,' says Sporle. 'He said, "Come here and look at this tub!" It was full of puke and Weeks went absolutely ape-shit. They were instantly removed.' Sporle thought no more about the tubs. He had enough on his plate as it was and, in any case, they were the responsibility of the department of leisure. The tubs disappeared, but not for long. Forty-two tree tubs, complete with vomit and West End detritus, sprang up along Walterton Road in the Labour stronghold of North Paddington. Jonathan Rosenberg of the WEAG says, 'It was mad. There were elderly people and

mothers with pushchairs who were finding it difficult if not impossible to get round these tubs. One woman living in a basement flat
complained that a tub blocked out her sunlight. No one saw them
being delivered, or even knew where they came from or who had
put them there.' The action had taken place at the behest of the
City Council in the early hours of two consecutive mornings at the
cost of £6,000. A senior official at the council's department of
leisure services wrote to Neale Coleman: 'I instructed my staff to
move some of the trees in planters to the Walterton estate as part of
the general redeployment of these planters which is taking place.'

Westminster seemed happier dealing with Fawsley's demands for
'redeployment' than the residents. Officers from the department of
leisure services met Jonathan Rosenberg. Later one of the officers
recorded what was discussed: 'At the conclusion of the meeting Mr
Rosenberg suggested we remove twenty-five of the forty-two containers. In my view this seems excessive and I have agreed that we
remove ten containers which are either inconveniently sited or contain trees in the poorest condition. The remaining trees, where
necessary, are to be pruned . . . and to be fed with an appropriate
fertilizer. The remaining thirty-two containers are to be planted
with flowers; this week with pansies which will then be replaced by
other flowers at the commencement of the summer bedding season.
It is proposed to move the other ten containers, after treatment, to
the Elgin Estate.'

Having upset Fawsley, Westminster had simply moved the tubs
from sensitive marginal wards to the black heart of the Labour-
voting enemy. It was hardly Category 1 BSC, but it did show
officers and Tory councillors thinking BSC and displaying BSC initiative. It had been a total BSC concept fiasco.

CHAPTER 16

Sid Sporle, Double Agent (1988)

S hirley Porter had few grounds to complain about her officers. She had asked them to do the unthinkable and, by and large, they were getting on with it. The marginal wards were being purged of 'HPs': in March 1988 eighty-two families were 'removed' 'due to enforcement action'; by February of the following year the housing department could proudly inform Porter: 'All Westminster families are now removed from hotels which were subject to planning actions.' The first designated sales were coming through, two years after they were first suggested. Porter was assured that she would soon be on target for 500 sales a year, although everyone agreed that keeping the properties empty was costing a fortune. There were now 500–600 empty properties sealed by Sitex doors waiting for sale, losing rent and rates payments by the week.

The losses were already huge and were mounting inexorably. If the District Auditor ever found evidence of her unlawful purpose, Porter would have to pay the money back in the form of a sur-charge: the £4 million setting-up costs of the Home Ownership Centre, the £4 million annual extra costs of deporting the homeless and the 500 homes a year sold at £30,000 discounts, i.e. £15 million a year. Renting 500 Sitex doors added £25,000 a week or £1.3 million a year, and pothole eating and Zipping did not come cheap.

By the middle of 1989, three months before the closure of the electoral register, there was a potential personal liability to Porter and her fellow plotters of more than £30 million.

Fear, either of Porter or of discovery, actually encouraged officers to take huge risks with the very things they thought they were protecting by their compliance: themselves, their families and their mortgages. Everyone could see what was in it for Porter and the politicians: if the plot came off and Westminster was saved for the Conservatives, there could be parliamentary seats and peerages for the victors. In contrast, no campaign medals would be struck for the officers because this was a story that could never be told. For them, personal danger of surcharge and disgrace depended on their proximity to the beast, on how far they had been pushed down the slippery slope. Bill Phillips tackled the slope with all the zest of a downhill skier, whereas Graham England appears to have tumbled down it unhappily, hoping against hope that something would arrest his fall. It never did.

The story of Sid Sporle goes a long way to explain the awful dilemma council officers suffered in the face of the conspiracy. Sporle's name appears in dozens of the secret documents recovered during subsequent inquiries into the affair, and Labour councillors considered him one of the architects of BSC. During much of the crucial gerrymandering period, Sid Sporle was the Council's Director of Planning and Transportation, or held the position in an acting capacity. The charge levelled against him can be put simply: he abused his position to rig the council's extensive planning powers, encouraging property developers to build the type of housing in marginal wards likely to attract potential Tory voters, and he chaired crucial meetings of his fellow officers, who were involved in the successful implementation and monitoring of pervasive gerrymandering. The appointment of Sid Sporle as Director of Planning and Transportation of Westminster in 1987 had a curious twist. There had been another Sid Sporle, his father, famous for his involvement in an earlier great council scandal of the twentieth century.

Sid Sporle senior was born in slum conditions in Battersea and left school at the age of twelve. He joined Battersea Council as a councillor, determined to improve the desperate housing conditions which had blighted his life. He went on to become mayor of the borough before it became part of Wandsworth and Labour leader of Wandsworth, and also served as Chairman of its Housing Committee.

In 1971 Sporle senior became involved in a scandal at his borough and was convicted for receiving a bribe of £500 from a construction engineer to award a contract worth £6.5 million to John Laing Ltd. Sporle was jailed for six years on seven counts of corruption, reduced to four after his wife Mabel got together a petition of 600 council tenants. 'I feel very sorry for my father,' says Sporle junior. 'It broke him as a man. He was never the same and he died not long after; I genuinely think he wasn't as guilty as he was found.'

Sid Sporle junior started his first stint as a local government officer at Westminster after leaving school at sixteen, and rose undramatically through the ranks of the planning department. He did not have a degree, as later became *de rigueur* for planning officers, nor was he a member of the Institute of Planning, but by common consent he was an instinctive and brilliant planner. He left Westminster in 1970 and had a brief spell at Salisbury District Council but it was too quiet for him so he returned to Westminster a year later. On his first day back, 12 February, the *Evening Standard* front page was devoted to the trial of his father: 'EX-MAYOR LIED IN HOUSING CONTRACT FIX'. The news went round City Hall and some people even phoned up Sporle to pull his leg. Everyone liked Sid junior. Sid was zany and madcap. Sid would sneak up behind junior officers at parties and give them a big cuddle. Sid was also ambitious and worked long hours. Not only were Mum and Dad Labour, but Sid junior was raised on a Peabody estate and was philosophically opposed to selling social housing. He was also a voluntary senior officer for the Social Democratic Party in Hampshire during the early 1980s. He was a strange choice as a chief gerrymanderer for Shirley Porter.

Few officials wield more power than those in the planning department. Their decisions, particularly in Westminster where land values are so high, can make or lose property developers millions of pounds and affect the lives of thousands of residents. In fact, the *Evening Standard* once described Sporle as one of the most powerful people in London. John Dyke joined Westminster as a young planner in 1982 and stayed for six years. Sporle was his boss throughout. Dyke says, 'To me he was the best planning officer I'd ever come across. I had unbounded time for Sid Sporle. He had enormous charm and enormous energy and charisma. I've probably only met four people in my life who I would say have charisma and I think Sid Sporle has charisma.' Sporle had the gift of often being to able to reconcile the irreconcilable. Dyke often saw him working a meeting where competing interests had to be appeased. He says, 'Sid Sporle had the fantastic kind of power of speaking to each person separately exactly according to their character and line of interest. Dealing with the developer he would be very much the man in the suit, the custodian protecting the City, aware that the planning system is there to facilitate development and therefore that he would do everything to make sure the development was something the City Council could approve. On the other hand, he would be very conscious of the woman sitting next to him objecting to the development. When he spoke to her, he responded very directly to her concerns. He had a great empathy for picking up people's concerns, making them feel their concerns were being recognised and would be dealt with. And he could do that with the flash of an eye.'

Sporle had been traumatised by what happened to his father. Despite the laughter and practical jokes, he made sure he was never alone when he met a developer to discuss a planning permission. Free opera tickets from builders were politely, but firmly, rejected. 'It conditioned me that you could sit down and have a cup of coffee with them,' says Sporle, 'but you couldn't sit down and break bread with them.' 'I think it's a bit like a child who experiences its parents' divorce,' says one of Sporle's former planning officers. 'It had this traumatic effect on Sid and it meant that he was incredibly sensitive to any whiff of allegation of corruption. So it is a very cruel irony that he should suffer the same experience in his own professional life and as a local government officer.'

The 1986 election results had an electrifying effect on the career prospects of Sid Sporle, who at the time was one of a handful of assistant directors of planning. Porter, David Weeks and others quickly realised that the planning department must play a major role in the gerrymandering. The social engineering possibilities with planning were extensive. Without paying a penny you could get developers to build the 'right type' of homes where you wanted them and stop housing associations building housing for the 'wrong sort of people' where you didn't.

Sporle's promotion brought him into regular contact with David Weeks, whose responsibilities included chairing the Planning Committee as well as driving through BSC. Weeks's ferocious temper was legendary. Nick Reiter always thought him one of the worst bullies in the council. John Dyke remembers Weeks as being particularly driven, and says, 'Weeks had this sort of sallow complexion of someone who has never seen sunlight.'

Porter understood the importance of planning to her overall political objectives. There was little use in selling off hundreds of council houses in the marginal wards, if a housing association built hundreds of homes in the same areas for likely Labour voters. The housing associations were already being told to build new homes outside Westminster, and the aim now was to facilitate the sort of private developments in the wards which would attract the 'right sort' of people. The District Auditor later found evidence that 'an element of the secret BSC policy was to dispose of council-owned properties and sites for the electoral advantage of the Conservative Party.'

Officers in the planning department were among the first to articulate in writing what gerrymandering would mean for the council in their 'Wandsworth Experience' paper: 'there is an immediate need to socially engineer the population in marginal wards.' James Thomas, then Planning Director, read the report and marked it 'STRICTLY CONFIDENTIAL' before passing it on to Bill Phillips, who, like Shirley Porter, had come to the same conclusion.

Thomas became progressively uncomfortable as the panic set in around him, and Porter grew increasingly unhappy with him. He was not helped by the fact that many of his planners thought he was stuffy. One former planning officer says, 'With hindsight I

understand that one of the reasons why James Thomas fell out of
favour with Porter was because he wasn't willing to pursue her
political agenda. James turns out to be more heroic than we planners thought at the time.' By March 1987 Thomas was expressing
concern that Porter was seeking out the help of Sporle, merely one
of his assistants. 'I understand your concern about the impact on
Mr Sporle's workload,' Phillips replied with lofty disdain, adding,
'I believe that Mr Sporle will have a lively, personal contribution to
make . . . If you remain at all uneasy about this, do let us have a
word.' In the spring Sporle was sent for by Rodney Brooke. 'James
Thomas is going,' said Brooke. 'Does he know yet?' asked Sporle.
'Not yet,' replied Brooke. On 29 May, following Thomas's departure, Sid Sporle was appointed Acting Director of Planning and
Transportation. The post itself would be his in a year's time, but in
the meantime he would have to prove he was worth it.

Initially, Porter wanted the council to establish a Westminster
Housing Trust with millions of pounds of ratepayers' money to buy
up sites in the marginal wards which could then be developed into
the type of housing required by BSC. But none of it could happen in
time for the next elections in May 1990, and, in any case, the proposals were vetoed by the government. According to an internal
planning department memo, subtle changes would be made to the
'City Plan', the development blueprint for Westminster, to 'include
the emerging corporate strategy of "Building Stable Communities".'
    Sporle's increasingly important role was spelt out a few months
later on 11 October 1987 in a note to David Weeks by Bill Phillips:
'There is a heavy burden . . . on the Chief Officers (Graham
England, Sid Sporle and myself) most directly concerned . . . we
need a centre of excellence. A small group of officers who totally
understand BSC: who work well together, who can pool their
resources to make sure that support is given where it is needed and
that the key actions actually happen.'
    To Porter and her chairmen, it appeared that Sporle was going
along with the conspiracy, but privately he had taken a decision.
He would keep up appearances, and even change the City Plan,
but, haunted by his father's experience, he had resolved not to

engage in the gerrymandering of the marginal wards or involve his hundred planning officers in the corruption of planning powers. The question is, how far did he succeed?

The major obstacle to rigging the planning process was the planning department itself. Planning officers were always regarded, and certainly regarded themselves, as far brighter than the average council official. They immediately suspected Porter's real motives. A joke swiftly spread through the department that BSC really stood for 'Building Safer Constituencies'. Furthermore, planning officers were hardly rabid Tories. Sporle says, 'You have to understand the planning department. A significant proportion of people in it are either Labour supporters or members of the Labour Party. So how could I have driven through a BSC strategy even if I wanted to?'

Sporle came under intense pressure from Porter and Weeks, as Nick Reiter observed at the time, 'Sid Sporle was very much under the same pressures Graham England was in, in the sense of feeling very pressured and threatened [by Porter]. Sid was perhaps a little better equipped, in terms of his character, to stand up and say, "Well, I'm not too sure about this." Sid was more prone to express doubts than some of the other officers. Sid was more extrovert; he had a wackier sense of humour and had better coping strategies.'

Sporle says he managed to cope partly by keeping out of Porter's way as much as possible. He would make a point of getting out of City Hall when he could for the sake of his sanity. He says, 'On average I was working a twelve–fourteen-hour day and I was knackered. On a Friday night I used to escape from the building as quick as I could by six o'clock, so that I couldn't be reached on the phone by Weeks or anyone else who would have me there until ten o' clock at night. I used to rush off and go to Choys in Kings Road and have a Chinese meal and then go to the pictures. It was gruesome. But it just wasn't me.'

The usually garrulous and chirpy Sporle became more remote, and his colleagues noticed that he had started smoking heavily. He charts his contraction of asthma back to the late 1980s at City Hall. Like most of his senior colleagues, he was scared of Shirley Porter. One young planner remembers seeing the pair together. 'I'm certain that Sid was bullied. Once I got in the lift and Sid was there with Shirley Porter. Sid was chatting away and joking around and he said, "Don't worry, Shirley; I'll have that report to you by Wednesday." She just looked at him and said, 'No you won't, you'll have it with me tonight.' Suddenly there's this Director of Planning, who scared the shit out of us, getting it, and we all stood there eyes glazed trying to desperately keep a straight face. Sid went bright pink and got out at the next stop. That's how she did things.' Sporle was in uncharted waters like everyone. 'I was scared,' he admits. Some of the pressures on him came from other council departments after his officers had innocently rejected an application on valid planning grounds, although the scheme fitted in with BSC. The angry memos would urge him: 'surely you can see the priority of BSC over planning issues.' Sporle says he would write back, 'No. Everything is subject to good planning criteria.'

Sporle had to wait months before the intricate interview process for his job began. First he took psychometric tests and then he was vetted by another 'Man With No Name', Michael Silverman, personnel consultant to Porter. Porter was clearly pleased with Sporle because, finally, she gave him the job.

Sporle found it increasingly difficult to avoid BSC. Up until March 1988 Bill Phillips had chaired the secret meetings of the BSC Officers Steering Group, which oversaw the gerrymandering strategy and monitored its progress, but then he relinquished the role to focus his efforts on his inquiry into the cemeteries sale. Phillips told Sporle that he would have to chair the BSC group for the next few months. Now Sid Sporle had no hiding place: not only would he have to chair meetings of officers actively engaged in the gerrymandering, but it fell to him to record all BSC activities in the marginal wards for Porter and her acolytes.

Sid Sporle tried to bring off a difficult balancing act. He had no choice but to participate in the secret BSC meetings, which were held in his office, and even help monitor actions in the key marginal wards, but he would try to protect his staff in the Planning Department. It was going to be difficult.

On 28 April Sporle reported that the 'necessary mechanisms, procedures and staff are now in place' and that 'the target of 500 sales for 1988/'89 will be achieved'. At this time too, the meetings viewed the new BSC block graphs which would now be produced every fortnight and would show the progress of all council activities in the marginal wards. The hand-drawn graphs unapologetically illustrated the gerrymandering strategy. They showed the number of council sales and the new residential units completed as a result of planning permissions in the eight areas. They also showed the total number of prospective new Tory voters achieved in each ward and any potential shortfall.

Despite Sporle's predictions, Porter still fretted about getting her 2,200 extra voters. The sale of council houses was not going as quickly as she planned. Now Sporle would have to make good the deficit in likely Tory voters by granting planning permission for more small residential developments in the key wards. On 13 July the pressure on him was made clear by the directive: 'in all wards, short-fall in residential units could be made good by concentrating on small schemes with planning permission.' Sporle says the planning permissions would have been granted anyway on proper grounds, but he simply recorded them to show that he was cooperating.

At the end of May the BSC officers' meeting chaired by Sporle decided that out of the eight wards the 'priority areas [are] now Cavendish, St James's and West End'. Good progress was being made towards fulfilling Porter's targets for new voters in five of the eight wards, but there was a projected shortfall in those three. A fourth, Victoria, would be added when Porter grew concerned that too little was happening there. The four wards would be the super marginals, the so-called 'stress wards', requiring extra love and attention. The gerrymandering in the other four was going to plan.

On 13 July 1988 a graph appeared to show the importance of planning permissions to BSC. In Cavendish, there had only been nineteen designated sales, but forty-three small planning permissions for new homes. By 1990 there would be 183 new voters, still sixty-seven short of Porter's target of 250. In St James's, there had been 142 planning permissions compared to sixteen designated sales. But there would be 241 new voters, nine short of the 250 target. In Victoria, where there had been no designated sales, the ninety-nine planning permissions alone were going to exceed the target of 150 more voters by 1990.

At one BSC officers' meeting Sporle insisted that planning permissions would be given for developments across the City, in marginals and non-marginals alike. Senior housing officers sniggered and said, 'Well, that's not concentrating on the key wards, is it?' 'It doesn't matter,' said Sporle. 'I'm applying BSC across the City and you should too.' According to Sporle, the eight marginal wards would 'get their fair share' of planning permissions but no more than elsewhere. He says, 'I went along with them to the extent that I did what they were seeking which was to secure additional housing, legitimately, through the planning process, but I did it over the City as well. I didn't differentiate; I didn't just focus in their eight key wards and you won't find anything in the planning control element where there is a focus on those eight areas. And if I found anyone focusing on it, I would have broken their bloody legs, simple as that.'

Far from uniting them in a common corporate enterprise, BSC isolated all senior officers in turn as they either wrestled with their consciences or attempted to limit their involvement. The secrecy and folly of the strategy poisoned relationships at City Hall. It became a 'spider's web', according to Sporle, and there was 'palpable hatred' between the council's most senior officials. Most of it was directed at Bill Phillips, who was increasingly viewed as a dishonest creep by several of his colleagues, and particularly by Sporle. An extremely well-placed official within Phillips's office told Sporle and Rodney Brooke, the chief executive, that their phones at City Hall were tapped. Sporle was genuinely shocked. 'What are you talking about?' he asked. His source told him, 'The technology is there now to tap the phones and yours will be one of them.' Both men decided to use outside phones to make important calls. Occasionally Sporle would have to call Aisla Robertson, the Labour planning spokesman, on one of the council's phones. 'Hello, Aisla,' he would say. Then, the joke, 'Are you listening, Bill?'

Throughout 1988 Porter believed Sporle was implementing BSC. By October monitoring reports showed that the situation in the four stress wards had improved vastly, largely thanks to planning permissions. The targets for all four looked likely to be exceeded by 1990. In Cavendish, there would be 295 new voters and in St

James's, which had been lagging behind, there would be 274. In the West End, where the target was also 250, planning permissions would help bring in 307 new voters. Despite the graphs showing how much of the gerrymandering was being achieved by Sporle's department, his officers confirm he placed them under no pressure to skew planning permissions to help BSC.

John Dyke says, 'He wasn't cooking the books because the statistics would no doubt be accurate but they were just the results of the normal free flow of planning decisions; they weren't planning decisions which were bent to achieve an objective and therefore, we in the planning department felt utterly protected by Sid. I think he did an absolutely masterful balancing exercise by apparently collaborating with the initiative, compiling tables and attending meetings and sending memos and producing statistics of residential developments in marginal wards. His fingerprints are all over the till. On the other hand he was soaking up all the stress so none of us in the planning department felt the least bit under pressure or had our arms twisted.'

David Weeks had ordered Sporle to speed up planning applications in the panic to achieve Porter's BSC objectives. Sporle agreed, but even then he was pulling the wool over Porter's eyes, according to one planner: 'One of the allegations was that we were fast-tracking applications. I looked back at what we did before this started and discovered that we dealt with seventeen per cent of planning applications within eight weeks; that rate did not change during this period. It remained at seventeen per cent in eight weeks, and that would not have been the case had there been pressure on us to speed up planning permissions in the marginal wards.'

Sporle insists that he was not gerrymandering: 'I don't believe any planning permissions were granted that were not legitimate. I was taking the job seriously. But I wasn't applying myself to a gerrymandering role and nor was the department. I was the punch bag, that was my sin, but by Christ, the integrity of the planning process at Westminster came out intact. I was just trying to be as skilful as possible, trying to protect the integrity of the planning process.'

Later the District Auditor declared that by August 1987 at the

latest, Sporle was aware of 'BSC targets' and of the electoral purpose of leading members in relation to the increased programme of
designated sales. The Auditor also declared that Sporle was
involved in monitoring of BSC targets. Sporle now regrets that he
did not speak up about what was happening, as the Auditor said
was his responsibility. In his final report on BSC in 2004, the
Auditor wrote: 'There is evidence that part of the secret BSC policy
was to use planning gain for the electoral advantage of the
Conservative Party.' One of Sporle's former senior colleagues says
he also heard the story about his extraordinary double bluff: 'He
said that but I didn't believe him. I like Sid, he's a smashing bloke
and we get on really well personally. But I'm not sure he was that
smart.'

To many people Sid Sporle remains an ambiguous figure in
Porter's gerrymandering plot: he went along with it, and yet he did
not; his double bluff succeeded, and yet it did not. He battled to
keep his integrity and he faced questions about his conduct. He
demonstrated that, despite his best intentions, he could no more
seek an accommodation with Building Stable Communities than
partially lose his virginity. The problem with ambiguity is that it
necessarily cuts both ways.

CHAPTER 17

Two Doctors, Two Cellos (1988)

The *Paddington Times* carried two articles featuring Councillor Michael Dutt, the joint Housing Chairman, on 26 May 1988. The first one was about Mary Montague, who bought her one-bedroom basement flat in Westbourne Gardens, worth £69,000, for just £34,000. It fell to Dutt to present her with a bouquet of flowers as the first person to buy a council home under the unlawful designated sales scheme. In the paper's photo Ms Montague looks pleased but slightly embarrassed; Dutt is a small man in a suit and glasses, and grimaces a sort of smile.

The other article reported a decision by Westminster City Council to designate for sale 126 flats in St John's Wood built specifically as sheltered housing for sick, elderly people. The flats on the Townsend estate near Regent's Park had wheelchair ramps, baths and lavatories for the disabled and handrails. Residents on the estate were outraged that the council could sell them off to first-time buyers looking for a *pied-à-terre* in a smart neighbourhood. Dutt was reported as the man who took the decision, and he defended it. He told the *Paddington Times*, 'There is a demand for home ownership on this particular estate.'

Jo Mahoney, press spokesman for the WAR cemeteries campaign, had given up her job as a singer when her mother, Emma, suffered a stroke at the age of eighty-six. 'I didn't sing a note for six years,' she says. 'I cared for Mum at home and existed on the Invalidity Care Allowance of £32 a week. I also used up an awful lot of my savings.' Emma Mahoney had been classified as a Category A medical patient by Westminster, which usually meant she would have top priority for a suitable council home when one became available. Someone told Jo Mahoney about the Townsend estate and said it would be ideal for her mother. It was also close to her flat in Maida Vale, so she paid a visit.

Mahoney peered through the windows of the flats to see that workmen from Westminster had ripped out the handrails and specially adapted loos. Elsewhere, the wheelchair ramps had been removed. Two flats had already been prepared for sale and lay gutted behind Sitex security doors. Mahoney says, 'They were obviously getting them ready to be flogged off and they appeared to be empty. I was devastated because they would have been ideal for Mum.' What made the decision more remarkable was that Michael Dutt was a practising doctor and by the time he decided to sell off the Townsend estate he was well on the way to qualifying as a consultant geriatrician, specialising in the care of sick, elderly people.

Aside from Shirley Porter and David Weeks, there was no greater BSC warrior than Dr Dutt; he took to the new cult of gerrymandering with alarming fanaticism. He stood out, even in the company he chose, as a determined deporter of the homeless and an obsessive salesman of their homes. He took decisions and supported policies which he knew would deny any chance of suitable housing to 600 chronically ill category A medical patients and hundreds of others with less serious conditions. People later dismissed Porter and Weeks as reckless and foolish, Bill Phillips as dishonest and incompetent, and men such as Graham England as weak and frightened, but the case of Dr Dutt is far more perplexing and unsettling.

Dutt first joined Westminster after the 1986 elections at the age of thirty-six, having stood successfully for the safe Tory ward of Knightsbridge, where he kept a flat in Ennismore Gardens. He was a senior doctor at several London hospitals, including St George's and the Brompton, before moving to St Albans to be near the local hospital where he worked as a geriatrician. Dutt was a mystery to his neighbours, his colleagues and fellow Tory councillors. All remember him as a loner who did not mix socially and, apparently, frequently spent holidays alone in his flat. His mother, Anne, was Swedish and his father, Anup Dutt, an eminent ear nose and throat specialist, originally from Calcutta. Michael Dutt decided early on to specialise in geriatrics, possibly one of the least glamorous of the medical specialities. Other than that, little was known about him. There had once been rumours of a girlfriend and even hopes of marriage, which never materialised. He was a devout Anglican who went few places without a bible. He played the cello but, rather significantly as it turned out, gave it up to concentrate on his new hobby of clay-pigeon shooting. He acquired a shotgun and mounted it in a cabinet. Eventually, when the District Auditor brought him to account for his actions, he would turn the gun on himself.

Porter picked out Dutt early on for advancement. Immediately after the 1986 elections, he was appointed Chairman of the Traffic and Works sub-committee and impressed Porter with a paper on car parking. He became vice-chairman of the Housing Committee in May 1987. Dutt had helped to soften up a reluctant Graham England before the fateful decision of the Housing Committee to go ahead with designated sales in July that year. With the fall of Peter Hartley in February 1988 over the cemeteries débâcle, Dutt became joint-chairman of the Housing Committee, along with his Tory colleague Judith Warner. Some senior officers referred to the pair as the 'Two-headed Hydra'. Within two years of joining the council, Dutt was a member of Porter's secret Chairmen's Group and at the very heart of her conspiracy. From this commanding height, he would exert a malign influence on the communities of Westminster, particularly in the marginal wards.

Graham England, who had regular contact with Dutt, found him exasperating. 'He does not listen,' he once confided to someone. 'He just doesn't want to know. He's a real hard-liner.' Peter Bradley, a Labour councillor, says, 'I think he was a man of deep insecurities who was probably quite bright and his inferiority

© Neville Chadwick photography

The mysterious and ambitious Doctor Dutt, pictured here as
parliamentary candidate with Prime Minister John Major, 1992.

complex made him a willing functionary through which the Tories
implemented their housing policies. They cared nothing for him
personally and probably quietly despised him, and then left him to
his own devices once he had fulfilled his usefulness.' Dutt may have
appeared inexplicable but it was clear that he was driven by political ambition. In the 1992 general election, he would stand
unsuccessfully as a Tory parliamentary candidate in Leicester
South.

During 1988 and 1989 Dutt's preoccupations were deporting
the homeless of Westminster and coping with the ruinously expensive results of cooping up vulnerable people for years at a time in
temporary accommodation. In his paper on 'Homelessness', he had
suggested: 'We should take a definite decision to look outside
Westminster for accommodation for the homeless, and be imaginative: prefabricated homes, mobile homes, houseboats, disused
holiday camps are all possibilities.' As many homeless as possible
should be exported outside Westminster, said Dutt, and 'indeed

outside London'. He urged more and more deportations and investigated other half-baked schemes which would help bring them
about. There were talks with British Rail about leasing properties
in Kent alongside the Channel Tunnel rail route, and research into
siting mobile homes in car parks outside the City. Anywhere but
Westminster.

Dutt agonised over the finer points of gerrymandering. He
thought it might be counterproductive for the council to give lump
sums of £15,000, called 'Assisted Purchase' grants, to council tenants to leave their homes and buy a place elsewhere so it could sell
off their flats to prospective Tory voters. He said that if people
wanted money to buy a property, they might well be just the sort of
people the Tories should keep. 'Where have they gone?' asked Dutt
during one meeting of the BSC Members' Steering Group. He said
'APs' might be 'the right stuff'.

Dutt oversaw the sale of 532 council homes in the two years
after designated sales were agreed; that alone meant a loss to the
ratepayers of around £15.4 million. Other huge costs accrued from
housing the homeless in temporary accommodation, losing local
taxpayers more than £4 million a year. By late 1988 the extra costs
were becoming so prohibitive that they had actually started to
impinge on the critical issue of the day: Westminster's ability to set
a low Poll Tax, a new form of local taxation officially described as
the Community Charge, to be introduced in April 1989. In August
1988 Barry Legg pointed out that 'the cost of homelessness would
take up to eight per cent of the Community Charge [poll tax]'. In
October Dutt was told that the 'escalating cost . . . must be dealt
with by 1990.' Porter was spending £10,500 on temporary two-
bedroom accommodation and £11,500 on three-bedroom
accommodation for homeless families a year, when council houses
cost little to provide.

The District Auditor would later calculate the loss of rent as a
result of keeping flats empty prior to sale at £7.72 million. By early
1989 it was clear that the council was also breaking the law on its
duties both to the homeless and the category A medical patients.
Dutt was not just trading in human misery, he was presiding over a
catastrophe for the council, and ultimately his own self-destruction.

The activities of Dutt and his Westminster City Council colleagues could not escape the attention of another doctor, a general
practitioner in the marginal ward of Bayswater called Richard
Stone. The two men never met, but Dr Stone would play a key role
in exposing his medical colleague operating in the shadows at City
Hall. The two men could not have been more different but they
had two things in common apart from their chosen profession: the
fathers of both had also been doctors and they both played the
cello. In fact Stone met his wife, Ruth, a talented musician, while
playing in the same quartet.

Stone came from the remarkable Silverstone family, who short-
ened their name to Stone. His father was Dr Joe Stone, married to
Beryl. Dr Joe, as everyone called him, was the personal physician to
Harold Wilson and six other cabinet members. He became Sir Joe
and later Lord Stone of Hendon. Joe's brother was Arnold
Silverstone, a property developer who made a fortune redeveloping
Victoria Street, opposite City Hall. He chose to remain as
Silverstone, before becoming Sir Arnold Silverstone, and later Lord
Ashdown of Chelwood. Both brothers ended up in the House of
Lords, on opposite benches. Arnold served as Tory Party Treasurer
under Edward Heath. He was married to Lillian, who also became
a senior Tory official and the first woman member of the Carlton
Club. She had been the one who had rejected Shirley Porter as a
possible parliamentary candidate in the late 1950s.

After leaving Oxford with a law degree, Richard Stone retrained
as a doctor. He built up a small practice in a house opposite the
Greek Orthodox cathedral in Westbourne Grove before moving to
Garway Road in Bayswater. He and Ruth had three children. Dr
Stone was a familiar and comforting sight around Bayswater. A
small man with a beard and pebble glasses, he could be seen cycling
through the council estates on his rounds to deal with heart conditions and bunions, or dashing up the stairs of tower blocks in his
bicycle clips, stopping off for some quick gossip or to dispense
friendly but stern lectures on the perils of smoking. He was an
effervescent and emotional man, passionate about his patients and
his community. In the early 1980s he became concerned at the
rising tide of homeless people in the City and the conditions they

were forced to endure in the grotty bed-and-breakfasts in Bayswater, so he became involved in a charity to help them.

In early 1988 Stone noticed the Sitex doors going up in the area. He did not know Bayswater was a marginal ward but he did know the effect it was having on his patients. He says, 'I thought, that's puzzling. When you're a GP, you're so busy dealing with heart attacks and so on, and you tend sometimes not to notice things. I went about my business and I saw there were grilles on the windows as well. I noticed it on the Hallfield estate because it was the nearest. Then it got to the point when there were two steel doors on the same landing and I began to see more and more of them around, even on some of the nice crescents, and I thought, I don't know what this is about.'

Stone was particularly anxious about one of his patients, a former wartime aircraft gunner with a serious heart condition, who lived on the top floor of a house in St Stephen's Gardens. He was classified as a category A patient, so he was supposed to stand a better chance of being moved by the council to accommodation that suited his needs. Stone says, 'He could walk downstairs to go shopping but he couldn't walk upstairs. I remember going to visit him once and I found him on one of those half-landings. He was puffing so hard that he was in danger of heart failure. His life was intolerable. I took his shopping in for him sometimes. He would telephone me and I would say, "Look, I'll come and visit you on my routine rounds this afternoon, what can I get for you?" If I hadn't done it, who else would have? Nobody, because Westminster City Council had taken away his home help.' Stone also saw the impact on people in temporary accommodation who were being denied homes as a result of designated sales. 'I could see people suffering as a result,' he says. 'These bed-and-breakfast hotels constitute the most health-damaging environment I've ever seen in my life. It's disgraceful and it's immensely damaging to family life.'

Stone rang the local council housing office and asked what was going on. An official cheerfully told him the homes with the security doors were part of Westminster's new policy of designated sales. Stone then wrote to the *Paddington Mercury*: 'The whole policy of using bed and breakfasts, instead of building homes, is an appalling waste of money. A new home costs £7,000 a year when part of a new estate or block. The cost of keeping the family in a nasty inadequate hotel is £15,000 for every year of the three or four years families are now wasting away there.' Stone realised that the council was losing rent and rates by keeping homes empty and contacted Neale Coleman to ask what could be done. Coleman said he should get in touch with the District Auditor, but it would be effective to complain only when the council's books were up for inspection. 'I didn't want to wait that long,' says Stone, 'because it was wrong, utterly wrong.'

Dr Stone sent a letter to the District Auditor, John Magill, claiming that the designated sales policy was unlawful, demanding action against the councillors and officers responsible. For months he heard nothing and then, in late 1988, he received a summons from the Auditor requesting his attendance at City Hall. The interview took place at a huge desk on the sixteenth floor. On one side sat Magill and his legal adviser, Tony Child, the solicitor to the Audit Commission, which oversees Auditors' inquiries; on the other, a nervous Stone flanked by two Labour councillors, Neale Coleman and Gavin Millar. Stone says, 'I felt just like the little boy in that famous painting "When did you last see your father?" My mouth was dry, my heart was pumping and I felt really nervous because above all, those people on the other side of the desk would find out that I didn't know much about these things.'

John Magill asked Stone what he knew. The GP spoke about the patients who were denied housing they needed and of the homeless in bed-and-breakfasts. He had done his own calculations and claimed the policy must be losing the council at least £5–£6 million a year, a huge underestimate as things turned out. Stone adds, 'At the end, Mr Magill asked me if I had any questions. I said, "Yes, what happens now?"' Magill promised to send him Section 15.2 of the 1982 Local Government Act, which spelt out the powers of the District Auditor. 'He was concerned about his patients,' says Magill. 'He wasn't saying this policy had the ulterior motive of altering the electorate, simply that this was a dreadful way to run a council.' Magill made inquiries but it would be another five years before he finally produced his devastating verdict on the Porter scandal.

Shortly after his interview, Richard Stone attended a reception at the House of Commons held by his mother Beryl, Lady Stone, for the All-Party Parliamentary Wives for Soviet Jewry, which campaigned on behalf of Jews suffering persecution, a cause dear to Porter's heart. Stone had recently been to Tel Aviv University to which both the Stones and the Porters gave money. At the reception Stone spotted a solitary Porter standing by the window, gazing silently across the Thames. The doctor approached the Leader of Westminster City Council: 'Hello, Shirley Porter, I'm Dr Richard Stone. I'm actually one of your constituents and I have been in Israel and I was at Tel Aviv University, and Yossi Carmel [university fundraiser] sends his kind regards to you.'

There had been no publicity surrounding Stone's interview with John Magill, but Magill had already written to the council about Stone's concerns and few things happened in City Hall without Porter's knowledge. 'Oh yes, Dr Stone,' said Porter almost absent-mindedly, 'I must go and get another glass of sherry.' With that, Porter turned her back on Stone and walked away.

CHAPTER 18

'The Dirt Squad'
(1988–early 1989)

To all intents and purposes, by the autumn of 1988 Westminster City Council was a municipal gangster state. Porter was convinced that secrecy and fear would not provide enough of a smokescreen either to hide the plot or to ensure victory in 1990. She knew what she needed to protect her conspiracy from exposure and Westminster from falling to Labour: dirty tricks. Porter decided to gather intelligence about her political enemies, for use against them whenever possible, and to deploy Tory activists in the key wards to undermine both them and her opponents within her own political party. She had already forced an informal and shadowy structure on the council and she believed that the only way to win the election was to do the same with the Conservative Party in Westminster.

The City of Westminster was made up of twenty-three council wards and two parliamentary constituencies occupying the north and the south: North Westminster and the Cities of Westminster and London, which also took in the few thousand residents of the neighbouring City of London Corporation. The two constituencies were roughly bisected by the Bayswater Road and Oxford Street, with north and south lying either side. In North Westminster Porter was extremely influential: it was her party power base and her

Hyde Park seat was there. According to a former senior Tory councillor, 'The party in North Westminster was her private domain. Even the local MP, John Wheeler, towed the line.'

The south was a different matter. There, many Tories, including councillors at Westminster and voluntary local party activists, had come to despise Porter and her cabal. Those who knew about the gerrymandering either recoiled from the idea or gritted their teeth. The last coup attempt against Porter had been mounted in late autumn 1987 from the south by Anthony Prendergast, who represented Knightsbridge.

Many party activists and councillors in the south found Porter's paranoia about Labour taking City Hall in 1990 excessive. 'I must say,' says one former Tory councillor from South Westminster, 'one did get rather fed up with the constant drum roll of "we must do this or that or we will lose Westminster." It would have been regrettable to lose Westminster but I didn't think there was much of a chance of that happening and frankly, in the grand sweep of history, it would hardly have been the end of the world if we had.'

Porter thought the party's complacency and sloppy organisation in 1986 had nearly cost her control of Westminster. She no longer trusted its officials and local activists to get their act together for the local elections in 1990. Half of the eight marginals – the West End, St James's, Victoria and Millbank – were in the south and local party members had to toe the BSC line if there was to be any chance of winning them. The gerrymandering would help, but there also had to be a professional fighting force of committed Tories in the marginal wards in the run-up to the polls. Porter concluded that victory could be guaranteed by fighting dirty, and if the local party activists were not up to it, then she had to bring in people who were.

In the spring of 1988 Shirley Porter set out her 1990 elections plans in her 'Keeping Westminster Conservative' paper which she presented to both north and south party associations. 'Imagine,' she wrote, 'socialists running Buckingham Palace, militants lording it over Parliament and controlling Downing Street, left-wing extremists interfering in the daily running of business, a horrible nightmare.' She added: 'There is only one solution to winning the local elections in 1990 and that is for a programme of political grassroots action to begin in the eight key battle zone wards as soon as possible. This can only be achieved by employing five paid political activists to work in the eight key wards, improving propaganda, making use of new technology, utilising political intelligence and managerial know how.' She calculated the cost of hiring the activists at £140,000 over the two years leading to the 1990 elections. Senior party officials received their copies courteously, and those who were conscientious enough to bother reading it properly were horrified.

Porter said the activists should build up a campaign team in each of the eight marginal wards and ensure likely Tory voters were put on to the electoral register, which was perfectly legitimate. However, she also demanded underhand political tactics: 'to cultivate good relations with residents associations both in public sector housing and private blocks of flats in each key ward. If necessary, infiltrate those which are hostile to Conservative initiatives. To monitor closely what the Labour Party is doing in each key ward and report back. To find out about the background of Labour councillors, candidates and activists for "skeletons in the cupboard" which can be publicly exposed.' She thought she could afford to antagonise the Labour Party, and even place intolerable pressure on council officials, but by suggesting members of her own party use dirty tricks she had chosen a particularly dangerous course of action.

Many of the Tories in the south still held fond memories of the old City of Westminster. Porter's leadership had transferred the City's political power from south to north. For many from the old City, the forced merger in 1965 with Paddington and Marylebone had been a mistake, embroiling them in the long-running battle between their counterparts on the other side of the Bayswater Road and the Labour strongholds in the north. They had not wanted too many details about the gerrymandering, but they disliked being asked to approve expensive dirty tricks which would undermine their more traditional election campaign methods. A former party worker in the old City says, 'The furthest we ever got to using underhand methods was during an election campaign when we would look after someone's children or helped prepare supper so they could leave the house and vote.'

During the course of 1988 Porter was repeatedly warned about her plans by senior Tory Party figures in the south. In late spring Anthony Prendergast gave a television interview for the *London Programme*, a documentary series, which had investigated the cemeteries débâcle, and made censorious criticisms of the Porter regime. Barry Legg was so angry that he withdrew a dinner invitation to Prendergast, and Porter demanded the attendance in City Hall of Prendergast's wife, Dame Simone.

Dame Simone Prendergast was one of the most respected figures in the Tory Party. She had been chairman of the London Conservatives and sometimes lent the Prime Minister her tasteful apartment in Warwick Square, SW1 for party political broadcasts. She was a Marks and Spencer heiress and Porter was a Tesco heiress, but the two women were like chalk and cheese, with markedly different views on ethics and politics. Their clash revealed much about Porter's approach and attitude to Westminster over the years. Porter clearly saw the council as an ersatz activity to compensate for her failure to secure her rightful inheritance, a seat on the Tesco board. She had conned herself into believing that BSC imposed corporate thinking on the City Council and she had pretensions to bring the same muddled thinking to the running of the Conservative Party in Westminster, which had always relied on the goodwill and free time of local members. 'Keeping Westminster Conservative' was as much an abnegation of the Tory Party ethos as BSC was of local government.

Dame Simone found Porter's aggression perturbing. A gentle and discreet woman, she felt Porter was almost lunging at her across the table 'like a lion'; she was not intimidated, she just did not like it. The meeting was held at Porter's request but there could have been few more suitable candidates to stand up to Porter than Dame Simone Prendergast. Porter opened the discussion by asking her, 'Why has Tony spoken out against me?' Dame Simone answered, 'Because he believes you did the wrong thing and he is entitled to his view.' The conversation turned to Porter's plans for 'Keeping Westminster Conservative'. Porter told Dame Simone that the Tory

Party in Westminster was not 'professional or efficient enough', and that it 'should be run like Tesco or Marks and Spencer'. Dame Simone reminded Porter that many Tory Party workers were well-meaning people who contributed by handing out leaflets and making chocolate fudge for jolly fundraising events. 'I know it's not efficient,' she told Porter, 'but you have to work with that and you know it's the hearts of people that matter. They are just people who want to be good Conservatives and help the Conservative government.' For the next hour and a half, the two women argued. Finally Dame Simone ended the interview. 'There's no point continuing this conversation. You have your way and I have mine.' She concluded that Porter simply did not understand how the Conservative Party worked, and that, perhaps more disconcertingly, she lacked 'humanity'.

Donald Stewart, Peter Brooke's agent, wrote tactfully to Porter on 6 June 1988: 'We share entirely your central aim, which is the successful conclusion of the 1990 City elections, but there are certain qualifications in the way in which we feel this can be done.' As the salaried agent of the local party, he did not like Porter's demand to bring outside activists into his constituency; he told her that any personnel employed to help the party in the south had to come under the control of the South Westminster constituency, adding, 'no matter from which source their remuneration is drawn'. Porter simply ignored the directive and vowed she would persuade the Conservatives to fire Stewart for his impertinence. She was determined to annex the party in the south.

Porter's 'strike force' of activists was recruited by her old friend Michael Ivens, who had proved crucial in her war against Ken Livingstone. In 1987 a company was created by a group of hard-right young Tories called Marketforce Communications Ltd, or MCL. Two directors, Mark MacGregor and David Saunders, had been chairman and vice-chairman of the highly controversial Federation of Conservative Students (FSC). Members of the FCS had been blamed for a nasty raid on the women's peace camp in Greenham Common, and there had been a drunken party at Loughborough University in 1985 at which frenzied young members of the FCS had rampaged through dormitories breaking down doors with fire extinguishers and shouting 'Kill the Wets'. Two of them had fought over a girl and in the resulting fracas the gutted carcass of her pet rabbit was nailed to a door. Another member's beanbag was set alight by arsonists. There were also rumours of a philosophical debate about Thatcherism in a Berlin bar, concluding in a serious assault on a German student. By 1987 the then Tory Party Chairman, Norman Tebbit, had wearied of such high jinks and forced the FCS to close by cutting its funds and shutting down its headquarters.

On the other hand, the former FCS leadership provided ideal material for Porter and Ivens. They were bright, committed and right wing – just the ticket to give the Westminster Tories the encouragement they needed to take on Labour. Initially, Marketforce Communications Ltd moved next door to Michael Ivens's office in Doughty Street, London, the base for his think-tank, the Foundation of Business Responsibilities, which he had technically classified as a charity for tax purposes. The law decrees that charities cannot raise money for political causes, but Ivens set up a secret slush fund which channelled £98,896 to Marketforce over a two-year period to help in Porter's fight to keep Westminster.

Money was raised by the Federation of Business Responsibilities mainly from concerned right-wing businessmen. Ivens then paid it to MCL through a company called Lifeasset Ltd. The contributors included the John Porter Foundation, another charity under the control of Porter's family. Fundraising events were organised through an organisation called 'the Friends of the City of Westminster', established to help Porter's campaign. One cocktail party was held at the House of Commons on 24 November 1988. Andrew Greystoke, a Tory councillor and close associate of Porter, selected potential donors, then told them that he had given their names to Lady Porter and that they would be receiving an invitation to a House of Commons cocktail party; he hoped that they would be willing to help preserve the Conservatives' majority on the council.

The slush fund broke the rules regulating charity status and the Charity Commission later declared that payments to MCL should not have been made by a charity. Ivens was later forced to pay back the money and resign from the FBR. The Charity Commission would hold two inquiries into the affair, but by then MCL, Ivens and Porter had done their worst. One former Tory councillor described it as 'subversion of democracy'. In the eyes of the Tory volunteers, particularly in the south, Porter had subverted the party as she had the council.

Meanwhile, Labour councillors were on the verge of uncovering the gerrymandering plot. A single piece of paper which showed that the housing department was 'monitoring' the sale of council homes in 'key wards' had been leaked to Neale Coleman. Paul Dimoldenberg, the Labour group leader, immediately informed the District Auditor, John Magill, who thought it was too little to act on. 'You need something more than a hint of something to go on,' says Magill. 'One has to remember that there was a climate at the time where the two main parties did not appear to have any civilised communication whatsoever. The climate was poisonous and I was getting letters from both sides; I was trying to figure out whether I was being used as a pawn in a game. Clearly, with the benefit of hindsight, a number of these documents were part of a big picture. But at the time, there was no way of knowing.'

Between March 1988 and April the following year, Paul Dimoldenberg wrote to Bill Phillips on no fewer than ten occasions to demand the truth. Porter's managing director replied on eight occasions, but his answers were later described by the High Court as 'deliberately misleading' and by the District Auditor as 'symptomatic of his dishonest approach'. The correspondence became progressively difficult. From the first, Dimoldenberg did not pull his punches: 'I have no idea why officers should have selected these wards and why they should be classified as "key". The only explanation I can think of is that the wards have been selected by Members of the Majority Party and that they are "key" because they are considered to be "marginal" by Members of the Majority Party.' He added: 'I insist on a full explanation of what is going on. I hold you completely responsible for disgraceful abuses which are clearly taking place . . .' In his response, Phillips, whose covert tasks included 'opposition handling', displayed his knowledge of the law governing the conduct of local government officers: 'I must make it absolutely clear that it would be unacceptable for any officer to discharge his or her duties in a way which favoured a political party. We are professional officers who take our professional responsibilities seriously. Those responsibilities include serving the council as a whole.'

Dimoldenberg and his colleagues concluded rightly that Phillips was not telling the truth, and the Labour leader felt confident enough to take the unprecedented step of accusing a council officer of lying: 'I think, also, that you and Mr England owe my colleagues and me a public apology for the clear untruth which is contained in the final two sentences of the third paragraph of your letter . . . In addition, I want to know what other policies are being monitored on a "key ward" basis. I suspect that officers in the Leisure and Planning Departments are also collecting figures on a similar basis. Please do not give me more "assurances", just give me facts.'

Within weeks of Dimoldenberg's discovery, Porter sent out the instruction to stop him or, in her own terms: 'Neutralise Dim'berg . . .' Porter did not only try to get at Dimoldenberg, she also attempted to smear other Labour councillors. She even tried to persuade the City Treasurer, David Hopkins, to hand over the personal local tax records of the Labour councillor Gavin Millar. Hopkins refused.

Peter Bradley had also been asking questions about 'key wards'. His persistence eventually came to the attention of Matthew Ives, the City Solicitor, whom Porter had carefully distanced from the conspiracy. In August 1988 an increasingly suspicious Ives demanded answers from Graham England, the Housing Director: 'The questions which I consider the Director of Housing should respond to are: Why were these eight wards chosen? By whom were these eight wards chosen? Why and by whom are these eight wards regarded as key?' These three pertinent questions were not answered honestly for another decade.

Relations between Labour and Tory councillors at Westminster were already sulphurous, but now Dimoldenberg and Bradley had entered personally dangerous territory. Not only were they fellow Labour councillors at Westminster, they both worked together as

public relations officers for Good Relations. Porter concluded that
if both men were fired from their jobs, they might be less preoccupied with her policies and more concerned about how they were
going to pay their mortgages. In her desperation she turned to her
oldest enemy, Patricia Kirwan.

Kirwan had worked as a press officer and knew Gethin Bradley,
one of the original directors of Good Relations. Porter steeled herself for a short audience with a baffled Kirwan. 'Right, you go and
tell them that we're not having his staff using his office rubbishing
me,' Porter told Kirwan. 'Shirley was absolutely spitting mad,'
remembers Kirwan. 'She wanted Gethin Bradley to sack Bradley
and Dimoldenberg because they were using his office to run a
public political campaign against Shirley.' Kirwan gossiped about
the episode with Rodney Brooke, who warned Dimoldenberg that
Porter was trying to destroy his career and would not give up until
she succeeded.

The London listings magazine *Time Out* was the first publication to allege that Porter was gerrymandering. In an article headed
'London Scandals', the magazine's correspondent Sarah Baxter
wrote on 3 October 1988: 'A new political storm is brewing at
Westminster following allegations that the ruling Conservative
group is channelling council resources into marginal wards, in a
bid to secure a safe return to power at the next local elections.
Housing department records obtained by the Labour opposition
suggest that Westminster's flagship policy of "Building Stable
Communities" by selling off council homes is being separately
monitored in eight "key wards", where the Tory vote is vulnerable.
In the 1986 local elections, Labour came close to snatching control
of the traditionally safe Conservative Council.'

It can be no coincidence that Shirley Porter wrote to Rodney
Brooke the day after the article appeared, enclosing a letter from a
local resident alleging that Dimoldenberg and Bradley were guilty
of using their status as councillors to get work for Good Relations.
'I have today received the attached letter from a concerned resident.
As you will see, it makes disturbing reading, raising as it does
important questions about the role of Councillors Dimoldenberg
and Bradley within the City Council. Should I order a thorough

inquiry? Has Councillor Dimoldenberg ever formally reported to the Authority that he is touting for business using the fact that he is the Opposition Leader of the City Council? Do you think I should contact the Fraud Squad? Serious issues are at stake. Who knows, perhaps Councillor Dimoldenberg has been involved in numerous planning matters that have been dealt with by the Council in the last couple of years. I am very worried about this. It would not help the good name of the City if we had a major corruption case on our hands.' Porter had no evidence to support the untrue allegations but on the strength of the letter ordered Rodney Brooke to hold an inquiry into the two Labour councillors.

The letter from the 'concerned resident' was a concoction, however, and Brooke saw right through it. He replied the following day: 'There is no evidence from the papers sent to me that either Councillor Dimoldenberg or Councillor Bradley has misused his Membership of the Council. A list of authorities in which Good Relations is said to have worked does not include the City of Westminster. There is no offence in stating that a person is a councillor as part of his curriculum vitae.'

Porter was infuriated by Brooke's refusal to back her. The relationship between her and her chief executive was already damaged beyond repair and heading towards meltdown so she had little hesitation in overriding him. At her behest, a week after his refusal, the Tory-controlled Policy and Resources Committee instructed Brooke to conduct 'an inquiry' into Porter's bogus allegations against Dimoldenberg and Bradley; she hoped that they would be damaged merely by publicising the fact that they were 'under investigation' and that they would stop asking questions about BSC. But the councillors did not stop asking questions, and for Brooke the episode was simply one more humiliation to endure.

While Brooke wearily looked into Porter's smear, other investigators were reaching their judgments over the sale of the cemeteries. On 4 November the District Auditor, John Magill, issued his interim report on the matter: 'In arriving at decisions, relevant factors were inadequately considered or not considered at all, and there were major weaknesses and errors in the implementation of those decisions.' Councillors forced officers to sell the cemeteries but Magill criticised 'the reluctance of officers to report what appeared to them to be facts which would be unpalatable to members'. He announced that public hearings would be held into the affair in the summer of 1989. Shortly afterwards, Dr David Yardley, the Local Government Ombudsman, found the City Council guilty of maladministration over the cemeteries sale. His report referred to 'a climate of fear' at City Hall and 'a great mistrust' between officers and council members.

The Tories' growing alarm at Porter's policies started to emerge in the press. On 7 November 1988 *The Times* reported that 'Senior Conservatives, including Mr Peter Brooke, the Party's Chairman, are to consider this week whether or not to intervene in the affairs of Tory-controlled Westminster City Council.' There was no intervention, but Tories leaked information about Porter anonymously. One told *The Times*, 'Lady Porter has the ability to turn even a minor problem into a national embarrassment.' Another said to the same newspaper, 'There is a feeling that Lady Porter is personally responsible for a lot of the mud flung at us.'

Porter had become recklessly self-sufficient. She had convinced herself that she was well on target to meet her gerrymandering objectives, but by the end of 1988 she was in grave trouble. Tens of millions of pounds had been squandered on unlawful policies and the council was breaking its legal obligations to sick and homeless people. She had antagonised senior council officers and senior members of her own party. Dirty tricks and paranoia had merged with institutionalised stupidity to create an atmosphere at City Hall in which anything was possible. Porter's downfall appeared inevitable and imminent, but there would be one more stop on the way. As the City Council spun ever faster out of control, it would start to take risks with people's lives.

CHAPTER 19

Two Towers (December 1988–February 1989)

On Saturday, 14 January 1989 City Council engineers discovered damaged ceiling tiles in the Kingsway underpass under the Strand. On further inspection, they spotted exposed asbestos and immediately closed the tunnel. Later, a council report commended the action taken to safeguard the safety of motorists: 'All emergency services were advised and arrangements put in hand to seal and secure the tunnel in order to safeguard the public and prevent unauthorised access.' Sid Sporle, whose duties included maintaining roads in Westminster, says, 'Chunks of asbestos were falling off and hitting cars. We knew we had to do something about it.' Laboratory tests showed the levels of asbestos fibres in the tunnel to be 'insignificant'. 'Nevertheless,' a further council report said, 'contamination would be likely to become worse if vehicles were permitted to continue to use the Underpass.' The tunnel was closed for two years while work was carried out to make it safe. The total cost was £5,322,000.

The underpass was in public view and the council's quick action commendable. However, when seeking a political advantage out of sight of the public eye, Shirley Porter displayed a terrible hypocrisy. In February, one month after the underpass was closed, she placed 122 homeless families into two tower blocks which she knew were riddled with asbestos and which one of her own officers once described as having the 'greatest potential for asbestos release within residential accommodation in Britain'.

Over the years, people have made all sorts of excuses for the actions of Shirley Porter, either through their happy ignorance of the facts and the law or their misapplication of both. People have said that she was the victim of a 'witch-hunt'; the homeless were deported to 'save money'; council property was sold to 'extend home ownership', and even if it was gerrymandering, it was simply pay-back time for Herbert Morrison; and even the sale of the cemeteries was 'good in principle' but poorly executed by incompetent officers. But no one has stepped forward to defend her decision to expose homeless young parents and their babies to the risk of lung cancer or mesothelioma as a tactic in a nasty political war.

The GLC finished building two tower blocks called Hermes Point and Chantry Point on a site off Elgin Avenue in North Paddington in 1968. At the time of their construction, the two towers were heralded as a groundbreaking experiment in residential accommodation, symbols of a New Britain which Harold Wilson described as being forged in the 'white heat of technology'. They were essentially built from kits: the component parts were made off-site and assembled by the GLC at the Elgin estate. What made the towers special was that each was constructed around a steel frame, a first for residential construction. Another innovation was the use of fibreglass panels to clad the buildings. The two completed towers loomed imperiously over North Paddington, glinting in their silvery fibreglass finery, twenty-two storeys high and containing 101 flats.

Serious technical problems emerged even before the builders packed up their tools and left the site. The window seals failed and the rain came into the flats; in some cases, the windows fell out of the frames altogether. These problems were dwarfed, however, by the worst design fault of all. To protect the towers' steel skeletons from fire, the architects had made extensive use of the retardant of choice at the time: asbestos. Approximately ten miles of the most dangerous type of the material, sprayed amosite asbestos, had been

© Philip Wolmuth

Hermes Point and Chantry Point, forged in the white heat of
technology and old before their time.

applied to each of the steel skeletons. But the workmen had neither
glued the asbestos on to the steel girders nor sealed it in afterwards
and there was nothing to prevent fibres detaching themselves as the
asbestos crumbled over the years. The heating system worked by
circulating hot air around the building through the duct work.
Because the panels designed to box in the steel frame were not air-
tight, asbestos fibres were carried into people's flats. In 1969, a
year after the towers were completed, such widespread use of
asbestos was banned. When Porter became Leader in April 1983,
asbestos had been discovered in homes across the City and there
was a full-scale scare. Shipyard workers and other industrial workers who endured long-term exposure to asbestos were dying from
lung diseases such as cancer, asbestosis and mesothelioma, which
have an incubation period of up to forty years.

In 1980 the Conservatives, in control of the GLC before Ken
Livingstone's takeover, divested themselves of their responsibilities
as landlords. They handed over entire estates to boroughs such as
Westminster, with the understanding that County Hall would be

responsible for major repairs and structural works but that the borough councils would be the actual landlords, collecting the rents, evicting the defaulters and undertaking minor repairs and works.

The two towers were included in the pact between the Tories at the GLC and Westminster, although neither side took into account the widespread use of asbestos and both seem to have forgotten all about it. A cursory glance at the architect's plans would have told them all they needed to know. Indeed, it came as a shock to Westminster when GLC workmen 'discovered' the asbestos in June 1981, but it was not until January 1983 that the full extent of its use became obvious to council workmen replacing the lifts.

On 10 February 1983 officials from Westminster's department of environmental health reported on the wide extent of the 'potentially hazardous' sprayed asbestos in the towers, necessitating its removal 'as a matter of urgency'. Exactly a month later there was a meeting between officials from the GLC and Westminster, including Charles Guy, the City's Housing Director and Graham England, his future successor. The officers discussed evacuating the tenants because of the 'loose asbestos apparently at large in the common parts which could present a health hazard to the tenants'. The council was already investigating the sums of money involved in removing asbestos from another estate in Lisson Green, and the City Architect 'was detailed to investigate the costs of removal' of asbestos from Hermes and Chantry.

These costs, as well as those which would be incurred in rehousing the evacuees, would be high. Shirley Porter became Leader a month after the meeting and during the next six years of her leadership she did little to solve the towers' problem. In late 1983, with the asbestos scare at its height and council tenants in the blocks and elsewhere across the City clamouring for action, the government advised all local councils about how to deal with the problem. The Department of the Environment issued circular 21/83, which made stark reading for local politicians like Porter having to cope with sprayed asbestos: 'It is . . . likely to release fibres especially if disturbed during repair and maintenance work. As it ages, sprayed asbestos may release more fibres and asbestos dust may accumulate in adjacent areas.' The circular recommended the regular inspection of sprayed asbestos, and added: 'if there is evidence of dust release it should be effectively sealed, enclosed or removed.' Residents and maintenance workers had to be 'made aware of the location of any asbestos materials and advised of appropriate precautions'. 'There is no known safe level for exposure to asbestos,' stated the circular, adding, 'the susceptibility to cancer may be increased in the very young', and ' In cases where there is potential daily twenty-four hours exposure, as in homes, or where children may be exposed, particular effort should be made to ensure that levels are as low as possible.'

According to Rodney Brooke, Porter was not happy about the advice, because of the potential costs. He says, 'She had just picked up the government guidance which officers were telling her meant that a number of multi-storey flats owned by the council had to be evacuated. There would be a substantial loss of income and she was very resentful of that and quizzed me a lot about it.' Brooke had little experience of housing before arriving at Westminster but he thought the council had few options: 'When I got into the job I found out that given the government guidance, there was no option but to evacuate the tenants from Hermes and Chantry as quickly as you reasonably could. It would take a few years for the asbestos to be removed. Asbestos can be all right if you don't poke about with it, but there's every reason that tenants would quite innocently while drilling holes in the wall and activities of that sort.'

For years, Brooke and Porter argued about the future of the blocks, and it was an important factor in their deteriorating relationship. The situation on the ground was also hindered by the souring of relations between officials from Westminster and the GLC at a time when cooperation between the two authorities responsible for the asbestos was crucial. The impact of the Ken and Shirley conflict filtered down the ranks at City Hall. On 2 September 1983 a GLC officer wrote to Westminster: 'it cannot be denied that . . . efforts to resolve the problems attaching to the discovery of asbestos have been totally frustrated by the City Council over a period of many months . . . This, I think you will agree is hardly conducive to the creation of a concerted strategy which is vital if we are to reassure the tenants that there is total accord between our two authorities as to how to proceed with the removal of the asbestos.' An official inquiry reported years later: 'The party political strife must have been a powerful influence on the officers, and institutionally it must have affected the relationships between the two local authorities with their different party controls.'

From 1984 onwards, Westminster did not relet newly vacant flats in the tower blocks to homeless people because of the asbestos risk, but it did choose to rent out some of the apartments on a short-term basis mainly to young people who liked them because they were cheap and close to central London. Eighty-seven flats were let to the so-called 'short lifers', who swiftly formed a strong community and knew enough about the asbestos to minimise the risks. Meanwhile, the GLC tried to tackle the crisis. On two separate occasions over the two-year period leading up to its abolition, the GLC applied to the Tory government for funds needed to carry out important schemes to deal with the problem. But on each occasion, the government rejected the GLC's application.

The expense involved in removing asbestos was the predominant factor in Patricia Kirwan's repeated efforts to privatise the two towers and the adjoining Walterton estate. Opposed by the WEAG, Kirwan's plans were almost rejected by Shirley Porter for totally different reasons. By the spring of 1987, when Kirwan put forward her new project for the estates, Porter was already planning to deport homeless people from Westminster as the first phase of her gerrymandering strategy. She also intended to decant them from the marginal wards into council property in Labour strongholds, where their votes would make no difference. She saw the two towers, situated in the safe Labour ward of Harrow Road, as a valuable dumping ground for up to 120 homeless families, despite knowing that the buildings were riddled with asbestos. Porter concluded that Kirwan's scheme contradicted the overriding objective of BSC and resolved to kill it off.

Kirwan's proposals were to be debated at the meeting of the Housing Committee on 1 April 1987. Porter, already in combat with Kirwan for the leadership, ordered her to withdraw the plan from the committee agenda. The Housing Chairman refused. On 30 March, two days before the committee, the women met. 'This was quite a vivid meeting,' Bill Phillips said later, 'because the principal protagonists, the Leader and Councillor Kirwan, were at each other's throats in a very personal way.' At the outset of this bad-tempered encounter, Porter made clear her antipathy towards Kirwan's scheme and accused her of stirring up the WEAG rebellion in the north. 'What on earth have you got us into?' she said. Kirwan told Porter that she could not put homeless families into the towers because, as everyone knew, they were filled with asbestos. She also argued that since the abolition of the GLC, the huge costs involved in removing the asbestos from the towers would fall to Westminster alone. The government had imposed tight spending restrictions on housing repairs and was never likely to allow Westminster enough money for the job; handing over the estates to property developers who would carry out the work as part of a redevelopment was the only course of action.

Kirwan says, 'The reason I had been told to pull this off the agenda was because it was going to affect the key wards. It seemed to me more important that the people in the Walterton Road area should live in decent conditions than some attempt to play political games in the eight marginal wards.' She thought the whole idea of pulling the scheme because it conflicted with the gerrymandering was 'exceedingly cynical and completely wrong'.

The asbestos issue itself forced Porter to allow Kirwan's plans to go to the Housing Committee for approval. Kirwan recorded their agreement in a note: 'Flats in Hermes and Chantry Points are not suitable for decanting from . . . key wards because they are riddled with asbestos and many of the flats are being kept empty.' In fact, wrote Kirwan, 'the Council could be criticised for having delayed so long [in dealing with the asbestos].' A further note of the meeting was made by Graham England in his filofax: 'No good for decant on present form from key wards' and 'Not relet because of asbestos.' According to the secret minutes of the meeting, Kirwan and England reassured Porter that the loss of the two towers for BSC 'would have no effect on the Council's strategic objectives before 1990'. In other words, it would not affect the gerrymandering. Six weeks later Kirwan failed to replace Porter as Leader and was herself deposed as Housing Chairman.

The decision by the Housing Committee to approve Kirwan's scheme was followed by intense warfare between the WEAG campaigners on one side, and the City Council and the developers on the other. The City Council told the residents that privatisation of the estates was the only way to pay for the necessary removal of the asbestos. In a leaflet to residents issued in April 1987, Patricia Kirwan said: 'Tenants in the Walterton area and from the asbestos-ridden Hermes and Chantry tower blocks will, at last, be living in homes worth calling home.' In a subsequent application to the Department of the Environment for approval of the works required under Kirwan's scheme, Westminster City Council proposed that 'Asbestos removal from Chantry Point, together with improvements to insulation, installation of off-peak heating, door entry systems and replacement of lifts, will all contribute to safer living conditions.' The estimated costs of the works were £38 million, much of it due to asbestos removal.

During the following twenty months, the scheme floundered. Patricia Kirwan, deprived of her chairmanship, was in no position to drive it forward; Porter was indifferent to it and preoccupied with the gerrymandering; it was fiercely resisted by the WEAG campaigners, who, despite their hostility to the City Council, still wanted the security of a council tenancy and thought that Westminster, rather than private developers, should repair the estates and remove the asbestos. In the face of the WEAG opposition, three out of four of the builders decided the development was trouble and pulled out of the scheme. Towards the end of 1988, despite its successes, the campaign was running into problems. As residents from the estates were gradually moved to prepare the way for the builders, it meant that the WEAG had fewer and fewer people to rally to the cause.

By chance, the Thatcher government came to the WEAG's rescue. The 1988 Housing Act allowed a private landlord to acquire compulsorily any council-owned homes. The council could be sacked as the landlord and forced to pay a 'dowry' which recognised the cost of putting right any disrepair. All that was needed was approval by the majority of the tenants on the estate and the Housing Corporation, the government quango which oversees housing associations. The Conservatives had designed the Tenants

Choice Act as a way of liberating tenants from their municipal landlords on incompetent Labour councils; it was not intended for use against Tory flagships. WEAG coordinator Jonathan Rosenberg and Neale Coleman laid the plans for the residents of Walterton and Elgin to take control of the estates from Westminster. If they succeeded, the privatisation deal would be dead and the council would have to hand over to a bitter enemy a dowry to repair the neglected properties and remove the asbestos, a bill then calculated by the campaigners at more than £30 million.

Rosenberg quietly gained the majority of the tenants' support for the break-away and received help in developing plans for the estates from the Paddington Churches Housing Association (PCHA), which had been originally founded by local vicars to provide decent social housing for the poor. The residents set up a new company called Walterton and Elgin Community Homes Ltd (WECH) and some 500 households, more than seventy per cent of the total, joined the company for £1 each. Rosenberg says, 'We kept everything we were doing quiet for as long as we could. The council had taken their eye off the ball and so we were able to go round and get organised.'

In December 1988 news of the residents' plan was reported in the press. Rosenberg told the *Tribune*, 'It's ironic that this legislation which was intended to help private landlords buy Labour council housing stock should be used by a group of tenants against a Tory council.' The news was a profound shock to Porter and her senior colleagues. They considered Rosenberg and the WEAG 'an old enemy', who had disrupted council meetings and opposed their plans, including designated sales, and were closely associated with the Labour councillors. Porter thought it would be a major defeat and humiliation for her personally if the residents succeeded in their plans to opt out of council control.

She was also disgusted by the idea of having to hand over as much as £30 million in a dowry to the WEAG/WECH. But she had a problem in disputing the amount because the council's own plans, to which she had been forced to give her reluctant approval, demanded that £38 million be spent on the estates, and the council itself had repeatedly emphasised the huge costs. Since 1983, countless council reports had spelt out in unambiguous terms the need to tackle the asbestos. Perhaps the starkest assessment was carried in a Masters thesis published in October 1986 by a senior Westminster environmental health officer, Graham Farrant: 'It is considered that these two tower blocks . . . may provide the greatest potential for asbestos release within residential accommodation in Britain. In particular, easy access to the common parts and the degree of vandalism encountered in these blocks give rise to concern among the tenants as to their exposure.'

On 12 December 1986 there had been a fire at 100 Hermes Point. Attempts were made to seal the abandoned flat but drug addicts broke in. More than three and a half years later, workmen discovered used syringes on the floor and pigeons flying in and out of missing windows and making nests out of asbestos. An official report later described the scene: 'The security door had been forced open, with large gaps around top, bottom and sides. The windows were unglazed, allowing the wind to blow through the flat into the common parts, and pigeons were contributing to the disturbance and distribution of the loose asbestos.' There were five other fires in damaged and empty flats in Hermes Point and Chantry Point. The scale of the crisis was so obvious that one housing officer expressed his concerns in an internal memo: '19th Floor Chantry Point is a wipeout . . . there is so much Asbestos Remedial work required . . .' Number 19, Chelwood House W2, it was not.

In total, there were approximately forty empty flats in the two towers in various degrees of dilapidation. Another internal memo from the housing department revealed that the kitchens were 'badly vandalised', the fittings were 'broken', the heating systems were 'defunct' and in many cases the plumbing had been 'removed', and that there was no hot water. Council workmen were instructed to render flats uninhabitable for squatters by vandalising them, which not only contributed to the increasingly squalid conditions within the towers but inevitably resulted in the release of more asbestos fibres. And there could be no doubt that conditions were not only terrible, but, as the council itself had recognised for years, dangerous as well.

Although publicly the council had used the risk of asbestos to promote its unpopular privatisation schemes to residents, Westminster's environmental health officers had sought to reassure existing tenants in the blocks by minimising the potential danger posed by the material. The officers had done this over the years by referring to the results of air tests periodically conducted to detect the possible presence of loose fibres, not in people's flats where household chores like drilling holes in the wall would disturb the asbestos, but in the communal parts of the blocks where people were just passing through. According to a later inquiry, Westminster's officers relied on these air tests 'to the point of perversity' despite knowing that they were next to useless in detecting fibres in occupied homes. In 1985 a GLC medical inspector said that 'far too much reliance was put on air tests . . . A recent report . . . had been very damning about air quality checks,' and that the sprayed asbestos represented a 'potential hazard'. On several occasions, even these inadequate checks had detected the presence of asbestos fibres above the recommended safety limit, but the significance was ignored when more reassuring results were obtained.

The air tests may have been worthless, but they would prove extremely useful to Shirley Porter and her chairmen as they contemplated one of the most disgraceful decisions ever taken by a British public body. On 20 December 1988, more than a fortnight after they learned of the WECH bid, Porter held yet another secret meeting with her chairmen to discuss ways of defeating her enemies in north Paddington. Increasingly, their gaze became fixed on the two potential death traps looming mournfully above the Harrow Road.

CHAPTER 20

Out of Control (1989)

There is no need to speculate about who took the unlawful decision to place deported Westminster families in the towers nor
why the decision was taken. When the shocking truth emerged
years later, the council conducted two exhaustive inquiries into the
affair which left no doubt as to what happened or Shirley Porter's
involvement.

Senior housing officers at Westminster had swiftly concluded
that the WEAG/WECH bid to own their estate was 'unstoppable'.
It was looking likely that the Housing Corporation would officially
approve WECH as a landlord when the new Tenants Choice Act
came into effect in April 1989. But Porter refused to admit defeat
and stepped up her 'war' against the campaigning residents. When
Porter met her chairmen on 20 December 1988, the councillors
decided 'the Council should publicly support the WEAG initiative',
but at the same time should do everything possible to defeat it.
Their weapon of choice would be homeless families.

Porter and her chairmen concluded that the best way to destroy
the bid would be to wreck the financial basis of WECH's plans to
refurbish the estates. For at least six years the council had been
emphasising the potential risks of asbestos in the blocks and the
need to remove it. Now Porter and her chairmen considered the

possibility of moving homeless families into Hermes Point and Chantry Point, a public act designed to demonstrate to everyone, not least to the Housing Corporation which would have to approve WECH as a landlord, that Hermes and Chantry did provide suitable accommodation for people, as the minutes of the meeting reveal: 'Another possibility to consider would be using some of the vacancies for short life accommodation for the homeless . . .'

The cynical theory held that, if the flats were safe enough for homeless families, then the asbestos problem was not as bad as had been stated and, therefore, that WECH's financial calculations, which included the asbestos repairs, were wrong. If this ruse worked, the Housing Corporation would have little option but to reject WECH's estimates and its bid for landlord status. Porter and the Chairmen's Group may have considered that their tactic would reduce costs for the local taxpayer but the predominant purpose was the defeat of a political enemy, as they themselves would acknowledge at subsequent secret gatherings.

In 1994 Bill Roots, Chief Executive of Westminster City Council, commissioned an official inquiry. It was conducted by John Barratt, the former Chief Executive of Cambridgeshire County Council, who stated in his report: 'If all that was known about the asbestos was ignored, the use of the Points for accommodating the homeless . . . provided an attractive solution.' But he added: 'I have to conclude that the real reason for the decision to accommodate Homeless Families in the Points was to assist the hoped for defeat of the WECH Ltd bid; that the decision was informally but powerfully taken by Chairmen, influenced by considerations of Party advantage; that the financial advantages were important but co-incidental; and that the use of delegated officer powers was a hypocritical smokescreen. Against such a background the chances of health risks caused by asbestos being considered were not realistic.'

What Porter and the others needed was a formal justification for the intended action. The meeting on 20 December delegated to Michael Dutt the responsibility of obtaining a report on 'the asbestos situation'. As John Barratt pointed out later: 'The Chairmen appear to have relied on Councillor Dutt's judgment about the importance of asbestos matters.' Not only was he the co-Chairman of the Housing Committee, he was also the only doctor in the Chairmen's Group. Who better?

Dutt's task was to get some sort of advice which the chairmen could use to defend the indefensible, and he more than adequately fulfilled his role. He demanded a report from the council's department of environmental health. Without waiting for the advice, the Chairmen's Group now emphatically took the decision to move the homeless into the tower blocks. At their meeting on 7 January 1989, attended by Dutt, Graham England recorded in his filofax that the chairmen had decided to 'relet tower blocks to homeless'.

Six days later, on 13 January, the council's department of environmental health produced the report ordered by Dutt. Prepared by a senior environmental health officer, it stated that the council had been 'carrying out air monitoring for asbestos in both Hermes and Chantry Points since November 1982'. The report approved the reletting 'provided that care is taken to ensure that the asbestos products within the flats remain in good condition'. The environmental health officer's assessment referred to the air tests conducted over the years: 'The standard adopted by the City Council at the Council Meeting on 24th October 1983 was that the level of 0.1 fibres 1m/air [sic] should not be exceeded in occupied dwellings.' The report added: 'None of the samples taken in Hermes or Chantry Points have exceeded this level,' although this was wrong because there had been at least two occasions on which the results, even of these worthless checks, had been higher than the acceptable levels.

The report did in fact highlight the critical point made by the GLC medical inspector more than three years previously and which was widely understood within Westminster's department of environmental health: 'Air monitoring however does not give a true indication of the potential risk from asbestos in a given location. In particular where asbestos-containing materials are damaged thereby producing dust with asbestos fibres a potentially hazardous situation could develop. Should that dust be disturbed, respirable size particles may be released giving rise to a localised yet potentially serious hazard.'

Dutt simply chose to ignore the serious caveats about the air tests and the risks posed by damaged asbestos. Instead, he plundered from the report snatches of vague assurances about the test results and the fact that the flats were 'essentially safe' if the asbestos was not damaged. Yet within ten days of the report being produced, Dutt knew that the two towers contained 'damaged asbestos'. On 23 January 1989 Dutt and his fellow Housing Committee Chairman, Judith Warner, as well as Graham England, received a report which referred to 'damaged asbestos' in the towers. In his inquiry, John Barratt concluded: 'It is abundantly clear that the bad condition of the Points was known to the Political decision-makers and that asbestos was a major factor . . . asbestos and the homeless, in relation to the Points, were now increasingly no more than abstractions in a strategic response to the Political dangers of the WECH Ltd bid.'

Porter and her chairmen relied on the air tests as proof that the asbestos posed little risk and that the flats were 'essentially safe'. But this 'line' held by the council for the next eighteen months as it moved 122 homeless families into the towers would be described by Barratt as 'phoney' and was known to be so. He added: 'It is difficult to see the point of monitoring in the undisturbed ambience of void flats, except to assess the safety of undisturbed asbestos materials. This was the purpose of the monitoring programme. As a universal measure of safety in the Points it was plainly absurd.' Perhaps one of the most depressing aspects of all was the silence of environmental health officers. One explanation charitably given by Barratt was that the council's department of environmental health was 'too weak within the internal politics of Westminster City Council to assert its judgment against the chosen policies . . .' but he added that whatever the explanation, it would not be 'adequate to excuse such a failure'. The only real conclusion is that cowardice caused a woeful dereliction of duty among the City's environmental health officers.

Bill Roots concluded that Dutt might have doctored the environmental health officer's advice in his eagerness to justify the decisions already taken. He says, 'I'm not sure to be fair to the members [Tory councillors] that they knew how bad it was. They had received certain environmental health reports and my suspicion was that they were doctored by senior officers. When Barratt started talking to the guys down the line, he discovered that they'd been giving quite clear advice that it was bad, but that's not what the members read. Whether certain members persuaded certain senior officers to doctor the report I don't know; you can never know.' However, Dutt continued to receive reports about the 'damaged asbestos' in the two towers and yet supported the use of the towers for homeless families.

By the end of January 1989 Porter and her fellow chairmen had come up with ever more implausible reasons for the path on which they had now embarked. Porter was also satisfied that using the blocks for dumping the homeless from marginal wards would fit in with her wider BSC objectives. Around this time, a secret 'political assessment' prepared by an anonymous Tory councillor analysed the risks to the Conservatives of a successful WECH bid: 'The embarrassment of a Left-Wing activist-led group opting out using a Conservative Government's legislation to do so . . . will halt the Council's aim of building stable communities in the area . . . No chance of Harrow Road Ward being won by the Conservatives.'

On 30 January a further report was written by a Tory councillor who was working closely with Shirley Porter at the time. He suggested that defeat by WECH would mean: 'We lose ability to implement BSC, create Socialist stronghold, and "lose" to an old enemy.' The main disadvantage in defeating Rosenberg, according to the report, was that it 'could create problems in tower blocks as we will have to rehouse the new tenants when we deal with the asbestos'. It asked, 'Do we want to stop JR at any price?' Clearly, the answer was yes. The report re-stated the main aim: 'Destroy the financial viability' of the WECH bid.

Neale Coleman had enough experience of the Porter regime to know that the real decisions were being taken, not by the council, but by the Chairmen's Group. On 21 February he heard from Ken Hackney, one of Graham England's deputies, that the chairmen were finally about to agree on the use of the towers for the homeless. Frantically, Coleman called Bill Phillips in an attempt to get any decision concerning the future of the towers referred to a public meeting of the Housing Committee. The managing director was deaf to his concerns.

Jonathan Rosenberg says, 'By February 1989 the Tories realised they had to pull their finger out because we were going to be far past the finishing post before there was any chance of stopping us from taking over the estates. They were running out of time. The decision to move in the homeless was quite a shock for us and we were very worried about that, partly because we hadn't been approved as a landlord and partly because we knew what a terrible state the blocks were in and that this was a terrible, terrible decision. The blocks by that stage were completely out of control; it was dangerous to go anywhere near them. People were throwing things out of the top of the towers; there was blood all over the place where there had been fights or addicts had been injecting themselves. It was really bad. The idea of putting homeless families in there was really shocking.'

The chairmen met on 21 February and according to Hackney, who was present and taking notes, they took the decision to 'use flats for homeless . . . ASAP'. According to the minutes, the meeting was chaired by Barry Legg, and other councillors present included Michael Dutt, Simon Milton, Judith Warner, Miles Young and Alex Segal. The District Auditor later declared that the decision, leaving aside the serious ethical concerns it raised, was unlawful because it was taken by a secret and unaccountable group. The group had secretly managed Westminster in the same way for so long that it no longer considered such legal niceties.

The decision took place a week after Porter had sacked her chief executive, Rodney Brooke. Porter and Brooke had argued bitterly about the two towers and Brooke is adamant he would have stopped it. 'What Shirley Porter did was simply criminal,' he says. The departure of Brooke took place one week exactly before the fateful decision. Brooke says, 'They would obviously know it would be a matter of principle and conscience to me, which I would certainly have opposed volubly. My going on Tuesday, 14 February 1989, the previous week, was connected to their decision to rehouse people the following Tuesday. I was told later by people at the council that they honestly believed that Shirley and the members did not understand what they were doing but that's a lot of nonsense. They knew bloody well what they were doing and I think that is dreadful.'

Although Porter was absent from the meeting, she had attended the clandestine gatherings which had come to the decision and had asked for a schedule of the move to be sent to her office by the following Friday. On 28 February Porter chaired a further meeting which rubber-stamped the decision of the previous week, as the minutes demonstrate: 'Properties in non-key areas and empty houses on the Walterton should be used.'

The chairmen decided to use every possible flat in the towers for homeless families, but one group of tenants stood in the way of this objective, the Short Lifers. On 1 March Porter and her chairmen decided: 'Short life groups to be terminated. By the end of the week.' A note of the meeting went on to record the following decision: 'All voids in tower blocks must be used inc. 16th, 19th floors Chantry & "fire damaged."' On 3 March the council dispatched eviction notices to the Short Lifers demanding their departure within twenty-eight days. They responded in writing to Westminster: 'The reason given for terminating our agreement is that you wish to use the properties for homeless families. We doubt however that they are suitable . . . the Council has acknowledged the safety risk posed by the high asbestos content of the buildings; add to this the poor state of repair of the estate and you have an environment which is clearly not suited to homeless families.'

Porter ignored this sensible warning and insisted they vacate their homes. Cynically, Michael Dutt suggested using the risk of the asbestos to scare the Short Lifers away, despite underplaying the danger to justify the influx of homeless families, as John Barratt later reported: 'Councillor Dutt expressly suggested it might be possible to gain complete possession by using the danger from the asbestos as a ground for gaining compulsory permanent possession.' Some Short Lifers did surrender their flats, but the majority resisted eviction for as long as they could.

Neale Coleman had not given up trying to prevent the use of the tower blocks for the homeless and he arranged a meeting with Bill Phillips, where he insisted the matter was debated in public by the Housing Committee. According to a record of the conversation between Phillips and Coleman on 2 March: 'The Managing Director stated that informal meetings of Chairmen cannot make such decisions, but only formulate views based on the professional advice of officers. The Managing Director also stated that the decision was not a departure from agreed policy and practice and that the decision did not need to go to Housing Committee . . .' But Phillips knew that executive decisions were being taken regularly by the Chairmen's Group. Furthermore, he knew that the council's former official policy was not to relet empty flats in the towers because of the known asbestos risk; now it had been decided, not by the council but by a secret group of politicians acting unlawfully, that the asbestos risk was so small that the apartments could be relet to homeless families. The managing director's failure to recognise the obvious change in policy can be partly explained in the light of his compliance with Porter's other policies and decisions.

Porter also deployed other dirty tricks to stop WECH. Simon Milton, a Tory councillor, was ordered to set up a bogus residents group to oppose Rosenberg, as is made clear in the minutes: 'Walterton Residents against Takeover to be set up with constitution.' The organisation, with the help of Porter's activists from Marketforce Communications, was duly formed. Two of the 'WRATs' were signed up members of the local Conservative Party and held a bizarre and extremely unconvincing press conference at the Coburg Hotel in Bayswater in March 1989 to argue against Rosenberg's scheme. The WRATs tried to smear Rosenberg, issuing a report which labelled him a 'left-wing extremist'. They also displayed photographs of Rosenberg being dragged away by members of the Territorial Support Group following his arrest at the Housing Committee meeting in September 1987. Rosenberg says, 'They obviously thought that if they could take me out, then the WECH bid would fail.' He suspected the whole thing was a council initiative but he had no evidence. WECH circulated a leaflet with the headline 'RESIDENTS SMELL A WRAT.'

Graham England was dispatched to lobby the Housing Corporation to reject Rosenberg as a landlord and Shirley Porter was planning to smear Paddington Churches, the local housing association supporting WECH, as the record of the meeting makes clear: 'SP to speak to John Wheeler [Tory MP for North Westminster] asking him to write to Council and to Housing Corporation about

complaints against Paddington Churches Housing Association.'
Porter also played an age-old trick against Rosenberg which her old
enemy Ken Livingstone had once used against her. Council officials
were instructed to investigate whether Rosenberg was in breach of his
council tenancy by using his home as an office. If it were, he could be
evicted or, at the very least, discredited. A junior officer refused to
carry out the instruction and referred the matter to a more senior
official, who in turn made an official protest to his boss. The insidious inspection did not take place, but an officer from the housing
department did timidly hand over for the chairmen the files on
Jonathan Rosenberg's council tenancy.

These dirty tricks pale beside the edict to move the homeless into
the towers. Predictably, chaos attended the decision: council workmen continued to smash up flats, knocking down internal walls
and stripping out the plumbing and electricity to prevent squatters
as previously instructed. Finally, they were ordered to stop the
destruction and prepare the properties for homeless families. John
Barratt said: 'The homeless families were rushed in, and attempts
were made to rush the Short Life licensees out ... to meet the
objectives of defeating WECH Ltd and of providing less costly
accommodation to homeless families. No adequate thought was
either given, nor adequate advice taken, in relation to current
asbestos risks.'

The first of 122 families were moved into the blocks in late
March and early April; for at least seven months the council took
no steps to inform them about the widespread extent of the
asbestos in homes or the measures necessary to protect themselves
from potential harm. Council officers told homeless families that
they would get no other offers of council accommodation if they
rejected the invitation to live in Hermes Point or Chantry Point.
There can be few more serious indictments of the behaviour of a
British local authority than the conclusion reached by John Barratt
in his exhaustive inquiry: 'This review will make very disturbing
reading for anyone concerned about the observance of proper
standards in the provision of public services, and especially for
former occupants of, and work people, in the Points. Despite the
availability of the clearest advice and instructions to the contrary,

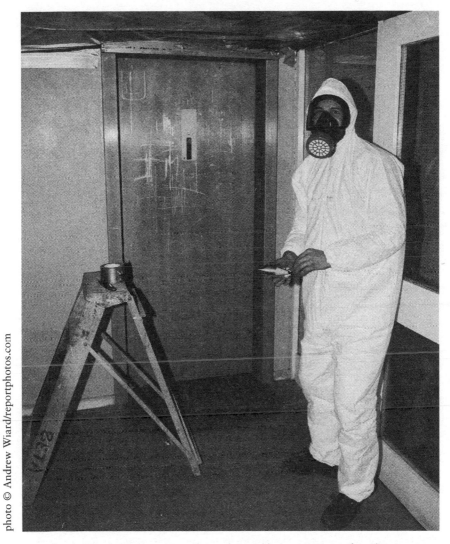

photo © Andrew Wiard/reportphotos.com

A Westminster council worker seeks to reassure families
moved into the two towers.

those acting on behalf of a public body repeatedly took risks, for a
variety of reasons, with the health of people who ought to have
been entitled to assume that such risks were not being taken.'

The decision to use the towers for homeless families was no
aberration; it was simply the continuation and, perhaps, the natural culmination of a pattern of behaviour which had become ever

more unstable and extreme. Porter had deported homeless families from Westminster as part of her strategy to beat Labour, and she used them again to defeat the WECH bid, even if that meant exposing them to a known risk. It is little wonder that most people would find it hard to comprehend such conduct when the truth emerged later, or even articulate a response to it. Now, surely, it was time that somebody, somewhere, lifted up the stone and peered beneath.

CHAPTER 21

A Glossary of Difficult Terms
(February–July 1989)

Shirley Porter triggered the events which led to her downfall by mishandling a piece of unfinished business. Since 1986 she had gone out of her way to humiliate and sideline her chief executive. She had blamed Rodney Brooke for her election near-defeat and brutally pushed him aside by appointing Bill Phillips as managing director. As the BSC machinery began to take grip, Brooke became increasingly isolated. Porter did not trust him with involvement in her conspiracy and those officers who were implicated felt it pointless to confide in him.

Brooke had refused to 'investigate' Paul Dimoldenberg and Peter Bradley and he exasperated Porter even further in February 1989 by once again declaring that her allegations against them were baseless. On the morning of 8 February Brooke told her he did not wish to renew his contract when it came to an end ten months later. Porter would have had no intention of renewing it, but now decided on his immediate ejection from City Hall. The dismissal itself was a predictably grubby affair, a botched assassination. Porter convened a gang, including the two other members of the ruling triumvirate, Barry Legg and David Weeks, to hammer out a financial settlement with Brooke. The bungled sacking of Rodney Brooke would cause such acute distress to Porter's senior officers and fellow Tories that few would have any qualms in betraying her. Crucially, it also attracted unwelcome attention to Porter at precisely the wrong time.

Matthew Ives arrived at City Hall late on the morning of 8 February and travelled up in the lift with a well-dressed man in a fine top coat. Ives got out on his floor to begin what he hoped would be a routine day in the office. At 3 p.m. the phone rang. It was Bill Phillips. Ives was required straightaway in Porter's office on the eighteenth floor and he was ordered to bring with him the official seal of Westminster City Council. A document had been prepared setting out the terms for Brooke's sacking but no one could sign it until the seal was affixed. Ives was horrified because the law decreed that any agreement with the chief executive had to be approved by the council and its committees. He told Phillips, 'Hang on a minute, you can't do this. This is something which requires proper consideration and it needs to be done by a body that's authorised; this is just madness.'

Ives rushed up to Porter's office where he was ambushed by the Leader, Phillips, Weeks, Legg and the man he had met in the lift a few hours earlier, Michael Silverman of Merton Associates. Once again Porter had called on him for help in the sacking of a senior officer. She was determined to dispose of Brooke with a generous financial package tied to an assurance that the secrets of City Hall would remain confidential.

For three and a half hours the gang tried to persuade Ives to fix the seal to the document. They cajoled, they threatened and they shouted at the City Solicitor in an attempt to force him to hand over the seal. Rather than be party to an unlawful decision, Ives weathered the storm. He remembers Silverman addressing him in tones of extreme irritation: 'No one need ever hear of Rodney Brooke again if the course which I have outlined, and indeed spent the whole day organising, is taken. Everything has been very carefully martialled and thought through and now at the very end, when all that is required is the seal to be impressed, you have the temerity to come and put the mockers on the whole arrangement.'

Ives told him, 'You can go on as much as you like, but it's not going to alter my view one jot. The council seal stays downstairs and if you want to sort this out, you have to go through the proper process. You know the law.' Legg and Weeks were furious. Legg was white with rage and banged the table with his fist. 'This is outrageous!' he told the defiant Ives. 'What you're saying is that this is not a matter which could be dealt with by an equivalent of a company by its board; you've got to go to the shareholders and get a general meeting resolution.' But Ives knew it was a council, not a company; there were no shareholders, only councillors and their committees, and only they were empowered to approve a deal. He stood his ground.

Curiously, one by one, the main protagonists abandoned the meeting. First Porter became bored and left, followed by Silverman and then Legg. Weeks was the last to burn out. Ives was left alone in eerie silence in Porter's office where he awaited a renewed assault. After twenty minutes he too left. He bumped into Porter on the way out. 'We haven't finished with you yet!' she snapped. A shaken Ives returned to his desk where he waited for ten minutes before picking up his briefcase and heading home. It had been a bad day at the office.

Ives's obstinacy meant that Brooke's sacking would have to be debated by the full council on 1 March. In the meantime, details of Porter's shabby treatment of the chief executive and the terms of his dismissal were leaked to the press and received the full glare of publicity. The newspapers alleged that Porter had bought Brooke's silence with a pay-off in exchange for his signature on a confidentiality agreement preventing him from disclosing what he knew about the cemeteries and other City Hall scandals.

Although the settlement was much less generous than reported, the affair upset many Tory councillors who detested Bill Phillips and thought that Porter had treated Brooke extremely badly. For the dissidents, such as Patricia Kirwan, the sacking was a *cause célèbre* to use against Porter. Kirwan had always been fond of Brooke and expressed her anger to her Tory colleagues. On 23 February Porter's supporters in the Westminster North Conservative Party passed a vote of confidence in her, and its chairman, Ronnie Raymond-Cox, wrote a menacing letter to Kirwan the following day, warning her not to vote against Porter at the council meeting in a week's time, and that the party would not stand for any sign of disunity.

Kirwan replied with a stinging attack on Porter: 'I have learnt that loyalty is a two-way thing; it cannot be imposed, it has to be earned. Leadership brings with it great responsibility; unfortunately at Westminster "Leadership" has come to mean autocratic rule, secrecy, an unfortunate tendency to see any criticism as "high treason", [and] a total ability to blame anyone and everyone for one's own shortcomings, mistakes or actions.'

The attempt by Tory officials to cow Kirwan and other rebels backfired at the council meeting, which vetoed Porter's plans for the 'reorganisation' of the City Hall's management in the wake of Brooke's expected departure. One Tory voted against Porter. Four others, including Kirwan and Elizabeth Flach, who as Lord Mayor was chairing the meeting, abstained. They baulked at actually voting against Porter because they did not want to be punished for disloyalty. Abstention was a way of making their anger public. Labour won the vote twenty-nine to twenty-six. It was Porter's first defeat in full council since becoming Leader. She did eventually get her reorganisation but it had been an extremely damaging imbroglio.

Following the headline news, Valerie Grove interviewed Porter for *The Times* and described a brash and arrogant woman. Porter said, 'Look, you've heard of my reign of terror, the number of people who leave because of me. But local authority work is no longer the polite, cushy, civil-service like profession. It's hard, tough, revolutionary . . . It's not like council work on Stow-on-the-Wold.' Stow-on-the-Wold Council was provoked into writing a formal letter of protest.

The Brooke affair whetted the interest of investigative journalist John Ware. Ware was a reporter for the BBC Television documentary series *Panorama*, and had established himself as one of its finest, with programmes on the IRA, the intelligence services and the activities of the extreme left in Liverpool. He decided to make his next programme about Shirley Porter and fixed up an appointment to see her. He met with Porter at her flat on a beautiful spring morning in mid-March and was surprised to discover that the tough Tory revolutionary had a passion for stuffed toys. 'I was shown to a waiting room, which was filled with dolls and teddy bears,' he remembers. 'I wondered if I had come to the right flat. I thought I was in a fairly affluent nursery by mistake. Eventually I was summoned to see her.'

According to the reporter, Porter was suspicious and her 'antennae were bristling'. She looked him squarely in the eye and asked, 'What do you want?' Ware replied, 'I want to make a programme about you.' 'Why? What sort of programme will it be?' Ware gave a reply he thought would cover every eventuality: 'I don't know because I don't know anything about you. It will be tough but fair.' Porter remained wary but allowed the *Panorama* crew to film a few sequences of her at City Hall while Ware hit the phones and began his research. When Barry Legg received a call from Ware, he was perturbed by the reporter's interest and asked how long the programme would be. On being told it was forty minutes, Legg replied cautiously, 'That's an awfully long time.' In the meantime, Ware dispatched Amanda Farnsworth, the researcher, and the producer, Mark Killick, to see what they could turn up. Farnsworth visited Patricia Kirwan at her basement flat in Amberley Road, North Paddington. She found a distressed and angry woman. Farnsworth says, 'Patricia used to get upset. You felt that she had been on the inside and that she had suddenly been cast off by Shirley Porter. So she was a woman scorned. But there was part of her that genuinely felt that Lady Porter was taking their Conservative Party down the wrong route and wasn't playing by the rules.'

Farnsworth returned from Kirwan with a letter Graham England had sent to Bill Phillips in the early months of the gerrymandering plot headed: 'Confidential: Designation of Council properties in Key wards – Supply of Accommodation'. In it, England wrote: 'it is not possible in professional terms to justify the designation of all properties in the eight wards.' Ware could not make head or tail of it. 'It didn't mean much to me,' he says. 'It was in local authority jargon and had something to do with housing stocks and wards and various other sorts of encrypted language that only local government officers understand.'

On 6 April Ware showed the letter to Paul Dimoldenberg, who explained his own suspicions that Porter had been gerrymandering.

By that time, Dimoldenberg had been engaged in fruitless correspondence with Bill Phillips for more than a year on the subject.
The Labour leader urged Ware to see Neale Coleman and Jonathan
Rosenberg for further help. Ware had planned to make a programme about a radical right-wing council leader but he soon
found himself investigating a possible corruption scandal. To his
amazement, he descended into an underworld of fear and paranoia. One Tory woman councillor told him how Porter kept her
troops in check: 'She doesn't like to be opposed and then with all
that money and power comes the viciousness . . . She always says
"I'll sue you!" That's her first phrase if anyone strays out of line.
And most of us can't afford to be sued and that's the problem.'
Ware discovered that the key senior officers were even more terrified and were convinced that their phones at City Hall were being
tapped, so he rang them at home outside office hours. 'They were
not friends of Shirley's,' says Ware, 'but they were in a good position to get access to material. I spent a lot of money on lunches
with senior officials.'

By the end of April further revelations were falling into Ware's
hands like ripe plums from a shaken tree. Brown envelopes arrived
at his office in Lime Grove; inside were secret BSC documents containing details of the gerrymandering, from the deportations of the
homeless and the Quality of Life Initiative to the targeting of designated sales in marginal wards. Ware says, 'It was extremely
complicated but I do remember one weekend in my back garden at
home which I spent with Westminster City Council's housing
inventory. I plotted the projected sales to see how that would
reduce the marginality of each of these wards to check if the thesis
made sense. I remember coming to a view by the end of the weekend that it did make sense. There were sales all over the borough
but the concentration of the sales without any question was
focused in these wards and at that point it clicked.' The reporter
wrote a draft script which he sent to Roger Law, a BBC lawyer.
Later, a worried looking Law came to see Ware. 'What's the matter,
Roger?' 'Just about everything,' replied the lawyer.

On 10 May a critical legal opinion from James Goudie QC was
delivered to the *Panorama* team. He had reviewed Ware's leaked

documents and an analysis showing the designated sales in Westminster. Goudie found that it was clear there was a 'bias in favour of the eight key wards'. The wards contained under a third of all the council properties, but more than half of all the properties designated for sale. He concluded that 'an utterly unlawful purpose' was 'the driving force'.

During his research, Ware had found the South Westminster Tories in turmoil over Porter's imposition of young activists from Marketforce and her orders to target Labour opponents with dirty tricks. Porter had grown impatient with the continued opposition and recalcitrance from the south, particularly from the constituency's agent, Donald Stewart. She warned Ian Walker, Chairman of the Westminster South Conservative Association, that she would engineer a vote to remove him from office unless he fired Stewart. Walker refused and so Porter resolved to oust Walker and replace him with one of her supporters, fellow Westminster Tory councillor Andrew Greystoke, when the Association held its annual meeting, set for 18 May.

Stewart had been confiding in Ware for several weeks and had kept him informed about the activities of the Marketforce workers. The agent feared Porter would use them to campaign for votes among the Association's members which were needed to depose Walker and place his own future in jeopardy. Three days before the annual meeting, on 15 May, Ware phoned Stewart, who had received a copy of Porter's paper 'Keeping Westminster Conservative' at a private meeting in the House of Commons on 3 March 1988. The document, which Porter had distributed among her enemies in the Conservative Party as well as her friends, carried her name and graphically detailed the gerrymandering activities in the eight key wards, as well as her unpopular plans to fund a campaign team to help win the 1990 elections. 'I didn't really read it in great depth,' Stewart told Ware. 'It really is a summary of the situation bit by bit, area by area, as they see it . . . and there's some sort of drum-banging section saying we've got to do this, we've got to do that.'

Ware believed this was possibly the most important document of all, but Stewart would not hand over his copy of 'Keeping

Westminster Conservative'. He agreed, however, to let Amanda Farnsworth see it. An appointment was made for the following day at the constituency office. Farnsworth says, 'He brought me this document and I had a dictaphone and I spent hours reading the document into the dictaphone, and feeling really quite scared. I knew I needed to get it perfectly right because he wouldn't give it to us, so I recorded exactly what it said and then we took that dictaphone and got that typed up until we had what we felt was a perfect replica down to the typing and everything, and you know that was for me a very big moment. That was the document that really set out the key wards' strategy and once you had that, everything else fitted in.'

But Porter was extremely rich and could easily afford to sue for libel, so the final legal hurdle for Ware was Richard Rampton QC, an expert in defamation. Rampton reviewed Ware's documents and suggested certain changes to the script. At one point, the QC lit up one of his Turkish cigarettes, leaned back in his chair, smiled wolfishly and used his favourite expression when announcing that a journalist had enough evidence to make serious allegations against someone with the resources to sue for libel: 'This is a true bill!' 'And I was hugely relieved at that moment,' explains Ware, 'because if he thought it was, then it was.'

The BBC team, bolstered by James Goudie's and Richard Rampton's legal opinions, had documents but as yet no whistle blower. They tried to persuade Kirwan to sit in front of the camera and go on record. She hesitated for weeks until she was shown the legal opinion from Goudie. She feared that she could be implicated when the scandal was exposed because, although she had tried to prevent the gerrymandering, she had known about it. Kirwan says, 'John Ware took me and my husband Peter out for dinner and we had a long, long talk. I knew it was going to be the end of my political career if I did the interview. He showed us the legal opinion on designated sales and things like that. He handled me very well; he's a crafty bugger! And Peter said "You know something, if John is right and this legal opinion is right, we could lose everything." And that's when we decided to go for it.'

As Ware's team set up the camera and lights in Kirwan's flat in Amberley Road, the phone rang. It was Barry Legg. Would Kirwan like to be Finance vice-chairman? Kirwan said 'yes', but of course never took up the post. It was astonishing timing by Legg, and Kirwan suspected that Ware had been followed to her flat and that Legg was trying to buy her silence.

John Ware and his team had planned a big filming schedule for 18 May. During the day, they were to visit Hermes and Chantry Points and in the evening, to record Porter's attempted annexation of the Westminster South Tories at their annual meeting in St Ermine's Hotel on Caxton Street, just around the corner from City Hall. Two weeks earlier, Ware's cameraman had been so concerned at the state of the two towers and the sight of exposed asbestos in the communal parts that he had refused to film for safety reasons. The BBC paid for checks before allowing staff back into the blocks. Unfortunately, the BBC also relied on air tests similar to those Westminster had cited and thus reassured the team filmed the exposed asbestos and the appalling conditions in the two towers. Ware also spoke to the homeless families moved in by Porter. Mary McDonald, a mother of two children, told the reporter that her new flat was infested with cockroaches. She was depressed and could not understand why she had had to live in an asbestos-filled tower block while the council was selling off hundreds of flats through designated sales. She recounted her discussion with the council's housing officers when she begged for a decent council home. 'Why don't you just give me one? That's all I am asking for . . . just somewhere decent to live.' She described the officers' response: 'No, no, sorry we're selling them off.'

Under the chandeliers of St Ermine's Hotel on 18 May, the BBC filmed Ian Walker's determined fight against Porter and her candidate, Andrew Greystoke, for control of the Westminster South Conservative Association. Walker emphasised the importance of the role of leader of the Tories in the south: 'It's something which must be earned, must be achieved, and must be prized.' In a clear attack on Porter's plans, he added, 'It's not in anyone's gift; it's not there to be hijacked at the whim of any individual or any organisation.' Greystoke bridled at the suggestion that he was 'Shirley Porter's poodle'. 'On the contrary, I am a loyal supporter of the work she has done to keep the council the way it is,' he said.

As Greystoke persisted with his unconvincing homily, Ware spotted Porter 'slinking' into the meeting and moving unobtrusively among the Tories. The reporter had written to Porter to outline the allegations but she had so far refused to give an interview and had ended all cooperation with *Panorama*. Ware determined to approach her in person and ask her for an interview. Suddenly she disappeared and he was distracted by the crucial vote for the Association chairmanship. Greystoke's challenge was crushed by 151 votes to just twenty-seven. The south had seen off Porter. A few minutes later Ware felt an elbow in his ribs. It was Porter. 'Never mind about the fair bits, what about the tough bits?' Ware replied, 'Well, those bits are quite tough and I want to talk to you about them.' Porter mused over the offer and thought of her supper engagement with her son John, a thirty-six-year-old businessman, and her daughter, Linda Marcus, a thirty-seven-year-old mother of two, visiting from Israel. 'I'm bored with this,' said Porter. 'I'm going to take my kids out to dinner.' She turned and left. Ware never spoke to her again.

Porter knew that *Panorama* planned to expose the gerrymandering plot and played for time by hinting that she might answer the charges in a recorded interview. On 6 June a genuine reason for delay arrived when her mother, Lady Cohen, died aged eighty-one. Porter insisted she needed a month to mourn. Ware says, 'I said we'd wait and so it went on and on and on and after about six weeks I said, "Doesn't the mourning end now? I'm not being disrespectful, but we must be getting close to the end of the mourning period."' But Porter continued to prevaricate.

The BBC ran out of patience and scheduled its programme for 19 July 1989. The final decision was taken by John Birt, then Deputy Director-General of the BBC. The Friday before transmission, Ware received a phone call while he sat in a management editorial meeting. It was Roger Rosewell. 'I am, as I speak, walking round Hyde Park with Shirley and we're trying to decide what to do and this is the deal. She will do an interview but she has to have the right to break off at the end of each question to consult with me or her lawyer.' Ware replied, 'I very much doubt whether that will be acceptable but I'll put it to the Deputy Director-General.' Birt told Ware, 'No.' Ware told Rosewell, 'No.' Rosewell said, 'Right.'

Ware said, 'Well, that's it then; is that it, John?' 'That's it,' said Birt. Ware said goodbye and put down the phone.

Wednesday, 19 July started badly for Porter and got progressively worse. It was the first day of the public hearings by the District Auditor, John Magill, and Tony Child, his legal adviser, into the cemeteries sale. The two men had already produced one damning interim report in November 1988, but July's public hearings were held to decide whether councillors and officers should be surcharged and disqualified from holding public office for five years. Magill had established himself at County Hall and during the first day submerged himself in the extraordinary transactions of John Whybrow, Clive Lewis, Peter Hartley, George Touchard and the rest. At the close of the day, Magill was preparing to return home to Wimbledon when he was approached by Neale Coleman and handed a note. It was a formal objection to the council's designated sales policy signed by Coleman and twelve other Westminster residents, including a number of other Labour councillors and Dr Richard Stone. The 'Objectors', as they became known, demanded an investigation into Porter's designated sales policy and the punishment of those responsible; their concerns were based on the revelations to be broadcast by *Panorama* that evening. Magill was perplexed and, once home, he settled into his armchair to watch the programme. Tony Child also tuned into BBC1 at his house in Essex.

Ware's *Panorama* film, entitled 'Lady Porter – the Pursuit of Power' opened with footage of Margaret Thatcher and Porter cleaning Downing Street with another of Westminster's gadgets. 'With a little help from Mrs Thatcher,' reported Ware, 'Shirley Porter is credited with cleaning up much of dirty London.' Twenty seconds into the programme, Ware got to the point: 'But tonight's *Panorama* discloses how she's spent millions of pounds of ratepayers' money to try to keep her Tory council in power, a policy which may be unlawful.' *Panorama* dispelled the myth of Porter as the radical Leader of a Tory flagship council, and, remaining faithful to the evidence which Ware meticulously deployed, presented the world with the unvarnished and unwholesome truth: gerrymandering, corruption and dirty tricks.

Porter invited her supporters and the press to a party at her flat to watch the broadcast, and affected a casual nonchalance to the public exposure of the decisions and actions she had worked so hard to disguise. She hoped her act of cheery stoicism would win her a favourable press. Dick Murray of the *Evening Standard* was present and reported on her reaction: 'the only anger came when Lady Porter realised the red and white table wine they had ordered had come from nearby Sainsbury's instead of her own store.'

Also watching nervously was Barry Legg, holding a similar *Panorama* party back at City Hall. Before the broadcast, he had left several messages on the answering machine of Patricia Kirwan inviting her along. When she had failed to return his calls, he had grown increasingly anxious, with good reason. Ware laid out before the viewers the full BSC gerrymandering strategy outlined by Porter in 'Keeping Westminster Conservative', but Kirwan's interview for *Panorama* was the most damaging part of the programme. In one exchange, she confirmed what BSC really meant:

KIRWAN: I remember Shirley once saying 'Now all of you listen here, whenever you see that word "Building Stable Communities", that means we're going to try and win that ward.'
WARE: Was it clear then, to you and to others that effectively Shirley Porter was talking about gerrymandering?
KIRWAN: I think gerrymandering is a not particularly pleasant word that the Conservative Party would not like to use.
WARE: Is it a fair description of those meetings?
KIRWAN: I think yes. I mean undoubtedly there . . . was [a plan] to increase the Conservative vote in those areas.
WARE: The principal overriding aim?
KIRWAN: Yes.

Kirwan's final analysis of Porter was: 'I hope she'll be remembered for a lot of the good things she has done in Westminster – and she has. I have a feeling that the good things may be overtaken by some of the less fortunate things that have happened.' When the programme ended, Kirwan, who watched the transmission at the Lime Grove studios, felt that Ware had not gone far enough in attacking Porter in a programme which was, by any standards, an astonishing denunciation of a public figure. On the following day Kirwan escaped both flak and the media spotlight by driving to the Languedoc in the south of France.

As for Porter, she described the programme as 'a series of attacks by a bunch of guttersniping screwballs' before also taking off, to Switzerland to meet up with her daughter, Linda. On her return, Porter commissioned Nick Reiter to compose a 'Glossary of Difficult Terms' which would explain away awkward expressions such as 'key wards' and 'Building Stable Communities'. According to the 'Glossary of Difficult Terms', the eight wards were 'identified as a result of discussions' and their choice was based 'on stress factors'. BSC was 'a corporate objective to increase and maintain permanent residency'; the 'numerical targets for electors' were 'guestimates of what might be achieved in the given ward in terms of getting additional electoral registrations, if BSC was fully and effectively implemented'.

Reiter had tendered his resignation by the time he received Porter's commission. He had become increasingly unhappy about what was going on, and when he received the inevitable call from John Ware during the making of *Panorama*, he had felt more dread than surprise. 'I never doubted that it would get out eventually,' says Reiter. 'I always wondered why Shirley Porter was doing it frankly. It wasn't for the money.' Reiter wrote the 'Glossary of Difficult Terms' on his last day at Westminster. He clearly did not put his heart into it; it is high on implausibility and low on enthusiasm.

The note from the Westminster Objectors, supported by the *Panorama* revelations, required the District Auditor to investigate. It would be the longest and most expensive inquiry by a District Auditor in history. From the beginning, attempts were made to confuse him. The 'Glossary of Difficult Terms' was produced to lie about what had happened; documents which told the truth would be destroyed.

But despite the evidence unearthed by *Panorama*, before numerous court appearances and her eventual exile, Porter would still be fêted as Lord Mayor of Westminster and receive a Damehood from the Conservative government.

CHAPTER 22

The Incredible Voyage of HMS Poll Tax Fiddle (July 1989–May 1990)

Panorama's investigation had an impact on City Hall even before the broadcast. A month earlier, in June, the senior members of the secret BSC Officers' Steering Committee held their regular meeting to discuss the gerrymandering initiatives and check the latest charts to see how the targets for new voters were being met in the marginal wards. At the close of business, their minutes recorded that: 'The Group agreed most of its functions were self-running and that there was no longer a need for regular general meetings.' It was their final gathering. Perhaps it was because the gerrymandering was now effectively on autopilot, but that seems unlikely. A realisation that the game was up is a more rational explanation. In the months following *Panorama*, the BSC machine was quietly dismantled as enthusiasm for the policy shrivelled, but the Sitex doors remained in place. The plotters had a choice: either admit the wrongdoing and cooperate with the authorities or lie and try to destroy the proof. They chose the second path without hesitation.

The letter from the Westminster Objectors had triggered the District Auditor's inquiry. *Panorama* had provided compelling evidence, but the Auditor had to prove that a loss to public funds had been incurred by councillors and officers who had wilfully abused public resources, knowing they were doing so unlawfully. The bar needed to prove guilt was set extremely high. The Auditor could not go by the allegations of a television programme, so he started a painstaking inquiry which would last four and a half years.

Meanwhile, the *Daily Mirror* suggested that if the BBC was wrong, the damages owing to Shirley Porter could exceed £2 million; if the BBC was right, added the paper, Porter should resign. Porter denied the allegations and made threatening noises about suing the BBC for defamation, but she had two big problems if she wanted to bring a libel case: firstly, she knew the allegations in the programme were true and secondly, Matthew Ives refused to support her.

After the programme, Porter summoned Ives to a meeting attended by solicitors from the firm of Peter Carter-Ruck. She had hired them to take on *Panorama* but she needed the City Solicitor on side. She told Ives, 'All these nasty things that are being said about what we're doing. I'm considering suing; what do you think?' Ives was appalled. As far as he was concerned, Porter could 'paddle her own canoe'. In his opinion, the Auditor's inquiry or the courts were the proper forums for the investigation and the last thing he wanted was another court action which would necessarily examine the *Panorama* allegations. It would be nothing but a dangerous distraction; libel juries were typically unstable beasts which condemned or exonerated both liars and their accusers alike with little obvious method. Ives advised against defamation proceedings.

The Objectors and Labour councillors again tried to force Porter to abandon designated sales by challenging the policy in the High Court, which ruled in Porter's favour. The same happened when the Objectors took their case to the Court of Appeal, which ruled that the investigation by the District Auditor was 'more apt to decide disputed issues of fact than is procedure by way of judicial review'.

Patricia Kirwan had returned from the Languedoc by September knowing that her interview for *Panorama* had been political suicide. 'It was like farting in public,' says Ware. 'In that febrile political climate that kind of disloyalty to the party was the worst thing to do.' By challenging Porter and exposing the wrongdoing,

Kirwan had become a non-person in the eyes of the City Council and the Tory Party. But she decided to go out with a bang. On her return, she resigned her council seat and attacked Porter further in the national press. Having already inflicted a heavy blow against her adversary over the gerrymandering, she now sought to undermine Porter's record on the one thing which everyone had assumed, despite the evidence of their eyes, Porter had defeated: rubbish.

Kirwan railed against the disgusting state of Westminster's streets. After more than six years of Porterism, Westminster had never looked so filthy. Kirwan told the *Sunday Times*, 'We have the best advertised leadership and the dirtiest Westminster ever.' By the autumn of 1989, most of Fleet Street had reached the same conclusion. The *Sunday Times* described the 220 miles of streets of Westminster as 'a litter choked disgrace'. In particular, Piccadilly: 'Eros statue surrounded by eighteen overflowing bins and a carpet of trampled food wrappers. There was no sign of the fulltime Piccadilly sweeper the council claims to employ'; Covent Garden: 'high piles of stinking rubbish bags against the market walls to the dismay of tourists strolling to restaurants'; Oxford Street: 'the pavement outside Marks and Spencer . . . barely visible beneath a sticky mass of discarded handbills and crushed food cartons', and Westminster Abbey and Parliament Square: 'Pavements and gutters . . . clogged with litter and bags of rubbish'. At night, rats were overrunning St James's Park, and according to the *Sun*, Leicester Square was 'shameful, dirty and squalid'. The *Daily Express* described Oxford Street as the 'filthiest road in Britain'. Outside Porter's home in Gloucester Square, the London Electricity Board had dug a huge hole and would not fill it in for another twelve months. Around the corner in Norfolk Square, exasperated hoteliers decided to pay for their own street cleaning. Despite the Pothole Eaters, WISP and ZIP, Westminster was undeniably grubby. The City Council had lost sight of its own purpose. In the topsy-turvy world of City Hall, the activities of dustmen were targeted not at rubbish, but at votes. Only the eight marginal wards had been well looked after, but even they had suffered neglect in the post-*Panorama* panic.

Porter's reaction to press criticism was another gimmick. The

Citizens' Task Force was formed in autumn 1989 to encourage Westminster residents to report any rubbish they happened to see lying around. Porter pressganged Margaret Thatcher into signing up for a photo-call but the launch of the Citizens' Task Force was boycotted by community organisations such as the Soho Society and the Covent Garden Community Association. The Residents' Association of Mayfair had no wish to be 'implicated in another of Lady Porter's initiatives' and pronounced that it had 'seen no evidence over the past years that the Council has been willing to tackle any of the problems and consider they are now expected to provide free labour to do the work the Council has so conspicuously failed to'. Little more was heard of the Citizens' Task Force.

Meanwhile, Margaret Thatcher was under pressure from the country and her party. One of the main reasons for Thatcher's eventual ejection from office was the introduction of a new form of local taxation, her personal obsession, shortly after her second election victory in 1987. She planned to replace the rates tax based on property values, with the community charge or poll tax, paid by everyone on the electoral register. The change would have a dramatic effect on Westminster, which had drawn part of its huge wealth from the expensive neighbourhoods in the City. Now every voter, except the poorest and the unemployed, would have to pay the same amount regardless of personal income. The inherent unfairness in the new system was apparent at once to people such as Gerald Grosvenor, the sixth Duke of Westminster and the country's richest man, who thought it so perverse that his poll tax would be the same as that of members of his staff that he immediately agreed to pay their bills.

As everyone had to pay the same to their council, a key element to the policy was to keep the tax low to deflect public criticism away from local councillors, the government and the Conservative Party. This vital point was recognised early on by Barry Legg, one of Porter's more astute acolytes. Legg feared that the rising costs of homelessness would fall on local taxpayers; and that, ironically, BSC might mean a higher poll tax, jeopardising Porter's chance of re-election in 1990. Nick Reiter says, 'I got the impression that Barry Legg convinced Shirley Porter that the battleground would

now be about local tax, and that the way for them to win would be
to play the old "Labour is high taxation and we are low taxation"
tactic. He thought they should stop concentrating so much on BSC
and really get the tax issue sorted out.'

In a confidential report Legg observed that 'the cost of homelessness would take up eight per cent of the community charge'.
The council was spending more than £7 million on extra temporary accommodation, as a result of designated sales, approximately
ten per cent of the council's spending at the time. On 9 May 1989,
two months before the *Panorama* programme, Graham England
and David Hopkins, the City Treasurer, warned Porter about the
extra costs involved in denying homeless families the chance to live
on estates earmarked for sale: 'We are taking more cases a year
than we are able to house. Unless the Government repeals the legislation, or we can supply more accommodation, this will have a
major impact on the City's Community Charge . . .' In their panic,
Porter and her chairmen 'de-designated' thousands of empty flats,
using them instead to house homeless families and cut down on the
exorbitant fees paid to bed-and-breakfasts. Even this climbdown,
essential to reduce the poll tax, was not to be allowed seriously to
undermine the gerrymandering: Porter decreed that the properties
to be used should be 'outside marginal wards. ASAP.' Although
scaled down, designated sales continued, but for Porter the poll tax
was now a more immediate priority in her fight to defeat Labour in
1990.

The poll tax disaster had been forecast long before its introduction in May 1990. The *Sunday Times* columnist Simon Jenkins
described it as 'a random visitation, like Aids, a virus vaguely
traceable to some long-past electoral promiscuity. Dozens of MPs
could be wiped out before a cure is found.' For the author Robert
Harris, writing in the same paper a month before the new tax's
imposition, it was 'an ugly, wicked, loathsome, bastard creation'.
Its introduction was planned for the week before the local council
elections in 1990 and Porter knew that high bills could wipe out all
the hard work of BSC. Home owners and even loyal Tories were up
in arms about the poll tax. Eighteen Conservative councillors in
West Oxfordshire were forced to set a poll tax of £412 in January

1990 and then promptly resigned in disgust, costing the party control of the local council. Nine Tory councillors in Beverley left their party, as did the Mayor of St Austell. In Truro, a woman on horseback ran a spear through a 20ft effigy of the Prime Minister before it was burned at the stake in front of hundreds of protesters. And eventually the poll tax would lead to one of the worst riots that Central London has ever experienced.

Secret papers showed that Westminster's poll tax would be set at £429, well in excess of the average for the old rates of £383. Such a hike of more than ten per cent would be political disaster. As usual, there was obsessive concern about the eight marginal wards. According to a paper by political lobbyists: 'In the two most marginal Conservative-held wards, Cavendish and St James's, the increases of . . . community charge over average rate bill per adult would be £43 and £66 respectively, and in the two most marginal Labour-held wards, Little Venice and Maida Vale, the increases would be £63 and £141 respectively . . . The Conservatives' chances of retaining control of Westminster by holding Cavendish and St James's wards in May 1990 are not likely to be helped by the projected community charge.' Porter and Legg believed that despite the success of BSC in bringing new voters into the marginal wards, a high tax would lose them Westminster.

The pair developed a secret strategy to scare the government into keeping down the tax with millions of extra pounds in Whitehall funds to make up the losses caused by BSC. After all, most of the money for local services still came from central government; local taxes were mainly a way of topping up finances and ensuring town hall accountability, but even the smallest fluctuation in a council's finances could make all the difference between a low and a high tax. The threat to Thatcher was simple: bail us out or you will lose the most important Tory flagship borough. Porter knew the Prime Minister was in deep trouble over the issue and perversely it meant the fate of the two women now became entwined.

Westminster hired a company of professional political lobbyists, Gifford Jeger Weeks (GJW), to keep the tax low by every possible means. GJW wrote briefing papers for Westminster such as

'Electoral Disaster', which were sent to the Prime Minister and virtually every government department and senior official at Central
Office. The Home Office was warned that Labour control of
Westminster represented a serious security threat. A GJW briefing
paper reported: 'The most acute embarrassment would be felt at
the Home Office where security arrangements for the Royal family,
Parliament and State visits depend heavily on the co-operation of
Westminster City Council. It is unlikely that the Home Secretary
would look forward with any alacrity to having to deal with a
Labour-controlled City Council.'

Other ministers were briefed by GJW including those at the
Departments of Education and Environment. Judith Chaplin, a
special adviser to Nigel Lawson, the Chancellor of the Exchequer,
was also lobbied and was perplexed by the notion that a particular
council, however self-important, should demand special treatment.
According to a GJW report, Chaplin did not act as expected: 'She
was not surprised or appalled by the Westminster political brief . . .
This may be partly because the Treasury has always opposed the
Community Charge and they may be privately pleased to see it running into trouble. She said it would be difficult to find extra money
[for Westminster] to bail out the Community Charge.' More powerful people would reach a different conclusion.

The extra money was found for Westminster through the various
agencies of central government. Richard Luce, the Arts Minister,
was warned that 'it might be difficult for Westminster to contemplate continued funding' for the English National Opera and the
English National Ballet, both based in the City. These national
institutions were already facing financial extinction, but Porter had
no hesitation in slashing their grants by ninety per cent in her bid
to retain power at the elections. Peter Palumbo, Chairman of the
Arts Council, described the decision as 'scandalous' and said the
council had failed to live up to its 'much vaunted support for the
arts'. He demanded a meeting with Porter. She refused to see him.
'It would not be proper,' explained a City spokesman, when asked
about Porter's haughty refusal. The government stepped in with
funds to save the two companies from closure and £17 came off the
Westminster poll tax.

The biggest ruse to prop up Westminster's finances was dressed up by the government as an 'error'. Westminster City Council was required to pay the National Rivers Authority £700,000 a year towards protecting the City against floods, but the council always got the money back from the government. Just before setting its first poll tax, Westminster received a cheque from the government for £7 million for flood relief. Apparently, someone had carelessly added another nought. The fiddle was exposed in the press two months before the introduction of the tax. Questions were asked in the House of Commons but a spokesman for the Department of the Environment said there was no need to 'reassess the figures at this late stage'. Porter could cut the bills by another £46.

The government now declared that the owners of second homes would have to pay the full tax on the properties. Although this applied across the country, it was felt keenly in Westminster where there were 14,000 second-home owners. The extra income for City Hall had an immediate effect: another £37 off the bill. A further £134 was shaved off the bill by a series of minor financial measures which went undetected by Labour councillors and the media.

At a press conference on 14 February 1990 Shirley Porter triumphantly announced the first poll tax to be charged by Westminster: £195. It was the lowest in the country at the time and would be bettered only by Wandsworth's charge of £148 a fortnight later. The average bill elsewhere in the country was £370. The *Daily Telegraph* described Mrs Thatcher as 'delighted' and said she would be holding up 'Wandsworth as well as Westminster to other Tory councillors as examples of the way efficient councils could give value for money and hold down their charges to local residents'. Shirley Porter brayed in the *Daily Mail* that it was all down to efficient housekeeping and cutting back on 'red tape and bureaucracy'. But she had achieved the low tax by a cunning combination of chicanery and threats, when her own corruption would later be calculated by the Labour Party at around £100 million.

Porter's poll tax triumph helped her fend off calls for her resignnation two days later when John Magill published his final report on the cemeteries sale, which he ruled had been unlawful on twenty counts and caused by 'negligence and misconduct'. Peter Hartley and George Touchard were criticised but escaped surcharge.

On 1 April new gates at the entrance to Downing Street approved by Sid Sporle protected Thatcher from the wrath of the poll tax rioters who flowed down Whitehall and around the West End. There were 341 arrests and damage was caused to over 350 businesses. The cost of the clean-up and repairs was put at more than a million pounds. Porter sent the clean-up bill to the Anti-poll Tax Federation. There was no chance of them paying of course; the organisation was largely made up of young anarchists, who did not believe in paying bills of any kind, particularly when sent by a woman so recently dubbed by *Time Out* magazine an 'Enemy of the People'.

As the local elections approached the pollsters were expecting an eight per cent swing from Thatcher to the Labour leader, Neil Kinnock. A week before polling, the *Times Educational Supplement* reported that if the swing were replicated across London, 'Labour will romp home in Wandsworth and Westminster, Mrs Thatcher's favourite councils.' All the newspapers agreed it would be a disaster for Thatcher if the Conservatives lost Westminster and Wandsworth. The *Telegraph* said: 'The opposition would interpret such defeats as the ultimate repudiation of Tory ideas for local government.' The *Financial Times* went further: 'For Labour, stealing the jewels in the Prime Minister's crown would be a damning verdict on the poll tax, and a damaging – perhaps fatal – blow to Mrs Thatcher's standing in her party.'

Porter planned one last publicity stunt before the critical local elections on 3 May 1990, to boast about the low £195 poll tax paid by residents in Westminster by comparing it to the £534 paid by people in the neighbouring Labour-controlled borough of Camden. She arranged for a press conference to take place at 9.15 a.m. on 1 May at a spot by the Grand Union Canal near Primrose Hill Bridge at the border of the two boroughs. Philip Wolmuth, the photographer, tipped off Jonathan Rosenberg, and the housing campaigner planned a retaliatory strike. He hastily requisitioned an eight-foot rowing boat, re-christened it *HMS Poll Tax Fiddle* and arranged to meet three friends, Piers Player, Will Rolt and Pete Stockwell, by the canal at Little Venice at 7.45 a.m.

It was a bright cool morning as the four men steered the boat into the canal. Rosenberg had prepared huge banners proclaiming 'Poll Tax Fiddle' and 'Never Forget Westminster's 15p Cemeteries'. The men carried a torch to light their way through the tunnel under the Edgware Road and managed to get a tow from a narrowboat most of the way to the target area. They then rowed *HMS Poll Tax Fiddle* behind some reeds and lurked in wait for Porter.

The press gathered at the designated time. Shirley Porter and David Hunt, the Local Government Minister who had agreed to participate in the stunt, strode past the media pack and stood with their backs to the canal while Porter held up a poster: 'Kilburn Toll-gate: Annual Toll, £534. You are now leaving Westminster and entering Camden.' *HMS Poll Tax Fiddle* went into action. Rosenberg shouted directions from the toll path as his three friends rowed the boat behind Porter and Hunt and unfurled their banners. According to Rosenberg's diary: 'The mob spotted the boat and, as one, the cameras swung down to the canal to get a good shot. Porter was furious and immediately turned and ran. Seeing that a routine publicity stunt had been transformed into something a little more spicey, the media got their shots, and then followed in hot pursuit.'

Porter and Hunt fled down the canal and took refuge in the *Lady Rose* barge. The crew of *HMS Poll Tax Fiddle* called through their megaphone: 'Aren't you ashamed, Mr Hunt, to be on a boat with Lady Porter?' and 'How can a council be efficient when it sells three cemeteries for fifteen pence?' Her stunt ruined, Porter left the sanctuary of the *Lady Rose* only to discover that a Westminster traffic warden had clamped her car. The following morning, all the newspapers carried photographs of Porter being torpedoed by three men in a boat.

Two days later, with the Tories more than twenty per cent behind Labour in some national polls, people voted in the local elections. It was to achieve victory at the polls that Shirley Porter had schemed for so long and despite the string of public scandals involving her, the electorate was not persuaded to vote Labour. According to the BSC graphs, her gerrymandering strategy had brought 2,200 potential new Tories into the marginal wards at a

HMS Poll Tax Fiddle in action; a Porter stunt is torpedoed.

huge cost to the council and the communities of Westminster, but victory was finally clinched by a low poll tax. 'When detected and exposed,' declared Lord Scott of Foscote a decade later, when he came to examine the Porter gerrymandering scandal in the House of Lords, 'it must be expected, or at least it must be hoped, that political corruption will receive its just desserts at the polls.' Lord Scott's high ideals were disappointed by the electorate of the City of Westminster who simply placed their sense of financial well-being before their sense of smell.

Paul Dimoldenberg had great plans for Westminster. If he had managed to achieve what he expected to be a decisive victory over Shirley Porter, he was going to sack Bill Phillips and had already sounded out David Hopkins, the City Treasurer, to take over as acting chief executive. Dimoldenberg also took the risk of standing in the critical ward of Cavendish, which Labour had so nearly won four years earlier. In the event, his plans came to nothing. Labour was virtually obliterated in Westminster. 'I suppose we were a bit naive in taking on both the Conservative

Council and the Conservative Party which had all the power necessary to help Westminster out of its financial mess,' says Dimoldenberg. 'They knew we were coming. With hindsight, it was a bit like the Charge of the Light Brigade. We were well organised but they were more so and got people in to do the canvassing and so on.'

Before the election, Porter had a majority of just four. There were twenty-seven Labour councillors, thirty-two Conservative councillors and one Independent. After 3 May 1990 she enjoyed a majority of thirty-six. Now there were forty-eight Tories and twelve Labour councillors. Lois Peltz, the only Independent councillor, lost her seat in the West End ward, one of the eight seats specifically targeted by Porter. Paul Dimoldenberg and his deputy, Neale Coleman, lost their seats, as did other leading figures such as David Pitt Watson. Porter had won seven of the eight crucial marginal wards; only Millbank remained Labour. Peter Bradley, the Millbank councillor, says, 'It was like standing in the wreckage of an aircraft disaster where thankfully you are unscathed but all your mates have gone down. It was quite traumatic and it took a long time for us to regather. Of course there was a lot of triumphalism amongst the Tories, and at a national level they managed to spin it that because they had held Wandsworth and Westminster somehow they had won the local elections nationwide which was far from the truth.'

The results were far better for Porter than any projections, despite the vital role played by Westminster's low poll tax. There were two other factors in her landslide. Porter's deployment of Marketforce had obviously paid dividends. In some marginal wards, the turnout reached unprecedented levels of more than fifty per cent, double the usual level. In one ward, it was 68.75 per cent. Most significantly, the gerrymandering had had its effects. An estimated 565 homeless families had been deported out of Westminster and hundreds of the 'right sort' of residential units had been given planning approval in the marginal wards, although it is impossible to know for certain how many additional voters this had produced by May 1990. Porter had also sold approximately 3,775 council homes, since 1986, of which 618 were designated sales.

photographs © Associated Newspapers/Solo Syndication

V for Victory? Porter offers some advice to a
defeated Labour opponent.

In her regular column for the *Paddington Mercury*, Porter wrote:
'Elections are a vital part of our democratic life, but for candidates
like me, they can also be a nerve-racking experience. She wanted to
run the City 'in the interests of every resident and not just those
who voted one way or another on May 3rd.' She also vowed to
continue her policy to sell as many council properties as possible,

despite the taint of gerrymandering: 'The city council will be using all its efforts in the next four years to make sure home ownership opportunities are just as widespread in Westminster as in the rest of the country.' John Wheeler, Tory MP for Porter's North Westminster, declared, 'I would like to congratulate and thank Shirley Porter for her courage in seeing through policies against the greatest political vilification from some in the Labour opposition. Her courage has been rewarded.'

CHAPTER 23

Pantomime Dame
(April 1990–September 1993)

Porter was planning her exit strategy from Westminster: she wanted a seat in the House of Lords and a job running London in Mrs Thatcher's government. Her desire for a peerage had become acute. Before the local elections, she had summoned Roger Bramble, the urbane and well-connected Tory councillor who had originally failed to persuade Margaret Thatcher's private parliamentary secretary Michael Alison to elevate Porter to the Lords. Porter told Bramble, 'I'm sure you agree I should have a peerage.' Bramble said, 'I'm no arbiter of these things, Shirley.' 'Well,' she said, 'you know all the right people. Let it be known that it would be appropriate.' He said he would 'take soundings'.

Bramble was dining at the Dutch embassy soon after when he spotted Willie Whitelaw, former deputy Prime Minister. 'Willie,' he said, 'I've got some bad news for you. Shirley Porter wants a peerage.' There was a moment's silence before Whitelaw suffered a violent coughing fit. The fit abated but further discussion was clearly out of the question. A confused Bramble later recounted the incident to a mutual friend who explained: 'Oh, that's a very old tactic of Willy's; when there's something he really can't handle, he has respiratory problems.'

Porter embarked on a political project to promote her peerage by commissioning two academics, Professor William Letwin and Keith Boyfield, to draft a paper called 'A Minister for London: A Capital Concept', which proposed a government minister for London. Neither Letwin nor Boyfield were in any doubt that she wanted the job as minister for herself, but to become a government minister, you need a seat in the House of Lords or the House of Commons, and Porter was not an MP.

Porter called a press conference on 19 April 1990 to promote the report. 'A Capital Concept' paints an abysmal picture of Thatcher's London in the wake of GLC abolition: 'Living and working in London is increasingly painful, tending towards the brutish.' It was now 'among the most squalid cities in Europe. Litter and rubbish are corroding the capital's image.' The number of burglaries had trebled between 1978 and 1988; 2,000 vagrants were sleeping rough each night on London streets; the schools were so bad that the capital was perceived as 'educationally subnormal'. But Porter did not identify the obvious culprits for the decay: a Conservative government which had been in power for eleven years and councils such as Westminster with responsibility for the capital. Porter's sudden concern for the whole of London seems to have struck few people as odd, even though she had shown no concern for it to date. She had deported her problems to other parts of London, and when it came to Westminster itself, obsessed for four years about only one third of it.

Porter planned to participate in a regional television programme to argue for a Minister for London, but first lobbied Thatcher. Boyfield says, 'Margaret Thatcher, as far as I understand it, left her in no doubt that she wasn't going to be put in the House of Lords and she wasn't going to become the first Minister for London.' Roger Rosewell rang Boyfield to say Porter had pulled out of the television debate and asked him to appear instead. 'We kind of went into reverse gear,' remembers Boyfield. 'We said the idea of a Minister for London was very good but it was an idea for not just yet.' In October 1990 Boyfield received a letter from Porter about his recommendations. She now felt that it would be rash to press ahead with Boyfield's proposals in case they divided rather than united the Conservative Party.

Harrowing events which demonstrated Porter's unfitness to rule Westminster, let alone London, were taking place in North Paddington. On 7 July 1990, Alastair Campbell, at that time political editor of the *Daily Mirror*, had exposed the deteriorating situation in Hermes Point and Chantry Point in a front-page article: 'Danger: These flats can kill.' Campbell's hard-hitting article hit a raw nerve, and the council decided suddenly that the asbestos situation in the two tower blocks was dangerous after all. Within two weeks of the *Daily Mirror* story, the council agreed to evacuate the flats. One expert report stated that: 'Asbestos contamination has been found throughout the building principally caused by the poor and raw condition of the sprayed asbestos.' It merely repeated what had already been known for years. Porter's flagship council sent workmen in protective suits and masks into the flats of young mothers to remove their babies' clothes from cupboards for decontamination. It was another year before the last tenant was moved out.

The only positive result of the tragic saga was that Walterton and Elgin Community Homes (WECH) was finally approved as landlord of the estates. In 1992 Westminster was forced to start handing out more than £22 million, a compromise sum significantly less than the £30 million originally demanded by residents towards repairs, and in April 1992 WECH took over the two estates. WECH took the view that the towers were in such poor condition that they could not be rehabilitated. In 1995 the asbestos was removed and the tower blocks were demolished to make way for new homes.

On 22 November 1990 Margaret Thatcher was forced from office and replaced by John Major, her Chancellor of the Exchequer. Within a few months Porter would follow, but not before her discredited policy of designated sales ran into further trouble from an unexpected quarter, at least in one part of the City. Four days after Thatcher's resignation, the Duke of Westminster won what became known as the 'Westminster versus Westminster' case in the High Court against Porter's City Council. Porter had designated for sale 532 flats in the brick-built black and white checkerboard Grosvenor Estate, off Page Street, in the marginal ward of Millbank. Although the leaseholds belonged to the council, the 999-year freehold had been retained by the Duke. The local Labour councillor, Peter

© Philip Wolmuth

Matthew Ives (left) receives an application from residents of WECH.

Bradley, had reminded His Grace that, according to a covenant safe-guarding the use of the buildings, they were to be used as 'dwellings for the working classes'. The Duke argued for the existence of the working classes against Porter's assertion that there was no such thing. In a nice twist, the *Evening Standard* portrayed the bout as 'The Duke *v* the barrow boy's daughter'. The Duke did not appreciate that he was targeting Porter's gerrymandering.

Sir Jeremiah Harman, a High Court judge and an Old Etonian, ruled in the Duke's favour and declared the working class alive and kicking, which provoked a fierce response by Porter in the letters column of the *Standard*: 'In a week when the son of a trapeze artist [John Major] has been battling to become Prime Minister, and less than a week after the British Communist party threw in the towel by lamenting "the fact of the working class is a thing of the past," the courts have ruled that we must remain wedded to an outdated class system.'

Bill Roots replaced David Hopkins as City Treasurer in November 1990, and much later, as chief executive, he would be the man responsible for sorting out Porter's mess. Roots had been treasurer of the London Borough of Bexley in south-east London when he was head-hunted by Westminster. 'It looked like a nightmare from where I was sitting. But,' he admits, 'I thought I'd like to meet Shirley Porter.' Roots was a tough local government accountant who did not take nonsense from anyone and liked to relax over a pint, a cigar and good gossip at his local rugby club. At his job interview, Porter introduced herself: 'We are not interested in messing around; take a seat.' Roots accepted the job as city treasurer and also assumed the role of deputy chief executive.

Soon after joining the council, Roots went to see Porter about the budget and found Roger Rosewell in the room. 'Who's he?' asked Roots. 'I'm sorry,' said Porter, 'I can't say.' Roots answered, 'Well, I can't talk to you, I'm here to talk about council business and he's not on the council, he's not a member or an officer; I'm not talking to him.' Porter asked Rosewell to leave. On another occasion, Porter sent for the city treasurer. 'I've had a hundred ideas,' she said. 'Can you come up?' Roots arrived and told her, 'Shirley, I'm only interested in the top three ideas that are do-able. I don't want to hear the other 97; I haven't got the time.'

Within a few weeks, Porter asked Roots to get rid of Bill Phillips. She had lost faith in Phillips during the crisis that followed *Panorama* and he was increasingly cast as the fall guy. Several senior officers and Tory councillors had come to loathe him: they concluded that his loyalty to Porter had blinded his own judgement and hers to the dangers inherent in the gerrymandering enterprise. Furthermore, in Porter's view, Phillips had 'failed to deliver', but on what was not clear. Certainly he had delivered on BSC, but perhaps that was the problem. Matthew Ives and Sid Sporle had long concluded that the managing director had provided disastrous advice and urged Porter to fire him. On being asked to manage the sacking, Roots told her, 'It's your job, you hired him. He's my boss!'

Phillips left in early 1991 after a regrettable mix-up over his expenses. He had forgotten that his salary included payment for organising elections and had claimed election remuneration of about £2,000 over and above his pay. Matthew Ives had been informed of the oversight by a worried clerk, and was himself so concerned that Phillips had been paid twice for the same role that he wanted to contact the police. Roots considered this course of action too drastic and agreed to handle the sensitive issue with Phillips directly. Phillips told Roots that it had been a misunderstanding. Roots said, 'Look, Bill, Shirley wants you out anyway. Either you pay this back with compound interest or I go to the police.' The two men agreed it would come out of Phillips' severance pay when he left as he did shortly afterwards. By any standards, Phillips's tenure had been calamitous.

The Conservative government knew about the gerrymandering allegations made by *Panorama* and that the District Auditor was in pursuit. Despite this, in January 1991 the new Prime Minister, John Major, made Porter a Dame of the British Empire in the New Year's Honours. She told the local press, 'I hope this honour has been made in recognition of the fact that the people of Westminster are now happy with the low community charge, cleaner streets and a brighter city and the emphasis on serving our customers.' A month later she went to Buckingham Palace with Sir Leslie to receive her honour from the Queen, who expressed her appreciation for the bottle banks supplied by Westminster City Council to help recycle the empties after state banquets. But a Damehood was not a seat in the House of Lords. Peter Bradley, deputy leader of the Labour group, scoffed that she had been 'Damed with faint praise' and further observed that 'every pantomime needs a Dame.'

Porter announced her resignation as Leader of Westminster City Council on 20 February 1991, after eight catastrophic years. On the same day she declared that Westminster residents would enjoy an even lower poll tax of £176, later reduced to just £36 when John Major slashed all bills by £140 to appease public wrath. The first editions of the *Evening Standard* led with Porter's triumph and carried a picture of her favourite stuffed toy, Paddington Bear. A few months later the government abolished the poll tax and said it would be replaced by a charge on property, to become known as the council tax.

Porter still clung to her dream of getting a peerage. She even pressed her claim directly to government ministers during meetings to discuss more important matters. Shortly before she handed over the leadership of the council, she met with Michael Heseltine, the new Environment Secretary, and Michael Portillo, one of his junior ministers, to discuss the central government grants. Westminster needed to balance the books. Roots had briefed Porter 'until the cows come home' on what to say, but before the meeting she told the Treasurer, 'I don't understand a word of it, can you deal with it?' Once at the meeting, she turned to Roots in front of the ministers and blurted out, 'Hurry up, Bill! What I'm really here for is: London needs a minister and I'm it.' Implicitly and constitutionally, this also meant she would have to be given a peerage. 'Right, I'm off!' announced an embarrassed Roots.

For many newspaper commentators, Porter's retirement as Leader of Westminster marked the final closure of the Thatcherite epoch. The *Daily Mail* said: 'Like the last rose of a Thatcherite summer, the redoubtable Dame Shirley Porter bows out as Leader of Westminster City Council.' The *Independent* observed: 'her departure, like the departure of Mrs Thatcher, does indicate the closing of a political era.' At City Hall, there was relief. At a meeting of chief officers, Matthew Ives said 'Crikey! She's gone now. Those of us who survived it should get a medal.' Graham England rejoined, remembering medals awarded to war veterans. 'What are we going to have?' he said. 'The "Porter Star"? ' Everyone laughed. They had survived. Sort of.

The leadership of Westminster was assumed by David Weeks, Porter's troubled deputy, in April. Law Lords would later describe Porter as the 'architect' of the corruption at City Hall and Weeks as the 'midwife'. Though Porter was no longer Leader, she remained a councillor. City Hall announced that she would become Lord Mayor in May 1991.

In both temperament and judgement, David Weeks proved to be unsuitable leadership material. His single most important achievement as Leader was the eventual reacquisition of the three cemeteries. Bill Roots in particular became exasperated with Weeks's prevarication over the issue. At one meeting, he asked him, 'Why can't I understand what the fuck's going on here?' He turned to Sid Sporle, slapped a coin down on the desk and said, 'Here's the twenty pence Sid, and I want five pence change.' Sporle negotiated directly with Wisland and reached an agreement on 29 June 1992. 'I got them back, didn't I?' says Sporle, but the relatives thought it a poor deal. The price was a nominal fifteen pence for the cemeteries themselves, but the land at Mill Hill, the crematorium at East Finchley and the properties, including all three lodge houses, were lost for ever. Furthermore, as part of the deal, the council awarded an annual maintenance contract to Cemetery Management Ltd, a company with close links to the owners, Wisland. Labour councillors felt Westminster was simply paying Wisland to look after the cemeteries. Peter Bradley described the deal as 'distasteful', telling the *Independent*: 'What it does is acquire for the Council all the liabilities and award Wisland all the public assets.' Labour councillors calculated that the affair had cost Westminster £4.25 million. 'Shirley Porter will go down in history as the woman who sold three council cemeteries for five pence each,' Bradley told the press, 'and David Weeks will go down in history as the man who bought them back for £4.25 million.'

Weeks's temper and conduct towards officers worsened. He failed to capture the public attention in the way Porter had. He hated his description in an unenthused press as the 'grey man of Westminster'. He would be deposed by his colleagues after just two years.

On 21 May Porter received her badge of office, lace mantle and funny hat as Lord Mayor from the Mace Bearer, Ernie Hodges, whose duties included driving Porter to official visits. Before long, he began to complain that she would urge him to break the speed limit to reach engagements on time. Porter occupied the Lord Mayor's parlour while the staff filled her diary with official engagements, which included receiving visiting foreign dignitaries, opening jumble sales and chairing council debates. The post was largely ceremonial but she threw herself with gusto into her new role. She launched a poetry competition, attended functions at local schools and took part in fun runs. It is a measure of how far *Panorama*'s allegations had faded from the public consciousness that Porter was invited to appear on Radio Four's *Desert Island Discs*, the nearest the BBC has to its own honour. Her choices included 'Maybe Because I'm a Londoner', the theme tune from the dance movie *Fame* and 'I'm Called Little Buttercup' from Gilbert and Sullivan's *HMS Pinafore*. The presenter, Sue Lawley, probed gently about the cemeteries but Porter argued that it would take too long to explain the background. Lawley did not mention designated sales or BSC.

While in office, Porter took the opportunity to appease her old school friends at the Warren, upset by her allegations of anti-Semitism against their old headmistress G. A. Ashworth. It is possible that Porter felt guilty or was perhaps concerned that members of the Old Girls Association might take their revenge in print. Whatever the reason, three of the Old Girls received an invitation from Porter to attend an official cocktail party at City Hall. Pru Moorcroft had not seen her since their school days but the Lord Mayor, dressed in full regalia, threw her arms around her and gossiped as if she were an old friend.

Porter's Lord Mayor's Parade on 1 January 1992 was one of the most spectacular in living memory. Some 3,500 performers took part, including marching bands, cheerleaders from America and an elephant. Porter waved at the crowds from her landau. Later, she took a group of pensioners to a special concert at the Albert Hall. The highlight of her year as Lord Mayor was the official ceremony at the Banqueting House in Whitehall to grant Margaret Thatcher the Freedom of the City of Westminster. Porter, in full regalia, handed Thatcher a huge carriage clock. A painting of the event was commissioned, which hung proudly in City Hall long after Porter's public disgrace. Tony Travers, a local government expert at the London School of Economics, who often sees the picture on visits to City Hall, says, 'It's a masterpiece of its kind. It sort of encapsulates everything. Shirley Porter is dolled up to the nines in ermine and tricorn hat and Mrs T is dolled up to the nines, Mrs T style, in radiant purple. And with all the council officers and things. It is a fascinating scene. In the same way that if suddenly you hear a piece of pop music, the painting can transport you back to 1988 in one step.'

Porter's year as Lord Mayor was marred by a few embarrassing events. There was the time Peter Bradley, hoping to wind her up and inject some laughter into a council meeting, produced a Sooty Sweep glove puppet which he waved at Porter. She banged her gavel furiously. The stunt earned Bradley an official reprimand from Porter and a headline in the *Sunday Sport* sarcastically implying that the Labour councillor may have brought his party into disrepute: 'Kinnock man has hand in Sooty shame.' Unlike his colleagues, who found the incident amusing, Matthew Ives regarded it as rather tedious and he gently counselled Porter against hauling Bradley before the courts; he did not want to go down in case law history as the instigator of 'Westminster City Council *vs.* Mr S. Sweep'. Porter managed to overspend the mayoral budget by £50,000, mainly through extra staffing costs and ceremonial functions. When the fearless Roots threatened to report the matter to the full council, Porter called him an 'awkward sod', but paid up the difference out of her own pocket.

Meanwhile, Porter's hidden past was gradually beginning to catch up with her. In November 1990 the *Observer* had broken the news about the secret slush fund for the 1990 elections, operated by Porter's political mentor Michael Ivens and his Foundation for Business Responsibilities (FBR). When the Charity Commission launched an inquiry into allegations that a charity's funds had been misused for party political purposes, Ivens paid back the money, some £98,000, and resigned from the FBR. But there was speculation as to who actually provided Ivens with the funds. The Charity Commission was content to let the matter rest when the money was returned.

Porter became known as the 'Backdoor Mayor' by the *Guardian* because she used the rear entrance at the Council House in Marylebone to avoid the cemetery campaigners from WAR who were insisting on the return of their dead relatives to council control. They protested peacefully in silence at council meetings and other functions holding banners which read: 'DEAD FOR SALE – 5p'. At her last meeting as Lord Mayor, she was goaded into walking past the relatives. Her mayoral limousine, WE1, drew up and Porter got out with Sir Leslie and her sister, Irene. As Porter walked up the steps, she turned to Jo Mahoney, the WAR press officer, and pronounced imperiously, 'I just want to say . . .' Suddenly, Irene tripped. Mahoney says, 'Her sister went down the steps, arse over tit. Porter never did finish her sentence. I have often wondered what it is she wanted to say to me.'

After handing back her regalia in May 1992, and with no prospect of a government job and a peerage, Porter drifted for the next six months without a role. She faded from political life at Westminster, and rarely attended council meetings. On 11 February 1993 Porter was at her home in Palm Springs, California, when she finally tendered her resignation as a councillor by fax to City Hall. 'The news swept through her old power base,' reported Dick Murray of the *Evening Standard*. 'Providing one did not work directly for her,' he added, 'she was impossible not to like; she was a journalist's dream. I believe she would have climbed unaided up Nelson's Column with a rose between her teeth if it meant a picture and a story in the *Evening Standard*.'

At a hushed council meeting, Matthew Ives announced 'the resignation of a councillor', whereupon the chamber was treated to a vitriolic eulogy on her reign from Peter Bradley. He told the council, 'She thought if you could make people homeless, make them live in cardboard boxes, take away their meals-on-wheels and home helps and their day nurseries and their jobs as well, then just watch their pinched little faces light up when you offer them a bedsit in Luton.' Porter was, according to Bradley, 'unfortunately unforgettable, thankfully irreplaceable and certainly unlamented'. The council announced that there would be a by-election for a new councillor in the Hyde Park ward on 25 March.

'I have no regrets,' said Porter, when asked about her resignation, citing a new challenge as the reason for her departure. Porter's son, John, and his business partner, Matthew Cartisser, had acquired a forty-nine per cent interest in the ailing London commercial radio station, LBC, for £7 million through a Porter family firm, Chelverton Investments, and had installed Shirley Porter as chairman. LBC occupied the first two floors in what staff described as a 'great big rotting hulk of a building' on Hammersmith Road next to the Olympia exhibition halls, with only a pub, a newsagent, a launderette and a shop selling bondage gear in the vicinity. Evidence of decline was everywhere: the station had huge debts and staffing levels had been cut right back.

Shirley Porter's takeover was greeted with astonishment by the seasoned hacks at LBC, who were worried about what effect this appointment would have on the new licence application in October 1993. Amanda Lewis, a former LBC producer, says, 'She was a bit of a joke really. We couldn't quite believe that we had been taken over by this really dodgy local politician. She'd stopped being Leader of the Council by then and apparently her husband was getting tired with her being at home all the time. The rumour was that he had bought her this radio station. It was clearly a toy, but we were going down the pan; we had no money; we were losing money hand over fist. We were a dead radio station.'

Porter took over a huge office on the ground floor and could sometimes be seen striding through the building in expensive jewellery, wearing a belt with a gold buckle bearing the motif 'SHIRLEY'. She meddled with the station's output almost immediately. John Allen, editor of LBC's FM programmes, remembers being approached by Porter with an idea for a new programme, which she had got from her chauffeur. He had suggested there should be a fishing programme at midday on Thursday, so he could plan his weekend's angling while waiting to drive her to her various engagements. 'I looked at her in astonishment,' says Allen. 'And I said, "But, we're doing the midday news at that time, from 12 to 1 p.m. every day. Perhaps we could do something on the Saturday morning breakfast programme," and I sort of left it there. The next thing I knew was that LBC was doing a fishing phone-in programme at midday on Thursday on our medium wave frequency.'

Critically, Porter also interfered with the station's political content, complaining about the way the Conservative Party was covered. 'I think that interference was of a different order,' says Allen. At least one former senior news executive is thought to have expressed his concern and word drifted back to members of the Radio Authority, the Government quango with the power to grant commercial radio licences. 'The Radio Authority was an absolute stickler on editorial independence,' says Allen. 'I'm quite sure that having someone like Porter as chairman was a huge liability when we were trying to get our licence renewed.'

The fate of LBC was not helped by the growing feverish anticipation surrounding John Magill's report into the gerrymandering allegations, which was postponed repeatedly throughout 1993. On

3 September the Radio Authority announced that LBC would lose its licence to another station, London News Radio. 'I fail to understand how this will lead to more choice and diversity for Londoners,' said a furious Porter, as she surveyed the wreckage of her brief media career. The Radio Authority's decision came as a blow to LBC staff, who lost their jobs, but, for Shirley Porter, it was simply a harbinger of a shocking and irreversible downturn in her life and fortunes.

CHAPTER 24

War of the Machines (1989–94)

The gerrymandering inquiry had been running for more than four years when Shirley Porter lost her radio franchise. John Magill would take another four months to complete his explosive first report and he was still in the courts fighting Porter at the end of 2001. It was the longest inquiry of its kind into the affairs of a local authority. Although the powers of the District Auditor were extensive – he could order people to appear before him and he had the run of City Hall and access to all its documents – it took that long because Porter, David Weeks and others did all they could to thwart Magill's progress.

The misdeeds of politicians at a national level can sometimes lose millions and sometimes billions of pounds of taxpayers' money and result in disgrace and resignation, but there is no requirement on them personally to make good the losses. At local level, it was different. But the need for the District Auditors to prove 'wilful misconduct' meant that they rarely used their power of surcharge. John Magill knew that only compelling documentary evidence could establish whether Porter and the rest had wilfully broken the law, either recklessly or in the full knowledge that their conduct was wrong. To observers, the inquiry seemed to be a battle between Porter's City Hall on one side and on the other, the District Auditor.

But ultimately, the inquiry came down to a war of machines: the photocopier and the shredder. In the age of email, inquiries can be swiftly concluded by the harvesting of incriminating material from the ether. In 1989 the important thing was paper and paper is easily destroyed. Both Porter and Bill Phillips shredded documents to conceal the conspiracy. But, though incriminating documents did vanish from City Hall, others kept copies. It was a question of knowing where to look.

From the night of the *Panorama* broadcast, John Magill and his legal adviser, Tony Child, the Solicitor to the Audit Commission, were at a serious disadvantage. The programme had based its investigation on approximately twenty documents, which were sufficient in fending off a libel action but they were not enough in themselves to convict Porter and her team on grounds of wilful misconduct; for that far more evidence would be necessary. In the days following the television programme, Magill asked for documents from the BBC. Peter Horrocks, the deputy editor of *Panorama*, refused to supply the actual documents used by the programme to protect the sources of the material. Horrocks wrote: 'All of these documents should be readily available to you from either Council members, or Council officers, or the Westminster Conservative Group. This would seem to be the best way of assisting your enquiry without compromising individuals or betraying confidences.'

John Magill is an honourable man and honourable people often find it difficult to comprehend that others may not be. In the early days of his inquiry, he laboured under the illusion that he was dealing with professional politically independent officers who would tell the truth. If there was incriminating material, he thought all he had to do was request it and and that those who realised they had everything to lose would readily agree to hand it over. Magill had taken great pride in his appointment as District Auditor for Westminster in 1986. He had worked closely with both Bill Phillips and Graham England and held both men in high regard. 'My starting point was that if they told me something then it was true,' says Magill. On several occasions, he met Porter and was impressed by her apparent drive and enthusiasm. But all the time, behind the smiles and common courtesies, Porter and Phillips hid from the District Auditor the endemic abuse of the council's resources for unlawful electoral advantage.

Inquiries by the District Auditor come under the jurisdiction of the Audit Commission, a semi-autonomous government body established to police public spending by councils and health authorities.

© Empics

The District Auditor, John Magill.

On 2 August 1989, nearly two weeks after the *Panorama* programme, Paul Dimoldenberg wrote to Howard Davies, the
Commission's controller, to demand quick action. The Labour
councillor had learned that Magill would be on holiday until 21
August, but he requested that a special investigation, led by a 'special auditor', should be instigated in Magill's temporary absence as
was allowed by law. Dimoldenberg believed that the corruption
exposed by *Panorama* was so widespread that such unprecedented
measures were required. He wrote to Davies: 'If the *Panorama* allegations are correct then Westminster City Council is acting contrary
to law and continues to do so. I believe it is your duty to act speedily and certainly within the next seven days.' Davies replied on 4
August: 'I do not propose to appoint a special auditor in these circumstances. It does not seem to me to be unreasonable that Mr
Magill goes on holiday from time to time, particularly in August.'
Dimoldenberg became increasingly frustrated with the progress of
the investigation as the days and weeks ebbed away and the shredders gorged themselves on documents inside City Hall. The Labour
councillor wrote again to the Audit Commission to express his concern about Magill's delay in dealing with the Objectors' concerns.
On 5 October Davies reported on Magill's progress to Dimoldenberg: 'I am satisfied that he is pursuing his enquiries into these
matters as speedily as possible.'

For the first year after the *Panorama* broadcast, Bill Phillips was
Magill's point of contact with City Hall. Magill little realised that
it was the managing director who had helped orchestrate the BSC
strategy for Shirley Porter. From the outset, Phillips misled Magill
about critical documents. In March 1990, eight months after
Panorama, Bill Phillips responded to Magill: 'I think I should formally point out that the City Council does not have a "key wards"
strategy or policy (notwithstanding the fact that the term 'key
wards' – which could mean different things in different contexts –
does appear in a number of documents). Accordingly there are no
Council documents under such a heading.' Later, Magill could not
comprehend how someone in Phillips's position could write something so 'fundamentally untrue'.

Magill's demand for copies of *Panorama*'s documents proved a gift to Phillips because, although it showed which documents Magill was aware of, it also revealed the hundreds of secret papers of which he had no knowledge. It was not until 22 May 1990, ten months after the programme, that Phillips finally wrote to the District Auditor inviting him to inspect documents at City Hall. Magill would later comment: 'The documentation assembled for my inspection was far from complete.'

Shortly before Phillips's departure in late 1990, Bill Roots received an anxious call from a secretary in the managing director's office: 'Bill Phillips is shredding everything.' Roots ordered her to 'copy everything' and bring the material to him. Roots handed the papers over to his internal audit team for safekeeping. But many reports and documents had already been destroyed, including a record of no fewer than forty secret meetings held either by politicians or officers, or both. The District Auditor's report later would be littered with such phrases as: 'The Council has been unable to locate any other reports to the meeting of . . .'

However, neither investigator nor investigated had taken into account the outpouring of the BSC machinery. Any successful conspiracy must have the cover-up carefully built into it from the start. A bank robber will devote as much attention to planning the getaway as the heist itself. But at Westminster Council, the conspirators implicated themselves with their meticulous records of the conspiracy, kept mainly at Porter's insistence, to make sure her orders were carried out. Memos, monitoring graphs and other documents were made out in triplicate and then photocopied multiple times until City Hall was awash with the stuff. The District Auditor would even recover documents which contained shredding instructions. Minutes from a key strategy weekend in September 1988 say: 'All papers shredded.' Clearly, not all were. Through a combination of contempt and carelessness, Porter had lost control of her plot. Evidence may not have been found in Bill Phillips's filing cabinet, because he had destroyed it, but much of it was lying around, forlorn and forgotten, elsewhere in City Hall.

By December 1990 Magill had finished his review of the documents, including the few supplied by Bill Phillips, and was ready to begin conducting interviews with Tony Child his legal adviser. John

Magill, a tall and cheerful Liverpudlian, was not only the District Auditor but a senior partner of Touche Ross, later Deloitte Touche, a top City accountancy company, where he had gained promotion as a formidable accountant. During his inquiry, he deliberately suppressed his natural exuberance behind a façade of austerity. He had a passion for golf and hill walking, and was a Francophile with a home in France and an occasional yearning for a game of *boules* with the locals on the Côte d' Azur. Tony Child, by his own admission, was a sports fanatic first and Solicitor to the Audit Commission second. He was player-manager of the Braintree and Brocking Football Club and a wicket-keeper batsman for Redbridge Parks Cricket team. In the decade before his appointment at the Audit Commission, he had acted as Solicitor to the London Borough of Greenwich. There was little Child did not know about either local government law or leg-side stumpings. To Shirley Porter, with her notorious ignorance of both accountancy and law, these punctilious men must have appeared as two Riders of the Apocalypse.

The first round of interviews, which began on 17 December 1990, took two years during which Magill spoke to forty-four officers and councillors. Patricia Kirwan was the first witness. With brutal candour, she repeated the allegations she had made on *Panorama* and went into more gory detail. She explained how estates in non-marginal wards were included as 'a cosmetic exercise so as not to make it look as though it was a complete political fix'.

Some interviewees were not so easily available. Magill had to hire private detectives to track down Peter Hartley. When the former Housing Chairman appeared before the Auditor, he was one of the few interviewees to confess the true purpose behind BSC and designated sales. 'Shirley was in the driving seat,' he told Magill. 'This, as far as I and others were concerned was very much her baby. She started this . . . she was determined to see it through. I was quite convinced in my own mind that her intent . . . was to increase home ownership in those key wards.' Her intention, Hartley continued, was to 'gain electoral advantage by selling more properties in marginal wards'. Magill could not help liking the amiable and candid Hartley, who had admitted that he was down on his luck financially, and later felt sad at having to include him on the list of those individuals to be surcharged and banned from office.

In April 1991 Matthew Ives gave evidence. He told Magill that he had received a note from the Leader's office in March 1987 with a series of handwritten questions about designating all estates in marginal wards for sale. His suspicions 'were aroused that there might be other than good reasons for the sales in members' minds at this stage'. He confessed that he had 'smelt a rat'. Andrew Arden QC, who later acted for the Objectors, would observe that with 'a rat that size, he should have pulled out a gun and shot at it'.

Soon, the team was immersed in the strange world of Porter's City Hall. They were intrigued about Porter's personal advisers, 'the men with no names'. Magill had identified Roger Rosewell as the 'man with no name Number One' and another Porter adviser, Stuart Greenman, as the 'Man With No Name Number Two'. The Auditor asked Lawrie Smith, Porter's administrative assistant, 'Was there a man with no name Number Three?' Smith replied, 'There was one further adviser that I think was probably recruited . . . in the lead up to the election, whose main job was, as far as I understand it, the PR machinery . . . and he was "the man with no name Number Three".' But Smith could not recall his name.

Beneath City Hall lay the archives known simply as 'Muniments', a vast catacomb of spiders, damp and secrets, stretching out under Victoria Street as far as the underbelly of Pizza Hut. The name traditionally refers to a place where legal deeds are stored but at City Hall it was simply the place where all the council's old papers were kept. Magill insisted on an inspection of Muniments and his team, including Tony Child, Judy Libovitch and Ian Gibson, were escorted down into the bowels of City Hall by a council clerk with a torch. Magill was particularly interested in finding the old battered green filing cabinet belonging to Nick Reiter. Reiter had told the District Auditor that he had not destroyed his files before leaving Westminster but his filing cabinet had vanished. Magill started his hunt for it as the rest made their way into the dank recesses among the spiders' webs and hot water pipes. Almost immediately, he spotted a battered green filing cabinet through the gloom. 'I remember thinking "Eureka!"' says

Magill. 'I thought we had found the key to the whole thing.' But the filing cabinet was full of innocuous material. Reiter's filing cabinet was never found.

In November 1991 Child and his assistant Judy Libovitch discovered documents relating to a critical meeting when Porter and her chairmen had worked out the details of the gerrymandering conspiracy. Child says, 'There were a series of papers that suggested, at a political level at least, that there was an unlawful purpose of altering the composition of the electorate for the advantage of the Majority Party. The first one of those papers was written by Dame Shirley Porter, and a number of the documents had her handwriting on them so she couldn't say convincingly that she wasn't aware of them.' Child and Libovitch took the precaution of photocopying the file. Later they wrote to the council asking for the original, but the council could not produce it. The following day they were told that the original file which they had photocopied had disappeared; it was never seen again.

By 1992 the interviews were yielding results but the team had failed to obtain some critical documents. Magill and Child switched their search to the individual council departments and made significant headway. Magill's team visited both planning and housing departments and discovered several copies of an important document in the files which the council had said did not exist. Child says, 'We went to different places in the Council and we found a number of copies of this document on file. To think the Council couldn't have found copies before if they wanted beggars belief.' Magill says, 'By this stage we had realised that although shredding had taken place it couldn't be done completely because of all the copies of documents which were made. It must have been quite difficult, because like a big fraud case, the more people you start telling and asking to do things, the more risks you're taking.'

The team was beginning to assemble the jigsaw, made up of the various documents and snippets of evidence gleaned from interviews and searches at City Hall. However, by the end of the year, Magill and Child realised that of the two teams in the field, only one was playing cricket. The realisation appears to have strengthened their determination – 1993 was breakthrough year.

Many of the people interviewed told lies or claimed a poor memory, but a few did tell the truth. Both Peter Hartley and Robert Lewis, the deputy City Solicitor, were candid to the point of naivety and implicated themselves, as well as others. Lewis spoke about the depth of 'the rot' at Westminster and honestly declared his belief that officers went along with the gerrymandering because they were scared about the repercussions of non-cooperation. Cooler characters were also vital witnesses. Both Child and Magill were impressed by Simon Mabey, a former Tory Social Services Chairman and Lord Mayor of Westminster. Like Magill, he was an accountant and one of the brighter Tory councillors at Westminster. Mabey had opposed designated sales and even stood against David Weeks for the deputy leadership when Kirwan, a friend, stood against Porter. He produced some critical documents and remembered that there were other papers which could prove important. Magill and Child found him a 'thorough and honest witness with a remarkable memory for events'.

Perhaps the most significant breakthrough came on 22 January 1993, when Graham England, the Housing Director, mentioned in passing that he was 'an inveterate jotter' of notes at meetings. He had kept a record of secret gatherings over the crucial three years when the plot had taken shape. The minutes of many meetings had been shredded and so England's notes were a contemporaneous account of events which officially never took place. He handed over his entire set. He seemed more concerned about some personal domestic details they contained than the incriminating records. With no trace of irony, he told the Auditor, 'I have all sorts of things that I got up to in there.' England's version of events changed subtly during the course of his many interviews as the evidence built up against him and he lost credibility as Magill uncovered what England had failed to mention. At an interview in May 1993, Child showed him a damning document proving that he had designated properties in marginal wards as part of the gerrymandering strategy. England, who had always answered questions facing Magill, turned sideways and would not look at the District Auditor for the rest of the interview. Magill's patience with England snapped a month later. He wanted to know details about

Bill Phillips's role in the whole affair: 'I think the loyalty thing, if that is worrying you, is past.'

Bill Phillips himself proved the most exasperating witness. He either lied or passed the buck. The eight wards had emerged in 'a delphic way', he said. By then, Magill and Child knew he was a pivotal figure. The news that he had shredded papers before his departure was the last straw. Phillips claimed they were mainly unimportant documents such as memos to Shirley Porter about 'slippery floors' in the foyer of City Hall or invitations to dine at the Royal Institute. Phillips had told Magill there were no copies of an important gerrymandering document written by Porter, 'Strategy to 1990'. Tony Child says, 'We had been told about this paper but we couldn't get hold of it for two or three years. Then we ended up with half a dozen copies from half a dozen different places, and Bill Phillips, who had circulated it to all chief officers, told us that the Council hadn't got it.' One response by the managing director provoked Child. 'Can I say to you, come off it?' he asked Phillips. 'No,' said Phillips, 'I will not come off it.' And he never did. Incredibly, this central figure in the saga claimed he was not trusted by Porter and was kept in the dark.

David Weeks also answered many questions incorrectly. Magill and Child were quietly dismayed at his foul language and his irrational loathing for officers. He once described the marginal wards as 'the fucking list of eight'. When asked about the deportations of the homeless, Weeks told Magill, 'To house Eritrean village dwellers in Westminster has never struck me as being very sensible.'

In June 1993 Bill Roots ordered his internal auditors to raid Weeks's office after reports that the leader had reportedly been continuing Westminster's unhappy tradition of abusing council facilities, on this occasion, sending begging letters to council contractors using City Hall stationery for money to fight the next local elections in 1994. Weeks was so furious about the raid that he tried to sack Merv Montacute, Phillips's successor as managing director. Roots and Matthew Ives briefed Tory councillors about Weeks's behaviour. In desperation, the leader summoned his colleagues for support, but was forced to sit, whey-faced, as his remaining authority drained away and his resignation was brutally extracted.

Shirley Porter faced Magill twelve times in under a year between August 1992 and July 1993 at the District Auditor's offices in Little New Street within the City of London, and dissembled at every encounter. She was not fooled by the cool politeness and the refreshments on offer. 'In spite of the biscuits and the fact there is a pleasant atmosphere,' she told Magill, 'it is an interview of a very serious nature.' She added, 'I feel as if I am in a dock, a charming dock, it may be fur lined.' She always appeared before the District Auditor with her lawyers, namely Stewart Cakebread, and, on one occasion, Anthony Scrivener QC. She told Magill, 'I do not plot and I do not dissemble,' adding, 'I would merely say that I was an exceptionally overworked, underpaid elected person trying to keep an extremely stroppy party under control, [and] a vicious opposition [and] overworking like mad to keep the citizens of Westminster happy.' She did not remember her document 'Keeping Westminster Conservative'. Perhaps it was anonymous. Like the *Iliad*, opined her legal adviser. Yes, said Porter, like the *Iliad*. Obviously, Cakebread did not know his Homer.

Porter became more elusive as further evidence came Magill's way. She often claimed she was too busy to attend interviews. Once she suggested that Magill and Child acquire a caravan and park it in the grounds of her Oxfordshire cottage at Worton so she would be close at hand to field their questions. Another time, Porter said she was too busy to be interviewed because she had to go to Israel to watch Sir Leslie being installed as Chancellor of Tel Aviv University. 'Does your remit allow you to travel if necessary with your entourage?' Porter asked the District Auditor, who responded, nonplussed, 'In connection with this inquiry?' 'I am being perfectly serious,' responded Porter. 'I leave at midnight.'

The Auditor was closing in by the summer of 1993. Too much evidence had been produced; too many people had confessed. Even Porter began to offer up others for the sacrificial slab, in an attempt to protect herself. 'This is not shopping people,' Magill told Porter when discussing Bill Phillips and his knowledge about the Tories' real intentions to target marginal wards, 'But you do have to say what you think.' With rare candour, Porter replied: 'I will put it like this. I think that Bill Phillips came from a civil servant background and, shall we say, he was economical with the truth.' Magill said, 'That is the same phrase I have used in interviews.' 'He viewed it [the truth] in a civil servant way,' observed Porter, '. . . he was most certainly aware.'

In one of her final interviews with Magill, Porter revealed her desperation. She appeared to compare the Auditor's treatment of her with the way the Nazis dealt with their victims: 'To me it smacks of another era which I shall not refer to. I do not like saying things about other people and going backwards and forwards. Let me leave it like this . . . I do not recall that I was particularly involved with a selection of wards.' Despite the bravado, Porter felt caught out. She rang Matthew Ives and said, 'I'd like to have a discussion with you. Can we go for a walk around St James's Park?' Ives met her outside City Hall and the pair walked slowly down Birdcage Walk and up towards the park via the Palace and Horse Guards Parade. Ives thought Porter was 'clearly rattled' by Magill and wanted to know about the possible worst case scenario. He laid out the potential dangers and she became more perturbed. 'Why didn't anyone tell me?' she asked. In fact, she had been warned repeatedly by officers about the folly of the course on which she had embarked, and time and again, she had chosen to override them.

As the inquiry continued, nervousness intensified in government and Conservative Party circles. Attempts were made to exert insidious influence on Andrew Foster, Controller of the Audit Commission, which oversaw Magill's inquiry. Foster remembers: 'There were parties who told me two or three times during the process to "back off" and asked me whether I was completely certain Magill was sound and that he didn't have ulterior motives.' Foster ignored the threats and supported the Auditor through thick and thin.

Porter came unstuck on every front in 1993. The District Auditor gathered irrefutable proof of her gerrymandering and her media career was destroyed by the loss of the LBC licence. Domestically, she suffered grievously. The marriage of her daughter Linda, broke down, and towards the end of the year, she and Sir Leslie had to move out of their flat in Gloucester Square after a fire.

The worst news of all came in November, just two months before Magill's report. Her twenty-one-year-old grandson, Daniel Marcus, Linda's son, had been killed in a car crash on the Arava Road north of Eilat while serving as a sergeant-major with the Israeli army.

Towards the end of the inquiry, Matthew Ives left a meeting of the Law Society and walked off down Victoria Street towards Westminster underground station. Ahead, he saw an elderly couple in deep and anxious conversation. It was Porter and Sir Leslie, and Ives concluded that the former Leader had emerged from yet another interview with the District Auditor. The City Solicitor thought, 'Should I say something?' He decided not to, and avoided them altogether by taking a rather more circuitous route to the Tube, past the Abbey and Parliament. He says, 'I still have a memory of this rather lonely couple walking off into the sunset.'

CHAPTER 25

A Series of Unfortunate Events (1993–2001)

Publication of the District Auditor's report on Porter's designated sales policy had been deferred nine times, as new incriminating documents were unearthed. Each time it was delayed, the sense of anticipation in the press heightened, while at City Hall, the gloom deepened. Mark Baylis, the head of communications for the City Council, developed a public relations strategy to handle its publication. 'I knew it was going to be a public relations disaster,' says Baylis, who had joined Westminster in May 1992 after a career as a journalist for BBC Television in Southampton. He quickly became aware of Porter's legacy at City Hall. He says, 'I remember everyone being shit scared of David Weeks and how bureaucratic everything was. It was the most inefficient, unbusinesslike and bureaucratic organisation I have ever worked for.'

In the summer of 1993, six months before the Auditor published his first report, Baylis sent Merv Montacute a confidential note on his strategy. He recommended that the council: 'Encourage the story to die down by being low-key in our response; blunt and deflect the inevitable media onslaught rather than tackle the Auditor head on; neither admit nor [sic] hint that we acknowledge any wrong doing.' Baylis also suggested that they 'draw attention discreetly to the passage of time since the alleged events took place.

This has two advantages, it raises a question over the report's validity and it places it in the past.' Baylis had prepared for a 'worst-case scenario'. 'The problem was', says Baylis, 'the actual report was worse than our worst-case scenario.'

John Magill and Tony Child released the report on 13 January 1994. They were so concerned about security that the report and interview transcripts were printed in-house by Magill's firm, Deloitte and Touche, and the papers were stored in a guarded room. The preparation was meticulous, down to punctuation. Child says, 'Even the commas were approved. Up to publication date, we were working till two or three in the morning getting everything ready. We had the documents printed at the last possible moment to avoid any risks of leaks.' Magill did not even tell his wife what was in his report. He explained to her: 'When all your friends ask you about it, you can genuinely say you don't know.'

On that January morning, nearly four and a half years after *Panorama*, all sides were preparing for an explosion of media interest. A 'war room' was established at City Hall where senior officers – among them – Graham England could read the report and prepare responses. Sid Sporle was also waiting, pen poised. At 8 a.m., the council clerks wheeled in trolleys piled high with copies of the report, bound in gleaming white lever arch files. As City Treasurer, Bill Roots was there to check the District Auditor's figures to see if they added up. He was aware of the *Panorama* allegations but, after more than three years at City Hall, had come to believe absolutely in the innocence of his colleagues. As he read through the report, words jumped out: 'guilty of wilful misconduct', 'guilty of gerrymandering', 'improper', 'disgraceful'. 'It was unreal,' he says. 'It was like a war room where you're expecting to say, "We've won!" Then you find out that we've lost. It was all out of the window.' Roots was profoundly shocked. 'Don't forget I hadn't been party to any interviews and I hadn't seen any draft notes,' he says. 'I knew when I joined the council that there had been audit objections. I didn't think too much of them, although there seemed to be rather more than usual, but I hadn't picked up the scale of the issue. I was just horrified; I couldn't believe it.' Roots feverishly flicked through the report and realised that people in the room were implicated. 'This can't work,' he thought. He ordered England out of the room and then Sid Sporle. At 9.52 a.m. LBC, Shirley Porter's soon-to-be defunct former radio station, received a 'flash report': 'Leading councillors and officers found responsible of wilful misconduct and actions. The cost to the authority: £21.25 million.'

John Magill held his own press conference in Covent Garden. The findings, transcripts and more than 6,000 pages of original documents were piled high on a table at his side. Magill emphasised that his report was 'provisional'; he would give ten officers and councillors a chance to explain why they should not be surcharged or disqualified from office for five years, in the public hearings set for October of that year. The District Auditor blinked through his huge glasses and read his statement to a gathering of excited journalists: 'My provisional view is that the council was engaged in gerrymandering, which I am minded to find is a disgraceful and improper purpose and not a purpose for which a local authority may act.'

Magill ruled that £21.25 million had been lost as a result of the unlawful gerrymandering. It had to be repaid from the pockets of the guilty, in the form of a surcharge: £13.3 million was the amount lost on selling off council homes at a huge discount to bring in Tory voters. Other losses included the £2.6 million Porter paid to council tenants to vacate their properties, £2 million of the extra costs of housing the homeless and £1.2 million spent on Sitex doors.

Councillors found provisionally guilty of wilful misconduct were: Shirley Porter, David Weeks, Barry Legg, Dr Michael Dutt, Peter Hartley and Judith Warner. Officers found guilty were: Bill Phillips, Graham England and his deputy, Paul Hayler, and Robert Lewis, the former deputy City Solicitor. A 'ruling triumvirate' of Porter, Weeks and Legg held particular responsibility.

Magill's report stated: 'In my provisional view, Councillor Lady Porter instigated the designated sales policy . . . smokescreens were erected to mask the purpose of that policy . . . Councillor Lady Porter was engaged in gerrymandering.' He added that she 'knew that it was wrong for the Council to exercise its powers to secure an electoral advantage for her party . . . [or] she was at least reck-lessly indifferent as to whether it was right or wrong.' She was guilty of 'wilful misconduct'.

In the House of Commons, Edward Heath described the findings as the 'heaviest blow to hit the Tory Party in living memory'. For Prime Minister John Major, the timing was particularly bad. He had launched his 'Back to Basics' campaign, urging a return to tra-ditional values, only three months previously. In turn, the press attacked the hypocrisy of an unpopular government, already on the ropes following Britain's humiliating ejection from the European Exchange Rate Mechanism on Black Wednesday, 16 September 1992. The media was already in a frenzy over Tory sleaze; there had been a string of scandals involving leading Conservatives. The papers were full of reports about the love child of Tim Yeo, the Environment Minister, and the five mistresses of Steven Norris, the Transport Minister. But the Porter scandal was on an altogether different scale. The corruption had been ingrained in a Tory flag-ship council, the sums of money involved were vast and the guilt reached into the Tory parliamentary party itself: Barry Legg was then Tory MP for Milton Keynes South West. According to Paul Beresford, now a Tory MP and a junior minister in Major's gov-ernment, it was 'one of the most destructive things that happened', and 'made some of Major's scandals seem pretty small.'

John Smith, the Labour leader, described the report as a 'devas-tating example of financial corruption and the abuse of power by senior members of the Tory Party'. He added: 'It is the stuff of banana republics. It shows the Tory Party is rotten and amoral to the core.' Smith insisted that Major apologise. The battered Prime Minister stated: 'If the allegations are confirmed, I condemn it unreservedly.' The findings would be confirmed but there is no record of an apology by John Major, or indeed any of his cabinet colleagues.

Shirley Porter was practising her golf swing near her Californian home, Rancho Mirage, in Palm Springs when the report was pub-lished. She vowed to fight on: 'This is a matter for the law. It will be fought through the courts. I shall come back fighting fit, ready for the battle which I expect to win.'

On the eve of publication of Magill's report, Dr Michael Dutt was at St Albans Hospital where he worked as a consultant geriatrician. He told his secretary, Anne Barnes, that he would be off the next day and to 'sound vague' if she received any calls from the press. Barnes had learned not to pry and courteously agreed. Dutt returned to his flat at 5 Garland Court, a small redbrick development of homes and offices in St Albans town centre and waited for the report. The following morning, men from the District Auditor delivered around thirty lever arch files. Dutt cut to the quick in the report and read what he must have known all along: he was guilty with the rest.

Over the next two days, Dutt faxed two rambling letters to the District Auditor, protesting his innocence: 'I had no interest in and was not influenced by considerations of gerrymandering at any time.' He had stood unsuccessfully for the Tories in the 1989 European elections for Strathclyde East and in the 1992 general election for Leicester South. His career in politics, and probably a lot more besides, was over. On 15 or 16 January, Dutt unplugged his phone and fax machine and wrote a third note addressed to 'police and others' which he placed under a bible. He took a scrubbing brush from the toilet and his shotgun from its cabinet and sat in a chair. He put the gun barrel in his mouth and pressed down on the trigger with the brush. According to Detective Sergeant James Mitchell, the local Coroner's officer, it was a 'straightforward' suicide.

Dutt's hospital colleagues became concerned with his absence and eventually rang the police. Ten days later police broke into the flat and discovered Dutt's body lying among papers from Magill's report. The suicide note read: 'My decision to end my life is due solely to the need to continue to fight this matter of designated sales further draining my energy and requiring resources I do not have. I could not do my demanding work properly and without this I do not choose to continue living.' The fact that Dutt's body remained undiscovered for more than a week added to Magill and Child's shock. For Magill's opponents, the suicide would be a powerful weapon.

Roger Rosewell told a radio interviewer that Magill had enjoyed his 'day of fame', now it was 'his day of shame'. Writing in the *Daily Mail*, Stuart Greenman, another adviser to Porter, launched a vicious attack on John Magill, claiming that the District Auditor and his three team members had hauled Dutt before them and crowded around him '. . . four against one.' Magill's inquiry had been 'Kafkaesque'. It would be a common charge levelled against the auditor by the Tories but unlike Porter, Herr K the hero in Franz Kafka's *The Trial* never discovered the reason for his arrest or trial, and remained baffled at the time of his execution.

Porter refused to recognise her own responsibility for Dutt's death. In an interview for LBC, she blamed Magill for the death: 'The strain which he must have felt at the savagery, the absurdity, the unsupportable attacks launched against him is absolutely dreadful.' It was the start of a long campaign of smears and lies against the Auditor which would ultimately fail. 'It was all water off a duck's back,' says Magill.

Merv Montacute, already battered by doing battle with David Weeks, had often displayed an intense dislike for strife. Shortly after the report was published, he told Bill Roots, 'I can't cope with this; I'm off.' Montacute moved to the US western seaboard for a new life in Seattle, and Roots was appointed chief executive, a role which had been briefly absorbed by Bill Phillips since Rodney Brooke's departure. Roots's main task now was to prevent Westminster City Council from collapsing under the weight of the scandal.

The Objectors, who had first officially demanded the inquiry, had also received the report and the thousands of accompanying documents. The Labour councillors now fully realised for the first time that council resources, which should have been directed towards local communities, had instead been targeted against them. Paul Dimoldenberg says, 'As I went through the papers, I actually felt physically sick not just about what had been going on but because we had been lied to so repeatedly by people like Bill Phillips.'

After reading Magill's report and understanding more fully the extent of the wrongdoing throughout all council departments, the Objectors submitted new demands to Magill for investigations into other BSC policies. The District Auditor decided he would wait until he had dealt with designated sales. In February 1994 Frank Dobson, the shadow Environment Secretary, and Andrew Dismore, the Labour group leader, called on the Audit Commission to launch an 'extraordinary audit' into Westminster City Council and send a whole team of auditors into City Hall to examine all the books. Dobson said: 'Urgent and decisive action is required to clear out corruption in the council.' Such an event was unprecedented but legislation allowed for such an action in exceptional circumstances. Bill Roots opposed the move, and, as he was untainted by the scandal, his word carried the day. He says, 'We were already in tatters when we heard about Labour's demand for an extraordinary audit. The government and the Audit Commission got on to me to ask if staff morale had collapsed because of the report and were our services failing as a result?' Roots assured them that the council staff were coping with the shock and were continuing to deliver good quality services. The Audit Commission decided against the extraordinary audit, confident that Magill could deal with all unresolved BSC issues.

On 2 March John Magill and Tony Child paid another unannounced visit to City Hall to seize and secure 360 separate council files, some 6,000 pages, relating to other BSC papers, which Magill would need for his subsequent inquiries. Roots loaned Magill a room at City Hall where the files could be held. A guard was placed at the door to prevent the files being removed and shredded and a trusted council clerk was given the key. 'You can have what you want,' Roots told Magill, 'but I'm not denying staff access if they need to see a file. We'll watch what goes on.' The Auditor's team later found that many documents relating to Quality of Life initiatives, an integral part of BSC, had been shredded in the months before the raid.

Roots set up a series of separate inquiries into related scandals, unearthed by the District Auditor. Roots appointed John Barratt, former Chief Executive for Cambridgeshire County Council, to investigate the move of homeless families into the two towers. With the leading Tory councillors in disarray, Roots effectively assumed control of the council. He says, 'I told the Tory group what I was doing. I think they were shell-shocked.' Roots refused calls from Labour councillors that he should at least suspend compromised officers such as England and Sporle. England was moved into a new role as head of External Relations, nominally in charge of the council's press office. Roots felt he could not sack him while the findings remained 'provisional', but Labour councillors thought it ridiculous that Graham England should oversee a press office handling media inquiries about Magill's report. Sporle stayed put as director of Planning and Transportation.

The Tory councillors were very uncomfortable that Roots instigated new inquiries into related scandals, but there was little they could do. Essentially, they consigned themselves to futile acts of protest. On one occasion, a group appeared outside Magill's accountancy firm holding a placard saying 'John Magill-Touche Ross'. They were a sorry spectacle, and looked more like minicab drivers in an airport arrivals lounge than seasoned protesters. Publicly, the Tories remained unrepentant, and even took comfort in their victory at the local elections in May 1994 when they retained control of the City. David Weeks not only secured his candidature in the Tory Party, but was also voted in again, despite the damning findings of the Auditor. Judith Warner resigned as housing chairman but also stood successfully as a Tory candidate in the elections.

Shirley Porter played for time. She was determined to fight the District Auditor through the highest courts in the land, in the hope that some judge would take pity on her. It almost worked. In the meantime, a small team overseen by Roger Rosewell campaigned against Magill. The campaign was led by two women, Nicola Woodhead-Page, a new Tory councillor at Westminster described as a 'former model', and her assistant Rowan Pelling, a former employee of *Private Eye* magazine, who would go on to edit the *Erotic Review*. The pair circulated the occasional newsletter to the press attacking the integrity of the District Auditor and the soundness of his findings. Their activities proved fairly harmless.

Porter's legal battle with the Auditor would last more than seven years. With her enormous wealth to back her, she employed teams of expert lawyers and took the battle all the way to the House of Lords. To a significant extent, her wealth and personal fame allowed her to dictate the news coverage. But it also acted against her. While the officers and other councillors would be unable to pay the surcharge, everyone knew that Porter alone could afford the enormous sum demanded by Magill.

The hearings began on 19 October 1994 at Marylebone Council House, where Porter had held sway for eight years. A large crowd of protesters gathered outside to greet Porter carrying placards with messages such as 'Tory corruption', 'What is a key ward?' and even 'Speak Up Porter!' 'We arranged to arrive in black cabs,' says Porter's barrister Anthony Scrivener QC. 'I didn't want to drive in my own car in case it was pelted with eggs. We had planned for Shirley to go up to the top of the steps and give a little speech.' Porter strode up the stairs defiantly past the baying mob. She turned and addressed the cameras and microphones: 'If you listen to all of the screaming and shouting, you must ask yourself: why do the people feel like this? It is because we have been judged guilty before the inquiry.'

photo © Andrew Wiard/reportphotos.com

Judgment Day. Porter arrives at the District Auditor's hearings, 1994.

At the start of proceedings, Tony Child read out Michael Dutt's suicide note. 'It was by far and away the most difficult thing at that public hearing,' says Child. Having protested her innocence at the entrance, Porter spoke no more. She spent two hours listening to the opening submissions and then she left. She did not give evidence. Roger Rosewell appeared as her press manager, but refused to answer the protesters' question: 'Are you the man with No Name?'

The Objectors were determined that the District Auditor's findings be upheld. So that their concerns should be represented, they raised more than £200,000 to pay for a legal team. Their barrister, Andrew Arden QC, told Magill, 'What went on here reflected a breakdown and contempt for democratic rule. This case is about contempt for the democratic rule. This case is about contempt for the resources of the authority. The greatest contempt of all was for the homeless . . . In Westminster, the party of law and order had become the party of deceit and distortion.'

On 8 November Patricia Kirwan gave a bravado performance at the hearings and was cheered from the public gallery. Magill warned that security guards would be ordered to attend if such disorder continued. Kirwan told Scrivener, 'The reason I stood against Dame Shirley was because I did not like her style, I did not like her attitude and I didn't like her way of working.' Porter's policies were politically 'crass'. At the end of her evidence, Kirwan burst into tears and was taken off to a nearby café for a cup of tea by the Labour councillor Jill Selbourne. Kirwan would later suffer a stroke, which she blamed on the stress she had been under during the hearing.

The Objectors wanted five more people surcharged for their alleged role in designated sales, including Miles Young, Weeks's replacement as leader, Sid Sporle and Matthew Ives, who had left for a new job with the Institute of Chartered Accountants a week before the Auditor's report. In July 1987 Ives had been working through a pile of papers on the train when he came across one written by Nick Reiter, which discussed targeting resources at marginal wards. The City Solicitor had hastily scribbled in the margin: 'This paper should not have been written by an officer. A much more subtle approach is required. This shows officers working for a Tory victory.' He put it to one side and forgot all about it. It reappeared in March 1994 and the Objectors claimed it implicated Ives. In 1995 the District Auditor ruled that as far as designated sales was concerned, no case of wilful misconduct could be made against any of the five including Ives and Sporle.

Magill's hearings were completed by the end of January 1995 but his final report would not be published until May the following year. In the interim, more skeletons broke loose from the cupboard. In early 1995 it emerged that Porter and her team had failed to charge council home buyers service charges for major repairs to their estates between 1987 and 1991. They had feared that repair bills might deter potential buyers. A secret paper said at the time that to charge for repairs might make buyers 'susceptible to pressure from the opposition'. Roots was mortified when he found out and insisted bills were sent out immediately. People who had bought into the dream of home ownership received unexpected bills of £20,000 to £30,000 for repairs to their estate. However, because any bill more than eighteen months old was unenforceable, many buyers were now out of reach of the council. Labour calculated the losses at £30 million but Roots insists the figure was £10 million. It would in the end be the national Labour Party who put a figure on the full cost of the corruption: they calculated that BSC had lost local taxpayers more than £100 million if all policies were included. Frank Dobson broadened his attack to include Porter's successful attempts to reduce the poll tax, adding, 'There is mounting evidence of the Tory party rigging of the 1990 grants which allowed Westminster to reduce its poll tax from £400 to £295.'

On 25 March 1996 John Barratt's report into housing the homeless in Hermes Point and Chantry Point was published. It concluded that the decision had been taken by Porter and her chairmen as part of their war against WECH and he found that officers had been 'trapped into defending the indefensible'. Those 'acting on behalf of a public body' had 'repeatedly' taken 'risks with the health of people who ought to have been entitled to assume that such risks were not being taken'. The asbestos saga, as

Steve Bell of the *Guardian* pays his respects to Gilbert Stuart of the Boston Sentinel. John Major tries to keep his head above water while Environment Secretary John Gummer looks on from his lily leaf. Like City Hall, Parliament lay within the marginal ward of Victoria.

described by Barratt, was for many of Porter's opponents the worst decision ever taken by a local council. The condemnation was led by the *Daily Mail*, which described the affair as a 'towering disgrace'. Still John Major refused to condemn Shirley Porter, or Barry Legg, who chaired the meeting which decided to use the tower blocks. Sid Sporle told Bill Roots he never again wanted to be in the same room as Graham England. Shortly after the report, Bill Roots received an anonymous package which had been sent to him at City Hall. It contained a lump of blue asbestos. He sent immediately for an officer from the environmental health department to take it away. In the meantime one of his secretaries placed it on top of an air-conditioning unit. 'Don't put it there!' said Roots. 'You'll send it all around the building.'

On 9 May 1996 Magill published his final report. With adjustments and interest, the surcharge was now £31.6 million. He cleared four people of wilful misconduct; the list had narrowed to Porter, Weeks, Hartley, Bill Phillips, Graham England and Paul Hayler. The surprise exception was Barry Legg, one of the three members of the 'triumvirate'. Magill found that Legg was 'aware of the party electoral reasons' behind designated sales and that he 'knew it was wrong for the Council to . . . secure an increase in the number of likely Tory voters in marginal wards'. However, Magill said there was insufficient evidence to prove Legg's personal involvement in the 'development of the policy'.

Although many remained unimpressed, Legg claimed to have been 'cleared'. In 1997 the Labour landslide swept him out of Milton Keynes South West and the House of Commons. Six years later, in February 2003, Iain Duncan Smith, then Conservative Party leader, demonstrated the remarkably short memories of politicians and appointed Legg as his chief executive, but Legg suffered the ignominy of a hasty ejection from his new job in May 2003, a day after the public was reminded of his role in the asbestos scandal.

Porter declared she would appeal to the High Court against the final report's findings. John Major again refused to condemn her and now said he would await the High Court ruling before commenting. Tony Blair, the Labour Party leader, asked Major in Parliament: 'Isn't your real problem that these were not a maverick

© Philip Wolmuth

Judgment postponed. Porter announces an appeal, May 1996.

group of obscure local councillors? This was the flagship Conservative council. Their activities were carried out with the knowledge and approval of the Conservative Party.'

On 19 December 1997 the High Court judges concluded that Porter 'lied to us as she lied to the District Auditor'; they found her and Weeks guilty while the remaining figures were depicted by the court as naive, misguided pawns and escaped surcharge. They included Paul Hayler, absent due to a nervous breakdown, his boss, Graham England, who 'did not appreciate the unlawfulness of his conduct' and Peter Hartley, who wept while giving evidence. Bill Phillips also avoided surcharge, which surprised Magill and Child. 'Phillips is an intelligent man, who no doubt appreciates the unsatisfactory nature of the answers he has given,' declared the judges, '. . . we find his account difficult to believe.' But such too was his apparent ignorance of the unlawfulness of his behaviour that the judges ruled that the former managing director could not be held financially accountable. One senior Audit Commission source says, 'The judges obviously put Bill Phillips in the second rank; in my view, he should have been in the first rank with Dame Shirley and David Weeks. I have some sympathy with the view that Graham England and Peter Hartley were in the wrong place at the wrong time and their involvement might be regarded with some mercy.'

Porter announced she would take her case onwards and upwards to the Court of Appeal, which elicited a weary question from a journalist to one of her lawyers, 'Does she plan on lying to the Court of Appeal as she did to the High Court?' The answer was yes and no. Dramatically, Porter changed tactics for the next legal battle. She had always claimed not to have been engaged in gerrymandering. Now for the first time, she admitted her gerrymandering strategy but tried to protect herself with the legal advice she had taken from Jeremy Sullivan QC. To universal surprise, two out of three Appeal Court judges agreed that she had been protected by Sullivan's advice given so hurriedly on that May afternoon in 1987. It was a victory for Porter but she would not have long to enjoy it.

John Magill was given leave to appeal against the judgment to the House of Lords, the highest court in the land. The hearing was set for December 2001. For the benefit of the five Law Lords, who would each give their own judgment, Tony Child drafted an 'Agreed Statement of Facts' to be signed by Shirley Porter. Here she admitted that she had been engaged in gerrymandering but again offered Sullivan's advice up as a defence for justification. In the Agreed Statement of Facts, Porter finally confessed: 'The intention of the majority party was to develop Council policies which would target marginal wards, including such housing policies as could affect the make up of the electorate in those wards.'

Porter sat at the back of the House of Lords for the crucial hearing. Proceedings were interrupted by the ring of a mobile phone. It was Porter's. She hastily switched it off and sat bent down with her hand over her face to avoid detection. The Law Lords were not fooled and dispatched an usher to exact an apology. 'I felt so sorry for her,' says Child genuinely.

The House of Lords announced that it would release the final written judgment on 13 December. Magill spent a sleepless night before making his way to the offices of the Audit Commission in Vincent Square, SW1, to receive the news. Tony Child strolled to the House of Lords with two assistants to pick up the written judgment. He had bought himself a maroon-coloured House of Lords baseball cap for the occasion. Despite being urged by his assistants to jump straight to the findings, he read the judgment slowly, smiled, donned his new cap and walked out of the House of Lords back to the Audit Commission. Child used his mobile to ring Magill: 'It's five nil.' 'Yes,' said the Auditor, 'but in whose favour?'

All five Law Lords had backed Magill and ordered Porter to pay a surcharge now standing at around £40 million because of interest. They expressed their judgment in the strongest language available: 'The passage of time, the familiarity of the accusations made against Dame Shirley Porter and Mr Weeks cannot and should not obscure the unpalatable truth that this was a deliberate, blatant and dishonest use of public power. There was an abuse of power by both of them not for the purpose of financial gain but that of electoral advantage; in that sense it was corrupt . . . Who can doubt that the selective use of municipal powers in order to obtain party political advantage represents political corruption? Political corruption, if unchecked, engenders cynicism about elections, about politicians and their motives and damages the reputation of democratic government.'

Porter had spent more than £3 million on legal fees since 1996. It had all come to nothing. She was ordered to pay a surcharge – an enormous sum of £43,321,644.

CHAPTER 26

Hiding the Money (1994–2003)

The decision by the House of Lords left Shirley Porter with the greatest debt owed to the public purse by any politician in British history, and she was no more prepared to pay it than she had been prepared to admit her guilt. The story of how she tried to hide her vast wealth from the clutches of her debtors, and its eventual discovery, is perhaps one of the most extraordinary chapters in her life.

The authority charged with the duty of recovering more than £43 million for local taxpayers from Shirley Porter was none other than Westminster City Council itself, which, like her, had been found guilty of gerrymandering, though in the decade following the Auditor's first report, not a single Westminster Tory either apologised for what had happened in their party's name or even acknowledged any wrongdoing. In October 1994 Simon Milton, the deputy Conservative leader, said, 'The council has never been engaged in a policy of social engineering for political purposes. That is not what the council is there for. The council has not done that. None of statistics, none of the facts, support that.' In the summer of 2001, six months before the Lords judgment, Simon Milton, by that time the Leader of the Council, dined with Porter and Sir Leslie in Tel Aviv while on holiday in Israel. Labour councillors concluded that the City Council would be reluctant to pursue the debt; for them it was as if the Roman Senate had demanded reparations from Attila the Hun and had instructed a band of his most loyal followers to wander into his fortified camp and demand instant payment.

The council did make attempts to get Porter to pay up. On 28 December 2001, fifteen days after the Lords ruling, Mr Justice Jacob, a High Court judge, granted the City Council a 'disclosure order' which required Porter to reveal: 'all her assets whether in or outside England and Wales and whether in her own name or owned beneficially by her and whether solely or jointly owned, giving the value, location and details of all such assets'. On 14 January the following year Porter declared assets worth approximately £300,000 including a half share in a flat in Rochester Row, Victoria, SW1, valued at £18,000, $271 in an account with Bank Leumi in Israel, £67.25 in a Coutts Bank account, thirty items of paintings and furniture, with no individual piece worth more than £300, two books of etchings valued at £500 each, and thirty other personal effects left behind in London worth around £4,000, including, it was reported, a gold-plated lavatory seat. The disclosure was greeted with derision by the City Council and her opponents alike. In the mid-1990s, the *Sunday Times* had estimated the joint fortune of Porter and Sir Leslie at £69 million. Where were the missing millions? Porter had lied about her assets on oath in an affidavit to the High Court. She had not only hidden her fortune, but was confident that it would never be located.

Shirley Porter concealed her wealth from the moment Magill's first report was published in January 1994. She knew that she, alone of all the accused, could afford to repay the £21.25 million surcharge. She spent more than £4 million on fighting Magill through the courts and her strategy was thorough and planned: if she eventually defeated the Auditor, she would escape the penalty and perhaps even get her costs paid; if she lost, the lengthy court actions would give her precious time to hide her fortune in offshore companies and trusts far from British jurisdiction. The council received legal advice that it could not freeze Porter's assets until the legal process had run its full course and Porter made sure that did not happen for nearly eight years.

In March 1994, two months after Magill's first report, Shirley
Porter flew into Israel and exile; she and Sir Leslie retreated to
Herzliya Pituach, a seaside town north of Tel Aviv, allegedly to be
close to their bereaved daughter, Linda Marcus. Porter was in such
a hurry to leave Britain that she left two pairs of shoes behind at
her local shoe repair shop in Bayswater. She also resigned as
Chairman of LBC, saying she had 'no more ideas' about how to
save the station from closure. The Porters and Cohens had long
been supporters of the state of Israel and, in their darkest hour, it
offered refuge from the courts and the District Auditor. Here they
had friends in high places; Tesco was one of Britain's biggest
importers of canned goods and fresh produce from Israel, particularly Jaffa oranges. In January 1986 Porter had chaired a reception
for the Israeli Prime Minister Shimon Peres and had become good
friends with Aura, wife of the country's President, Chaim Herzog.
In 1987, while Porter was cleaning up the marginal wards, she was
Chairman of the British Friends of the Council for a Beautiful
Israel. She congratulated both Arabs and Israelis alike on tidying
up the highly contested West Bank and suggested that Automatic
Public Conveniences should be introduced to Tel Aviv. 'If we don't
train up the future generation now for these standards,' Porter told
the *Jewish Chronicle*, 'we will only have ourselves to blame if Israel
looks dirty.'

Between 1987 and 2003, the family gave £13 million to charities,
including many in Israel. Jack Cohen had started the largesse in the
1950s by funding the Porter Senior Citizen Centre in Old Jaffa, and
it was continued by the Porters long after his death. The family paid
for the UK Building of Life Sciences and the Porter Super Centre for
Environmental and Ecological Research at Tel Aviv University; the
university repaid its gratitude by making Sir Leslie its chancellor,
and Shirley Porter a governor. Their charities, particularly the Porter
Foundation, funded the Porter Institute for Poetics and Semiotics,
the Shirley and Leslie School of Cultural Studies and the Cohen-
Porter Family Swimming Pool. A park in Tel Aviv is named after
Cissie Cohen. After John Magill's first report, Porter's opponents
argued that the money had not been hers to give away, however
noble the cause. The money belonged to the ratepayers of

Westminster. One prominent British Jewish immigrant to Israel once asked the Israeli newspaper *Haa'retz*: 'Why should Israel act as a laundry service for Jews from abroad who wish to revamp their image and get respectability they lack from Israeli institutions?' It was a good question, but not many appeared to ask it in Israel.

In contrast to their high profile and society lifestyle in London, the couple remained unknown to ninety-eight per cent of Israelis according to local journalists, and the remaining two per cent who knew of them considered the Porters as extremely rich and generous benefactors. Sir Leslie kept a yacht, *Legasea*, in the Herzliya marina, and Shirley Porter could sometimes be seen smashing balls around the tennis courts at the Arcadia Hotel nearby.

The *Sunday Times* estimate of Porter's personal fortune at £69 million was an exaggeration; it was an educated guess of the total worth of the Porter family, including Sir Leslie, whose successful stewardship of Tesco had left him a seriously wealthy man. Porter had inherited £10 million in Tesco shares on the death of Sir Jack in 1979 [worth £36.7 million – 24 October 2005] and she and her sister, Irene, were left more than £17 million in shares by their mother, Lady Cissie. In 1990 Porter held £4.8 million Tesco shares; by early 1994 she had reduced her shareholding to £3 million. She continued to sell shares through that year and on 24 October 1994, ten months after Magill's report, she sold her last tranche of 150,387 shares. There was nothing the council could do to stop it. One man above all would help Porter shield her wealth from the investigators: Peter Green, her financial adviser.

Green began his career with a small practice in Tunbridge Wells in Kent. He had advised the Porters since the late 1980s, and his business flourished under their patronage; gradually, the fate and finances of his companies and those of the Porters became increasingly entwined. By the time Porter was in trouble with the Auditor, he had established the headquarters of his companies, principally Personal Finance Management, PFM, at 79 Mount Street in the heart of Mayfair.

As Porter sank ever deeper into the mire, she was forced to rely on Green's ingenuity and discretion. The financial adviser built a bewildering structure of offshore trusts, companies and foreign bank accounts designed to shield Porter's wealth from the authorities. On paper, independent trustees controlled these so-called 'sham trusts', but in reality they dispensed vast funds on the instruction of Peter Green, who, in turn, was responding directly to demands for money from Porter. These trusts owned companies and held bank accounts in the British Virgin Islands, Guernsey and Switzerland, countries where the authorities allow the greatest possible discretion to attend the financial transactions of the seriously wealthy. Millions of pounds changed hands, either in loans or investments, which served to baffle and confuse anyone trying to discover Porter's true worth.

There was an early demonstration of this operation in 1994 when Porter and Sir Leslie sold their penthouse flat at 19 Chelwood House. Their son, John, bought it from them after borrowing £1,250,000 from Trawden, a company in the British Virgin Islands, the same company which also owned half of the couple's property Porterho! in Rancho Mirage, California. Essentially, John had borrowed the money from his parents, but the transaction meant the flat was no longer in Shirley Porter's name and could not be seized to help pay her debt. The Porter family still controlled the property, and it was in safe hands until the unlikely event that Porter was able to defeat Magill and return to her London home.

In 1996 Bill Roots hired financial and legal experts to trace the Porters' hidden assets in the eventuality that she would be forced to pay up. He chose Stephenson Harwood, a company which specialised in tracing offshore assets of wealthy debtors. They in turn commissioned KPMG accountants to carry out an investigation into Porter's wealth. Roots had not been authorised by a council committee to pay for such an inquiry. He hid his decision, fearing that supporters of Shirley Porter might tip off the former Leader. He asked John Magill for the all-clear, worried that he might be surcharged if he spent money without proper approval: 'Look, if I don't do something to show that I've started to track this then somebody's going to turn round and say I've got to do it. By the way I've got no authority, so don't surcharge me for it, but I'm going to do it.' Magill replied, 'I'll back you up.' Roots disguised the money he spent on the hunt in a fund to pay external consultants. The Tories never suspected a thing.

Roots also sought legal advice on whether he could take out an injunction to block all transfers of Porter's assets pending final judgment day to prevent her spending her money or moving it away. The answer was 'no'. Labour councillors accused Roots of not doing enough and demonstrated at Westminster's annual civic dinner in April 1996 along with Cedric the Pig, a huge sow they had borrowed from the GMB union. Cedric had a history of activism and had been used with great effect in the protest against the huge pay rise that the Chairman of British Gas, Cedric Brown, had awarded himself. Cedric scoffed her pig nuts while, at the dinner in the Dorchester hotel, the Tories feasted on *noisettes d'agneau* and *sauce tamarinde et noix de cajou*, at a total cost to local taxpayers of £20,000. Andrew Dismore, the Labour Leader, sat with Cedric on the pavement outside the hotel holding a placard: 'TORY SNOUTS HOG THE TROUGH!' Bill Roots had to ignore the protest. Unable to trust the Tories with the news of his secret inquiry into Porter's wealth, he felt that he could not confide in the Labour councillors either because they were bound to leak any information about Porter to the newspapers.

Roots's agents at Stephenson Harwood reported on their search shortly after the High Court ruling against Porter in December 1997. On 27 January 1998 John Fordham, a senior lawyer at the company, wrote to Colin Wilson, the City Solicitor, that the investigation 'had not identified any assets belonging to Dame Shirley Porter remaining within the jurisdiction of any English court'.

Porter would have been delighted by the assessment; she had gone to extraordinary lengths to hide her wealth. Many companies and trusts handled her secret millions. They often had obscure names and were nominally controlled by people with no apparent link to her: Koori, Lionheart, Palmerston and Henley. Her greatest secret was an obscure company registered as Whitecoast Investments Ltd in the British Virgin Islands (BVI). A separate firm, Patton, Moreno and Asvat, was the registered agent for Whitecoast and its funds were kept in a bank account with Credit Suisse in Guernsey. There was nothing in writing to suggest any link with her. Whenever she needed funds to pay her mounting legal bills or invest in business enterprises, Porter would request the money from Peter Green who would contact her representative at Whitecoast. Then, the funds would be moved from Whitecoast through a series of offshore family trusts including Richmond and Marlow, which also had no direct link with Porter, into one of her several bank accounts in Israel or Guernsey. Porter's money was hidden from view by a complex patchwork quilt which might be unravelled by a sharp tug on a single exposed loose thread. If the investigators discovered just one part of her financial network, they could apply for a disclosure order from the courts and force it to yield up its secret transactions going back years. That would implicate other seemingly innocent companies, banks and trusts and compel them to do the same.

On 8 April 1998, two months after its bleak conclusion that no significant Porter assets could be found, Stephenson Harwood made an important discovery. She appeared to have forgotten that she owned at least three large forests in Scotland including 885 acres of the South Quintall Forest near Caithness, 344.8 hectares of woods known as Coille am Sealbach near Dalangwell, and a small patch of woodland at Strachan near Kincardine. She had bought the forests of Sitka Spruce woodland as part of a government-approved tax avoidance scheme to plant trees on barren land, predominantly in the Scottish Highlands.

On 14 April Porter sold the forests in a bid to dispose of any assets which could be seized by British courts. In her panic, she almost blundered. She had intended to sell them to her own company, Whitecoast, which paid for a valuation, but a purchase of the woodlands by Whitecoast could have led the investigators straight to the bulk of her personal fortune. Peter Green changed his mind about transferring the forests to the company, but the disposal of the land later led newspapers to conclude that one of Porter's friends at City Hall had told her about the Stephenson Harwood discovery.

Green established another bogus British Virgin Isles company, called Oakum Association Ltd, to buy the woodlands but the money for the purchase was supplied by Whitecoast, and therefore by Porter. Oakum was 'owned by the same trustees that owned Whitecoast', reported Green. In other words, Porter still owned the forests and had simply sold them to herself to throw her pursuers off the scent. As Peter Green told Porter in a note: 'this was to separate the ownership away from Whitecoast.' The money from the sale, £319,643.65, went to Richmond, one of Shirley Porter's family trusts, and then on to Whitecoast.

Porter demonstrated remarkable nerve by phoning Bill Roots a month later. 'I'm coming to England. Are you going to have me arrested?' She was not joking. 'I can't arrest you, Shirley,' Roots replied, 'we are still in a judicial process.' 'Can I come and see you?' she asked the chief executive. 'Yes,' replied Roots, 'but I can't do anything with you.' They could talk, but they could not discuss a deal.

At 10 a.m. on 21 July 1998, Porter arrived in Roots's office. It seemed to the chief executive that her brash, irrepressible force had dissolved. Porter persisted in her claim that she had not done anything wrong and appeared self-pitying. 'If only people had told me and been stronger,' she said to Roots. 'From what I understand, Shirley,' he replied, 'you weren't easy to stand up to.' 'I know, Bill,' she said. 'But if they were good, they would have done it.' Porter played the hunted, vulnerable woman. Her reputation was in tatters and her husband was descending into the long night of Alzheimer's. She told Roots she wanted to return to England with Sir Leslie. She was haunted by her loss of face with the Jewish community in London and she wanted to sort out whatever it was she was supposed to have done. She yearned for rehabilitation.

Porter now asked if she could make a deal. Roots told her, 'I'm not in that position Shirley; you're going through the courts and we don't know what the outcome will be but if you've got to pay, then presumably some sensible compromise will appear.' Porter had played a double bluff; although apparently opening up her heart to Roots, she never mentioned the forests nor the huge efforts she had made to confuse his investigators.

After her meeting with Roots, Porter flew with Sir Leslie to Monte Carlo. They ensconced themselves at the magnificent Hotel Armitage, where rooms cost £350 a night. The *Evening Standard* reported how Porter 'headed for the main shopping street where she scurried between Cartier, Yves Saint Laurent and Christian Dior'. On 25 August the *Daily Express* revealed that Porter had sold Scottish forests to a company called Oakum. 'Attempts to trace Oakum Association Ltd have proved fruitless,' its reporter, Martin Tomkinson, stated. 'Westminster Council has refused to tell the *Express* who precisely was privy to this information,' he added. 'The strong suspicion must remain that someone at the Council leaked the information to Lady Porter, who promptly sold the land.'

On the same day, Alan Lazarus, the Labour leader, wrote to Roots, demanding 'the fullest investigation to establish whether the discovery of these assets was leaked to Dame Shirley and, if so, who by.' A mystified Roots was none the wiser and the inquiry yielded nothing. Without inside information, Green's judgement to change the purchaser of the land from Whitecoast to Oakum appears unbelievably prescient. Shortly afterwards, Porter called Roots and further abused his generous and open nature to claim that that she did not even know she owned them. The ownership of the forests were unimportant; vitally for Porter the existence of Whitecoast had been kept a secret.

The forests scare and the investigators' pursuit fuelled Porter's paranoia and her unhealthy reliance on Green. In August she wrote to him asking whether she could store personal items at his company's headquarters in 79 Mount Street. She was worried about how discreet his staff would be and was thinking about employing the architect Peter Mischcon to design a separate entrance so her comings and goings would pass unnoticed. She instructed Green to sweep the premises for bugs. She kept a small office there for her periodic visits and was provided with a laptop, which she said should be 'cleaned' before anyone else used it. Sarah Hunt, an employee of Green's, worked as Porter's assistant and was paid a salary directly by her. Porter fretted constantly to Green about getting a credit card without her name; she was fearful of any payments being traced to her.

The finances and fortunes of Green and the Porters became inextricably entwined in a way unusual for financial advisers and their clients, so much so that Green and Porter's other family members had as much to lose as Shirley Porter at the hands of the council's investigators. On 10 March 2000 79 Mount Street was bought by Orion Financial Holdings Inc. via Credit Suisse Guernsey, which also held Shirley Porter's main secret bank accounts. Orion was owned by two offshore trusts: the Tower Settlement and the Robert Settlement, both funded by Porter and Sir Leslie. John Porter's company Telos, also based at Mount Street, and other companies owned by family members, including Sir Leslie's Sunset Corporation, invested heavily in Green's financial advice companies. The interdependence of Green and Shirley Porter was underpinned by the overriding objective of keeping Westminster City Council in the dark about her financial affairs.

Increasingly and recklessly, Porter used Whitecoast to make investments in other companies in the confidence that no one would suspect that the company was her *alter ego*. Through Whitecoast, she invested in I-Spire, a dotcom company, and Call Manage, a firm developing telephone software. She was particularly keen to buy shares in Call Manage and emailed Green: 'I would like my company to make a new investment which requires funds of $500,000. Accordingly, I authorise the sale of sufficient investments to raise any money as required.' Call Manage suffered large losses and made no sales.

Green did a brilliant job in hiding Whitecoast for years and would probably have succeeded completely had it not been for the business activities of John Porter. Once, both Porter and Sir Leslie had high hopes that John Porter would take over Tesco. After graduating from Stanford University, he decided he would 'pay my dues to a well-known supermarket chain'. For eighteen months, he worked as an assistant general manager for the Tesco store at Trowbridge in Wiltshire and was sent on a course to learn about butchery, bakery and grocery floor management. It had all been 'very interesting', but John Porter wanted to branch out as an entrepreneur in his own right. Later, Sir Leslie accused the Chairman of Tesco, Ian MacLaurin, of refusing to honour a pledge to put John Porter on the company board; the same MacLaurin who had already infuriated the family by rejecting Shirley Porter as

a director in the mid-1980s. In a letter to *The Times* in 1999, Sir
Leslie wrote: 'We accepted his word that our son, who is a suc-
cessful businessman in his own right, should be appointed . . .
Unfortunately, Ian subsequently decided not to keep his promise.'

In the early 1980s John Porter invested $400,000 in Verifone, a
company which made credit card-swipe machines and was sold
later to Hewlett-Packard for $1.4 billion. John Porter was reported
to have made $50 million or so on the sale and his net worth was
valued at approximately £60 million. His main company was
Telos, described as a 'privately owned enterprise integration business'. John Porter liked quick profits and he once said that he felt
comfortable only in an environment 'which is growing at forty per
cent or so'. He was someone in a hurry. 'I've got a strong sense of
urgency,' he once said. 'There should be a feeling of do it today,
rather than tomorrow.' Like his mother, he quickly fell in love with
the internet and saw its money-making potential.

In 1994 John Porter was introduced to the businessman Cliff
Stanford by a mutual associate, Anthony Rothschild. Stanford was
brought up in Southend-on-Sea by his mother, a bookkeeper and the
first woman in England to run a bookmaker's office. After leaving

photo © Andrew Wiard/reportphotos.com

Porter and her children, John and Linda, April 1999.

school, he trained as an accountant and at the time of his introduction to John Porter was a designer of accountancy software, operating out of a small office in Finchley. Stanford had heard about the development in the US of the internet, to which only big corporations and universities had access. Kent University was selling access to the net to corporate customers for £20,000 and so he paid up and then sold on access to wannabe surfers for £10 a month. Soon, he was deluged by a huge demand and his company, Demon, Britain's first internet provider for ordinary people, was born.

In 1997 Stanford was embroiled in a battle with other investors and needed £500,000 to retain control of Demon. John Porter loaned him the money at the critical time. Stanford sold Demon to Scottish Telecom in 1998 and made an instant £33 million. He celebrated for four days in a pub in Finchley, buying drinks for his staff. Stanford had always lived frugally but on becoming rich beyond his wildest dreams he acquired a taste for the high life. 'You can never have enough money,' he proclaimed. John Porter made a £2 million profit. Four days later, the two men decided to go into business with each other and set up another dotcom company, Redbus Interhouse, in which they both invested £2 million. John Porter was so delighted with his huge profit that he introduced Stanford to Peter Green who agreed to become Stanford's financial adviser. 'I don't normally handle people with sums as low as £33 million,' said Green pompously to Stanford, 'but I am prepared to make an exception in your case as a favour to the Porter family.' He said he would structure Stanford's wealth in the same way as he had done with Shirley Porter: offshore companies in the British Virgin Islands, trusts with Swiss trustees and bank accounts in tax havens such as Guernsey and Jersey. John Porter took Stanford to Porter Ho! in California and introduced him to his parents. 'It was immediately clear to me that John Porter was treated like a little boy by them,' remembers Stanford. 'The father spoke to John Porter and me as if we were five years old.'

By 2000 John Porter was a dotcom emperor, and according to the *Daily Telegraph* had developed the 'capacity to speak in a pure stream of e-language using endless "techy" acronyms and expressions'. Disastrously for Stanford and John Porter, and ultimately for Shirley Porter, the two business partners fell out around this time, not only about the future direction of Redbus Interhouse but over other joint ventures. John Porter was the chairman of Redbus, and Stanford heard stories of him meddling in the running of the company, despite the fact that the pair had agreed to let the managers run it after it was floated on the stock market. Stanford concluded that his business partner was a disruptive influence and resolved to depose him as chairman, but received assurances that there would be no more interference. The two men agreed a temporary truce, which swiftly collapsed.

During this period Shirley Porter began to assume direct responsibility for managing and controlling her wealth. Sir Leslie had until then dominated the organisation of the family financial affairs with the help of Green. As Alzheimer's took an ever tighter grip, Sir Leslie faded from the scene, leaving Porter to deal with the myriad complexities of the family fortune which left her increasingly exposed to the investigators. Exiled in Israel, Shirley Porter carelessly began to use email for her business transactions. In April 2001, when the Porters had not received shares from companies in which John had invested their money, Shirley Porter sent her son an email, copied, of course, to Peter Green.

First she reprimanded John Porter for his failure to deliver his share of cash for an investment in a company called Lampol, which was developing property in Birmingham: 'Whenever a call has been made for further cash injection . . . you have never wished to put in further cash,' she wrote. '. . . the interest running on your non-payments has nearly wiped out your investment in the company . . . not that we are all absolutely certain we will get anything in the end.' Sir Leslie added his contribution to the email: 'At the moment I find it very difficult to understand why IN NO CASE HAVE EITHER OF US RECEIVED ANY SHARES for all the different companies that either I or your Mother have advanced monies to . . . I cannot understand the reason. I had to sell Tesco shares because you wanted delivery immediately. I have never failed to provide the money and you have always taken it for granted and failed to deliver the shares . . . I love you as a son and for the sake of our future relationship let us regularize [sic] the current situation and in the future, as Sam Goldwyn said, "include me out." Hope you enjoyed the skiing and the Stock Market improves. Love from both of us.'

It later transpired that John Porter had helped his mother to invest $225,000 in an internet classical music business, The Classical Alliance, based in New York. The money was supplied by Whitecoast Investments Ltd in February 2001 and the transaction was confirmed by email, under the acronyms 'WIL-DSP' or 'Whitecoast Investments Ltd-Dame Shirley Porter'. John H. Glanville, the company's chairman, wrote a note to John Porter confirming the investment: 'I have included several items that have been part of the ongoing dialogue for this investment; eg, a board seat for your mother.'

Porter was feeling confident that she could move her money around undetected. On 17 August 2001, just four months before the House of Lords judgment, she received a report from Peter Green: 'All in all a good year with WCC [Westminster City Council] seemingly making little progress legally and apparently no closer to tracking down SP's [Shirley Porter's] assets.' On 30 September Green estimated Shirley Porter's wealth as follows: 'Money in the bank, £2,303,128, realisable assets, £13,233,253, not immediately realisable, £3,925,487. Total: £19,461,868. Green estimated Sir Leslie's total assets at £33,489,032.

In the weeks immediately after the House of Lords judgment, Shirley and Leslie Porter loaned $1.75 million from Whitecoast and Sunset either to John Porter directly or to Toxford, another one of his companies. The couple wanted the interest payments on the loan to be paid into their accounts at Credit Suisse in Guernsey. Sarah Hunt handled the transactions for the 'Porter family loans', which were paid into John's account at Rabo Bank Nominees, Guernsey. All told, the family had parked approximately £34 million in the Channel Island.

While this money was moving among family members, Shirley Porter was supposed to be existing on £1,500 a week, the living allowance set by the High Court to try to prevent her from disposing of her assets at will. The investigation into her wealth was now public knowledge and funded openly by the council. Fordham's inquiry was overseen at City Hall by the 'Urgency

Committee', which, according to one former Labour councillor, was 'somewhat bizarrely named', given that the group, controlled by Tory councillors, did not meet for the first time to discuss the investigation until 6 November 2002, almost eleven months after the House of Lords decision. Labour councillors were convinced that the pursuit of Porter's millions was not in earnest and that it would soon be abandoned on grounds of 'cost'. Porter, meanwhile, confident in the security of Whitecoast and her other companies and trusts, continued to demonstrate her overwhelming contempt towards her pursuers. At this stage, the woman who owed about £43 million to the British taxpayer was claiming her UK state pension of £301.40 per month.

There was outrage when it emerged in January 2002, a month after the House of Lords ruling, that Leslie and Shirley Porter had gone on a luxury cruise around the Pacific aboard *Silver Wind*. They had taken all 1,314 square feet of the Grand Suite, complete with two full-time servants, three balconies and a bathroom decked out in Italian marble. Cost: a total of £90,000. It was hardly the behaviour of a woman down to her last few hundred thousand pounds. The *Daily Mirror* asked: 'Where did the money come from? The DSS [Department of Social Security]?'

By this time Bill Roots had retired and been replaced by Peter Rogers. Stephenson Harwood remained as the council's investigators but they were making little inroad into Porter's wealth. They had received a few of her near-worthless items valued at around £4,000, but there was little more they could do in ignorance of her financial network. John Fordham, still heading the Stephenson Harwood investigators, told the press, 'She has had a long time to rearrange her affairs and make it difficult for the City of Westminster to recover the money.' He added, 'We believe she is still an immensely wealthy woman.'

On 14 May 2002 £1 million-worth of Tesco shares was sold in the names of Shirley Porter and Irene Kreitman, her sister. They were shares held on trust for a relative but this lapse in security showed that Porter held assets in excess of £300,000. This transaction, which appeared on the Tesco share register, appears to have gone undetected by the investigators.

With interest, the Westminster Council surcharge grew ever larger and eventually reached more than £48 million. Porter pinned her hopes on an appeal to the European Court of Human Rights in July 2002. Before the hearing, she arranged a meeting with legal advisers and her supporters. Roger Rosewell had come up with names for an internet 'Porter is innocent' campaign: 'friendsof-shirleyporter.com-net' or 'shirleyporter.net'. Porter wrote to John Porter for his advice: 'What do you think? We have supporters who we try to keep informed. I am thinking ahead for rehab (rehabilitation) if you understand me. Should Roger attend the meeting . . .?' John replied: 'I am not sure about this . . . [It] needs to be a spontaneous unfunded initiative by people who genuinely believe it . . . YOU MUST NOT BE INVOLVED IN ANY WAY. PARTICULARLY NOT FINANCIAL SUPPORT.'

As the months went by in 2002, Shirley was becoming ever more frantic about the state of John Porter's finances, which were suffering some short-term turbulence, and, in fact, her fate would not in the end be decided by the council or its expensive investigators, but by the boardroom fight between Stanford and her son. In August 2002 John Porter persuaded his fellow directors to force Cliff Stanford's resignation from the board of Redbus. Stanford was determined to regain control of the company from John Porter by fair means or foul. On 5 August he was contacted by an ex-Metropolitan policeman, George Liddell, who described himself as a 'corporate troubleshooter', specialising in boardroom feuds. He promised Stanford return of the chairmanship of Redbus and said he would demand no payment if he failed. Stanford initially agreed to pay Liddell £150,000 plus expenses if he succeeded. To help Liddell, Stanford ordered a contact at Redbus to access emails from the company's old computer server and copy them on to a CD which he gave to the former police officer to analyse. On 6 September Stanford asked his loyal contact within Redbus to divert all the company's emails to a hotmail address supplied by Liddell. Four days later, on the evening of 10 September, all emails coming in and out of Redbus headquarters were sent to Liddell's secret email account.

Some of John Porter's investments, including his dotcoms, had not performed as well as had been hoped. Shirley made a note about a conversation regarding her son's money on 3 September 2002: 'All his property is charged [mortgaged],' she wrote. 'Only the farm in Vermont is available, worth about half a million dollars. He requires about $2 million now to get out of trouble – that will cost me $4 million, [he] has promised to sell Telos which will take six–nine months. He is not liquid . . . I have asked for an account of his holdings and what security he will put up and when he will pay back.' On 24 September she wrote to her son: 'I am very over extended with many topics at this moment and wish to come to proper conclusions. You may not have appreciated what a difference your request for help will make to my own future plans, how much it will curtail my activities . . . I will not decide anything without proper information. As mummy used to say "I'm not as young as I used to be." How well I appreciate her sentiments.' On 25 September Shirley Porter emailed John Porter again: 'Just to keep you informed, I am leaving for NY [New York] on Sunday and staying at the Waldorf Astoria until 5 October.'

In January 2003 Shirley Porter had surprised her son with a party for his fiftieth birthday and he had given her flowers in thanks. On 10 January she wrote to him: 'Thank you for the beautiful flowers. We really enjoyed preparing the party, and worrying that you would find out. In the event you appeared to be totally surprised, unless of course, you have inherited my genes and know how to lie . . . Love from sunny Israel.' Porter would have been wiser to pass on her gratitude by phone or face to face. Her private correspondence was going straight to George Liddell.

CHAPTER 27

Chasing the Money
(January 2003–July 2004)

Cliff Stanford was ever more desperate to unseat John Porter, whose Redbus supporters had in turn acquired more shares to stave off a counter-attack from his business adversary. On 16 January 2003 Stanford wrote to George Liddell restating the original objective of the interception plot: to give the press emails showing John Porter's financial reliance on his mother and embarrass him in the eyes of the Redbus shareholders: 'Disgrace JP [John Porter] and the institutions will turn to CMS [Cliff Stanford].' However, Stanford was worried that this might not work: 'Even disgraced he still owns forty per cent of the shares.'

During the autumn of 2002 Liddell had reportedly posted some of the information he gleaned from the emails on the internet, in an attempt to smear John Porter using the pseudonym 'Wolff'. At the start of the following year panic broke out within Redbus as the directors' suspicions that their email traffic was being diverted were awakened; they sent emails to each other asking 'Who is Wolff?', which, naturally, were being read by Liddell. On 23 January Liddell realised that John Porter and the others might trace the diverted correspondence to his computer and urged Stanford to 'pull the plug on this as a matter of urgency'. On the same day Stanford noticed that the directors had changed the password and a little later, that they had discovered the email diverts at Redbus, and removed them. Within a week of the discovery, Liddell was being interviewed by the police about the identity of a certain 'Wolff'.

But the operation was by no means a failure, as Stanford and Liddell had obtained more than 20,000 confidential emails from two separate sources: the download on to CD of internet traffic over a two-year period up to September 2002 and the diverted emails from 10 September 2002 to 23 January 2003. Secreted in this treasure trove of documentation were approximately seventy emails containing vital information about Shirley Porter's wealth. They included details about Whitecoast and her secret bank accounts in Guernsey and Switzerland, down to the sort codes and account numbers. Some emails showed Porter transferring millions of pounds from Whitecoast to her son's companies. Several emails proved that Shirley Porter was Whitecoast and revealed her investments in companies such as Classical Alliance. Cliff Stanford now had a dossier containing emails relating to the financial dealings of Shirley Porter and her son. 'It wasn't as comprehensive as I had hoped,' he said, 'and I had difficulty in understanding it fully.'

Porter may have suspected a leak but initially believed it was the council's investigators. She still retained enough confidence to antagonise both the council and the courts. On 11 February Stephenson Harwood obtained a wider disclosure order against Porter in the High Court from Mr Justice Lightman, ordering her to disclose all her assets including those in offshore banks, companies and trusts. The judge issued a further order freezing worldwide assets up to £37 million, to come into effect should such assets ever be located. This prevented her from selling her homes in Israel and Palm Springs, any shares in Tesco and any jewellery, including her engagement and wedding rings. Of course, it made no mention of her real and substantial assets in companies such as Whitecoast because nothing much was known about them.

At 2.43 p.m. on 18 February 2003 Porter faxed an imperious letter to City Hall for the attention of Peter Rogers, the new chief executive, announcing her refusal to cooperate with an order issued by the High Court. 'Last November,' she wrote, 'I was seventy-two. I am no longer prepared to be immersed in the costs and emotions of a case which has now lasted a quarter of my adult life when the process seems so pointless and my family need me more than ever. As a result I have decided not to participate in the latest proceedings any further.' In her letter she told some of her more audacious lies: 'There is no mystery about my finances – despite newspaper attempts to suggest otherwise.' She added: 'I have made a full declaration of my assets and accepted a worldwide freeze of those assets. I have also cooperated with the forfeiture of personal possessions – even arranging for household goods to be delivered to the City Council's solicitors.' Porter mentioned recent press coverage and suggested that 'the City Council seems to be boasting about their use of private detectives to rifle through my household rubbish.' She concluded: 'As you know, and the courts have accepted, I have never made any personal gain from what I have been accused of doing . . . I remain extremely grateful of having had the opportunity of serving the people of Westminster and am proud of my achievements in public life. I have nothing further to add.'

Peter Rogers replied: 'You state there is no mystery about your finances. In fact, you have refused to answer our question as to what became of your previous wealth, about which you have said nothing in your disclosure to the court . . . your failure to provide further disclosure suggests we are on the right track. Your breach of the order places you in contempt of the English Court.' Rogers did not send his reply to Porter until 25 April, more than two months after her letter, with the precise lack of urgency which so infuriated the Labour councillors. Even when Rogers did reply, his letter was inexplicably sent to Israel from City Hall with a nineteen pence domestic second-class stamp, which would have been 'returned to sender' had he written his address on the back of the envelope. Thanks to the Royal Mail and its sister organisations between London and Herzliya Pituach, Rogers's letter travelled by surface mail across mainland Europe and Turkey in an amazing journey of around 2,500 miles lasting sixty-eight days, at an average speed of 1.53 miles mph. In a statement later, greeted with incredulity by Labour councillors and the local press, the council said this letter was part of its 'strategy' to recover the huge debt from Shirley Porter.

Throughout January and February 2003, Cliff Stanford and

George Liddell tried to interest the City Council and its investigators at Stephenson Harwood in the material they had obtained as a result of their activities. Neither man had anything against Shirley Porter but both thought their information could prove useful in applying pressure on John Porter to leave Redbus. Stanford wanted to let his adversary know that he had 'damaging information' and 'if this persuaded him to step down I would not have been unhappy about this.' Stanford did not consider this 'blackmail' as was later alleged by Shirley Porter and her son, but 'normal behaviour in these types of business situations'.

'I was not looking for anything relating to Shirley Porter,' says Stanford. 'Indeed, at the outset I felt Shirley Porter had been wronged. It was only later that it became clear that she had been blatantly breaking the gerrymandering rules.' Stanford and Liddell concluded that if John was receiving funds from Shirley Porter to buy shares in Redbus, as indicated by the emails, then the council's investigation into her assets could provide a great opportunity. Perhaps, if all else failed, they could supply the investigators at Stephenson Harwood with the evidence they needed to freeze John Porter's assets or his mother's. Stanford would then call an Emergency General Meeting (EGM) of Redbus and force his business partner off the board.

On 3 January 2003 Liddell wrote an email to John Fordham of Stephenson Harwood to say that he had certain information relating to Westminster's pursuit of Shirley Porter's assets. In his note, Liddell referred to both Whitecoast and the Sunset Corporation, Sir Leslie's BVI company. Fordham claims he had already heard about both companies, but he did not have enough evidence to take action to freeze their assets. He was also suspicious about Liddell and concerned that he had obtained the documents unlawfully. Over the next two months, both Liddell and Stanford say they made persistent attempts to interest Fordham in the evidence that they had obtained about Porter's missing millions, but on 28 February Liddell reported to Stanford that Fordham did not want to meet them.

On 12 March 2003 Stanford tried another tactic on Peter Green, his financial adviser. 'We were discussing how my own trusts had performed so badly,' says Stanford. 'One of the comments Peter made was that he was spending an awful lot of time working on Shirley's affairs.' Stanford was not pleased that his finances were suffering because his adviser was busy trying to reorganise Porter's funds. As Green put on his coat to leave, Stanford made an extraordinary offer: he said he wanted to meet Shirley Porter to try 'and talk some sense' into her. Stanford says, 'I explained that John Porter was acting foolishly and doing a lot of damage to the company. I suggested that I bring my mother out to Israel to meet Shirley Porter. There was certainly no threat by me in relation to Shirley Porter. I was quite open in wanting to try and persuade her to rein in her son. My suggestion of taking my mother was a genuine one. My mother is Jewish like Shirley Porter and has lots of nerve. She is more Shirley Porter's age and I thought would be respected by her.' Green, who, by now, knew about the Stanford–Liddell operation, rejected the offer.

Apparently without Stanford's knowledge, Liddell also made contact with Green that month and made it clear that he was in possession of some extremely damaging information. Liddell sent a note to Green's private email address regarding the information he held on Shirley and John Porter: 'I am not the one who has breached their collective security.' Then, he said mysteriously, possibly alluding to Stanford or his contact at Redbus: 'That is another and he or she is much closer to home.' Liddell added: 'John Porter is rapidly making enemies within RBI [Redbus Interhouse] and this has in turn compromised his and his mother's situation.' Liddell, who was hoping to come to some deal with Green and Shirley Porter, wrote to Stanford on 17 March: 'Don't make any calls to any of the parties as you might queer my pitch, in fact I would make yourself incommunicado. We are negotiating on a knife edge, but I think you have more of an advantage here and at least they are talking.'

The following morning Liddell met Green in the lounge of the Grosvenor Hotel. Green was dressed in an expensive dark suit and looked fit and tanned but struck Liddell as uncomfortable and extremely nervous. As the pair sat on a sofa and talked, Liddell noticed the furtive glances of two men drinking coffee nearby. Green said he was speaking on behalf of the 'family', that Shirley

Porter wanted the problem cleared up and she had even advised John Porter to stand down from the Redbus board. Green said he would see what could be done to sort out the problem. Suddenly, the financial adviser moved away from Liddell and signalled to the two coffee drinkers by waving some papers. They were plain clothes detectives, who approached Liddell and arrested him. He was later charged with attempting to blackmail Shirley and John Porter, a charge which would hang over his head for two years before it was dropped by the Crown Prosecution Service.

Shirley Porter and Green were badly mistaken if they thought that they had silenced Liddell. For nearly two months, he felt increasingly frustrated that his hard work had come to nothing and angry about being set up by Green. Late at night on 7 May Liddell 'threw a spanner in the works' by sending an email to Karen Buck, a former Westminster Labour councillor and the MP for Regent's Park and Kensington North, revealing that he had been investigating John Porter for his client Cliff Stanford: 'During my investigation I have by sheer necessity had to investigate matters relating to Dame Shirley Porter . . . I'm sorry to have to tell you that I got a lot further than WCC's [Westminster City Council] lawyers investigating the matter. We told them [Stephenson Harwood] that we could prove John Porter had in the past two years carried out investment business on DSP's behalf. Did they ask to see the evidence? No! I offered to hand over my entire investigation and continue to develop the leads we had made. Did they want to know? No!' Liddell went on: 'Peter Green, the man who most definitely "moved" her money has never been interviewed to my certain knowledge . . . So scared was Peter Green and DSP that they have used every trick in the book to keep me quiet. I dislike telling you this but DSP's money is alive and well and running around London in the form of her son John Porter. We can show the trail from her to him and we can certainly prove he acts on her behalf . . . You will see that there is little doubt of my commitment in this matter; it is a shame the same cannot be said for WCC.' The following morning Karen Buck forwarded the email to Paul Dimoldenberg, who had been re-elected to the council in 1997, and to Jonathan Rosenberg, who sent it on to me.

By this time, I had been working as a reporter for BBC Radio 4's *Today* programme for five and a half years, and had covered the emerging Porter scandals in the early to mid-1990s as local government correspondent for BBC South East. A few days before Liddell's email, both I and the *Guardian* had run stories exposing the role of Barry Legg, in the decision to move homeless families into Hermes and Chantry Points, forcing him to resign as Chief Executive of the Conservative Party under Iain Duncan Smith. On 9 May Rosenberg sent me the Liddell email. Initially, I sent an email to Liddell asking for help, but received no response. On 13 May I rang Cliff Stanford at his home at Costas Mijas, just south of Malaga on the Costa del Sol. 'You could not have called at a better time,' he told me. He gave me some background detail about his dispute with John Porter and mentioned that he knew a lot about Shirley Porter's secret wealth and her company Whitecoast. He told me he did not have any documents with him but thought he might be able to obtain some copies. We agreed to meet up at his villa in Spain.

In the meantime, Porter's legal fight had come to an end at the European Court, which rejected her appeal as 'manifestly ill-founded'. On 22 May the Court also said: 'Given that the applicant is now living out of the country and has failed to comply with the orders issued against her, the Court would note that the applicant has no intention of paying the surcharge, or any part of it, in any event.' Despite its knowledge of the Stanford/Liddell material, the council had all but given up hope of recovering any money from Shirley Porter. On 20 May 2003, the city solicitor Colin Wilson wrote to John Fordham asking him to delegate work on the inquiry 'to the most junior member of the team', to save money, 'wherever practicable'. Wilson wondered 'if it makes any sense to spend much more money on pursuing this debt.'

I flew out to Spain on 28 May. The following morning I arrived at Cliff Stanford's palatial villa, complete with swimming pool and jacuzzi, overlooking the sun-baked beaches of the Costa del Sol. Stanford, a short squat man with a beard and a mop of curly greying hair, dressed in short-sleeved shirt, shorts and flip-flops, came across as an open and talkative man, proud of his business

achievements. He burned with an intense resentment towards John
Porter and spoke bitterly about the man he considered 'a serial
destroyer of other people's wealth'. Once, John persuaded Stanford
to invest £250,000 in Lasik Vision, a US-based optics company.
But the company had huge liabilities as a result of legal actions
from former customers and went bust, and Stanford lost every
penny he had invested. He said that Redbus was once worth £100
million; now it was worth just £2 million. He told me about the
involvement of Peter Green in managing the Porter wealth.
Stanford said that if the council could be forced to seize the assets
of Shirley and John Porter, he still hoped to call an extraordinary
general meeting. He promised to try to get me the documentation
I needed for the story and I flew back to London on the same day.

Coincidentally, on 29 May Westminster City Council had started
to consider abandoning its pursuit of Porter. Colin Wilson met Rod
Ainsworth, Solicitor to the Audit Commission, to discuss the council's flagging investigation. In a note four days later to Chief
Executive Peter Rogers, Wilson wrote: 'Bearing in mind the considerable expenditure to date, and the lack of substantial recovery,
one option would clearly be to conclude that no further action
should be taken.' Wilson's note referred to no other options;
Labour's fears that Westminster would call off its hunt for Porter's
assets were being realised.

I met Stanford again on 9 June at his London office in Covent
Garden, which, by a strange coincidence, was above a pub called
Porters. Stanford, in short sleeves and a pair of braces decorated
with images of liquorice allsorts, was holding a bundle of documents. He asked jokingly, 'How do I know you're not going to go
to Peter Green and demand £2 million for this?' 'Because I'm an
idiot,' I answered. Stanford laughed. 'Yes, you are!' He handed me
approximately thirty confidential emails which established that
Shirley Porter was in control of funds worth substantially more
than the £300,000 she had claimed and that she had forwarded
large sums of money to John Porter. Crucially, the documents
proved that Shirley Porter was Whitecoast and that she had used
the company to transfer these funds to her son. The emails contained the most sensitive details about Porter's missing millions,

including bank account numbers and the whereabouts of hidden funds. The documents also established the heavy involvement of Peter Green and showed how his company handled her wealth.

I had agreed to work on the story with Paul Dimoldenberg and two other Westminster contacts, Jonathan Rosenberg and Neale Coleman. I was surprised at the claims made by both Liddell and Stanford that the council had rejected their offer of help, and I had heard about the Scottish forests and the suspicion that someone at City Hall had tipped off Porter, so I took the precaution of not approaching City Hall with my information. Dimoldenberg agreed to let me have anything else he could find out. He entered into email correspondence with Colin Wilson, the city solicitor. Without knowing that Dimoldenberg was passing on the information to me, Wilson revealed that the High Court had issued a disclosure order against Green and that he 'had complied' with it, and that there was 'no basis' for proceeding against John Porter and other members of the family.

On receipt of the High Court disclosure order Green had lied on oath by failing to mention any of Porter's secret companies. Not only had Green lied but he had also submitted a bill of £27,911 to the City Council for the time and trouble he had been put to by the disclosure orders. 'In addition to this firm's costs,' Green's lawyers wrote, 'Mr Green has himself spent 95.5 hours on this matter. His normal charge is £275 per hour and we invite your proposals for the settlement of these fees.'

For the following three weeks I worked on the story with my BBC colleague Malcolm Borthwick and investigated the web of companies and trusts established by Peter Green to hide Porter's wealth. We sent off requests to authorities in the Channel Islands and the BVI for further information on companies, particularly Whitecoast. Often, the information which came back cast little light on Porter's involvement with these organisations, but at least it proved they existed. We applied through Companies House for the accounts and details of other firms located in the UK, particularly those belonging to Peter Green. The financial adviser had gone to enormous lengths to disguise the ownership of his own companies, but the records showed that Porter family members, particularly John and Sir Leslie Porter, owned big chunks of Peter Green's business. This helped to explain why he was prepared to take such significant risks in lying on Porter's behalf.

We went to experts for their opinions on the evidence that we had accumulated. Both Raj Bairoliya, a forensic accountant, and Michael Ashe QC, an expert on trust law and money-laundering, said the material appeared to confirm Shirley Porter's control of substantial funds. The most important document was a short email confirming that Shirley Porter wanted her company, Whitecoast, to invest in the Classical Alliance. This investment linked her to other documents showing that Whitecoast transferred millions of dollars to John Porter via Peter Green's companies.

We planned to broadcast the story on Monday, 30 June 2003, and sent letters to Shirley Porter in Israel and John Porter and Peter Green asking them for their response. They received our notes late on Friday afternoon, as the markets were about to close, to prevent Green from moving the money out of harm's way. In a last bid to cast suspicion on the details of the impending broadcast, Green told *The Times*, which was also making inquiries, that computers had been stolen from his offices in Mount Street. He hoped this false statement would convince people that the real story was how the BBC had acquired stolen documentation to support their story. Few believed it.

On 30 June the *Today* progamme broadcast a piece lasting more than ten minutes exposing the whereabouts of Shirley Porter's missing millions and raising questions about the council's attempts to recover the debt. Shortly after *Today* came off the air, my editor, Kevin Marsh, received the following fax, marked 'URGENT', from John Fordham: 'It would be of assistance to our client if you would provide us with all such documents in your possession and we should be grateful if these could be provided as a matter of urgency.' Peter Bradley, former Westminster Labour councillor and later MP for Wrekin, would later tell the House of Commons: 'The *Today* programme had discovered more in two weeks than Westminster City Council and its expensive lawyers had discovered in two years.'

Later that day Fordham attended a crisis meeting with Colin

Wilson, Peter Rogers and a council press officer, to discuss the *Today* story. The minutes of the encounter exude an air of poorly suppressed panic and injured pride. Rogers positively bristled at the suggestion that the City Council had not done enough to recover the debt from Porter. 'Can they prove it is Shirley's money? Can they show it's recoverable?' he asked. The chief executive was upset at the implication that he had been 'leaned on politically' not to go after Porter, although *Today* had not made the allegation. Fordham was more measured. 'The link with John Porter is new,' he said, before warning the others about the risks of dealing with Liddell, because he 'probably got the material unlawfully'. He added: 'I don't want the council to become embroiled with this.'

An hour later, Dimoldenberg strolled into the meeting and demanded action, little realising that Rogers and Wilson had been discussing the possibility of closing down the Porter inquiry. He handed over a copy of the crucial emails which I had obtained from Cliff Stanford and which had been offered to the City Council nearly six months previously. 'Shirley Porter is in contempt of court,' Dimoldenberg stated angrily. 'What are we doing about it?' He pointed to the documents and said, 'These contain the details of bank accounts. We should freeze assets imminently.' Fordham suggested that it was 'more appropriate to proceed if we could use the information we found'. 'But the police don't operate like that!' said Dimoldenberg, who insisted that the information be used to pursue the debt.

After the broadcast, Jean Claude Depuis and Craig Renaud, two former employees of Green, came forward with information. Depuis said of Porter that 'All her money is in a bank in Guernsey in Peter Green's account.' Renaud, who had fallen out badly with Green, was happy to confirm the details contained in the Stanford emails. On 2 July representatives of Stephenson Harwood arrived at the *Today* programme offices at BBC Television Centre in Wood Lane and spent most of the day photocopying records and research contained in seven lever arch files. On 4 July Porter sent Peter Rogers an email: 'Thank you for your letter of the 25 April which unfortunately I did not receive until 1 July due to inadequate postage. I am considering the contents and will revert back to you as soon as possible.'

Peter Green, Shirley Porter and members of her family were now stuck like flies to fly-paper. The Stanford documents not only revealed Porter's hidden wealth but also proved that Peter Green had lied on oath. Because of the council's earlier freezing order, Green was impotent to move Porter's wealth out of the way. Over the ensuing few weeks both he and members of the Porter family were hit by an array of court orders. In his second email to Karen Buck on 6 July, Liddell cautiously anticipated what was about to follow: 'I have even noticed renewed vigour on the part of John Fordham at Stephenson Harwood. I am worried however, that in all the niceties and the hogging of the limelight by Uncle Cliff et al, the real issues may not be addressed and with the best will in the world John Fordham has little chance of finding her money. For instance, he mailed me on Friday evening looking for John Porter's address, asking for his current whereabouts and where he [John Porter] was spending the majority of his time. For a team of lawyers who have spent upwards of £500,000 not to know these things is pretty appalling.'

In the end, Liddell was wrong about Fordham. Despite their slow start, on 9 July Stephenson Harwood used the documents provided by *Today* to secure a freezing and disclosure order against John Porter, prohibiting him from dealing with his mother's assets and requiring him to provide information about her. On 15 July the Guernsey Court granted orders against Whitecoast and Credit Suisse (Guernsey) Ltd, restraining Porter from selling her assets on the Channel Island. It granted more disclosure orders against Credit Suisse (Guernsey) Ltd on 18 July and 5 August. The bank was ordered to relay information concerning Whitecoast's account. Two senior bank officials provided affidavits along with six box files containing client information.

On 17 July the British Virgin Islands Court granted a disclosure order on behalf of Westminster against the agent for Whitecoast, Patton, Mareno and Asvat. Further court orders were obtained in the UK, Guernsey and the BVI about twelve sham family trusts and other companies, including Sir Leslie's Sunset Corporation. On 21 July the High Court granted further disclosure orders against Green and Sarah Hunt, Porter's personal assistant. Other orders were granted on the same day against the accountants Citroen Wells, who had acted for Porter. Green's computers were seized and specialist consultants, Vogon, examined the hard drives to recover incriminating emails between Porter and her financial adviser.

Porter's only known response to this series of heavy blows was a further letter to Peter Rogers on 31 July: 'Further to my recent correspondence I write to advise you that I have instructed Dr Jacob Weinrot, my attorney in Israel, to represent me. His contact details are attached.'

On 5 September Cliff Stanford was arrested, questioned about his alleged role in a computer-hacking operation and released on bail. 'There has been no crime,' he told the *Daily Telegraph*. 'It just needs explaining.' He was also charged with blackmailing Shirley and John Porter. The charge was dropped in April 2005.

On 4 November the City Council announced that the courts in the British Virgin Islands and Guernsey had granted disclosure orders against fourteen companies and individuals, requiring respondents to disclose to the council information about Porter's past and present wealth. The courts had also granted orders freezing approximately £34 million of Porter family funds held in Guernsey under various trustees. No one came forward to protest that their £34 million had been frozen. This was the most conclusive proof that the money belonged to Porter and her family, because, had it belonged to anyone else, they would surely have protested. Porter could not complain because that would prove what everyone else knew anyway: the money belonged to her.

On past experience these events might have encouraged Shirley Porter to embark on yet another legal battle lasting many years. However, the complete freezing of assets in Guernsey meant that her entire family's wealth would be inaccessible. At least £9.3 million of the £34 million in Guernsey had been definitely identified as belonging to Shirley Porter, but an additional result of the court orders was that members of Porter family could not gain access to their funds either. Shirley Porter's granddaughter, Joanna Landau, was forced to borrow money from her mother, Linda Streit (née Porter), while her own funds were frozen in Guernsey. The council now had a choice: if Porter were declared bankrupt in Israel, they would have total

photograph by Flash90

Leslie and Shirley at Herzliya Marina. The sun's out but
the money's frozen, July 2003.

access to her financial transactions, which may have proved her
control over other family funds and not just her own £20 million.
That could take time but might yield millions more for the
Westminster taxpayers. Alternatively, the council could settle for a
substantial sum. In early 2004 rumours of a deal started to circulate. 'Shirley Porter responded immediately to the offer of
negotiations,' according to Kit Malthouse, deputy leader of the

Tories at City Hall. Malthouse would lead the talks on behalf of Westminster, and in great secrecy.

On Wednesday, 21 April 2004 the City Council team flew out to Brussels on British Airways flight 398, touching down at 6.35 p.m. They made their way to the Radisson SAS Hotel in the Rue Fossé-aux-Loups, in the heart of the Belgian capital, where rooms cost between €105 and €625 a night. There, in three small meeting rooms, they met Shirley Porter, family members and her lawyers on 22 and 23 April for talks to hammer out a settlement. The discussions lasted from 9 a.m. to 3.30 p.m., with a break at lunch for sandwiches. Porter's position as stated by the family was a poor one: 'You need to understand that until the last few years, Leslie has been the person who has dominated the organisation of the family's financial affairs. Shirley has never been interested in finance, and is unable to remember anything in detail. As you will be aware, for the last two–three years Leslie has been suffering increasingly from Alzheimer's and related conditions. He does not understand at all what is going on in relation to the litigation. Shirley, Linda and the rest of the family have had to try to understand the financial affairs which Leslie formerly attended to, but are heavily dependent on their financial advisers and the family trustees for information.'

The deal was so secret that Porter insisted that documents relating to it be shredded. At the time of the Brussels conference, the debt owed to Westminster taxpayers, with accrued interest, stood at £48,719,334. She agreed to pay Westminster £12.3 million, a deficit of more than £36.5 million, but a great deal better than the gold-plated lavatory seat which the City Council had allegedly secured from Chelwood House in part-payment.

On Saturday, 24 April I was interviewing Patricia Kirwan for this book on her veranda overlooking the rugged vineyards of a village called Montyperoux, her home near Montpellier in Languedoc. My mobile phone rang. It was Paul Dimoldenberg to tell me that Shirley Porter had agreed to pay £12.3 million in a 'full and final settlement'. 'I think of it as a down payment,' said Dimoldenberg. In a statement, Porter said: 'I have decided that it is time to bring this case to an end, despite my belief that I did nothing wrong. As Leader of the Council, I was repeatedly assured the policies we followed were lawful.' I passed the news on to Kirwan, who looked stunned. We logged on to a news website to read the details. Kirwan gripped my arm and said, 'Is it over?' 'Yes,' I said, 'I think it is.' Later, Kirwan broke open a bottle of Languedoc bubbly to celebrate and we drank it as the sun set over the castle ruins on the distant hills. On my return to London the following night, I received a call at home from Kit Malthouse, who briefed me on the deal. 'We pretty much cleaned her out,' he observed brusquely.

At 3.44 p.m. on 1 July an email from Colin Wilson to Dimoldenberg announced: 'We have just received confirmation that our bank has received the £12.3 million pursuant to the settlement agreement.' Later, Malthouse told the *Guardian*, 'The highest court in the land found her guilty of gerrymandering. There isn't a much worse offence than that in politics. It is definitely up there in the hall of infamy.'

The money was paid to the council by Sunset Trading Corporation, one of its last acts before it was dissolved, along with Whitecoast and the rest of the financial structure created by Peter Green. Sunset belonged to Sir Leslie Porter, who released the cash to repay the debt by selling Tesco shares. To the bitter end, Shirley Porter had neither shown a single shred of remorse nor, at least on paper, had she repaid her debt to the taxpayers of Westminster with a single penny of her own money.

West End Final

Ibumped into Roger Rosewell outside the Houses of Parliament on a windy day in September 2004 and asked him if he had received my email request for an interview. He was still mulling it over and wondered why I wanted to talk to him. 'You were Shirley Porter's right-hand man,' I said, 'you were the "Man With No Name Number One, the thing in the lift".' He smiled in weary acknowledgement. 'There's no mystery about me,' he said. 'I used to drive with Shirley in her Mini from her flat to the underground car park at City Hall and we would use the service lift together because it was the nearest.' We chatted amicably for an hour and Rosewell fielded my questions with courtesy and good humour. He still felt Porter had been badly treated by the District Auditor and the courts and insisted that she had believed Sullivan's advice would protect her. I asked him whether Porter would be prepared to talk to me. 'I'll put it to her,' he said, 'but I doubt it. Leslie's dying and Shirley's a little shaky at the moment.' I never heard from Rosewell again but he was right: Porter did not want to talk to me after receiving legal advice and her husband was dying.

Sir Leslie Porter succumbed to Alzheimer's on 20 March 2005, and was buried not in the Jewish cemetery in Willesden, as Shirley Porter had hoped, but in Israel. It seems she felt she could not return to London, even to visit her husband's grave. According to the *Independent* obituary writer Nicholas Faith, Sir Leslie 'was dominated by his wife and after he retired he shared her disgrace and life in exile from Britain . . . Her difficulties must have contributed to the heart problems from which he suffered for the last years of his life.' Porter suffered two further bereavements in the same year. Her sister, Irene Kreitman, aged seventy-eight, died from a degenerative disease in a London hospital just three months later on 14 May. *The Times* reported the £15 million she and her husband, Hyman, had contributed to the arts over the years, particularly the Tate: 'She made a deep and lasting mark on the artistic life of this country.' The third and surprising loss which occurred in the months following Porter's settlement with Westminster City Council, happened a few days before I met Rosewell. Her financial adviser Peter Green suffered a fatal heart attack at home. He was just sixty-two.

Six months before my chance encounter with Rosewell, and a month before the secret Brussels talks where Shirley Porter agreed her £12.3 million settlement, I hopped on a coach in Walterton Road that had been specially laid on by WECH to take residents to a meeting of Westminster City Council, where the final stage of John Magill's inquiry into the gerrymandering was to be discussed. The District Auditor had published a 'Public Interest Report' into the outstanding aspects of Building Stable Communities. It had been almost exactly a decade since Magill and Child had raided City Hall and requisitioned a room from Bill Roots to save from the shredder documents regarding BSC policies related to the gerrymandering, which extended into almost every department at Westminster Council. This stage of the inquiry had been delayed while Porter challenged Magill's designated sales report through the courts, but these particular aspects of the BSC policy were unfinished business and Magill now drew a line under the whole affair. In his final report, he included Porter's 'Statement of Agreed Facts' and pronounced as unlawful various BSC-related actions, including the misuse of planning powers, the sale of Bruce House, the deportation of the homeless and the use made of Hermes Point and Chantry Point, but could find no further financial loss. The ruling Tories of the City Council extracted comfort from Magill's report, which completed the judicial process. A statement by Westminster Council declared: 'It is not considered that any specific action needs to be taken by the Council now about these aspects which are, of course, entirely historical.'

As ever, the Westminster Tories showed little contrition during the debate about Magill's final report at the Marylebone Council House. Simon Milton, the Leader of the Council, emphasised that the events had occurred a long time ago, and apologised on behalf of his 'predecessors', which presumably included Shirley Porter with whom he worked in the late 1980s and visited in 2001 while on holiday in Israel. The local hacks in the press gallery looked too young to remember Porter and scratched the odd quote absent-mindedly as they gazed at their watches. Judith Warner, who served as joint Chairman of Housing with Michael Dutt, referred to her well-thumbed copy of the Barratt Report as she protested her innocence. It is strange to think that Warner was still a councillor at Westminster nearly eight years after John Barratt's report revealed her attendance at the meeting of the Chairmen's Group which took the decision to move homeless families into the two asbestos-riddled towers. Her Tory colleagues attacked Labour councillors when they raised what they considered tedious ancient history during the meeting and even suggested they 'get a life'. The cemeteries stalwarts, Jo Mahoney and Eileen Sheppard, had heard it all before. Sheppard gave a resigned smile and whispered to me, 'They haven't changed, you know.'

Nearly half of the £12.3 million paid by Porter was used to cover the costs of the Audit Commission and other legal fees. The rest went into the housing budget to help Westminster provide 'affordable homes'. Following the settlement, the City Council also reached agreement with the forgotten man of the scandal, Porter's co-defendant and former deputy David Weeks. He paid £48,000 towards his debt of £48 million, but kept his tasteful flat in Dolphin Square, by the river at Pimlico. Some of the original Objectors believe the City Council could have recovered many millions more from Porter, but failed to do so because of their sympathies for her. They have made a formal objection about the deal, and at the time of writing a new district auditor is gathering the material necessary for an investigation. The Objectors believe their case has been strengthened by the evidence that the council initially rejected the Stanford material and was contemplating stopping its pursuit of Porter's assets.

A wretched development followed the broadcast of the *Today* programme. The BBC had given Stephenson Harwood the material it needed to freeze Porter's worldwide assets, particularly the £34 million in Guernsey. Among the hundreds of documents supplied was a short email between Paul Dimoldenberg and me which proved that the councillor had provided me with information relating to the council's secret disclosure orders against Peter Green, which in any event had elicited only misleading information from the financial adviser. Dimoldenberg also gave me evidence which proved the council had not been contemplating any action against John Porter or other members of the family. John Fordham of Stephenson and Harwood handed over the email to the Council Chief Executive Peter Rogers, who made an official complaint to the Standards Board for England – a body created by the government in 2001 with the power to disqualify any errant councillor for up to five years – for allegedly leaking confidential information relating to the council's secret court actions to a journalist.

Ironically, the Standards Board was established largely in response to criticisms about the time taken to bring Shirley Porter to account, a process which Dimoldenberg did more than most to bring about. At the same time, the government abolished the power to surcharge councillors in England for deliberately abusing public resources, as they had learnt from Porter's case that it took too long to bring people to account. Instead they gave the Board extensive investigatory powers which could result in the public disgrace and disqualification of local politicians.

The Standards Board investigated Dimoldenberg for nearly two years before presenting its case against him to a three-day tribunal which began on 18 May 2005. Gavin Millar QC, Dimoldenberg's barrister and a former councillor, argued that Dimoldenberg had a public interest defence in supplying the BBC with the information it needed. 'I was getting angry and concerned,' Dimoldenberg told the tribunal. 'The fact that Liddell had apparently offered the

Council such vital evidence and been treated in such a half-hearted manner again made me think that the Council was preparing to throw in the towel. I thought that, at best, it would do a deal with Porter and then hope finally to sweep the embarrassing "Homes for Votes Scandal" under the carpet.'

The Standards Board employed a high-profile legal team in its attempts to argue its case against Dimoldenberg. Before my own cross-examination by Antony White QC, the Standards Board barrister, I read to the Tribunal a press release issued by Stephenson Harwood when it won the Dispute Resolution Team of the Year prize in the 2005 Legal Business Awards for its part in recovering £12.3 million from Porter. This underlined the importance of the material supplied by the *Today* Programme and its broadcast supported by important information from Dimoldenberg: 'Great care was needed, given the legal, reputational and evidential issues that arose. In one case, the information was eventually broadcast by BBC Radio 4's *Today* Programme, and was then skilfully used to good effect in further applications to the Courts.' I described as 'outrageous' Stephenson Harwood's use of my material to help Peter Rogers to make an official complaint against Dimoldenberg, who had clearly been acting in the public interest particularly in light of the fact that the firm earned a further £1.3 million in fees in the ten months following the *Today* broadcast.

The Tribunal decided that Dimoldenberg had not brought Westminster City Council into disrepute – if by now such a thing were possible – and further ruled that Westminster's recovery efforts 'might well have been assisted by Councillor Dimoldenberg's action'. But it found that he had technically breached the rules by supplying me with information relating to Peter Green's secret disclosure orders. Steve Wells, the chairman of the Tribunal, leant forward to pronounce sentence: 'The Case Tribunal has decided that no sanction should be imposed on Councillor Dimoldenberg.' A loud cheer went up in the public gallery; the Tribunal members clearly recognised a plate of tripe when it was placed before them. This fiasco of the Board's pursuit of a man who had helped expose Porter's gerrymandering and helped City Hall recover £12.3 million had cost the public purse approximately £100,000. On

15 September 2005, Cliff Stanford and George Liddell were convicted at Southwark Crown Court of 'unlawful and unauthorised
interception of electronic communications' and received six-month
suspended prison sentences. Stanford, who was also fined £20,000,
announced an immediate appeal against his conviction.

Shirley Porter is now an elderly widow living in Herzliya Pituach,
and makes occasional discreet visits to London. She cuts a sad
figure, but the *Panorama* reporter John Ware has little sympathy:
'The natural humanity one has for somebody being pursued for a
long time, although it was largely of her own making since she contested the findings of the courts and the Auditor, is tempered by the
fact that she has never shown real contrition. I think that makes
her an arrogant person, lacking in a degree of humanity, which
puts her beyond the pale.'

The great gerrymandering scandal would not have happened but
for its constituent causes: the collapse of political consensus in the
1980s, the erosion of the officers' political independence, the critical importance of Westminster to the Conservative Party and the
demographic changes within the City itself. But Shirley Porter was
the catalyst. The fates conspired to produce precisely the wrong
person at the wrong time in the wrong place. Some people praise
Porter's achievements – which included attempts with her 'One
Stop Shops' and other measures to treat local taxpayers as 'customers' – but how do these policies sit with her willingness to
abuse their resources and communities? There are a few who still
insist she did not know she was doing wrong.

In her 'Agreed Statement of Facts', she has admitted the corrupt
reasons for her actions, although she does not recognise that her
betrayal of public trust was absolute. It is likely that she never will.
Porter attempted to hide her unlawful actions by dissembling and
shredding incriminating documents, but she was undone by the
meticulous documentation that she kept of her own actions. She
has left behind a unique and irrefutable record of corruption and
dishonesty in British public life. It is not the legacy she wanted, but
it is the one she deserves.

Index